Guide to Naval Writing

Robert Shenk

Guide to Naval Writing

Naval Institute Press   Annapolis, Maryland

Library of Congress Cataloging-in-Publication Data

Shenk, Robert, 1943-
Guide to Naval writing/
Robert Shenk.
p. cm.
Includes index.
ISBN 0-87021-438-1
1. United States. Navy—Records and correspondence. 2. United States. Marine Corps—Records and correspondence. 3. Naval art and science—Authorship. 4. Military art and science—Authorship.
I. Title.
VB255.S54 1990
808'.066359—dc20 90-6139
CIP

Printed in the United States of America on acid-free paper ♾

9 8 7 6 5 4 3 2
First printing

Page 351 is a continuation of the copyright page.

For Paula

Every successful guy in the E, D, and down to the A ring in the Pentagon, or out in the Fleet and in the Corps, is a writer.

—Admiral Jeremy D. Taylor

At least 90 percent of an officer's work is paperwork. Take the ops officer, chief engineer, reactor officer—very little of their time is spent on the wing of the bridge with binoculars, watching airplanes take off.

—LDO, Admin Officer on a Carrier

People who can write make their opinions go.

—Naval Aviator

Contents

Foreword

Two things need to be said in this foreword. The first is that this book focuses primarily on the *principles* of writing: getting the purpose straight, marshaling the arguments, writing in a natural style—above all, *communicating*. That's our main goal.

Of course there are many occasions for writing, so it seemed good to organize this book around the common naval genres: naval letters, messages, point papers, evals, and so on. However, in each case this text stresses principles rather than formats. Although many samples of documents and some page-guides appear here, this text cannot give comprehensive guidance on every detail of the myriad of naval forms we all have to use. There are simply too many such formats and they change too often. Moreover, by pressing too hard on format (or on another possible focus, "correctness") one often avoids or overlooks the really hard (and vital) parts of writing—*what* to say and *how* to say it, along with such ancillary subjects as purpose, occasion, audience, persona, revision, and editing.

Format and correctness, of course, do have important parts to play. If you don't get the format right or if you make too many errors, you'll get a document sent right back to you. These latter two topics, however, are by no means the most important aspects of communicating. Instead, how to write so your points will *get across* and *make things happen* should always be the central concerns.

Having made that point, I ought immediately to add the second one—*use this book as you see fit*. Use it as a handy reference guide, as a primer on various genres of naval writing (fitreps, award writing, JAGMAN Investigations, etc.), or even as a whole course of instruction on naval writing. The text has been designed to accommodate many different purposes.

That is, while some people may want to consider the subject of naval writing from start to finish, I expect others will have picked up this book because they need help with writing a particular kind of naval document. If the latter description fits you, simply start with the type of writing you need to work on now. Each chapter in this text is pretty much self-contained. The chapter on messages doesn't depend too greatly on the text's introduction, for example. Similarly, if you've just been given a POM issue paper to write for the first time, you can go right to that section and begin reading there.

Further, when you need quick reminders of format, a checklist, or a list of the standard headings for a particular document, you can often consult that section directly, with the help of the page headings and the index. Do read a bit before and after, to make sure you have the context right. Later, when you have time, you can read further.

On the other hand, some chapters or major parts of chapters in this book have been composed to be read from beginning to end. For instance, if you have just been assigned to a staff, you would do well to read from the start of "Staff Writing," which has been designed for a person new to a staff. Similarly, "Writing for the News Media" and "The Professional Article" are designed to guide new collateral duty PAOs or budding professional writers, respectively, in their work. Read each of these chapters from start to finish.

A couple of early sections—like "Naval Writing Standards" or "Rules for Naval Editing"—can guide naval professionals in almost all the writing or editing they do. These sections would benefit most naval readers who haven't studied such topics in depth before. Leaf through these sections to see what I mean. For that matter, leaf through the whole book to get a good idea as to what's here.

Finally, use this book in one other way as well—to give me a piece of your mind. Yes, many eyes looked at this book before it went to print, and the best of the counsel comes from the many officers, enlisted people, and civil servants who gave freely of their time, their expertise, and their good advice. However, no text of this sort is anywhere as good as it can be until it has been digested and sorted out by its larger audience, and until members of that audience have given the author a thorough professional critique.

So if you have some specific criticism and can tell me how to make this book better in a later edition, please pen me a quick note and send it to me, care of the Naval Institute Press. Thanks for your help. If we work together we can make all of our writing much more effective.

Acknowledgments

A great many people gave me help on this text, in a variety of circumstances.

There was the engineering officer on a carrier, for instance, who—drawn away from busy duties because his executive officer wanted him to see me—straightened me out on the need for references in naval messages. A limited duty officer on a destroyer offered sea stories and excellent advice on casualty reports, while other junior officers around the wardroom chimed in. Aviators sat around their briefing tables, offering me pointers from their experience, and then later sent examples of award recommendations and other such documents.

Marine officers at the Marine Corps Development and Education Command discussed with me the whole range of Marine Corps writing and gave me excellent examples to boot. A captain who headed a Navy training command shared with me his strategy on writing fitness reports (which I think he had kept very guarded before). Navy chiefs who were admirals' writers shared examples and strategies. A civilian secretary on a major staff in the Pentagon shared her hard-won expertise on correspondence folders. The list goes on and on.

My debt to all of those who helped me is very great. I can name only a few. Among those who read major portions of the manuscript, who aided me over extended periods with this project, or who gave especially vital assistance were Lieutenant Commander Steve Bannow, Captain Harry Benter (USN, Retired), Major Thomas Bowman (USMC), Captain John L. Byron, Commander Dave Courter, Lieutenant Walter East, Lieutenant Colonel Brian Faunce (USMC), Lieutenant Jill Garzone, Lieutenant David Hayes, Lieutenant Johnny Hopkins, Lieutenant Commander Austin Jordan, Lieutenant Jeff MacFadden, Commander Mike Mullen, Captain

Keith Oliver (USMC), Commander Ron Ratcliff, Captain T. H. Reynolds, Jr., Commander Warren Rohlfs, Lieutenant General E. H. Simmons (USMC, Retired), Lieutenant Mike Stranno, Lieutenant Commander J. B. Strott, Commander Bruce Stubbs (USCG), Captain Frank Snyder (USN, Retired) of the Naval War College, Commander Rich Virgilio, Master Chief David Watson, Commander Tom Webber, Lieutenant Commander Mike Weglicki, Commander Ken Weinberg, and Professor Nancy Wilds of the Armed Forces Staff College.

In addition, journal editors John Greenwood, John Miller, Fred Rainbow, and Frank Uhlig, Jr., provided invaluable help. Not only did they give me permission to use material from their journals but they offered good advice, sometimes read a chapter, and referred me to experts throughout the services.

Thanks of course to those at the Naval Institute who worked closely with me, especially Deborah Guberti Estes, who guided me expertly through the greater part of this project.

And thanks, finally, to my family, who supported me through the many long months of this project. Thanks to Paula, of course, but also to my teenagers Mary, Stephanie, Henry, and Peter, for keeping my spirits up, and for providing endless variety to my life.

Guide to Naval Writing

> I feel that much of my success in the Navy has come from being able to write instructions, point papers, major planning documents, and other reports that my peers could not, or were reluctant to write.
>
> —Navy Captain

1

Introduction

When interviewed, naval professionals of all ranks often commented on how important it is for them to write well.

Who Is Doing Important Writing?

It is not surprising, perhaps, that the writing done by senior officers carries great weight. But it is rather remarkable how important writing can be for junior people. The duties of three lieutenants, a Marine major, two civil servants, a Marine staff sergeant, and a Navy chief stand out. These people's responsibilities demonstrate how important writing can be at almost any level.

For example, consider the duties of a lieutenant on a destroyer squadron staff. Only three years out of the Naval Academy, he drafted a great many messages for the command. That is highly significant, since messages are the very lifeblood of the communications of an operational staff. But the lieutenant also had other important writing responsibilities. For example, when interviewed, he had just been put to work drafting the remarks of his Commodore for the change of command of the ship that helped save the USS STARK.

Another lieutenant (junior grade) was made administrative officer of a destroyer late in his tour because he was such a good writer. He ended up writing all of the award nominations, many evaluations, frequent press releases, and much of the command correspondence aboard ship. He felt he had gained invaluable perspective from working directly for the commanding officer (CO) and executive officer (XO). Like a civilian executive assistant (EA), he was at the living center of the organization and was being trained to step up.

Then there was the lieutenant who had become the officer in charge (OinC) of a Personnel Support Detachment. She had to compose enlisted evaluations, award justifications, instructions, correspondence, and messages for her unit with no one around except her first class yeoman to offer guidance and criticism.

Another officer had the opposite problem—working under many eyes. This Marine major was the EA to an 0-6 division head at a schools command. Like many EAs, he wrote a good deal, but he edited and coordinated much more. Besides drafting messages, letters, memos, and performance evaluations for the colonel's signature, the major had a hand in JAG Manual (JAGMAN) Investigations and letters replying to congressional inquiries. He coordinated award ceremonies, dinings-in, and other social functions—all of which also required a good deal of writing. And he supervised a team of civilian secretaries.

Civil servants can also have important writing responsibilities. At a fairly high rank, a civil servant in the Navy's budget-writing office was an unsung individual whose writing had major impact on the Navy. His ability to rewrite budget justifications ("POM issue papers") submitted from throughout the service—without time to query officials at major commands as to the exact meaning of their sometimes unclear terminology—had a vital effect on the success of Navy budget requests. At a somewhat lower level, another civil servant wrote Pentagon "blue blazers" and accompanying correspondence. Her paperwork often reached up to and was signed off by two- and three-star admirals.

Among enlisted writers, a boatswain's mate chief found he had a big writing burden when he reported aboard ship. He was assigned as the first lieutenant on a frigate, duty that required writing many instructions and messages, recording some counseling sessions, and even putting together a JAGMAN Investigation, besides doing the evaluations and award write-ups that were already very familiar to him. Indeed, as one of the vessel's dozen or so division officers, he found himself doing far more division paperwork than work in his own rating—not an uncommon experience for senior enlisted men and women.

And a Marine administrative chief spoke of the job he once had as a staff sergeant in the Secretary of the Navy's office. Although his position was in security, he happened to work alongside officers who drafted answers to service members who had written the President. When the officer staff suddenly got overloaded, the sergeant was asked to contribute. Guided by a senior civilian secretary, he learned the required style over many weeks of practice, and soon he was researching and drafting 8–10 letters a week, many for the signature of the President of the United States. This experience later served him well in the adjutant's office of a Marine division, where he supervised Marines writing responses to congressional inquiries and supervised many other kinds of correspondence and staff work.

"Few of my young lieutenants could write well. They had little concept of detail, style, spelling, or grammar. Duty in the Fleet Marine Force, particularly in staff billets, requires an ability to write."—Marine Lieutenant Colonel

Some service members have major writing responsibilities very early in their careers. Others do not—many junior enlisted aboard ship may not write very much, and some junior officers may not either. Junior Marine Corps officers assigned to a battery may never write a letter or speedletter or message, and some naval aviators in squadrons may not have to write much in their initial tours.

"Most of the paperwork falls on the shoulders of *those who can*—which usually means those individuals have lots of face time with the XO and CO."—LDO, Admin Officer on a Carrier

Eventually most of these situations will change. When junior enlisted become senior they will at the very minimum have to draft enlisted evaluations and award nominations for their people and contribute to messages, letters, and instructions. Often they will have much more writing to do. As for officers, sooner or later almost all of them will join staffs on which writing becomes a major personal responsibility. In short, virtually all naval professionals should learn the principles of good writing early in their careers.

What Are They Writing, and Why?

The purposes of naval documents are multifold; a brief description of the uses of the major types of service writing can illustrate how vital they are.

Of course, almost everyone writes naval and business letters and memos in daily work—documents that serve virtually all the administrative functions you can name. In addition, ships, units, and staffs run themselves by directives, whether called instructions and notices (in the Navy) or orders and bulletins (in the Marine Corps).

Beyond that, personnel evaluations ensure that the services promote the best individuals and help place the right people in key positions, while award justifications, letters of commendation, and award citations recognize individuals for their achievements. In a related area, sooner or later service members all have to write letters to request changes of designator, entry into new programs, and so on. Such letters and their required endorsements allow service members to find good places to use their skills, helping the services to funnel talent into needed areas.

News features in base papers help keep up morale and spread the word about the good jobs people are doing. Hard news releases, letters responding to congressional inquiries, and formal position papers present news and naval perspectives to the public and to public officials. In a different area, JAGMAN Investigations and other legal writing efforts help ensure that justice is done both for service members and for the services they serve.

On staffs, point papers and briefing folders articulate naval policies and procedures, while budget justifications and technical reports help build and maintain the services. Staff reports and messages feed and equip fleet units, while messages sent by operational units back to a staff inform commanders of the situation in the field. Without the messages, letters, after-action reports, and many other reports that originate from ships and Marine operational units, shore staffs would have precious little information with which to form impressions, solve problems, and make changes to guide the Navy and Marine Corps. Finally, documents such as war-fighting doctrine, night orders, battle orders, operation orders, and operational messages directly assist the naval services in fighting a conflict or war.

This text presents guidance on most of the topics outlined above. However, the various kinds of actual writing situations beggar description. In interviews service members mentioned all sorts of occasions for writing about which they had no guidance at all. Such out-of-the-ordinary writing responsibilities just begin to suggest the great need for naval professionals to be generally good writers, good enough to adapt to greatly varied needs.

For example, one junior officer commented that hard as he might try to draft a personal letter to an admiral to invite him to the ship's change of command, he couldn't get to first base. His commander eventually had to write it. Another officer said that after writing so much navalese, addressing a civilian in a letter was like trying to change gears in her mind—and she couldn't do it. Such inability is unfortunate. At the very least almost every officer has occasion to write recommendations for enlisted men and women leaving the service. If you don't know how to address civilians about the talents of your subordinates, your letter probably won't help your people very much.

No official guidance tells you how to communicate with a previous CO or other official on missing evaluations or fitness reports, or, more touchy yet, how to request evaluations be removed from your record. In a related area, whether or not to write to the selection board is often argued at happy hour but seldom discussed in print (it is discussed briefly in this text).

"As you proceed up the ladder of seniority, the need to write effectively increases greatly."—Marine Colonel

Senior officers also mentioned quandaries. A destroyer squadron staff officer pointed out that the budget reports he wrote for his boss were always freehand. No one told him how to write them, nor how to compose the "justification" section of a request to convince Commander, Naval Surface Force, Atlantic (SURFLANT) to augment the staff's OPTAR ("Operating Target") by $100,000. A destroyer's XO said that letters of indebtedness were usually but not always pro forma. After two or three form letters to an individual you'd have to spell the situation out very clearly, or the problem might result in a congressional inquiry.

Enlisted service members' struggles with specialized writing tasks were similar. Besides situations like those described above, in which sailors and Marines have to write evals, letters, point papers, technical descriptions, and so on, many a chief or top sergeant has tried to offer written words of wisdom to sailors or Marines about to go ashore at Hong Kong or in the Mediterranean. Often the content of their advice as to what to do (and, sometimes more important, what *not* to do) is very good. But if it is not written well, or isn't written or placed so as to catch people's attention, it may have little effect.

Further, many a sailor has a good idea on streamlining procedures in his or her specialty and saving the Navy some money. The Navy has a program for presenting these ideas—but someone must write up the service members' suggestions. Writing a "Beneficial Suggestion" or "Pricefighter" is usually an unfamiliar task. If both the sailor and the sailor's junior officer lack confidence in their writing abilities, no one will submit the good ideas, even though service members can sometimes earn hundreds of dollars for their suggestions, and the services can often save thousands.

Clearly, if a person has confidence in writing, he or she can adapt to a great many writing situations and can master all kinds of documents that neither this nor any writing text can discuss individually. You cannot prepare for anywhere near all the specific documents you'll have to compose in a naval career, nor can this text offer instruction on every possible eventuality. What you can do is to master the principles of good writing, to practice them in all the kinds of writing situations that are covered here, and with these same principles as guides, to adapt to other circumstances by using your head.

Principles of Good Writing—A Writer's Triangulation

As in navigation, good writers look for fixed points of reference from which to plot their positions and ideal headings. The classic writer's (or speaker's) triangle looks like this:

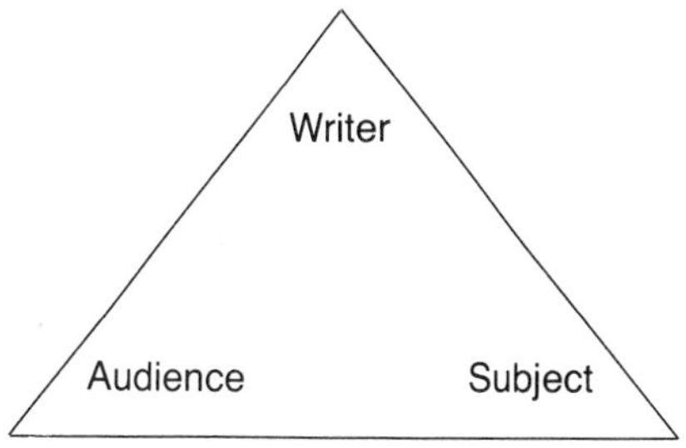

Knowing your audience, your subject, and yourself (including how others will see you in the writing situation), you can gauge your position with respect to any particular communication.

Know Your Audience

To start with, the nature of your *audience* is obviously important, beginning with its rank, position, or billet. Whether you're writing to someone senior or junior to you makes a difference in how you'll pitch a letter or memo. Also critical is the position your correspondent holds—is he or she higher up in the organization, at your same level but in a different branch, or in a different organization altogether? The possible complexities in organizational relationships beggar description, especially on staffs in Washington, D.C.

You should also consider how important the boss of the person you're writing to is, "politically" speaking. Knowing the standard positions of the organization he or she works in can be vital. Your attention to such things can affect whether your letter or memo receives standard routing, gets put on the back burner, or merits immediate command attention (for better or for worse).

"The best ships build credibility by not hesitating to report bad news along with the good. As one officer put it, 'They put their marker down,' meaning they let their boss know exactly where they stand."—Gullickson and Chenette, *Excellence in the Surface Navy*

Besides the organizational and "political" realities of your communication, you have to recognize the personality of the person you're writing to, or your correspondent's known opinions on the issue you're bringing up. For instance, knowing an admiral's personal preferences and normal way of working can be vital if you have to get the admiral on your side. Remembering the principle of audience will also help you adjust your style. Unless your readers will all be aviators, for example, you'll do well to forgo terms like "painting bogies," "out of knots," "losing a hop," and "strapping on the jet." Even when writing to aviators, you probably won't want to use such jargon for official correspondence that leaves your command—you don't know who is likely to read those terms and to view them as too informal to be used outside the briefing room.

Writing to nonmilitary audiences requires even more adjustment, explanation, and simplification. As a naval official writing to a civilian, you'll usually have to explain more than you do to fellow service members and to do without all those Navy-specific or bureaucratic terms we all use so widely in-house. In short, *know whom you're writing to*—that's the very first principle of good writing awareness.

Know Your Subject

Secondly, you must make adjustments for *the subject matter* you are dealing with. Those who live or die by whether what they write is actually read—recruiters, for example—know this principle very well. "As a recruiter I learned that as soon as my recruiting document went beyond a paragraph or a paragraph and a half, it was thrown away," said a Navy chief. "So I had to get a reader's attention in that opening paragraph." Depending on the subject, a writer doesn't always need to be so immediate with the message. Almost all of us will study discussions of changes in pay and benefits with some care, since such subjects arouse natural interest.

Knowing the way readers usually treat a document can also be valuable. Naval directives are typically scanned, not read word for word—so headings can help alert readers to key information. On the other hand, extremely technical material requires great patience on the part of readers, and a manual writer must be careful to go slow and give readers many aids—summaries, visuals, section reviews, etc. Obviously, there are many other such considerations.

It should go without saying that you should know your argument inside out. Lapses in logic or in documentation, failures to explain or to exemplify, or omissions of crucial details can all sink your recommendation before you get out of harbor. Because of space limitations, very little of your knowledge may show up in a briefing memo or message. But in tabs, appendixes, or material held in reserve you should be able to support any position. Make use of examples, statistics, pertinent testimony, comparison and contrast, definition and analysis—all the furniture of standard argument.

Know Yourself

Third, you should always remember *who you are* and the self-image you want to project when composing your letter, message, or speech.

Some service members forget this principle when they compose letters to selection boards, criticizing the service or their superiors to explain away some low rankings. The writers come across as malcontents to board members, who just as quickly toss their records on the "nonselect" pile.

Clearly, deference and respect are always good qualities in juniors speaking to seniors. But keep your wits about you here. You are sometimes in a position to speak *for the command*, not just for yourself. Even if you're relatively junior, if you're representing your command at a conference you can be very forceful in your expressions of opinion. E-7s or E-8s from a staff may speak decisively and with strong credibility even among senior officers, for they know the admiral will back them up.

Naturally seniors are expected to be forceful. In a recent inspection, a senior Navy inspector often heard the commanding officer criticized for not taking charge or giving strong direction. "He didn't act like a Navy captain," commented one of his officers, and this complaint was widespread. That impression hurt the captain's credibility both with enlisted and officer members of his command—and in turn with the inspecting party. The point: *Act so as to be believed and respected* whenever you speak or write.

Being aware of the impression you make can have wide application. If you are appearing before Congress to support a budget request, you'll be expected to wear your uniform proudly and speak forcefully to the needs of the service. On the other hand, if as a base commander you have to address civilians in the local community about projected school closings that could affect service members' children, you might consider toning down your customary military manner to meet the civilians halfway.

To be sure, one's purposes in all circumstances will affect that adjustment—one may or may not want to be conciliatory; one may or may not want to portray a strongly military image in any particular case. The point is to remember that the way you come across to others in manner and tone can influence how they receive your message. If you know what you sound like when you speak or write, you can make use of that knowledge to help get your message across.

A Special Case of Knowing "Yourself": Writing for the Boss

One other aspect of speaking with credibility, or of remembering who you are when you write, is especially important in naval service. Many times (*most* times aboard ship) you don't write for your own signature but for someone else's. In many a letter, directive, message, and other document, the drafter disappears, and the only name that appears (or is assumed) is that of the commanding officer. This principle is even more true of major staffs where staff action officers are writing for very senior officers.

Writing for seniors can require considerable adjustment. A chief yeoman was given special training to be a flag writer. His whole work was writing for the signature of a two-star admiral. When interviewed, he commented that even after his schooling, he needed *six months* to learn to write like the admiral before his work began progressing smoothly.

"The major requirement for contact with senior officials is the ability to write."—Navy Commander

Whatever time it takes, sooner or later not only specialists like flag writers and staff action officers but almost all naval professionals must learn to write for their superiors. A lieutenant commander, executive officer of a helicopter squadron, often encountered difficulty in writing for "the command." Once he finally mastered the process, he made this suggestion: "Keep the facts in, and leave the adverbs out. Let the Old Man put in the modifiers." He also advised giving the skipper *more* than needed, to allow the CO to decide how much is necessary and just chop out any extra parts. Not giving him enough makes him come back to you to complete the paperwork; if all he has to do is chop something out, he can give the document to the yeoman immediately, thereby cutting out an extra step. However, the XO continued, you must not assume such a review. The letter or message should be ready to go out as written, for many times there will be no change.

The situation sounds complex—and writing for the boss or bosses can be extremely complex. After working in a high-level office in the Office of the Chief of Naval Operations (OPNAV), a commander reported, "I became somewhat frustrated in my previous job because the deputy director and director had radically different writing styles from myself and each other. The result was an awful lot of 'wordsmithing.' "

Then she went on: "I think that every new tour puts you in the position of writing for a new senior who has his own writing style—good or bad. You have to learn the basics of expressing yourself clearly and succinctly in writing, but you have to learn to be flexible and not to take the rewriting/reediting by your seniors too personally. The bottom line is to find the best way to communicate your points effectively so that you get the support or approval you're seeking."

Not everyone finds writing for a senior an aggravation. A limited duty officer found a special usefulness in a senior's signature: "My biggest problem is electrical safety. But who will listen to me? My working for the engineering officer carries weight; I use the boss's signature for added authority." And a lieutenant on a surface division staff advised that junior service members try to imitate the boss: "Work at writing like the Captain writes; learn his key phrases," he advised. He thought this practice had improved his own writing, for by doing so he had learned another style.

Indeed, seniors should assign juniors to write for them not only to lower the workload but to help juniors learn. This type of writing not only helps a junior master naval style but also teaches a commander's perspective. Drafting night orders for a destroyer's commanding officer while the ship is underway can become an exercise in thinking as the commander has to think, in seeing through the Old Man's eyes, as it were. If you see how the commanding officer modifies what you've written, then you've shared a CO's general outlook and operational perspective.

Another surface line officer thought that drafting messages and letters from a ship to a staff offered great opportunities for learning. His ship was the test platform for a new sonar, and the testing required lots of free-flowing status reports. When an apparatus didn't work, he found he had to choose words carefully so as not blame anyone. He wanted to avoid putting a senior in a tight spot or stepping on anyone's toes, but still he always had to get his message across.

He learned that there are subtle ways of presenting a case—hints, hidden bottom lines, etc.—that are the fruit of strong "political" awareness, tricks that you normally pick up on staff tours as you get more senior. He didn't have that awareness, but seniors did. So his standard way of operating was to present the facts as he saw them. Then the XO wordsmithed the document, and the CO polished it. He found this process very educational, for the CO had the political awareness to know *exactly how to say* what had to be said.

This officer had made a point of comparing the smooth copy of documents the CO had signed with his own rough drafts. Other drafters would also find this practice educational. Seniors are typically glad to share the reasons for substantive revisions, and they appreciate juniors showing the interest. But such individual initiative isn't enough, and executive officers and others in the chain of command would do well to incorporate this kind of feedback into formal training programs. At the very least, seniors can make a policy of routing a copy of outgoing correspondence back down to the person who first drafted it.

Naval Writing—The Basic Steps

Knowledge of the basic communication triangle outlined above—the three fixes from which to plot your course—gives you good perspective for any particular writing situation. But there is a great deal more to understand, particularly about the steps we take or *processes* we go through in writing—researching, brainstorming, drafting, revising, and editing. Although you may take only a few moments for each particular step or process when you compose any particular document, you can inform your whole perspective on naval writing if you consider each step in some depth.

Check the Basic Reference

Before proceeding with any kind of writing assignment, take one essential preliminary step—*become thoroughly familiar with the basic reference.* In the service we're too accustomed to going by "the gouge," whether official or not. Don't let patterns laid out in this book or any other unofficial writing guide govern your writing exclusively. Regulations change often, and no published text can keep up with all the changes. Remember you're accountable to what is *official*—know the official instruction, and use it.

When you write Navy enlisted evaluations, as just one example, first get a thorough knowledge of NAVMILPERSCOMINST 1616.1 (of course, as with any directive, always make sure it's the effective version and that it incorporates the latest changes). You can then use the enlisted evaluation guidance found in this or any other text to help you generate ideas, freshen your writing, or clean up the format. Similarly with fitness reports, letters, messages, staff papers—above all, get the basic reference down first.

Use Other Guides, as Available

Make use of any informal guidance that is available, either personal help from experts or written guidance such as comes later in this book. You can learn a great deal from such informal material. For example, the "bullet format" that we have become so accustomed to was almost entirely an *unofficial* development. We learned to write that way from seeing and talking about others' innovations. Used judiciously, unofficial guidance—word of mouth from selection boards, good examples of a point paper you've seen, printed guides of various kinds—can give a writer invaluable help.

Of course, never just take phrases from a pamphlet or book like this one and plant them in your argument without adaptation. Not only is doing so dishonest, but it also usually doesn't work, coming across as foreign matter in the midst of your thoughts. Use writing guides to give you *perspective,* not to replace your own thoughts.

Do the Necessary Research

By searching out official and unofficial guides to the kinds of documents you must write (and checking with any local experts), you will have solved a major part of the writing problem. Having done so, take account of all the notes, documents, directives, messages, and other written information you already have on hand, and consider what more you require. Then *do the required research.*

When writing messages aboard ship or ashore, the standard means of research is to search message and other shipboard files. When writing naval letters, one often looks to directives, office files, regulations, manuals, policy letters, and operating instructions. Writing a performance evaluation, on the other hand, primarily requires knowledge of a service member's performance. Similarly with award nominations—the research required is to get the facts about what an individual has done. JAGMAN Investigations can call for a variety of kinds of research, from conducting interviews to looking into regulations to evaluating procedures and logs, and so forth.

Library research such as one learns in high school or college is occasionally called for in naval writing—when writing a professional article or drafting a speech, for example. Guided by a standard tool such as the *Air University Library Index to Military Periodicals,* you can look into past articles to see what has already been said about your subject. There are many other guides to periodicals, as well as card catalogs for book information. Base or station librarians can guide you in this research.

The point is that your situation and writing task govern the kind of research you must do. Be sure to talk to experts at your command or nearby about new writing tasks. For example, see the executive officer about writing letters and directives; consult a local staff judge advocate on JAGMAN Investigations; and see staff librarians and civilian consultants often when you work on major staffs. Don't forget to consult past files of reports of the same kind you have to do, and the people who once put those reports together if still on station or reachable by phone. These sources can offer invaluable suggestions on where to start and how to proceed.

Draw Up an Outline

Once convinced you have enough material (admittedly, sometimes hard to tell), prepare to write. At this point, unless you have only a short memo to draft, pause long enough to *write out a rough outline*. Don't make it so formal that you focus more on outlining than on writing, but use it to set your sights.

By going through your notes and listing specifics in an outline, you're checking the road map and putting the car in gear. Use this organizing as a starting technique, whereby you review all the material you have, getting it fresh in mind. As you read through your material, your mind will unconsciously begin structuring beyond what you've put down on paper; the engine will be revving up more than you realize. Once you've got an outline down on paper, you can usually begin writing.

Of course, there are other "brainstorming" or "freewriting" or "first-drafting" techniques, all of them methods of what used to be called "rhetorical invention," of finding the important things to say, and then beginning to say them on paper. These launching techniques have been studied in depth by modern rhetoricians, and if you've been taught a particular method in a composition class, go to it. Use whatever launching technique works best for you. Outlining is simply one of the classic ways to begin.

Incidentally, there's no magic to that first outline. If it proves faulty later, you can change it. And sometimes it will be premature. If you see holes in your argument and realize you haven't done enough spadework, stop and do further research, but then come back and rework the outline again.

The reviewing, rereading, and reflection you do to prepare an outline will also subconsciously prepare you to begin to write. The outline itself will become a compass by which you can arrange your notes, orient each section, and keep your perspective as you steam along.

Write the First Drafts

Once begun, go ahead and *draft as much as you can* of the point paper or letter or whatever you're composing. Try not to let anything stop you from getting the bulk of your argument down on paper. You can always go back and alter what you've written, but there's a momentum to writing, a "heat of composition," and if you stop the momentum, you may not be able to get back into the mood.

That is, bulling your way through a rough draft is always better than getting sidetracked by looking up dates, figures, names, or other technical details. Don't consider grammar, spelling, punctuation, or style while writing the basic draft. You may have learned that you tend to write in the passive voice, and that using passive verbs keeps you from speaking forthrightly and adds needless bulk (good advice)—but don't worry about that problem now. You can go back and fix the passives and other errors later, when you're tired, for example, or between watches, musters, phone calls, meetings, or inspections. Getting a draft of an important document on paper is not easy to do in hassled minutes late in the day.

Even if you know your organization is faulty, don't stop short to fix it, but keep writing the sections you find on the tip of your tongue. You'll usually find some place for what you're writing now, or at least for what you'll eventually get into by not stopping now. Ideas can come and go very quickly. Get them down on paper, and wait to polish and revise them. *Capture the raw material,* and leave the finished product till later.

Once you've got a pretty full draft on paper, take a bit more time to go back and clean it up. Fill in the names and figures (always double check the figures), flesh out passages you left sketchy, correct the errors, add needed transitions, and look up whatever you need to. In other words, fill out your draft and smooth it a bit. Make that first draft a *complete* draft. Once you've gotten that far, the rest is all revision.

Let it Rest a While

One of the keys to a good revision is rest—a time for your composition to stew. A limited duty officer working for a three-star in OPNAV remarked in frustration, "If they'd only let the paper ferment a half hour, anyway. But they're caught up in the rush, and as a result they don't get to the major topic until page three."

On a large writing project, *let your first draft sit for a week or two,* if you can, before you come back to it. If it's a smaller project, maybe a day or two will do. If you simply don't have the time, at least try to *wait thirty minutes* before proceeding. You'll often be surprised how different your text will look with just that much time separation. As yet one other alternative, if you literally have no time and you still have to make it good, there's a standard device practiced by many staffers that you might try:

- Have one person write the document.
- Have two others immediately edit.

Next time, don't wait till the very last moment.

Revise for Content and Organization

Whenever you look back at the document, providing it has any length or importance at all (and isn't just a brief memo), *go through the whole piece quickly several times,* scanning for the following:

- **First, ensure the document "answers the mail,"** or accomplishes its basic purpose. If it is an award justification, does it show off the special quality of the service member's performance? If it's a CASREP, will the addressees know exactly what equipment has failed and why (if you know why), what you are doing about the problem, and what your ship can and cannot accomplish?

"Lots of staffers produce packages that look terrific and are formatted perfectly, but *don't answer the original question.*"—Navy Captain in OPNAV

> **Paperwork Reduction?**
>
> **We want your suggestions as to paperwork reduction. It may take some courage for us to say we don't need that piece of paper, but it will help all of us reduce our administrative burden. So give us your suggestions. In triplicate.**
>
> **—Overheard at a staff briefing**

If you don't think you've served your basic purpose, add information or revise the wording until you are sure the specific audience you're addressing will get the *very key points*.

- **Second, correct major problems in structure and length.** Presenting your major points clearly is important, but putting them in a logical order is just as crucial. *Beginning quickly* and *writing short* are particularly vital to most naval documents. Usually keep background sections very brief, and get on to your key statement or argument very early on. Briefing memos throughout OPNAV, for example, are typically too lengthy and wait too long to express the point. With all kinds of documents, do your best to get your major request, answer, conclusion, or argument *at the very beginning* of your paper, leaving details and explanations to follow.

Of course, there can be other problems in structure besides not starting fast. See that all the paragraphs link with the ones before and after and that your overall structure is clear and easy to follow. Then make sure there's no extraneous material.

- **Third, look at each paragraph's structure and support.** Having placed the paragraphs correctly, make sure that the evidence justifies your points. Do you need to add details, figures, or other support? Check all supporting material for pertinence, completeness, and proper order. Also check to see if you can use topic sentences better within your paragraphs to guide the reader and help shape information.

Remember that sometimes a written paragraph may not be the right way to present information. You can often render detailed support best in the form of bullets or lists, providing that those bullets are grammatically parallel in form, hard-hitting, and not too numerous. See "Naval Editing," below, for more on this topic.

- **Finally, check the sentences**. They should be clear, straightforward, and grammatically correct. Make sure they link naturally to the sentences that precede and follow, are varied in structure (although primarily subject-verb-object), and are also varied in length (but not too long).

If you take all of these major steps, you can be pretty sure to have a sound document, in substance and organization.

Rules for Naval Editing

Confident that your content is correct and your organization straightforward, you have yet to check for correctness of format, correctness of details, and overall effectiveness. We usually term this process *editing*.

Sea Language

There seems to be an idea abroad that Secretary Josephus Daniels abolished *starboard* and *port* in the United States Navy. That is not true. Even with the enormous infiltration of landsmen in World War II, the Navy, like the Merchant Marine, still uses *forward* and *aft*, *starboard* and *port*, *above* and *aloft* and *below*. Ships still have *bulkheads*, not walls; *cabins* or *compartments*, not rooms (except in composition like wardroom, storeroom, etc.); *overheads*, not ceilings, and *decks*, not floors. What Mr. Daniels did change (and it was all to the good) was the form of orders to helmsmen, who no longer have to translate "port your helm!" into a right turn on the wheel, or "starboard helm!" into a left turn. Orders are now given as "left" or "right" so many degrees, or "left" or "right standard rudder" with variations, assuming the helmsman to be facing forward.

It will be a sad day when sea language leaves English literature. . . .

—from Samuel Eliot Morison, "Notes on Writing Naval (*not* Navy) English," *The American Neptune*, Vol. 9, January 1949, p. 10.

You can edit your own work, and you often do with shorter documents. For lengthy items or any document of major importance, editing is a crucial process that should not be left to the necessarily shortsighted drafter.

Many people edit others' documents more often than they write their own. Division officers typically draft more than they edit, while executive officers usually edit much more than they write (and spend a great deal of time proofreading documents). All should know the basic principles of editing. Those principles include, first, the Naval Writing Standards, referred to above and outlined later in this chapter, and second, the naval editing rules, discussed below.

Of course, not all these rules will apply to any particular document. On shorter documents, you can look for several problems at once. With written material several pages long or with a document that is extremely important, you may want to go through the writing several times, looking for different problems each reading. Seldom should you check all ten items in the following section one by one when analyzing any particular document. However, if (along with the Naval Writing Standards) you also master the ten rules discussed below, you can be pretty confident you know the basics for making writing both *correct* and *effective*.

1. Check that the Document Follows the Prescribed Formatting

Even if the Navy or Marine Corps has no particular format for a certain document, your own command may have. Most letters, messages, correspondence folders, and formal reports require a standard format, especially at major commands. (If a local format differs from any format outlined in this book, follow the local practice.) The quickest way to get a piece of correspondence on a ship or a staff sent back to you is to make simple technical errors that a YNSN or PFC admin clerk can catch.

In fact, if funding is scarce or time is short, harassed senior officials on staffs may use simple errors in formatting or documentation to reduce the number of substantive decisions they have to make. If they find an error, say, in a POM issue paper or other funding request, they may simply cancel your request with a stamp: "Standard Procedures Not Followed." This matter is not a joke; budget requests of major monetary proportions (and *months* in the processing) have failed simply because the format or documentation was not exactly right.

2. See if You Can Use Bullets, Lists, or Other Visual Signposts

Almost every naval author now knows the usefulness of "bullet" format. A "bullet" is a piece of type used to introduce each element of a list or series; it is shaped like a bullet seen head-on: •. Bullets should be grammatically parallel in form and in sentence order, like this:

- Bullets help a reader to skim.
- Bullets emphasize key ideas.
- Bullets often enliven a text.

If you use sentence fragments instead of complete sentences, head them with an introductory statement. Ensure each such bullet

— completes the clause,
— contains the same basic structure, and
— expresses its content concisely.

Many typewriters and some word processors don't have bullets, in which case

* hyphens (-),
* asterisks (*), or
* small Os (o)

will do just as well.

Other means of drawing attention to particular data visually are boxes, →pointers←, <u>underlining</u>,

vertical spacing,

bold print, larger type, or ALL CAPS. Of course, there are stars, pointing hands, and many other devices.

The degree you can freely use such visual formatting devices varies with the formality of the document you're writing and whom you're writing for. Bullet format, of course, has now gained wide acceptance and can be used in all except the most formal documents (hardly ever in award citations or letters to Congress members, but almost anywhere else).

Remember to use strategic placement in any list of information. Normally the *first* item in a series of bullets (and to a lesser extent the last) will attract the eye and be much more obvious than an item buried in the middle. Of course, don't overdo your use of typographic devices or you'll make your document more difficult to read (rather than less), and you'll be accused of being "cute" too.

3. Add Headings for Readability

Headings (of several levels) can help readers immensely to skim a text, to find material, and simply to comprehend. Consider using them on any documents longer than a couple of paragraphs (including memos, messages, staff documents, and directives). Use them even on very short pieces if you need to catch a reader's eye.

Also make them as interesting and pointed as possible, to draw readers' attention. Make sure they're grammatically parallel—match a full sentence with a full sentence, a noun phrase with a noun phrase, and so on, within each level of heading. See the headings in this text as examples.

4. Make Subject Lines Brief but Descriptive

The special kind of heading called a subject line is standard to many naval documents, but it can be crafted well or poorly. Make your subject line a sentence fragment that announces the specific subject of your communication. Without using more than ten words or so, make it as genuinely informative as possible.

For example, instead of "Engine Failure" as a subject line for a speedletter, write "H-3 Engine Failure Data" or, better yet, "Request for H-3 Engine Failure Data." That phrase is more specific but still brief.

Be careful not to use acronyms in subject lines, unless to identify a standard term parenthetically, as in "Global Positioning System (GPS) Requirements." Remember, there are thirty to forty uses for some abbreviations (like "IT" or "EIC") in the government; several acronyms have many meanings even within the naval services. Don't lose or confuse your readers.

Try to avoid long noun strings (hut-2-3-4 phrases) here. The subject line "Approved Joint Air Defense Operations Manual Position Reporting System" is very hard to follow, stringing together as it does some nine adjectives and nouns in a row. Is the subject a Position Reporting System for an Operations Manual on Approved Joint Air Defense? Or is it a Manual Position Reporting System for Approved Joint Air Defense Operations? Strung together in this way, no one but an insider will know.

5. Preface Long Documents with Summaries

Regulations require that writers use summaries to preface technical reports, research reports, correspondence packages, and many staff documents—but we could use summaries more widely still. This text discusses several common methods of summarizing that are highly useful for naval writers. *Briefing memos*, *executive summaries*, and *abstracts* find wide use at commands and staffs, for they help busy senior officials quickly get the gist of any particular document. And *letters of transmittal* are helpful in pointing out key information in the complex documents or the thick correspondence packages that they introduce.

Also useful are the standard ways of organizing what follows the summary. For example, consider the *inverted pyramid* used by news writers to organize material following the news lead (also discussed in this text). This technique accustoms journalists to state the vital facts first, then to add other information in descending order of importance, a habit that can be useful in naval documents as diverse as performance evaluations, briefing memos, and naval messages.

6. Add Visuals, if Appropriate

Charts, graphs, and drawings may help explain your topic or convince your audience. They're normally most appropriate in oral briefings, technical reports, and professional articles rather than correspondence. However, they may find places as appendixes to correspondence packages and occasionally in instructions. Make sure they are simple and clear in presentation—cluttered visuals only confuse and slow the reader.

7. Check for Grammar

You can best check for errors in grammar if you have a good knowledge of it. Second best is to keep at hand a standard grammar handbook and to use it often to check your writing. A good yeoman or secretary can also help, but you may not always have such an expert to consult. A grammar check on your computer is also an intriguing possibility, but the current software can't check everything. So have a handbook on hand, and know it well.

8. Proof for Errors in Spelling, Punctuation, Capitalization, and Figures

Computer spell-checkers can pick up spelling errors, but those programs won't find homonyms and technical terms not in their files. A good dictionary (a collegiate dictionary, not a pocket one) will help. The "Handbook" later in this text provides a short guide to punctuation, capitalization, and proper use of numbers, with naval examples.

In the process of reading, we all naturally anticipate and skip a great deal. We skip even more while editing our own writing. When editing you should work to break this habit, and learn to *proof* rather than just read.

How to proof? One way is to use a pointer (like a letter opener) and systematically move it from word to word while you read, pausing to look at each punctuation mark. This method will ensure you don't inadvertently skip over any word, number, or mark on the page. A second method is to read *out loud* as you edit—that will also help you pay close attention to the text. A third way is to work backwards sentence by sentence through each paragraph, purposely upsetting your ordinary reading custom. This process will help you look at each sentence with a fresh eye.

9. Check the Visual Impression Your Document Makes

Make sure the type is clean and dark and the margins are reasonable—normally one and one-half inch on the left, one inch at top and bottom, and an inch on the right (but you can adjust the margins to center short documents on the page). The sharp appearance of paperwork can make as much of an impression as a sharp uniform and be even more important in its impact.

10. Notwithstanding All the Above—*Get the Work Out*

"Don't fine-tune all you write, but only the most important things. *Get the work out*. Adapt existing documents to your purposes—don't reinvent the wheel."—Lieutenant Commander

As a commander advised, "Before you order a revision, count the cost. 'A few minutes' on a single document easily becomes 30; a 'few minutes' on everything works into hours. You end up taking three or four days before you get a document on its way." Even Naval Writing Standards (described later in this chapter) are not sacred compared to getting work through the top of an organization. As a limited duty officer who once worked in the office of the Vice Chief of Naval Operations commented, mild problems of passive voice, doublings, and the like in a briefing memo or letter for signature would not stop a package from going forward for signature if everything else was right.

At sea, this penchant for getting the job done is perhaps even more pronounced. As one senior captain commented, "Those who really operate don't overedit; those who really edit don't operate." To *operate* is naval jargon for to *perform*; and almost everywhere in the naval services, performance is what really counts. Of course, bad writing can profoundly inhibit performance. That's why editing is so important. But everything has its season—and sometimes meticulous editing is out of season.

The Mode of Writing: By Hand, By Typewriter, or By Word Processor?

Word processing has revolutionized naval paperwork. Formats can be loaded into word processors, reducing the need for yeomen, secretaries, and clerks. Networks and electronic bulletin boards have replaced the printed memo at some offices, and "paperless ships" have become possible in conception. In such circumstances, naval professionals who can only write by hand are living in the horse-and-buggy days, and those who can type but have never used a word processor would seem to have a "fear of flying" of some kind. Enter the modern era and don't handicap yourself: *Learn word processing.*

"A most important ability for an officer is the ability to type, and to type a good draft the first time, instead of relying on external admin support. It's the difference between getting something out in an hour or two and getting it out in three to four *days*."—Commander in OPNAV

Of course, many questions have yet to be sorted out. Lots of officers are bringing personal computers aboard ship—can they be used to process classified material? Many senior officers, on the other hand, are still more comfortable with pen and paper than with an electronic keyboard—should they have to use a screen and hard disc? It is important to sort out

> **On Editing *Quickly***
>
> Many naval writers do a great deal of editing—executive officers, executive assistants, yeomen, administrative clerks, etc. Sometimes they need to get through piles of paperwork quickly. Here's a procedure for *editing short documents quickly*, adapted from copy editors in a newsroom.
>
> Read the document three times—once for familiarization, once while you edit it, and once to check your work. This is an old rule, but it's a good one.
>
> 1. *For the first reading,* put your pencil down and just try to understand the document. If it makes no sense or has major gaps in information or logic, send it back for a rewrite or simply disapprove it. But if it holds together and has no glaring problems, move on to the second reading.
>
> 2. *The second time,* read slowly and scrutinize the text. Make sure the writing is concise and to the point. Above all, see to it that *the main point comes early and that it is fully supported,* proven, or explained.
>
> Do each stage of your work only once. After checking for thesis and support, *decide what should be cut out, and cut it* before editing the details. Don't waste time meticulously rewriting sentences and combining paragraphs only to cut them later.
>
> Then *look for errors* in spelling, grammar, punctuation, and style. Look at every sentence, every word, every letter. Make sure every word gives exactly the meaning desired. Decide if one word can do the job of two or three or four, and if so, chop fearlessly. Also look for places to use bullets or lists in place of dense paragraphs. Of course, know Naval Writing Standards, and edit to comply with them, too.
>
> *Check for accuracy.* Add all figures; calculate percentages too. Don't leave anything for later. Also get the format right. See to it now that the document does the best possible job of communicating.
>
> 3. *Do the third reading,* again at a normal pace to ensure your editing hasn't botched the meaning. Sometimes when editing you think faster than you can write. Your good ideas often go down as incomplete thoughts or sentences or as sloppy transitions. You've checked the writer's work; now check your own.
>
> If, after three readings, you're satisfied you have a sound document, sign or initial it, and send it on.

exactly what advantages word processors do and do not have and how best to fit them into the naval paperwork world.

What Computers Can Help Us Do

Computers can help us revise much more quickly and more effortlessly. With a computer instead of a typewriter, you won't be erasing or using white-out or correction tape, and you won't spend hours completely retyping documents. True, revising requires many key strokes and is not totally painless, but, in general, the computer helps us to revise and modify *before* we print.

It also helps in formatting and producing documents. You can alter format and the general appearance with a keystroke or two. Margins, spacing, type fonts, underlining, bold face, italics, superscripts, etc., are all within a computer operator's command, not left as they once were to the typesetter and the printing press. As a result, with the aid of high-quality dot-matrix or laser printers, professional-appearing documents are well within any computer operator's reach.

And who is that computer operator? Nowadays, virtually anyone with typing skills and the ability to read. Yes, some programs can take hours and days to learn and can be very troublesome—but many computers are extremely user friendly. As long ago as 1985 midshipmen in a class at the Naval Academy were assigned to walk into the basement of Nimitz Library, review the instructions on a MacIntosh computer, and type a two-page assignment, using that word processor. Many had typed and printed out a professional-appearing document in just over an hour, though they had never used a word processor before. Word-processing programs have been simplified even more since then. Although mastering a whole program still takes time, as long as you possess basic typing skills, word processing comes quickly to hand.

Increasingly, word-processing programs possess special features besides typing and revising. Spell-checkers find all but homonyms and seldom-used terms; style-checkers let you adjust sentence length and passive voice; and programs for outlining, note taking, and indexing help with all these processes. Graphics and desk-top publishing find use in many naval offices.

So which should be your normal mode of operation:

- Paper drafts personally handwritten for others to type up smooth?

or

- Machine drafts personally typed on a word processor for a secretary or yeoman to review and print out?

Where possible, opt for the latter. As one senior naval officer commented:

> The latter mode is more than just a change of medium. It introduces a much fuller control over the finished product and permits a tightening of the production loop from *days* (for multiple iterations) to *hours or minutes*. The official who selects the machine mode is far more capable of rapid response when that is called for, and is functioning in the same language and vocabulary as his yeoman. My experience as an executive assistant says that the official who uses the machine will be *significantly* more effective in correspondence.

Are there any downers to the machine mode? Of course. Or perhaps we should call them *limitations*.

Limits That Computers Have

- **They will not solve all your problems.** "Garbage in, garbage out" remains a standard rule. Service members must still learn composition, research, editing, drafting, revising, and all manner of other communication skills. The word processor remains *a tool* and can't substitute for thorough research, clear expression, and good reviews.

• **They will not find all common errors.** Spell-checkers and style-checkers will neither locate nor correct incomplete sentences, apostrophe misuse, dangling modifiers, agreement problems, or other common writing errors all of us tend to make.

• **They still take time to use.** Though revising is much easier on a word processor than by hand or typewriter, the time to type a document into the machine hasn't changed appreciably from standard typing. Initializing discs, saving text, numbering and naming documents, or a myriad of other standard word-processing operations can all consume minutes or hours of the day.

• **They don't eliminate the yeoman or admin clerk.** If originators don't use a word processor, a yeoman must enter the document into a computer, format it, and so on. And administrative personnel must still make copies, distribute, file, collate, and perform myriads of other tasks besides typing.

• **They sometimes lose documents.** If you forget to save the document and haven't printed any hard copy, you can lose hours or even days of work. The computer viruses talked of recently can even destroy documents you have saved.

• **They invite over-revision.** "The word-processor is a two-edged sword," an XO remarked. "A CO would like to see things different ways, so you'll run a document three, four, five, six times, even if it's a POD that circulates only within the command. We easily become subjugated to the word processor." The XO was right. Thirty seconds of pen-and-ink changes can easily become ten minutes when you have to put the disc back in, retype, resave, command to print, and reshuffle the pages—and longer if the pagination and paragraphing change. Moreover, when revising "just a word or two" you can easily forget about the automatic word-wrapping function of a word processor and thus lose or misplace a few words or a whole line.

Procedures You Should Follow

Because we have word processors, and since secretaries and clerk-typists are a fast-disappearing species throughout government, more and more of us have become our own word processors. Advice on details of word processing should be taken to heart by everyone who manages, edits, writes, or otherwise uses computers for writing. Follow this advice:

• **Save files frequently** (at least every 15 minutes), and **make both disc and hard-copy backups.** A power surge can erase hours of work, and poor labeling, an inadvertent mistroke, or a computer gremlin of some sort can delete a whole file from a disc. Periodically save the file on a backup disc, and also keep a hard copy. Intermittently print out hard copy when engaged in long projects.

• **Revise on hard copy.** Spelling and other typos tend to be more noticeable on paper copies than on computer screens. Moreover, some features of a programmed document do not appear on the screen but only become obvious when printed.

• **Make sure the printer makes readable, professional copy.** Low-quality dot matrix often looks unprofessional (like cash register tape) and is hard to read. Some high-quality dot matrix is almost indistinguishable from type and is highly professional in appearance. Laser printers put out better copy than anything a typewriter can produce.

• ***Use* but *don't overuse* typographical features** such as formatting, underlining, bold print, font style, etc. Used judiciously, such functions can help a busy reader get the key points. Overuse of fancy type styles and changes in size of type can make a page resemble an old-time billboard advertisement for a circus rather than a professional document.

• **Use the spell-checker and thesaurus.** While it will not eliminate the need to proof, a spell-checker will help you catch errors. A computer thesaurus can help you improve your style.

• **Make pen-and-ink changes** with word processing as well as typing. The Correspondence Manual allows for a couple of pen-and-ink corrections per page, and advises, "Rarely retype correspondence already in final form merely to correct typographical errors, word omissions, or other mistakes." Apply this counsel to word processing as well as typing. Of course, make corrections neatly, whatever the method.

• **Remember to use a dark ribbon.** Don't make readers strain their eyes on faint print.

• **Use ample margins**, usually at least an inch on all sides. Don't crowd.

• **Use good quality paper.** Some computer paper is of poorer quality than others; you may have to feed your printer bond paper page by page for very important documents (adjusting to letterhead as needed).

Gender in Writing: Some Quick Pointers

The Correspondence Manual directs us to avoid stereotyping men and women on the basis of gender and suggests that, where possible, we use pronouns and titles that include either sex. As it points out, "Such [gender-free] language fosters mutual understanding and demonstrates the Navy and Marine Corps' commitment to equal opportunity for all members." However, the manual also recognizes some complexity when it advises to "avoid creating curiosities such as 'freshwoman' for freshman and 'seaperson' for 'seaman.' Such awkward terms only invite ridicule."

Legal issues further complicate this subject. For instance, a Joint Chiefs of Staff directive stipulates that titles established in directives or law, such as "airman" or "Chairman, Joint Chiefs of Staff," should be used *as is* (though the directive counsels selecting sex-neutral titles when establishing new positions). And since there are laws limiting combat roles to men, the exclusive use of male pronouns in reference to combat personnel seems perfectly appropriate. A problem occurs when male service members come back from combat exercises or sea time in combat ships: often they lapse and forget to use the more generic terms. Also, more and more ships and military units include women as temporary or permanent members of their crews.

One other important factor is tradition. Tradition reaches deep in the naval services, and naval authorities wisely foster tradition, knowing the great part it plays in human communities. Partly from tradition, no doubt, when women first entered the Navy Academy the Superintendent decided that the term "midshipman" would not be changed, but that the proper terms to use would be "male midshipman" and "female midshipman." Many similar decisions are even now being made throughout the services, and universal rules are hard to come by.

Complicating the situation is the occasional poor choice of alternatives. Few naval professionals would want to step away from all traditional terms immediately if the alternative is (as it once was) use of terms such as "Unaccompanied Officer Personnel Housing" (UOPH) in place of the time-honored "Bachelor Officers' Quarters" (BOQ).

In the face of such complexities, *keep your wits about you*. Realize that certain choices of pronouns or titles may offend, thereby proving obstacles to effective communication. Remember also that the specific way they offend may differ, depending on the situation and the audience. Both males and females can take offense—and rightly and wrongly in either case, depending on the situation.

Follow the advice outlined below (based on the Correspondence Manual, among other sources) when you need to change single-gender references to gender-neutral ones.

- **Write directives as if talking to a group of readers, or one typical reader.** Use "you," stated or implied. Instead of "The young officer must take his training seriously," write "Take your training seriously," or just "Take training seriously."
- **Choose plural pronouns such as "they," "their," or "them."** Replace "A chief can submit his request to his division officer" with "Chiefs can submit their requests to division officers." Note, however, that the use of "their" with a *singular* antecedent, as in "Anyone can take their laundry off base for cleaning," is technically incorrect ("anyone" is singular). While usage is changing and we use such reference very often in speech, in formal writing you will be safer to say, "All sailors can take their laundry off base for cleaning."
- **Reword sentences to eliminate pronouns.** In place of "The private should return to his barracks," say, "The private should return to barracks." Instead of "None of the Marines was proud of his performance in the exercise," say, "None of the Marines was proud of the exercise." (Be alert to subtle shifts of meaning, as in this revision.)
- **Substitute articles for possessive pronouns.** As an alternative to "Every petty officer must be assigned her watch station by Friday," write, "Every petty officer should be assigned a watch station by Friday."
- **Use terms referring to a particular sex in reference to a particular person.** Although it is often wise to use job titles that include both sexes, such as "service member" instead of "serviceman," "chair" rather than "chairman," etc., you may still refer to "Spokeswoman McCarthy" and "Chairman Jones" in reference to the actual sex of the person cited.
- **Occasionally write "he or she,"** as in "He or she must choose a place of duty carefully." Don't overuse this method. Repeated reference of this kind, as in "He or she should take his or her seabag with him or her," becomes very awkward and tiresome.

Famous Phrases *in Navalese*

Here are five famous phrases, as some naval bureaucrats would have written them. See p. 26 for the original phrases.

1. **Argumentative contesting by originator has not yet commenced.**
2. **May the metallic underwater explosive devices be execrated. Let maximum velocity in a forward direction be achieved forthwith.**
3. **When the subordinates desire, permission is hereby authorized for the expeditious emission of ordnance.**
4. **Upon arrival in the theater of operations, an overview of the environment was conducted, and the conflict situation was subsequently resolved in my favor.**
5. **Expenditure of ammunition is to be withheld pending the detection of whiteness in the ocular organs.**

One final note: don't allow concern over the gender issue to interfere with your rough drafts—wait till you edit to adjust all such references.

Naval Writing Standards

Naval writers must often edit to cut out "navalese"—bureaucratic prose. There is no reason to start from scratch in identifying or correcting such bad writing habits. The 1983 edition of the Correspondence Manual (SECNAVINST 5216.5C) identifies faults and how to correct them by setting what it terms "Naval Writing Standards."

Refer to the first chapter of the Correspondence Manual for the fullest account of these good stylistic practices. Reproduced below is a condensed version of that chapter, a series of summaries and a short editing procedure drawn from the workbook for the Correspondence Manual, entitled Better Naval Writing: A Workbook for Chapter I of SECNAVINST 5216.5C (OPNAV 09B-P1-84).

Rules for Organized Writing

Start Fast, Explain as Necessary, then Stop

When you write a letter, think about the one sentence you would keep if you could keep only one. It should appear by the end of the first paragraph. The strongest letter highlights the main point in a one-sentence paragraph at the very beginning. Put requests *before* justifications, answers *before* explanations, conclusions *before* discussions, summaries *before* details, and the general *before* the specific. Avoid mere chronology.

"If you were to put the word 'Motherhood' at the heading of every instruction, you could eliminate 'Background,' 'Purpose,' and 'Discussion' altogether and go right to 'Action.' As currently written, instructions and notices *never get to the point.*"—Commander

Delay your main point to soften bad news, for example, or to introduce a controversial proposal. But don't delay routinely. In most cases, plunge right in.

To end most letters, just stop. When writing to persuade rather than just to inform, you may want to end strongly—with a forecast, appeal, or implication. When feelings are involved, you may want to exit gracefully—with an expression of good will. When in doubt, offer your help or the name of a contact.

Downplay References

Reading slows down with every glance from the text to the reference caption. Justify such distractions by using only references that bear directly on the subject. Avoid unnecessary or complicated references. Many letters need no references at all, while others are complete with a reference to only the latest communication in a series.

When you respond to an earlier communication, subordinate it to your main point. Don't waste the opening—the strongest place in a letter—to merely summarize a reference or say you received or reviewed something.

Be sure to mention in the text any reference cited in the reference block. List references in the reference block by following the order of their appearance in the text.

Use Short Paragraphs

Long paragraphs swamp ideas. Cover one topic completely before starting another, and let a topic take several paragraphs if necessary. But keep paragraphs short, down to roughly four or five sentences. Call attention to lists of items or instructions by displaying them in subparagraphs.

Now and then use one-sentence paragraphs to highlight important ideas.

Take Advantage of Topic Sentences

A paragraph may need a topic sentence, a generalization explained by the rest of the paragraph. Then again, it may not. In a short paragraph a topic sentence may be unnecessary if a reader can follow the writer's thinking without it.

Be alert to the advantages of topic sentences, for they help shape masses of information. Without them, some paragraphs make readers shrug and say, "So what?"

Write Disciplined Sentences

Here are four ways to write sentences that call attention to important ideas:

— Subordinate minor ideas. Subordination clarifies the relationship between ideas and prevents the overuse of *and*, the weakest of all conjunctions.

The Famous Phrases Key

1. **I have not yet begun to fight.**
2. **Damn the torpedoes; . . . Go ahead, Jouett—Full speed.**
3. **You may fire when ready, Gridley.**
4. **I came, I saw, I conquered.***
5. **Don't fire until you see the whites of their eyes.**

*The navalese version was used as epigraph to CAPT Carvel Blair, USN. "Effective Writing, Navy or Civilian." U.S. Naval Institute *Proceedings* (July 1968):131.

— Place ideas deliberately. An idea gains emphasis when it appears at either end of a sentence. To mute an idea, put it in the middle.
— Use more parallelism. Look for opportunities to arrange two or more equally important ideas so they look equal. Parallelism saves words, clarifies ideas, and provides balance. Go by the first words of the series; all should use the same parts of speech (verbs in the previous sentence).
— Try some mini-sentences. An occasional sentence of six words or less slows down readers and emphasizes ideas.

Rules for Natural Writing

Speak on Paper

Make your writing as formal or informal as the situation requires, but do so with language you might use in speaking. Because readers *hear* writing, the most readable writing sounds like people talking to people. Begin by imagining your reader is sitting across from your desk. Then write with personal pronouns, everyday words, and short sentences—the best of speaking.

Use Personal Pronouns

Though you needn't go out of your way to use personal pronouns, you mustn't go out of your way to avoid them. Avoiding natural references to people is false modesty. Speak of your activity, command, or office as *we, us, our*. These words are more exact than the vague *it*. Use *you*, stated or implied, to refer to the reader. Use *I, me, my* less often, usually in correspondence signed by the commanding officer and then only to show special concern or warmth.

Rely on Everyday Words

The complexity of our work and the need for precision require some big words. But don't use big words when little ones will do. For example, deflate *utilize* to *use*, *commence* to *start*, and *promulgate* to *issue*. Prefer short, spoken transitions over long, bookish ones. Use *but* more than *however* and *still* more than *nevertheless*. Avoid the needless complica-

Banned Bombast

The Terrible Ten Bureaucratic Verbs

Instead of	Try
commence	begin, start
disseminate	give, issue, pass, send
facilitate	ease, help
implement	carry out, start
necessitate	cause, need
obligate	bind, compel
prioritize	rank
promulgate	issue, publish
terminate	end, stop
utilize	use

The Awful Eight Long-Winded Phrases

Instead of	Try
at the present time	at present, now
due to the fact that	due to, since, because
for a period of	for
for the purpose of	for, to
in accordance with	by, following, per, under
in the amount of	for
in the event that	if
until such time as	until

For a comprehensive list of overdressed, bookish, and legalistic language to avoid, see Section F of the Correspondence Manual, "Simpler Words and Phrases."

tions of legalistic lingo; let a directive's number or a letter's signature carry the authority. Use *here's* for *herewith is* and *in spite of* for *notwithstanding*. Write to express, not to impress.

Use Some Contractions

Contractions link pronouns with verbs (*we'd, I'll, you're*) and make verbs negative (*don't, can't, won't*). They are appropriate in less formal writing situations. Day-to-day naval writing should be informal enough for contractions to fit naturally. If you are comfortable with contractions, your writing is likely to read easily, for you will be speaking on paper. If contractions seem out of place, you may need to deflate the rest of what you say.

Keep Sentences Short

For variety mix long sentences and short ones, but keep the average under twenty words. Though short sentences won't guarantee clarity, they are usually less confusing than long ones. Try the eye test: average under two typed lines. Or try the ear test: break up most of the sentences you can't finish in one breath.

Naturally Written Night Orders

Seldom is there more need for clarity than in drafting night orders. The set of night orders shown below, which dates from World War II, is admirably terse and clear.

Thursday Night 23–24 December

1. **On the Truk-Rabaul line.**
2. **Course 100°T**
3. **Speed: About 10.2 kts (Aux load and propulsion on #4 main eng.)**
4. **At 2130 CC to 190°T (this should put us right along the line).**
5. **Stop and listen each half hour, as last night.**
6. **This is a hot spot! Men of war are making the transit. They have radar. We do not. We *must* see or hear them. I will be in the fish grotto. Wallop me at any suspicion of contact.**
7. **Moonrise 0354. Zig Zag if it is bright.**
8. **Call me at 0530.**

Respy
R. J. Foley

—Transcribed from the Night Order Book of 23–24 December 1943 of USS GATO (SS 212), commanded by Robert Joseph Foley. Used by permission of the Nautilus Memorial Submarine Force Library and Museum.

Ask More Questions

A request gains emphasis when it ends with a question mark. Do you hear how spoken a question is?

Be Concrete

Without generalizations and abstractions, lots of them, we would drown in detail. We sum up vast amounts of experience when we speak of dedication, programs, hardware, and lines of authority. But lazy writing overuses such vague terms. Often it weakens them further by substituting adjectives for examples: immense dedication, enhanced programs, viable hardware, and responsive lines of authority. Don't use a general word if the context allows for a specific one; be as definite as the situation permits. Work to avoid vague, high-sounding language in job descriptions and personnel evaluations.

Listen to Your Tone

Tone—a writer's attitude toward the subject or readers—causes few problems in routine letters. You may pay special attention to tone, however, when the matter is delicate. The more sensitive the reader or issue, the more careful you must be to promote good will. Tactlessness in writing suggests clumsiness in general. When feelings are involved, one misused word can make an enemy. To avoid tactlessness, use positive language.

Cutting the Fat

Here's a memorandum that one naval office sent to another, along with a revision of that memorandum by someone fed up with "budget-speak."

ORIGINAL MEMORANDUM:

1. Your request for $750, as stated reference (a), is approved. Contact Mr. John Jeffries, X4442, to coordinate the appropriate procedures for utilization of funds from Account 15B of the Foundation Support Fund.

2. Liaison with the Foundation Support Committee Associate Budget Officer indicates that this item will be supported out of departmental funds in the future, and, therefore, is not considered a routine budget item for Foundation Support Funds.

REVISED MEMORANDUM:

1. You can have the $750. John Jeffries at X4442 will tell you how to get the money.

2. In the future, though, your department will have to pay for this, instead of the Foundation Support Fund.

COMMENT:

Problems of passive voice, long words, and officialese plague the original memorandum. The writer should shorten it, make it more direct, and speak more naturally.

Rules for Compact Writing

Cut the Fat

Give your ideas no more words than they deserve. The longer you take to say things, the weaker you come across and the more you risk blurring important ideas.

Suspect wordiness in everything you write. When you revise, tighten paragraphs to sentences, sentences to clauses, clauses to phrases, phrases to words, words to pictures—or strike the ideas entirely. To be easy on your readers, you must be hard on yourself.

Avoid "It Is" and "There Is"

No two words hurt naval writing more than *it is*. They stretch sentences, delay meaning, hide responsibility, and encourage passive verbs.

Like *it is* constructions, forms of *there is* make sentences start slowly. Don't write these delayers without trying to avoid them.

Prune Wordy Expressions

Wordy expressions don't give writing impressive bulk; they clutter it by getting in the way of the words that carry the meaning. *In order to* and *in accordance with*, for example, are minor ideas that don't deserve three words.

Free Smothered Verbs

The most important word in a sentence is the verb, the action word, the only word that can *do* something. Weak writing relies on general verbs, which take extra words to complete their meaning. When you write a general verb such as *is* or *make*, check to see if you can turn a nearby word into a verb (not *is applicable to* but *applies to*, not *make use of* but *use*).

Splice Doublings

As the writer, you may see some differences between *advise* and *assist*, *interest* and *concern*, or *thanks* and *gratitude*. But your readers won't. Repeating a general idea can't make it any more precise.

Shun "The -ion of" and "The -ment of"

Most words ending in *-ion* and *-ment* are verbs turned into nouns. Whenever the context permits, change these words to verb forms (not *for the accomplishment*, but *to accomplish*, not *for the development of*, but *for developing*).

Prevent Hut-2-3-4 Phrases

"They'll come to see the Admin Officer. Sheepishly they say, 'I have to write this thing.' It's almost like they're coming to see the priest. They come quietly. They show me this document, this. . . . After a while, with some work and criticism, they get a little better."—LDO, Admin Officer on a Carrier

Though you should cut needless words, sometimes you can go too far. Avoid hut-2-3-4 phrases, long clots of nouns and modifiers. Readers can't tell how the parts fit together or where they all will end.

We must live with some established hut-2-3-4 phrases such as *standard subject identification codes* for *subject codes*, but you can keep them out of whatever you originate by adding some words or rewriting entirely.

Avoid Excessive Abbreviating

Excessive abbreviating is false economy. Use abbreviations no more than you must with insiders and avoid them entirely with outsiders. Spell out an unfamiliar abbreviation the first time it appears.

If an abbreviation would appear only twice or infrequently, spell out the term every time and avoid the abbreviation entirely. Put clarity before economy.

Captain Queeg Hides Behind the Passive Voice

Captain Queeg of Herman Wouk's novel, *The Caine Mutiny*, writes in the same peculiar way that he thinks. Among several methods of evading responsibility that he employs in the Grounding Report printed below is a wide use of the passive voice. One wants to ask—of the passages in italics—*by whom* were these things all done?

Grounding of USS CAINE (DMS 22) in West Loch, 25 September 1943—Report on.

1. Subject vessel ran slightly aground on mudbank in subject area on subject date at 0932. It was floated off by YT 137 at 1005. There were no casualties or damage.
2. The reason for the grounding was failure of the engine room to respond in time to engine orders telegraphed from the bridge.
3. This command *has recently been relieved*. The state of training aboard *is believed* to warrant a drastic drilling program to bring performance of crew up to proper standards. Such a program *has been instituted*.
4. It *was intended* to submit a grounding report in full tomorrow morning by messenger. Report *was not made* by despatch to ComServPac at the time because help was at hand, damage was nil, and the matter appeared to be disposable without troubling higher authority unnecessarily. Regret *is expressed* if this estimate was erroneous.
5. It *is believed* that the intensive drilling already instituted in this command will rapidly bring about competent performance, and such incidents will not recur.

PHILIP FRANCIS QUEEG

—From Herman Wouk's *The Caine Mutiny (New York: Pocket Books, 1951), pp. 183-84*. Used by permission.

Rules for Active Writing

Avoid Dead Verbs

Passives cause problems. They make writing wordy, roundabout, and sometimes downright confusing. To avoid this infectious disease, learn how to spot passives and make them active. Most of your sentences should use a who-does-what order. By leading with the doer you automatically avoid a passive verb.

Learn the Symptoms of Passive Voice

A verb in the passive voice uses any form of *to be* plus the past participle of a main verb:

am is are was were be being been

> **So Much for the Active Voice**
>
> **The following excerpt is from a certain headquarters' supplement to the Correspondence Manual (italics added):**
>
> **2.c. The writer should favor the active voice over the passive voice. . . .**
> ***The very next sentence*:**
> **2.d. The repetition of words and phrases *should be avoided.* . . .**

PLUS

a main verb usually ending in *en* or *ed*

Sentences with passives don't need to show who or what has done the verb's action. If a doer appears at all, it follows the verb. But most passives in naval writing just imply the doer, sometimes a severe problem when the context doesn't make the doer clear.

Know the Three Cures

- Put a doer before the verb:
  The part must have been broken by *the handlers.*
  The handlers must have broken the part.
- Drop part of the verb:
  The results *are listed* in enclosure (2).
  The results *are* in enclosure (2).
- Change the verb:
  Letter formats *are shown* in the Correspondence Manual.
  Letter formats *appear* in the Correspondence Manual.

Write Passively Only for Good Reason

Write passively if you have good reason to avoid saying who or what has done the verb's action. This situation may occur when the doer is unknown, unimportant, obvious, or better left unsaid:

Presidents are elected every four years.
(doer obvious)

The part was shipped on 1 June.
(doer perhaps unimportant)

Christmas has been scheduled as a work day.
(doer better left unsaid)

When in doubt, write actively, even though the doer may seen obvious or unimportant. You will write livelier sentences (not, livelier sentences will be written by you).

On Revising to Naval Writing Standards

Here's a method of revision designed for making sure a document conforms to Naval Writing Standards. This short, step-by-step method of revision helps to enliven your writing, unburdening it of navalese:

1. Read through the writing quickly.
2. Circle the main point and make sure it's early.
3. Flag unnecessary words and ideas:
   —"it is," "there are"
   —smothered verbs
   —doublings
   —excessive abbreviating
   —wordy and unnatural expressions
   —hut-2-3-4 phrases
   —"the -ion of" and "the -ment of"
   —passive constructions
4. Revise ruthlessly, editing out what you've flagged.
5. Read through for continuity and smooth flow, checking for topic sentences and clear transitions.
6. Use visual guideposts—subject lines, subparagraphs, white space, parallelism—to highlight key ideas and their relationships.
7. Read the writing out loud. Does it sound like people talking to people? Have you used personal pronouns and an occasional contraction or question?
8. Put the writing down and come back later for a final edit.
   —From Better Naval Writing, OPNAV 09B-P1-84, p. 56.

Some commands have the philosophy that "anything we write is OK as long as it gets the job done." But commands are known by their external communications. We know the best boats by what crosses our desks.

—Flag Lieutenant of a SUBGROUP

In the peacetime Navy, we evaluate a ship only by inspections—and by *correspondence and messages.* So the writing is absolutely vital.

—Navy Lieutenant on a DESRON Staff

2

Letters, Memos, and Directives

Naval correspondence does not suffer from a lack of good guidance. The 1983 edition of the Department of the Navy Correspondence Manual (SECNAVINST 5216.5C) not only improved the old manual but, as we have seen, it set excellent new Naval Writing Standards. It also exemplified those standards in its writing style and examples. If that manual is not already on your desk, get your command to order you a copy or photocopy short parts of it for your own use. Don't use just the manual's guidance on formats: also consult its wide-ranging advice on writing and on paperwork management.

This chapter presents advice and examples following the guidance of the Correspondence Manual but focuses on subjects not given thorough discussion there. It pays much less attention to format (exact line spacing, window-envelope procedure, details of assembling multipage letters, etc.) than that text. A short treatment of the style, content, and format of a standard naval letter begins this chapter. Advice on particular kinds of naval letters follows. Then comes a discussion of business letters of several types, succeeded by some pointers on memos. A short section on naval directives ends the chapter.

The naval examples shown here are based on actual documents (as they are throughout this text), although some individual and ship names have been changed for privacy and some examples have been edited slightly. The advice has been gathered from wide interviewing and research.

Standard Naval Letters

Use standard naval letters to write to organizations within the Department of Defense. Both commands and individual service members write standard naval letters, the marks of which are formality, the use of standard naval terminology and abbreviations, and a businesslike tone.

Standard Naval Letter—Its Format, Style, and Use

Here's some advice on how to compose the standard naval letter.

5216
N13
1 Jan 90

From: Author, USNI Textbook
To: Navy and Marine Corps Officers (All Codes)

Subj: HOW TO COMPOSE THE STANDARD NAVAL LETTER

Ref: (a) SECNAVINST 5216.5C, Dept. of the Navy Correspondence Manual

1. Follow reference (a)'s superb advice: *Jump right in* with the main point in a *brief* opening paragraph.

2. Putting your chief request or conclusion somewhere in the opening three or four lines helps get the attention of the right people from the very first. As reference (a) puts it,

> When you write a letter, think about the one sentence you would keep if you could keep only one. Many letters are short and simple enough to have such a key sentence. It should appear by the end of the first paragraph. The strongest letter highlights the main point in a one-sentence paragraph at the very beginning. Put requests <u>before</u> justifications, answers <u>before</u> explanations, conclusions <u>before</u> discussions, summaries <u>before</u> details, and the general <u>before</u> the specific. (CM, 1–3)

3. After the opening, spell out the details. Write in relatively brief paragraphs—normally no more than four or five sentences apiece. Writing short paragraphs and punctuating them by white space makes reading easier; long paragraphs can discourage the reader and encourage skimming.

4. Keep most letters down to a single page. Try using enclosures to spell out additional material, if more than a page is necessary. In longer letters use headings to keep the reader oriented and to help in ready reference (see paragraph 6, below).

5. Use the standard naval letter to correspond with DOD activities, primarily, but also with the Coast Guard and some contractors. Send business letters to other external addressees. Of course, before you even write the letter, make sure some other means won't suffice. Telephone calls documented by memos for record can often take the place of formal correspondence.

6. Follow this additional guidance:

a. Show Codes and Titles in Addresses. Whenever practical, indicate the office that will act on your letter by including a code or person's title in parentheses right after the activity's name.

b. Compose a Good Subject Line. Craft the subject line to make it genuinely informative. Try to limit it to 10 words or less. In a reply, normally make the subject line the same as that of the incoming letter.

c. Make Pen and Ink Changes. Rarely redo correspondence already in final form just for a rare typo, an omitted word, or other minor error. Unless the importance of the subject or addressee justifies the time of retyping, make neat pen and ink changes—up to two per page, and to all copies—and send the correspondence on. This advice holds for word processing as well as typing. Although some features of word processors (like spell-checkers) can help you avoid errors in the first place, making minor changes with word-processing equipment still takes time and can also introduce unnoticed errors in pagination or spacing.

d. Reply Promptly. Answer most received correspondence within 15 days. If you don't anticipate being able to answer within that time, inform your correspondent of the expected delay (by phone, if possible).

e. Get All the Other Details Right. See reference (a) for further details as to standard-letter format, window-envelope format, markings on classified letters, and joint letters.

7. Include your phone number and name when your correspondence might prompt a reply or inquiry, and make sure you include your own office code. Use no complimentary close ("Sincerely," etc.) on a standard naval letter. For rules on signatures (on who signs the letter, on "by direction" authority, on how to put together a signature block, etc.), see reference (a), page 2–9.

R. E. SHENK

Copy to:
USS ALLHANDS (NAV 1)

Official Personal Letter

The technical details of communicating with higher commands on personal matters (such as enlisted applications for warrant officer or LDO, officer applications for augmentation or change of designator, and so on) are spelled out pretty clearly in the Correspondence Manual. It recommends this procedure for Navy people:

> Prepare your letter on plain bond paper in standard-letter format. . . . Address the letter to the higher authority and send it via your commanding officer and any other commands as circumstances require. The commanding officer prepares an endorsement on letterhead paper and forwards the correspondence to the next via addressee, if any, or to the higher authority. (CM, 9–1)

Marine Corps personnel use NAVMC 10274, Administrative Action (AA) Form, as prescribed in MCO 5210.2.

Normally, the format to use in such letters is thoroughly specified by the responsible authority. In all blocks requiring precise data, the only way a person can go wrong is to leave something out, supply faulty information, or make errors in grammar or spelling. Any such mistakes might admittedly call into question the administrative ability of the person applying. If you pay attention, it's difficult for you to go wrong in supplying that information.

However, what gets said in the "remarks" section, if there is one, can influence those who take action on your request. How well you write this paragraph (or paragraphs) is crucial to your letter's success.

Writing a Good Remarks Section

Usually you craft this section to add key information and express the nature of your interest or desire. There are several possible approaches. One approach is to recount, in brief summary form, what special qualifications or interests make you well suited for the position for which you are applying.

For instance, in the following excerpt a Surface Warfare Officer justifies his request for a change of designator to Supply by emphasizing his strong academic background, his experience and course work in business, and his operational experience. He manages to work into this paragraph many of the pertinent highlights of his naval service. True, these highlights might be picked up by board members in their review of his service record, but he *makes sure* the board sees them by mentioning them in his letter.

Having completed nearly four years of service as an Unrestricted Line Officer, I strongly desire to broaden my career by transfer to the Naval Supply Corps. My civilian experience includes a strong academic background:

- B.A. (summa cum laude, Phi Beta Kappa), Univ. of Pennsylvania
- M.A., Cambridge University, England

- Several positions in the business and arts management fields, often involving considerable fiscal responsibility

Following graduation with honors from Surface Warfare Officer School in April 1982 I began a tour of duty aboard USS EL PASO (LKA 117), holding demanding billets in engineering and operations. As both Auxiliaries Officer and Administrative Department Head, I have worked closely with the ship's Supply Department and have gained much insight into Supply procedures.

The officer might have made his background even more impressive by naming the positions he held in business and arts management, or perhaps by specifying the fiscal responsibility he has had ("I was responsible for a $400,000 budget," etc.).

Besides mentioning your *own* accomplishments as in the letter above, you can also cite *command* accomplishments to which you've made a significant contribution. The lieutenant who authored the "closing statement" below thought his command's good maintenance record reflected well on his own performance as Maintenance Material Control Officer and enhanced his request for augmentation.

During my tenure as Maintenance Material Control Officer (MMCO), Fighter Squadron THIRTY-THREE has been recognized as one of the top commands in Fighter Wing One. Functioning during a post-deployment period with the lowest requisition priority in CFW-1, the oldest F-14A aircraft in the naval inventory, and substantial Fleet Maintenance Fund reduction, VF-33 has aggressively pursued operational commitments rivaling those of any deployed unit. Significant accomplishments while I have been MMCO include:

(a) 100% sortie completion rate during FFARP.
(b) Best missile expenditure record in fighter community for FY 1987.
(c) Overall FY 1987 sortie completion rate of 97.2% during 3657.6 flight hours, with mission capability rate high of 87.2% (CNAL average is 74.4%).
(d) Achievement of zero NMCS/PMCS requisitions on three occasions, and maintenance of zero FOD rate during CY 1987.
(e) Lowest XRAY message error rate CY 1987 (highest in CY 1986), and finest aircraft logbooks in Fighter Wing One.

These achievements reflect my commitment to aviation maintenance duty. I am resolute in my career intentions and respectfully request augmentation to the regular Navy.

Although perhaps somewhat more technical than it need be (not all the members of the augmentation board will be aviators, nor will everyone understand all the abbreviations), this closing statement does spell out impressive specifics, accomplishments that stemmed in part from this officer's own work. He even supplies comparative data for the board's information, and his closing comments sound forthright.

Figure 2.1 is an example of a complete letter of application. As the writer explains, he was originally rejected for pilot training because his eyesight, while good, was less than perfect. Now, having been a Naval Flight Officer for several years, he is applying for pilot training in a "transition" program that does not require quite the same degree of visual acuity as the original program. This officer's letter does well both in listing specific details supporting his request and in expressing the desire and aptitude for the requested program.

Endorsement to a Personal Request

In official requests, sometimes only a paragraph or two is for general remarks. In contrast, the endorsement to such a request is usually free-form. A commander can write endorsements as a few short paragraphs or can use bullet form (as adapted to standard naval letters). Like performance evaluations, the endorsement does best when it begins with an overall opinion, then sketches specifics, and ends with a recommendation.

However, the endorsement will usually have a much stronger impact than any single performance evaluation on whether the request is approved. For one thing, rather than being filed away in the service record with all the other evaluations, the recommendation remains attached to the request while it is being processed. For another, although the service record may be on hand for those who make the decisions, the command's recommendation will usually be the only evaluative document on hand to comment on the specific request being made.

Clearly, it is very important to craft the endorsement well. Not only commanders but also juniors who make requests should know how to write endorsements. Juniors should normally submit a draft endorsement along with the request letter.

What steps should you take in composing an endorsement? First of all, **speak specifically to the particular request being made**. Specific comments are relatively easy to make if the member's past service has been related in any way to the request at hand. The paragraph below endcrses an unrestricted line officer's application for redesignation as an intelligence officer (163X). Since the officer has been the squadron's intelligence officer, the endorser can speak directly to the officer's intelligence-related duties:

He is the proven performer who has substantially enhanced the squadron's intelligence and radar identification training program. In his role as an intelligence instructor, he has provided positive, aggressive leadership and technical guidance during the intelligence/mission-planning phase of fleet replacement aircrew training. He has also performed expertly during the

Figure 2.1 Official Personal Request. The writer expresses a good attitude while narrating many pertinent details.

26 June 1987

From: Lieutenant ____________, USN, XXX-XX-XXXX/1320
To: Commander, Naval Military Personnel Command (NMPC-432N)
Via: Commanding Officer, Attack Squadron SIXTY-FIVE

Subj: REQUEST FOR BOMBARDIER/NAVIGATOR TO PILOT TRANSITION

Ref: (a) BUPERSMAN 6610360

Encl: (1) Current Flight Physical (forms 88 and 93)

1. I hereby apply for Pilot Training, under the provisions of reference (a).

2. Enclosure (1) is forwarded per reference (a). The date of my birth is 14 May 1958.

3. I certify that I have not been previously separated from any Flight Training Program of the Army, the Navy, or the Air Force.

4. Throughout my childhood I made every effort to follow in my father's footsteps and pursue a career in Naval Aviation. My strongest desire throughout my Naval Career is to become a Naval Aviator. After graduating from the United States Naval Academy in May 1981, I reported to Flight School at Pensacola in January 1982. I was not physically qualified for Student Naval Aviator because my visual acuity was less than 20/20; however, I aggressively accepted training as a Naval Flight Officer. Upon completion of my training I received my first choice of communities because of my class standing. In April 1983 I reported to Attack Squadron FORTY-TWO, home of the A-6 Intruder. I completed the training syllabus at the top of my class and also as the number four CAT I Bombardier/Navigator for FY 1984. I again received my first choice of orders and reported in June 1984 to Attack Squadron SIXTY-FIVE, the "World Famous Fighting Tigers." I complete my tour with Attack Squadron SIXTY-FIVE in August 1987, and I am in receipt of orders back to Attack Squadron FORTY-TWO as an instructor for replacement aircrews.

5. I have accumulated 1080 hours of total flight time, of which 920 are in the A-6. I have 235 carrier landings on four aircraft carriers. I qualified and was designated a Post-Maintenance Functional Check Flight Crew Member within 18 months of reporting to Attack Squadron SIXTY-FIVE. I was designated as a Mission Commander as a junior LTJG. My experience and accomplishments in both my ground job and role as a crewmember increased rapidly, and I was rewarded with added responsibilities. Based on my proven aeronautical abilities and superb knowledge of the A-6 Intruder flight and weapon systems, I have been assigned to fly with the inexperienced replacement pilots as well as visiting senior Naval Aviators.

6. The "All Weather Attack Community" in my mind is the most important and exciting branch of U.S. Naval Carrier Aviation. There is nothing more rewarding to me than to fly the Intruder in its environment, the way it is meant to be flown, and put bombs on target, on time. I have tremendously enjoyed the A-6 Intruder as a Bombardier/Navigator. I feel that the Co-Pilot and Mission Commander experience that I have obtained in the A-6 Intruder have

Figure 2.1 *(continued)*

Subj: REQUEST FOR BOMBARDIER/NAVIGATOR TO PILOT TRANSITION

prepared me well and would greatly facilitate my transition to the pilot program. I am a proven performer. I have excelled at every challenge presented to me and am confident that, if selected for transition, I will be able to do the job exceedingly well. I will continue to be an asset to the U.S. Navy and to the A-6 community after completion of flight training.

Medium Attack Tactical Employment School (MATES 1-85/2-85) and during weekly intelligence training briefs to staff and replacement aviators.

In many other cases—applications for subspecialty, requests for entry into technical programs, and so on—a commander can, with profit, cite specific experience directly related to the request.

At other times, **try to connect the individual's general qualities with the particular request**. Below, in an endorsement to the letter cited earlier in which a surface line officer requested a change of designator to Supply, the ship's captain points out aspects of the lieutenant's past performance that make him particularly apt for a Supply career:

A recent squadron command inspection rated his Admin Department OUTSTANDING, with Lieutenant ___ receiving special praise for his superb organizational skills, close attention to detail, and dedication to the concept of "service to the crew." All these qualities should serve him well in the Supply community.

Another possibility is to **make specific comparisons to others**. This technique is used well in the following endorsement to an officer's request for selection to civilian postgraduate school:

Although Lieutenant ___ is ninth in seniority among thirteen talented lieutenants in this command, he is this squadron's <u>number three lieutenant</u>, a rating all the more remarkable since the two officers rated above him are board-eligible for lieutenant commander this fall while Lieutenant ___ has only recently been promoted to lieutenant.

Then you might **try other ways to state the degree of your support**, for these statements can also help the selection board. Here, in endorsing a chief's request to be considered for limited duty officer, the commander makes it clear that he'd want that chief working for him:

I would be pleased to have Chief ___ under my command as a commissioned officer, proud to have her in my wardroom, and gratified to know that the support establishment was in the hands of someone as capable as she.

Finally, it may be important to **let the board know the length and closeness of your observation** of the person in question, if not already obvious. For instance, although the Marine lieutenant colonel writing below was not in the direct chain of command, the officer making the request for augmentation called him and asked for a letter. He gladly responded, speaking in the first sentences of the circumstances of his knowledge of the lieutenant:

During my recent tour as the Consolidated Public Affairs Officer in Okinawa, Japan, I observed 2ndLt ____'s performance of duty—as Media Operations Officer for one of the Corps' largest and most complex public affairs offices—for over six months.

Example of a Complete Endorsement

Overall, the best endorsements are ones in which *the facts themselves speak*. The endorsement in Figure 2.2, of the request for pilot transition shown above in Figure 2.1, doesn't depend just on the commander's reputation and expressed opinion. Instead, at crucial moments the writer adduces strong evidence that the officer possesses qualities appropriate to a pilot. Because of the presence of convincing details, the readers can *see for themselves* both the quality of the person being recommended and the fit between the person and the qualification being sought.

Letter to a Promotion Board

When there is no format to a particular "request" letter, you must do your best to write with the particular communication situation in mind.

For example, neither in the Naval Military Personnel Manual (MILPERSMAN) nor in the U.S. Marine Corps Promotion Manual (MCO P1400.31, Vol. 1) is there any standard format prescribed for writing a letter to a promotion board. These references simply direct you to use a standard naval letter. MILPERSMAN article 2220110—the reference on Navy officer boards—does stipulate that any "third-party correspondence" must contain a written acknowledgment by the eligible officer that he or she desires it in the record. Besides setting out such standard procedures and listing an address, neither MILPERSMAN nor the Marine Corps order helps by telling you how or when to write such a letter.

In contrast to most evals or fitreps, letters to the board may be read by the whole board and not just by the briefers (there is no universality here; each board sets its own policy). Hence, such letters can make a very strong impression, for better or for worse. What governs the impression you make? Let's look at those three keys to any writing situation—whom you're writing to, who you are, and the nature of your message.

To whom are you writing? Remember, a promotion board is composed of individuals senior to those under consideration. These individuals have wide naval experience, so you don't need to explain to them how the service works. On the other hand, they will not all be experts in your particular career field. On a Navy chief's board, for instance, some rates will be unrepresented, and so a few technical details may have to be explained. But always remember that board members typically have a great deal to do in a very short time.

Who are you? Obviously you are someone under consideration, and junior to your audience. You are a member of the Navy or Marine Corps, and should sound like one. Respectfulness is your proper demeanor. You

Figure 2.2 Endorsement to a Personal Request. This endorsement—to the officer's letter in Figure 2.1—provides a commander's perspective on the officer making the request.

DEPARTMENT OF THE NAVY
ATTACK SQUADRON SIXTY FIVE
FPO NEW YORK 09501-6212

1542
Ser 00/272
13 JUL 1987

FIRST ENDORSEMENT on LT ____________, USN, XXX-XX-XXXX/1320 ltr of 12 July 87

From: Commanding Officer, Attack Squadron SIXTY-FIVE
To: Commander, Naval Military Personnel Command (NMPC-432N)
Via: Commander, Carrier Air Wing THIRTEEN

Subj: REQUEST FOR BOMBARDIER/NAVIGATOR TO PILOT TRANSITION

1. Forwarded, most strongly recommending approval.

2. LT _______ has been assigned to Attack Squadron SIXTY-FIVE throughout my entire tour as Executive Officer and Commanding Officer. From the start he set the standard for professional excellence in this command. He has consistently ranked as one of the top lieutenants since reporting to the "Fighting Tigers." He has held nearly every major junior officer billet, producing flawless results. He was handpicked by Commander, Medium Attack Wing ONE to augment VA-176 during deployed Mediterranean Operations in order to bridge aircrew manning shortages and experience. During this short-fuzed deployment, he exceeded every expectation. His performance and tactical acumen underscored his versatility and "comfort level" with the all-weather attack mission. He is a proven leader who produces under pressure, and he currently holds the VA-65 Austin-Inglis Award for professional leadership.

3. LT _______'s outstanding aeronautical skills coupled with his ardent desire make him a logical choice for selection as a student Naval Aviator. I have no doubt that he will maintain the highest levels of performance as a pilot. His enthusiasm, determination, and naval instincts will enhance the "competitive edge" he must maintain while under instruction. He is command material. In my eighteen years of naval service I can think of no finer candidate for this program. He has my strongest possible recommendation for Pilot Training and ultimate reassignment as an A-6 Pilot.

____

must not appear to be looking for any advantages but just fair treatment. On the other hand, you have a right to your say, and from your firsthand knowledge may be able to contribute what no one else can.

Finally, what is your message? Your message is *not* that you should be promoted. That's the board's decision, and, in fact, only the board is in the best position to make that decision. Your goal, if you write, is to explain circumstances in your record that do not stand on their own. You really have no business writing at all unless there are some special circumstances or facts the board doesn't know or might overlook about your past performance, items not discoverable or not well explained in your service record. What kinds of circumstances? Unusual duty, for example, or an unusual pattern of career assignments. A logical explanation of broken service might be well received. Of course, there are many other possibilities.

The communication situation suggests a number of dos and don'ts, outlined below. No doubt your knowledge of the particular kind of board to which you are writing, your knowledge of yourself as an officer or enlisted person, and your knowledge of the particular case you need to make will suggest many additional points:

Do:

- Be as brief as the subject matter allows (long letters, regardless of content, are viewed dimly). Write at most a page or a page and a half.
- Write respectfully to the board members.
- Assume they are scrupulously fair.
- Get to the point quickly.
- Spell out explicitly and clearly the vital facts; put them in logical order.
- Explain unusual circumstances.
- Explain the positive aspects of any negative facts.
- Have your letter read by former selection board members, if you can, or other experts such as senior officers and leading chiefs.

Don't:

- Explain what board members will already know.
- Make grammatical or spelling errors.
- Express negative opinions or emotions either toward naval service or toward particular individuals.
- Write a letter to the board *at all* if you have no clear reason to do so.

Figure 2.3 is a letter submitted by a Navy lieutenant to a lieutenant commander board. He sent it because he had been out of the service for three years and wanted to explain the circumstances. Respectful, to the point, and clear, this letter spends its main effort explaining the unusual circumstances of the lieutenant's leaving, then returning to Navy duty. It makes the most of positive aspects of those circumstances—that he had stayed in the government even though he had left the Navy; that he returned to the Navy as soon as his three-year FBI obligation allowed; that he excelled even when in the FBI; and that he immediately began renewing his qualifications once he returned to Navy duty. Overall, the letter makes a very positive impression.

Figure 2.3 Letter to a Promotion Board. An officer explains the special circumstances of his leaving and then returning to active duty.

27 April 1987

From: Lieutenant ____________________, USN, XXX-XX-XXXX/1320
To: President, FY 88 Lieutenant Commander Line Promotion Board

Subj: FY 88 LIEUTENANT COMMANDER LINE PROMOTION BOARD

1. I would like to submit to the board the following information for consideration in addition to my record on file:

a. I have faithfully served the U.S. Government since my original commissioning in May 1974, having accumulated 13 years of consecutive government service, uninterrupted by terminal leave of any sort.

b. I had a life-long desire to serve both in the U.S. Navy and as a Special Agent in the Federal Bureau of Investigation (FBI). Unfortunately, I had to leave the employ of one to pursue the other. I enjoyed a very successful career with the U.S. Navy from May 1974 until January 1981. It was only after much vacillation that I elected to pursue a career in the FBI. Early during my three-year obligation to the FBI I decided that I wanted to return to the U.S. Navy. Throughout my FBI tour I continued to perform to the best of my ability, receiving seven letters of commendation for my performance, including two from the Director of the FBI, the Honorable William H. Webster. I point this out to show that my desire and ambition to excel have never diminished.

c. The FBI restricts a Special Agent from participating in the military reserve, making it impossible for me to retain a reserve commission with the U.S. Naval Reserve during those three years.

d. In the spring of 1984 I received my reserve commission, which was necessary to reapply for recall to active duty. I was informed, though, that there were no quotas for recall back to U.S. Navy (Regular). However, the TAR program was available, and I was subsequently selected for this program and assigned to the Naval Air Reserve, Norfolk. I immediately took it upon myself to get refresher training and then NATOPS qualified in the F-14A Tomcat, eventually receiving orders as a staff instructor to the F-14 FRS in August 1985.

e. I applied for augmentation at my earliest qualification date, August 1985, and was selected in September 1985 with redesignation to the Regular Navy on 3 January 1986.

2. I sincerely believe my record speaks for itself. I have maintained the highest standards of excellence through both careers, and my goal is clear - to SERVE, ADVANCE, and COMMAND in the U.S. Navy. I feel I have demonstrated the talents and abilities required for success in the U.S. Navy and respectfully request the board deliberate these when deciding upon my selection for promotion to lieutenant commander.

____

Letter of Instruction

The personnel-related letter of instruction (LOI) is a nonpunitive warning to a service member about subpar performance (another letter of instruction is a preexercise directive—we won't cover that here). You can issue the LOI either to an enlisted person or to an officer. It amounts to very formal counseling, counseling combined with a "memo for record" kind of documentation. This letter is a variation of a Navy Page Thirteen or a Marine Corps Page Eleven entry in a service record, though the LOI is somewhat more formal than either since it is issued directly to the individual.

Some commanders issue an LOI only when it documents performance poor enough to lead to the service member's relief or transfer to other duties. Others prefer to issue the LOI as early as possible, when the service member's performance first begins to degrade. Those who issue LOIs early argue that issuing one at the eleventh hour is a way to get rid of a problem, not to solve it.

Composing an LOI serves two major purposes. (1) *Having to write one* forces superiors to determine and describe the specific behaviors that need to be corrected. (2) *Having to read one* requires the service member to direct attention to particular problem areas and to explicit methods of improvement. In the best case, the formality of such a written set of instructions, including very well defined goals and final attainment dates, can help galvanize a service member into great effort.

The cardinal rule in writing an LOI is to *be specific.* To generalize in the comments, to say no more than "you're a poor performer and need to build up your character and to improve in discipline," just demeans the individual and offers no real assistance. But detailing both the particulars of past deficiencies and the specifics of the needed improvement can make the LOI a highly effective counseling tool.

To summarize, the LOI should outline these five matters:

1. **The specific failures** in performance: **when, where, and what**.
2. **Actions the command has taken** to correct this problem.
3. **Steps to be taken** by the service member, **or goals to be met**, for each area of failing performance.
4. **Individuals who can help**.
5. **Not-later-than dates** for each step.

If well thought out and accompanied by the right kind of personal counseling, an LOI can genuinely aid the service member, helping greatly to turn his or her performance around. On the other hand, if the service member refuses to be helped, or for some other reason cannot meet the goals on the dates specified, this letter serves as specific documentation of the failure. It then becomes formal grounds for subsequent relief, separation, transfer, disenrollment, or other such proceedings.

Here is an example of an LOI written to an officer who has gotten behind in his warfare qualifications, including division officer administration. To be most helpful in their specific guidance, letters must usually run at least a page and a half or two pages in length. The example below is a bit shorter than the usual LOI.

1611
21 Dec 86

From: Commanding Officer, USS VESSEL (DDG XYZ)
To: Ensign J. R. Officer, USN, XXX-XX-XXXX/1160
Via: (1) Executive Officer, USS VESSEL
(2) Weapons Officer, USS VESSEL

Subj: LETTER OF INSTRUCTION TO CORRECT SUBSTANDARD PERFORMANCE

1. Your professional growth as a Surface Warfare Officer has been substandard. Specific deficiencies include:

a. Lack of satisfactory progress toward surface warfare qualification.

b. Inadequate knowledge of the 5″/54 gun system and its operation and maintenance requirements, despite your having attended Gunnery Officer School and Ammunition Administration School.

c. Inadequate knowledge of the 3-M system, manifested by improper planned maintenance scheduling and performance.

d. Inability to develop, plan, and execute a basic division training program despite specific direction from your department head.

2. To improve your performance and help you become competitive with your contemporaries, I direct you to complete the following actions by the dates specified:

a. Learn the mechanics, operation, and capabilities of the 5″/54 MK 42 MOD 10 gun, and be prepared to demonstrate that knowledge no later than 31 Jan 87 at an oral board composed of LCDR Howe, LT Soderman, and LTJG Griepentrog.

b. Complete Basic 3-M PQS (NAVEDTRA 43241D) prior to 31 Jan 87.

c. Demonstrate significant progress toward Surface Warfare Officer qualification in the areas of division officer and warfare qualification. You will establish a qualification timetable and submit it to the Senior Watch Officer, the Weapons Officer, and the Executive Officer no later than 5 Jan 87.

d. Complete the Gunner's Mate Guns (GMG) Petty Officer 3 & 2 correspondence course no later than 28 Feb 87.

3. These requirements constitute the bare minimum necessary to improve your SWO knowledge and skills. Completing these requirements

will also help you gain a more confident demeanor when dealing with juniors and seniors.

4. Individuals in your chain of command are always already to assist you or provide additional guidance. Request help from me, from the Executive Officer, or from the Weapons Officer, whenever you need it.

D. D. SKIPPER

Business Letters

The business letter should really be called "the business or personal letter," for besides sending it to businesses, you can also use it for sending thanks, congratulations, or condolence. As the Correspondence Manual points out, it can even be used "for official correspondence between individuals within the Department of the Navy when the occasion calls for a personal approach" (CM, 7–1).

You can vary the format of a business letter somewhat so that, say, a letter of condolence isn't encumbered with serial numbers or so the text of a very short letter fits in the middle of the page. The main variations, however, result from the differing *uses* of a business letter. We'll discuss several particular cases, beginning with what is probably the most common use.

Business Letter to a Business or Other Organization

Here is guidance on how to write a business letter—in the form of a business letter.

Department of the Navy
USS HALEAKALA (AE 25)
FPO SAN FRANCISCO 96667-3004

5216
Ser AE 25/28
January 10, 1990

Business or Company Name
Attn: Person Within the Company
Street Address
City, State, ZIP

THE FORMAT, STYLE, AND USE OF A BUSINESS LETTER

State the purpose of your business letter in the first paragraph unless the occasion calls for delay to soften bad news or you are introducing a controversial proposal. Don't delay routinely.

See to it that your paragraphs are no longer than about 10 lines each—the first much shorter than that. Work at writing even more clearly in letters to civilian audiences than in standard naval letters. In particular, avoid all unfamiliar military terminology, including acronyms. If you must use such specialized language, make sure to explain each term the first time you use it. A great deal that we take for granted in our internal correspondence is unfamiliar to a civilian audience.

Other things that differentiate a business letter from a standard naval letter:

1. You **don't number main paragraphs**. You may number subparagraphs (like this one).

2. There is no "From" line on a naval business letter, so you **must use a letterhead** (printed, stamped, or typed) to show the letter's origin.

3. You can express dates in month-day-year order if your readers are likely to be most familiar with that format. Whatever the order, always **spell out or abbreviate the month** rather than designate it by number. (If you express the date as 3/4/89 or 11/12/90, some readers may mistake the day for the month, or vice versa.)

4. If writing to a company in general but directing the letter to a particular person or office within it, **use an attention line** between the company's name and address. See above.

5. You may use either a salutation or a subject line in a business letter. If you use a salutation, "Make the salutation agree with the first line of the address. If the first line is a company name, the salutation is <u>Gentlemen</u> even if the attention line directs the letter to an individual" (CM, 7–3). On routine administrative matters you may replace the salutation with a subject line (as above). As the Correspondence Manual points out, "a subject line has three advantages: it orients readers to the

topic; it skirts questions of gender; and when a file number is included, it unburdens the text" of having to refer to that number (CM, 7–4).

6. Business letters typically use the complimentary close "Sincerely," whereas standard naval letters omit the complimentary close entirely. If you wish to show special deference to a high public official, you may replace "Sincerely" with "Respectfully" or the like.

Sincerely,

O. H. PERRY
Lieutenant, U.S. Navy
Administrative Officer
By direction of
the Commanding Officer

Encl:
(1) Correspondence Manual (sep cover)

Figure 2.4 is a good example of a business letter—and it gives clear guidance on the relationship of the Department of the Navy, the Navy, and the Marine Corps.

Good Will Letter

You will often want to express thanks to a person in or outside the military who has done you a favor. You might be thanking someone for a talk, for a personal favor of some kind (such as an introduction), for hospitality, or for a number of other services.

Whatever the circumstances, *be genuine*. Avoid form letters in this kind of writing, and strive especially to express genuine gratitude. The latter takes some care. Sometimes informality will help you write genuinely, the degree of informality depending on your relationship with the correspondent and the particular situation. Recount some of the details of the service rendered or what specific good it did, if you can.

Make sure your letter doesn't appear to have been written just to conform to the rules of service etiquette. To this end, *avoid the passive voice*. Saying "it was appreciated" instead of "we appreciated" will communicate aloofness, not gratitude. Of course, be timely in thanking someone; write quickly so you won't forget to write—at least within 48 hours of the occasion.

Here's the text of a letter of thanks written to a Japanese restaurant owner by the officer in charge of a small Navy unit. The writer speaks her gratitude warmly and simply.

Figure 2.4 Example of a Business Letter. A senior Marine Corps official outlines to a civilian the relationship of the Department of the Navy, the Navy, and the Marine Corps.

DEPARTMENT OF THE NAVY
HEADQUARTERS UNITED STATES MARINE CORPS
WASHINGTON, D.C. 20380-0001

IN REPLY REFER TO
1.11
HD:EHS
29 Dec 86

Ms. Fran Lazerow
Vice President
Toborg Associates, Inc.
1725 K Street, NW, Ste 803
Washington, DC 20006

Dear Ms. Lazerow:

Thank you for your letter of December 23.

Adjusting the program to make it read "Navy and Marine Corps" wherever it now reads "Navy" and then insuring that "Naval representation" includes Navy and Marine Corps representation will probably take care of my earlier misgivings.

If the conference accomplishes nothing more than an understanding of the Marine Corps as a service within the Department of the Navy and how that affects its role in joint operations, the conference, from my point of view, will have accomplished a good deal.

Permit me to elucidate a bit:

It is not merely that the Marine Corps "may consider itself somewhat of a separate branch of the service" as you state in your letter; it is a matter of law. The Marine Corps is a separate service within the Department of the Navy. "Department of the Navy" (nor, for that matter "Navy Department") is not synonymous with "U.S. Navy." The U.S. Navy is a separate service within the Department of the Navy.

Nor is it correct to say that "administratively the Corps is attached to the Navy." There are many linkages, both administrative and operational, between the Navy and Marine Corps, but in no sense is the Marine Corps "administratively attached" to the Navy. These relationships have been hammered out in law and practice over nearly a two-hundred year period, and the well-indoctrinated Marine does not regard them lightly.

"Naval," properly used, does subsume both the Navy and the Marine Corps; as for example, a Marine aviator is a Naval aviator, and Marine Corps aviation forms part of Naval aviation.

All of this is well understood by Dr. Christopher Jehn, the Vice President, Marine Corps Programs, Center for Naval Analyses. Dr. Jehn is immediately subordinate to Dr. DePoy and directs CNA's Marine Corps Operations Analysis Group.

Figure 2.4 *(continued)*

Now that we have cut away the underbrush and have good clear fields of fire, I will be pleased to help with your conference in any way I can, including the suggestion or nomination of participants, if you will let me know at what levels and with what groups you want Marine Corps participation.

From looking at your tentative agenda, I would suggest we participate in the following work groups:

1) Military History Data Availability and Accessibility;

2) Uses of Military History for Operational Planning;

3) Military History Education.

I myself would like to attend the plenary sessions.

With all best wishes for the success of the conference,

Sincerely,

E. H. SIMMONS
Brigadier General
U.S. Marine Corps, Retired
Director of Marine Corps
History and Museums

Dear Mr. Narita:

On behalf of the men and women of the Personnel Support Activity Detachment, I want to thank you for your gracious hospitality on Saturday, October 10.

From the moment you met us at the train station until our departure from your lovely restaurant, we knew we were in excellent hands. We will never forget the warmth of your reception. As a result of this trip, we are all eager to visit more places in your beautiful country.

Please extend our gratitude to your family, especially your son who so willingly took us to our destination. The day was truly blessed with good weather, good food, and good memories.

Sincerely,

The memo below on Thank-You Letters, once put out at the Naval War College, offers guidance on how *not* to write such letters.

"THANK YOU FOR YOUR THANK YOU?"

December 29, 1978

MEMORANDUM FOR DISTRIBUTION

Subj: LETTER-WRITING TECHNIQUES: THANK-YOU LETTERS

1. Special lectures, field trips, conferences, etc., require us to write thank-you letters. In the past, many draft thank-you letters submitted to the President for signature have fallen into the category of "insincere letters."

2. To reduce rewrites, here are some suggestions:

a. Determine if the letter is necessary. Some letters have come up saying essentially, "Thank you for your thank-you letter." Needless to say, they were not sent. If two recipients of letters work at the same activity, perhaps a single letter to the head of the activity will suffice.

b. Do:
- Keep it short.
- Keep it simple.
- Use short declarative sentences.
- Use adjectives that accurately describe what you are praising (e.g., the lecture was "informative," not "delightful").
- Use "Sincerely" as the closing.

c. Don't:
- Use "thanks" and "appreciation" over and over, and don't say, "Please accept my thanks." (In most cases I think they will without your having to ask.)
- Use the phrase "from your busy schedule." We are all busy—having to read that phrase only adds to our workload.
- Use the phrase "I want to take this opportunity." It's obvious you are taking the opportunity.
- Use the phrase "This is a short note." The recipient can see it's a short note.
- Dwell on the obvious (as in the phrases above).
- Try to be cute. Make your writing simple and sincere.

3. This list is not exhaustive, but it does provide a starting point. While these guidelines apply specifically to thank-you letters, they also apply generally to all types of correspondence prepared for Admiral Stockdale's signature.

[Signed]
R. Crayton
Chief of Staff

Letter to Parents

> One of the most rewarding and successful parts of my command was, surprisingly, the form letters I sent to parents. I wrote each parent of the fifty people up for awards and promotions, modifying each letter slightly. The parents fired back letters to their kids, and morale zoomed up. It was a building block for success.
>
> Such letters don't have to be long, or sexy, or even grammatically correct, but they have a great payoff.
>
> —Navy Commander, after a command tour

Parents of sailors and Marines are an interesting audience. Supportive of their children, usually patriotic, and also very understanding of the scrapes their children get into, parents will usually be very responsive if commanders treat them well. Assume in your writing that your audience is mature, intelligent, and understanding.

Write to them often. Welcome them to the unit's family. Praise their young service members on their promotions and awards. These letters will help keep up morale and will establish a relationship between the command and the parents. On more difficult subjects that might come up later, it is always easier to write to a familiar audience, one with whom you have already established contact.

Here are two good examples. Figure 2.5 is a letter from the commanding officer of a Coast Guard cutter; it congratulates the parents of a petty officer on his recent promotion to second class.

The letter whose text is shown below is based on one written to a serviceman's parents in a difficult period (the 1970s). It does pretty well with a tough subject.

Dear Mr. and Mrs. A____ :

I am writing to inform you that your son John has petitioned the government for discharge as a conscientious objector.

Petitions such as John's are handled in a prescribed manner. First, John will be interviewed by a chaplain and Navy doctor, preferably a psychiatrist, if available. Then a lengthy, formal hearing will be conducted by an officer, usually a lieutenant commander, to consider the merits of the application. A final determination will be made by the Chief of Naval Personnel in Washington, D.C.

If successful in his petition, John will be discharged, but he will be ineligible for any veterans' benefits. If unsuccessful, he will be required to serve out the full term of his enlistment. As these cases require a substantial amount of documentation, it will be some months before a final decision is rendered. Additionally, I should point out that the burden of proving the case will be John's. He must show that the ethical

Figure 2.5 Letter to Parents. The commanding officer of a Coast Guard vessel informs parents of their son's recent advancement.

COMMANDING OFFICER
USCGC HARRIET LANE (WMEC-903)
4000 COAST GUARD BLVD.
PORTSMOUTH, VIRGINIA
23703-2199

October 12, 1988

Dear Mr. and Mrs. Kempton:

I would like to take this opportunity to inform you of your son Mark's recent advancement to Boatswain's Mate Second Class (E-5). He has demonstrated exceptional initiative and personal effort in reaching this goal on the advancement ladder.

His appointment as a Second Class Petty Officer carries with it the obligation of exercising increased responsibility. I have every confidence that he will discharge the duties of his new position with the same dedication to duty he has displayed in the past.

Mark is an outstanding HARRIET LANE sailor who has set an excellent example for the junior personnel. The Coast Guard needs men of his caliber. I am sure you are as proud of Mark's achievement as we are. Best wishes to you.

Sincerely,

B. B. STUBBS
Commander, U. S. Coast Guard

convictions he holds have directed his life in the same manner as traditional religious convictions, and that the belief upon which the conscientious objection is based has been the primary controlling force in his life. Further, he must show that he gained his ethical convictions through training, study, contemplation, etc., comparable in rigor and dedication to the processes by which traditional religious convictions are formulated.

Until final resolution, John will be assigned duties other than those in the Electronics Technician rating for which he was trained. These duties will mostly consist of general cleanup and maintenance here at the naval facility.

I have talked with John at some length about the probabilities of success for his petition and about his driving philosophical outlook. In this day of an all-volunteer military, the success rate for this sort of petition is not very high. I am concerned about John because his strong aversion to participate in war (or, for that matter, even to assist a war effort) was present prior to his enlisting in the Navy. I find him a very confused young man who is frustrated with his present assignment as an Electronics Technician and quite upset with what the future holds for him. He does not appear to realize that his contract with the Navy was voluntary on his part and is a two-way one and that, to date, the Navy has completely made good its side. After reflecting on our conversation, I find John extremely idealistic and am doubtful that the world will ever be capable of meeting his expectations.

I hope this letter will assist you in understanding the process John will be undergoing. It is a difficult path he has chosen, and one that will require him to bare his soul if he is to be convincing at his hearing. If you have any questions, please write me.

Sincerely,

Letter of Condolence

> Few will go through a career without the loss of a person in a unit—a friend, a shipmate, or a subordinate. The parents, spouse, and children may have very little to comfort them; sometimes a sincere letter that expresses what the loved one meant to another will be treasured. But expressions of insincerity may be worse than not being heard from at all.
>
> —Navy Captain

If a service member has died and you must write to express your sympathy to a spouse, parents, or children, how do you go about it? There are no places for formulas here—no form letters, no canned phrases. Don't copy an example from a book, including this one. Anything that sounds insincere will be worse than writing nothing at all.

Express sympathy, sadness, or compassion. Say what you can say about the dead; say what you can in the way of sympathy with the living. You might mention the loss that shipmates feel. Perhaps the best guide is to search your own feelings and to remember your experiences with the person who has died. Reflecting on something you've shared with their loved one or something you know of the family might provide you a subject to speak on.

Be brief. Don't philosophize on the meaning of life and death; quote scripture or poetry only if you know your particular audience will receive it well. Service to country or shipmates might be appropriate subjects—or the service member's cheerfulness, dedication, good deeds. Use your best judgment. You might express your willingness to do whatever you can to help. Usually your own sympathy for the bereaved, your shared knowledge of their loved one, and your understanding of their pain are the chief expressions that might be of comfort.

Keep your tone familiar. Speak in the first person and use first names where appropriate. Show the letter to others, if you have any doubts, to see how what you have written strikes them. Sometimes chaplains can help with the writing. Pay particular care to the preparation of the letter, whether you type it or write in longhand. Keep the format simple; don't include a serial number or otherwise clutter the letter with bureaucratese.

Besides your letter there will probably be an official one from the command discussing funeral arrangements, shipping of personal effects, a command memorial service, and so on. The person who writes that letter will have to pay scrupulous attention to the accuracy of all of the details and should express sympathy too. But as a commander, leader, or friend, take the extra step of writing a personal letter. Don't mix up your genuine condolence with mere officialdom.

The first example below is a fictional passage from *Flight of the Intruder*, in which Lieutenant Jake Grafton expresses his condolence to the wife of Lieutenant (jg) Morgan McPherson.

Jake began to write. After three drafts he had the semblance of an acceptable letter. It wasn't really acceptable, but it was the best he could manage. Two more drafts in ink gave him a letter he was prepared to sign.

Dear Sharon,

By now you have been notified of Morgan's death in action. He was killed on a night strike on a target in North Vietnam, doing the best he could for his country. That fact will never fill the emptiness that his passing leaves but it will make him shine even brighter in my memory.

I flew with Morgan for over two years. We spent over six hundred hours together in the air. I knew him perhaps as well as any man can know another. We both loved flying and that shared love sealed our friendship.

Since I knew him so well, I am well aware of the depth of his love for you and Bobby and realize the magnitude of the tragedy of his passing. You have my deepest and most sincere sympathy.

Jake

The second example is an actual letter to the editor of the United Kingdom's *Navy News*. More of a tribute than a letter of condolence, it praises a Royal Navy officer named "Stuart Honour," who has just died. The Royal Navy captain who wrote it remarked later, "Perhaps the key factor in writing such letters is to mean what one says. I certainly did. Stuart's selflessness and courage are quite unforgettable."

Dear Editor:

There will be many who mourn Lieut-Cdr. Stuart Honour, who died on June 13 after a long fight against cancer.

A large number of officers and men, while passing through Haslar, formed a brief but memorable acquaintance with him at one time or another during his long spell in that hospital.

I write to pay tribute to a man whom I knew for only two short weeks, but who made such a profound impression upon me that news of his death struck hard.

Stuart displayed the good humour, resilience, and determination that are the hallmarks of the very courageous when faced with immense physical suffering. He was, quite unwittingly, the sort of man we would all like to be—physically tough, uncomplaining, and invariably considerate for those around him.

His many acquaintances will share a peculiar sense of loss. In a Service not given to expressing emotion they will nonetheless feel it, but they will also feel privileged to have known Stuart Honour and to be enriched by the experience.

G. M. S. Sayer
Captain, R.N.
Ministry of Defence, London

Letter to a New Command

Good manners are never out of style.

—Traditional

A type of business letter often taught in senior enlisted or officer indoctrination classes is the letter to a new command. New ensigns or second lieutenants will often slave over their first such letters feverishly, but later either will not spend much time on them or will fail to send them at all. Don't make that mistake; write a letter each time you transfer to a new command, and craft each letter with special care.

Such a letter is not just a courtesy but serves several distinct purposes. To start with, it alerts a ship or other station to the pending arrival of someone's relief. Normally, the command will have already heard through the personnel system of an assignment. But even if they know your name, they usually won't have much information on your specific qualifications, background, or interests. Nor will they necessarily know anything about your family status, your need for knowledge of the area (for housing, schools, etc.), or your plans for leave and arrival dates.

If you can fill in your future senior and shipmates on this kind of information, it may help them fit you into billets, ensure for a contact relief, arrange a sponsor to help you find housing, and so on. They might be able to schedule various kinds of helpful temporary duty, if you give them enough information.

Moreover, by penning such a letter, both officers and enlisted can create positive first impressions. Recently a Navy lieutenant with orders to CINCLANTFLT Staff sent a short letter to the admiral, a letter very well crafted and professional in appearance. The letter impressed the deputy, who sent it on to his boss. The admiral responded: "I want to meet this lieutenant when he comes in. Give this officer an arrival call." This lieutenant's letter set him on a fast track.

Realize, however, that a letter can backfire if it is not well conceived. The commander of an aircraft squadron sent a message to another squadron, where he knew there was a young officer who had orders to his own command. The informal message read something like this:

TO LTJG SMITH: WELCOME ABOARD. VIOLA SENDS.

The young officer wrote back, and his response was quickly admired by all those with whom he would soon be working, something he probably would *not* have appreciated. Why not? The opening of his written response was

Dear Commander Sends: I'm looking forward to coming to your command. . . .

Clearly, here as elsewhere, it's often a good idea to have your drafts reviewed before you print them and send them on.

Below is a letter of introduction from a warrant officer who has orders to report to a naval weapons station. He includes his plans to visit the area before reporting, an address and phone number while there, some details about his past duty, and other useful information.

Officer Indoctrination School
Naval Aviation Schools Command
Naval Air Station
Pensacola, FL 32508-5400
19 January 1989

John B. Smith, CDR, USN
Executive Officer
Naval Weapons Station
Yorktown, VA 23691-5959

Dear Commander Smith:

I have received orders to report to the command as relief for LTJG Arthur after graduating from LDO/CWO Indoctrination School. Although my reporting date is not until 20 February, I expect to be in the Yorktown area on ten days' leave beginning 2 February. My wife, Martha, and I will be staying at her parents' home at 1500 Cornwallis Road in Williamsburg, Virginia 23491 (phone 765-4321).

As a Chief Gunner's Mate-Technician, I supervised the performance of 38 technical personnel for the Special Weapons Intermediate Maintenance Facility at Naval Weapons Station, Concord, California, just prior to coming to school. I have also served aboard three destroyers—USS BRISCOE (DD 977), USS COCHRANE (DDG 21), and USS DAHLGREN

(DDG 43). This duty has given me experience as an ASW Work-Center Supervisor, 3-M Coordinator, and Assistant Training Coordinator.

Martha and I have two daughters, ages seven and five, and a son who is three. Since my wife is originally from the Yorktown area and has many friends and family living in the local community, we are eagerly looking forward to the move. Given our familiarity with the area, it doesn't appear we will need any special help from my sponsor.

I feel that this assignment to Naval Weapons Station, Yorktown, will provide me an excellent opportunity to use my supervisory and technical skills. Also, beginning in the summer or fall I would like to pursue a master's degree during off-duty hours, workload and detachments permitting.

Very Respectfully,

J. F. Richardson
CWO W2, USN

Yet one more example is the following letter based on one written by a Coast Guard lieutenant commander to his prospective CO. Like the letter above, it includes important information that the command ought to know. But it's a bit more informal, since the writer has met the commander before.

April 2, 1982

Dear Commander Yeaton,

As you know, I am under orders to be your executive officer. I am extremely pleased with these orders and look forward to serving in DAUNTLESS.

My previous afloat experience has been in USCGC WACHUSETT (WHEC 44), USCGC RUSH (WHEC 723), and USS HAROLD E. HOLT (FF 1070), all on the West Coast. This will be my first time in the Seventh District, and I can't wait!

I expect to detach from my present assignment on 1 July and report about mid-August. I cannot attend the Shipboard Helicopter Training Course at Mobile since its convening date conflicts with the PXO course. Unfortunately, that is the only week the course is offered. I have already passed the Rules of the Road test.

Patricia and Spenser are as excited about moving as I am. I suspect it's because Disney World is so close. Our baby, Joan, is too young to know.

Once again, I am very happy with my orders and enthusiastically look forward to serving in DAUNTLESS.

Sincerely,

Harlan B. Badger
Lieutenant Commander, USCG

Commander H. Yeaton, USCG
Commanding Officer
USCGC DAUNTLESS (WMEC 624)
U.S. COAST GUARD BASE
MIAMI BEACH, FL 33139

Incidentally, the format shown in the Coast Guard letter above (with date centered at the top, comma after the salutation, address at the bottom left, no serial number, etc.) is known as personal-correspondence format. This format is typically used by flag officers (and sometimes their aides, as was the case here) on personal flag stationery.

Letter to Answer a Congressional Inquiry

> Anyone with a 25-cent stamp can provoke a congressional inquiry.
>
> —Marine Corps General

A special kind of letter that virtually all commands must write sooner or later is the response to a congressional inquiry. Being able to write such a letter quickly and fluently is obviously a very important skill, and not just for senior officers. Commands of all sizes can receive such letters, and they must respond in very short order. While the final letter is usually honed by the XO or CO, a senior enlisted person or a junior officer could be assigned the first draft.

The Typical Situation

Most congressional inquiries to commands outside Washington, D.C., have to do with personnel. Ships' captains or unit commanders will not have to defend large issues of naval policy to members of Congress. Instead, they will normally have to handle inquiries about particular individuals' complaints.

Perhaps a sailor has been turned down for the Navy diving program and has written a letter of complaint to his local congressman about that refusal. A petty officer may have complained to her representative about not being able to strike for a particular rating, or a Marine may have written his senator, contending that he hasn't received the correct pay.

In such cases, the Congress member's staff will send a letter of inquiry either directly to the service member's command or to Navy or Marine Corps Headquarters, which will then write to the command. Sometimes the complaint originally sent to the member of Congress is vague, emotional, and clouded in perception. Indeed, the service member may not even have been the prime mover in the letter's being written. A spouse or parent may have convinced the sailor to write and may even have ghostwritten the letter.

Whatever the circumstances of the service member's writing, the Congress member normally is simply asking for information with which to respond to the complaint. True, such correspondence can have great visibility. But typically the Congress member simply needs some perspective as to the problem, and the ship or station need not be on the defensive.

In 9 out of 10 cases, all that has to be done is to fill in all the missing information and the command's perspective, to give the Congress member what he or she needs for a reply.

Follow a few simple rules when receiving a congressional inquiry (typically abbreviated "CONGRINT," signifying that someone in the U.S. Congress—either the House or Senate—has "interest" in the matter at hand). Follow the same procedures when receiving a letter of inquiry from the White House—people write the President too, and the same kind of response is required. The situations considered here are mainly the most common, those involving personnel—but with only slight modifications the guidelines below will apply to other cases too.

Respond Quickly

Members of Congress like to respond to their constituents quickly. After receiving a letter, the Congress member's staff has to write to the naval command. When it gets the letter, the naval command must investigate and write back to the Congress member; then the staff must write back to the constituent. (If there is an intermediate step via a liaison office in Washington, D.C., even more time is lost.) With time counted for mail, for weekends, and for operations, you can see that months could easily elapse were each stage not executed quickly. The rule is for a command *to respond within five days of receipt of the inquiry* (you may respond with an "interim" reply if some information is not available within those five days). Many commands get most of their "final" replies out within *a day* of receipt.

Be Factual

Research the facts and then lay out in order the actions that both sides have taken—as well as the rationale behind the command's actions. If the problem is a long-standing one, a history of actions on the ship's or unit's part may exist, and you can catalog those actions. Often the XO and CO have been involved with the issue before and will have lots of information on hand. Maybe the division officer has recorded some information in a division officer's notebook, or perhaps someone has written a memo for record about a particular sailor's request or complaint or about a key counseling session.

Whatever the situation, *be accurate, research and re-research the facts,* and *be sure of what you're writing.*

Explain the Command's Perspective

A sailor may have written out of concern for his rights. The command certainly respects those rights, but it is also the custodian of the service's rights—the sailor's obligations. Usually those obligations will not have been spelled out in the original letter. The Congress member will want to see the command's perspective on *all sides* of the issue.

To show that perspective in full, you may need to explain some key regulations or procedures, and also to outline exactly what violations of procedures may have occurred. Don't overexplain. Your correspondent is usually a very busy person who may handle more congressional inquiries in a day than your command does in a year. But remember to delineate the service-specific information needed to understand this particular problem.

Start with the facts, and proceed to explain the rationale for the command's actions. As you write, account as best you can for the service member's point of view and feelings. Admit forthrightly any mistakes that the command has made. Being straightforward, evenhanded, unemotional, and factually oriented are good ways to keep the tone right, to shun being overly defensive on the one hand and to avoid negative attitudes toward a service member on the other.

Try Seeing the Problem from the Congress Member's Point of View

Here, as in many kinds of writing, you can enhance your credibility by trying to help the reader in whatever way you can. Besides explaining the facts, do your best to try to see things from the Congress member's position.

The member of Congress will, of course, want to do whatever he or she can to address the service member's valid concerns. How can you aid the Congress member in that task? Here's one way: quite often, whether a complaint is justified or not, all the means for redressing that complaint within the service have not been exhausted. You can be very helpful by explaining to the Congress member exactly what the service member's options are, including the service member's very next move. Moreover, you might be able to provide a point of contact (with phone number) or send along forms the service member may need to pursue a further option, thus giving the member of Congress *specific aid* in responding helpfully to the original complaint.

Write in Civilian

Be careful not to confuse your reader with naval jargon or acronyms. Switch gears, step back a bit, and speak to an intelligent civilian, not a service member. Explain any acronyms you *must* use, but try to do without them. Also, use civilian-style dates (month-day-year) in the heading and throughout the letter.

Check with the Right People to Review the Situation

Occasionally, the command may need to consult a naval lawyer, officers up the chain of command, or the respective office that handles legislative liaison in Washington, D.C. (Navy: Office of Legislative Affairs [OLA]; Marine Corps: Office of the Legislative Assistant to the Commandant). Again, sometimes congressional inquiries will come via the Washington office in the first place, and a ship or unit will be asked to respond to that office instead of writing directly to the Congress member. (This procedure is standard in the Marine Corps; it is somewhat less standard for Navy units, which most often have to write the member of Congress directly.)

In any case, the best advice is to *start immediately* with the research and writing. That way you'll find the problem areas early and can get help quickly.

Once you have written your response, have it reviewed by your command's writing experts. Should anyone look at it beyond the command? Aboard a ship or squadron, while a commanding officer is often required to let the commodore know there has been a congressional inquiry, there is usually no formal requirement that the correspondence be routed through the group or squadron staff. Still, on sensitive issues, a prudent commander will ask if the boss wants to see a hard copy before it's sent out.

In the Marine Corps, normally a command's Office of the Inspector will prepare the smooth draft from the information it is given. In addition, as mentioned above, almost all responses are sent via the Congressional Inquiry Section of Headquarters, Marine Corps rather than going directly to the member of Congress from the command. Whatever the process, the responsible officer should ask to see a copy of the smooth draft before it leaves the command. That way he or she can make sure no errors have been made and can check to make sure the inspector's drafter has not taken too much license with the facts provided.

Get the Details Right

- Be sure to address the Congress member correctly:
  - Senator = "Dear Senator [last name]:"
  - Congress[man/woman] = "Dear Mr./Mrs./Ms./Miss [last name]:"
  - Chairman or Chairwoman = "Dear Mr. Chairman:" or "Dear Madam Chairman:"

See Appendix B of the Correspondence Manual for a comprehensive description of inside addresses and salutations.

• Normally begin a letter to a member of Congress with a thank-you phrase, such as "Thank you for your letter of February 21 concerning Petty Officer November's pay problem." This first thank-you paragraph serves the same function as subject and reference lines in a from-to letter. By stating here the subject the letter will discuss, the date of the Congress member's letter, and the constituent's name, you help the congressional staff to find the right file.

• Write the letter in *business*-letter style. (Some commands prefer you use a comma rather than a colon after the salutation.)

• Enclose an additional courtesy copy along with the original when you send it to the member of Congress.

• Navy commands replying directly to the Congress member are required to send a blind copy of the final reply and copies of all substantive interim replies to the Office of Legislative Affairs in Washington, D.C.

Example: Letter to a Congresswoman

Below is a fictionalized letter to a congresswoman. The congresswoman had inquired about the serviceman's loss of leave and asked why he had not been allowed to reenlist, despite his receiving an honorable discharge. The person upon whose behalf Congresswoman Capitol has inquired is addressed as "Mr." in the letter since he is no longer in the Navy. (Note that current policies or regulations concerning illegal drug use may differ from those outlined below.)

LETTERHEAD STATIONERY

March 15, 1989

The Honorable Dorothy Capitol
House of Representatives
Washington, D.C. 20515

Dear Mrs. Capitol:

Thank you for your letter of March 10, 1989 about Mr. Charles Sailor's discharge from the Navy due to marijuana use.

Some details of Mr. Sailor's case may help clarify the circumstances of his discharge. The urine sample he submitted on June 18, 1988 tested positive for tetrahydrocannabinol (THC). The Navy Drug Testing Laboratory used radioimmunoassay for the initial sample screening and gas chromatography for confirmation. These tests yield results in which we have high confidence, with no false positives in over three years of quality-control testing.

After initially exercising his right for court-martial, Mr. Sailor changed his mind and requested his case be heard at a nonjudicial hearing under Article 15 of the Uniform Code of Military Justice. I found that he had committed the offense of illegal drug use with which he was charged, and I awarded punishment. Mr. Sailor did not exercise his right to appeal this punishment.

Care for due process and granting Mr. Sailor's requests, including a polygraph examination that he terminated prematurely, resulted in an adjudication period of July 1 to October 13, 1988. This period is longer than usual but is still within the 120 days required by the Manual for Courts-Martial. During this period I did not allow Mr. Sailor to take leave because he was in a disciplinary status. (My command policy is not to grant leave to individuals awaiting disciplinary action, placed on restriction, or serving extra duty unless an emergency or hardship is involved.) As required by statute, Mr. Sailor lost all accrued leave in excess of 60 days at the beginning of the fiscal year.

We retested Mr. Sailor for drug use two days prior to his October 22 discharge, and his urine sample again tested positive for THC. We did not receive the results until after his discharge and therefore took no further action. Although he received an honorable discharge, we assigned an RE-4 (not recommended) reenlistment code because of drug use, in accordance with Navy policy.

Mr. Sailor has the right to petition the Board for the Correction of Naval Records (BCNR) regarding his reenlistment code and loss of accrued leave. I am enclosing the necessary forms should he desire to do so. We established the BCNR for the purpose of reviewing naval records and correcting possible injustices.

Sincerely,

L. N. OFFICER
Commanding Officer

Enclosure

Comments on This Letter

- The letter adduces strong evidence supporting the reasons for the "not recommended" reenlistment code, and it explains the apparent discrepancies clearly (honorable discharge but not recommended to reenlist; seemingly unjust loss of leave).
- The letter sketches the main details of the chronology, without going into every detail.

- The writer does not try to justify the Navy's policy on drug use (an explanation would be unnecessary).
- The writer adds credibility by citing "three years of quality-control testing" (which suggests to the congresswoman that the Navy is attuned to the possibilities of injustice) and by citing Navy rules (the assignment of a "not recommended" enlistment code; the statute on loss of accrued leave).
- The discussion of rights and of the ex-serviceman's logical next step manifests the command's concern for the individual's rights. Including the forms is also helpful both to the congresswoman and to the correspondent.
- Overall, the letter is to-the-point, factual, and relatively brief.

Some Other Examples

Here are some passages from similar letters, illustrating various tacks you may want to take in a particular case.

Write to Explain the History of Events

We approved Petty Officer Unitas's request to work in Public Works at Naval Station, Long Beach, in the hope that he could receive better training and be more productive in a large, maintenance-oriented organization. However, he was apprehended in an attempted theft of government gasoline, and for this action he was subsequently awarded punishment at nonjudicial punishment ("Captain's Mast"). Because of this incident and his generally poor professional reputation, the Naval Station Public Works Officer disapproved his temporary transfer.

Write to Explain How a Specific Policy Applies to an Individual's Situation

The 4th Marine Division's policy gives commanders authority to reduce Marines in grade administratively because of unexcused absences. The unit commander sent to Lance Corporal Doubletree via certified mail a letter of intent to reduce him in grade. That letter informed the service member that he had 20 days to respond to his officer in charge about the unexcused absence allegations, but he made no attempt in that period to appeal the reduction. Lance Corporal Doubletree was then reduced to his present grade.

OR

Department of Defense policy states that when members are involuntarily separated for substandard performance of duty, they shall receive separation pay equal to one-half that to which they would normally be entitled, to a maximum of $15,000. We can see nothing to support an exception in Lieutenant Threefoot's situation.

Write to Explain What Options the Service Member Has Not Yet Pursued

Petty Officer Quarterman is not eligible for normal reassignment until March 1989. Until then he may consider a self-negotiated exchange of duty with another sailor of identical paygrade and specialty who would like an assignment to Alaska. We have the necessary information if he is interested in pursuing this option.

Write to Explain the Command's Perspective

I wish to reiterate that we have made a concerted attempt to train Petty Officer Quintilla to perform satisfactorily at the first class petty officer level. However, he must be prepared to dedicate a large amount of effort to self-study and to learning the basic tenents of leadership if he is to pursue a successful naval career.

Write to Set the Facts Straight

We process enlisted performance evaluations through the division officer, department head, and executive officer; then they are signed by the commanding officer. Each level of leadership thoroughly examined Petty Officer Sexton's performance record as did a review board of chief petty officers. He was, in fact, ranked as the worst second class petty officer in this command, and his performance was judged unsatisfactory. Despite Petty Officer Sexton's assertions to the contrary, he is the only Seabee to receive an unsatisfactory performance evaluation during my 20 months of command.

Other Dos and Don'ts

Do:

- Conduct thorough research quickly.
- Check files for past inquiries on the same or similar topics.
- Assemble those officials familiar with the issue, and have them compare notes rather than preparing separate responses. This discussion will help you to get information quickly and to resolve discrepancies on the spot.
- Log (in a memo for record) any information gained from telephone inquiries, with date, a full account of the information provided, and the name of whoever provided it.
- Be candid.
- Address every point in the inquiry.
- Omit the originator's code and the letter serial.
- Get the final reply off within five days, if possible; if not, send an interim reply.

Don't:

- Be defensive or emotional.
- Compose stereotyped replies.
- Refer to documents not held by the Congress member.
- Use jargon or navalese.
- Use acronyms unless unavoidable—then spell them out the first time, as in Plan of the Day (POD).
- Hide the matter from the implicated sailor or Marine. (Instead, tell the service member that you have received the congressional inquiry and that you plan to respond.)
- Go on any longer than necessary, adding unessential details. (Obviously, deciding how much detail to include is very much a judgment call.)

Checklist for Preparing Answers to Congressional Inquiries

Technical Details

- Have you written this response in business-letter format?
- Have you double-checked the addressee and address?
  — Did you use "The Honorable"? Have you addressed a Committee Chair properly?
  — Is the ZIP Code correct (House=20515; Senate=20510)? (See the Correspondence Manual for slightly different format for home district address.)
- Is the salutation correct?
- Is the letter's opening stated properly?
- Have you included extra copies, as required?
- Have you checked for unnecessary jargon or acronyms?

The Substance

- Does the letter get to the point, stating the basic response right after the thank-you sentence?
- If the letter cites a chronology, does that chronology run smoothly and completely?
- Is the explanation sharp and pointed, rather than rambling?
- Is the letter fair to the service member, and does it also *appear* to be fair?
- Is the letter fair to the needs of the service?
- If mistakes have been made, have you stated them forthrightly and apologized or stated future compensatory action, as appropriate?
- Does the letter raise any issues it doesn't have to raise?
- Does the letter obligate the service to do something? If so, have you checked to make sure that the service both *can* and *will* do it?
- Have you given the member of Congress sufficient perspective on this issue?
- Finally, does the letter answer all the Congress member's inquiries?

Memos

I wrote lots of memos as an XO and as a Department Head—but I seldom put "Memorandum" at the top of one. It's my style to understate and be less formal. I was afraid to put "memo" at the top for fear of scaring my subordinates (or boss) into thinking my notes were always recorded to hang them with later.

Sometimes I did write (or type) "Memorandum"—I was *sure* they'd read that one.

—Navy Commander

Memoranda range from brief notes to vital policy initiatives. They are mainly for internal use aboard staffs and operational commands but can occasionally be used externally, between commands.

A preprinted form or a plain-paper memorandum is the least formal memo and is often handwritten. A memorandum on ship or station letterhead is about the same in structure but is somewhat more formal and can be sent from one activity to another (routine business only). A special memorandum is a memo for record, by which you record information that might otherwise be lost. It has wide potential usefulness—and could be used much more than it is. The memorandum-for is the most formal of all memoranda and is arguably the most important.

One other kind of memorandum, the briefing memo, is widely used on staffs in briefing folders. The chapter "Staff Writing" discusses the briefing memo, for staffs use it much more than anyone else.

Become familiar with all the formats and uses of memos, especially the common ones. Realize that although the Correspondence Manual does not so specify, common naval usage in the past was to add a complimentary close to many informal memos. That is, a senior would often close with "Respectfully" or "R" before signing or initialing a memo to a junior or someone of the equivalent rank, and a junior would pen "Very Respectfully" or "VR" before his or her signature when writing to a senior. This custom is not as widespread as it once was but still holds force in many circumstances.

The Informal Memo

Below is guidance on an informal memo.

MEMORANDUM 10 January 1990

From: Writer's name, title or code
To: Reader's name, title or code

Subj: KEY POINTS ABOUT WRITING AN INFORMAL MEMO

1. Plan Ahead. Whether using a preprinted form or this plain-paper memorandum, don't write thoughtlessly. Always plan out a memo; at least jot down a few points and then organize them before writing. On complicated matters, write up a full outline. A few seconds spent in planning will help make the writing go quickly and the correspondence be effective.

2. Get to the Point Quickly. Craft the subject line to state the essential matter briefly, and elaborate on your main point in the first paragraph. Normally, keep your memo to one page.

3. Remember Your Audience; Watch Tone. Figure out, in light of your audience and purpose, what tone to adopt. Tone can be especially important in informal memos because memos are often very personal.

4. Use Formatting as Needed. Formatting helps in memos as in many other kinds of writing. Examples of such formatting include:

a. Lists (in a, b, c order or in bullets).
b. Headings (as in this memo).
c. Occasional underlining, *italics*, **boldface**, or ALL CAPS.

5. Remember These Shortcuts. Very informal memos can be penned, and you need not keep a file copy if the matter is insignificant or short-lived. You can sign a memorandum without an authority line.

T. X. AUTHOR

Here's an informal memo on a routine manner, written in appropriately informal style.

20 February 1987

MEMORANDUM

From: Admin Officer
To: Department Heads

Subj: LETTERS OF DESIGNATION

1. There are numerous requirements laid on by this command and higher authorities to "designate in writing" individuals to perform certain tasks/responsibilities/accountabilities. It would behoove us to know exactly who all these folks are and "track 'em."

2. I'm requesting that each department review its working instructions, CVWR-30, and higher instructions (such as 4790.2) and forward a list of all such requirements to Admin NLT Friday, 28 February.

3. Admin will collate your responses into a notice, and we will thus be assured that all requirements to designate are met.

P. D. BRADY

A note of caution as to the methodology outlined in the above memo: Whenever you collate the requirements of many diverse authorities, your notice becomes obsolete as soon as *just one* of these authorities changes its requirements. An apparent shortcut can easily become a trap.

Don't Try to Lead by Memo

You're following a gutless path if you try to lead by memo. Don't use memos in lieu of face-to-face discussions. You can write lots of bad stuff in memos, which becomes *permanent in impact*, the reaction to which *you cannot control.* A commanding officer of a ship was losing faith in his XO and therefore directed that all their communications be in writing, not face to face. But that "solution" helped to *create* the problem, not deal with it. Remember the old lines—

Say it with flowers,
Say it with mink,
But never, no never, say it in ink.

Memos within a shipboard command should be seen primarily as records, not communications—and *never* as leadership.

—Navy Captain

The Memo for Record

Do you want to ensure some key information is recorded, but are you afraid that because of the informal circumstances in which it came up, it won't be? Then pen a memorandum for the record (or memo for record or MFR).

The information might be from a meeting, a telephone conversation, or an informal discussion held on a staff. You can use the memo for record to record an agreement among several parties at a conference, or to record decisions made at decision briefings. The memo for record resembles the minutes of a meeting in some respects—and can be used for minutes—but is more the gist of the meeting than a formal set of minutes.

On a ship, in a squadron, or in a field unit, the memo for record can also be effective. Use it to document an informal investigation and its results or an important counseling session conducted with a subordinate along with the factors that led to the counseling. (Note, however, that some commands prefer to record such formal counseling in a letter of instruction. See pp. 46–48). Another common use of memos for record is to document information from a phone call or from the informal discussion that an investigator conducts in the process of a JAGMAN Investigation.

Usually you file a memo for record for future reference, but you can route it to your staff if everyone needs to know the information it contains. Staff officers can forward memos for record up the chain to keep seniors informed of what's happening down below.

Whatever you use it for, keep this memo informal. It's an in-house document, to help keep track of business. Do remember to sign and date it, but always keep it easy to use.

The example of a memo for record below is fictional, but it is based on MFRs that were used as exhibits in a JAGMAN investigation. It documents a discussion that the investigating officer had with an expert about funds that had been stolen from a postal safe. Specifically, the officer wanted to know who had been assigned the responsibility for the safe's security.

11 August 1989

MEMORANDUM FOR RECORD

From: LT J. R. BLACK, USNR, Investigating Officer

Subj: RESPONSIBILITY FOR CHANGE OF POSTAL SAFE COMBINATIONS ON USS OVERHAUL (FFG 999)

1. On 10 August 1989 I discussed this investigation with PCC Gray of the COMCENTGULF Postal Assist Team. Specifically, I asked PCC Gray what the responsibility of the postal officer in this case would have been. He said that a postal officer must oversee the entire postal operation of the command. Therefore, ENS Brown did have a duty to make sure safe combinations were changed. However, he also pointed out that ENS Brown's responsibility was oversight only, and that the primary responsibility for changing the combinations remained that of the Custodian of Postal Effects (COPE) aboard USS OVERHAUL, that is, PC2 White.

J. R. BLACK

Clearly, it is important that such a discussion as is illustrated above be recorded right after the discussion takes place, and the memo for record provides a good way of doing that.

The next (again fictional) example is somewhat more formal than the one above. It resembles a memo for record that might be put out by an office in OPNAV or at another major staff. Rather than documenting information discovered in an investigation, here a division director sends cost figures on two major equipment procurements to individuals in the chain of command and to members of his own staff.

15 May 89

MEMORANDUM FOR THE RECORD

Subj: TARGET ANCHORS AND SALVO RETRIEVERS

1. I have been asked the following questions by OP-88Z and by Mr. A. C. E. Shooter of SASC staff:

a. What are the quantity and funding profile for target anchors and salvo retrievers for FY 88 and prior through FY 91?

b. What would be the cost of 300 target anchors in FY 91?

2. I provided the following information:

	FY 88 & Prior	FY 89	FY 90	FY 91
Target Anchors	150/$3.0M	300/$5.4M	400/$7M	50/$0.8M
Salvo Retrievers	250/$15M	400/$23M	550/$32M	800/$46M

The cost of 300 target anchors in FY 91 would be $4.8 million. The inventory objective for target anchors remains 1,500; the inventory objective for salvo retrievers is 3,000.

3. This inquiry is probably the first of many on this subject. We should be consistent in our answers.

E. PREBLE
Director, Targeting Division

Copy to:
OP-OX
OP-OXA
OP-OXB

The Memorandum For

Here is some guidance on the memorandum-for, common to OPNAV and other high-level staffs.

LETTERHEAD STATIONERY

5216
Ser 943D/345507
10 Jan 90

MEMORANDUM FOR THE DEPUTY CHIEF OF NAVAL
OPERATIONS (OP-XX)

Subj: PROFESSIONAL PREPARATION OF THE MEMORANDUM-FOR

Ref: (a) CNO Supplement to DON Correspondence Manual
(b) HQMC Supplement to DON Correspondence Manual

1. The memorandum-for is a very formal memorandum. Its normal use is to communicate with very senior officials such as the Secretary of Defense, the Secretary of the Navy, the Chief of Naval Operations, one of the Assistant Secretaries or Deputy Chiefs, or an Executive Assistant (EA) for any one of these officials.

2. Take great care in the preparation of memoranda-for. These documents have high visibility and require thorough staffing and tactful expression. Make sure each of them has:

— a subject line that best describes the memo's purpose;
— headings, if useful;
— brevity, always—normally keep the memorandum-for to one page.

3. If you use tabs, be sure not to let those tabs substitute for good staffing. Do your best to pull the relevant information out of the references and weave it into your memorandum rather than asking a senior official to plow through the tabbed material.

4. Protocol is important. List the addressees in the established order of precedence.

5. Prepare the memorandum-for on letterhead stationery. Because it lacks a "From" line, show the signer's title below the typed name.

6. Various offices have issued additional guidance on preparing this document. For example, the Secretary of Defense asked recently that "ACTION MEMORANDUM" or "INFORMATION MEMORANDUM" be placed at the end of the subject line of each memorandum-for addressed to or from his office. See current versions of references (a) and (b) and other local information for up-to-date guidance.

J. Memorandum
Deputy Chief of Naval Operations

Figure 2.6 is an example of an actual memorandum-for concerning a change of command at SURFLANT. Note the "Very Respectfully" complimentary close, and the "Yes ____ NO ____" line at the bottom left. The latter is a very good staff device when all you want is a yes or no answer—the boss can give you the go-ahead with a simple stroke of the pen.

A document of the same family as the memorandum-for is a formal, multiple-address memorandum for a staff, usually called a "MEMORANDUM FOR DISTRIBUTION" or a "MEMORANDUM FOR ALL HANDS (OP-XX STAFF)."

Other staff examples are the memorandum for the OPNAV writer (in the Staff Writing chapter), the memorandum for distribution on thank-you letters earlier in this chapter, and Figure 2.7. The latter, directed to detailers and others in the "customer service" business, gives useful advice about making commitments over the phone.

Figure 2.6 Memorandum For. This memorandum prepared for a change of command at SURFLANT.

DEPARTMENT OF THE NAVY

COMMANDER NAVAL SURFACE FORCE
UNITED STATES ATLANTIC FLEET
NORFOLK, VIRGINIA 23511-6292

4 December 1987

MEMORANDUM FOR VICE ADMIRAL ____________

Via: N3 ___ 02 ___

Subj: CHANGE OF COMMAND HONORS

Encl: (1) OPNAVINST 1710.7 of JUL 79 (Change of Command Guidance)
(2) OPNAVINST 1701.7 of JUL 79 (Change of Command Sample Program)
(3) CNSL Change of Command 1982 SOE
(4) CNSL Change of Command 1984 SOE

1. The Navy Protocol Manual OPNAVINST 1710.7 indicates that each principal should receive full arrival honors (gun salute for the senior official). Arrival honors for the principals have been conducted differently for the last two CNSL Changes of Command. In the 1982 version Admiral ________, VADM ________, and VADM ________ each received full honors upon his independent arrival (gun salute for ADM ________ only). In 1984 VADMs ________ and ________ received side honors only and awaited ADM ________'s arrival on the quarterdeck; ADM ________ received full honors (including gun salute).

2. Separate full honors are required by Navy Regulations for the relieved officer and the relieving officer at the hauling down and breaking of each officer's respective flag.

3. Enclosures (1) and (2) are highlighted excerpts of the Change of Command section of the Protocol Manual. Enclosures (3) and (4) are the schedules for the previous two CNSL Changes of Command.

4. Recommend that we proceed as last time: Side honors only upon arrival of VADM ________ and RADM ________ and full honors for ADM ________ and for hauling down and breaking of flags.

Very respectfully,

CDR, USN, N00X

YES ____ NO ____

Figure 2.7 Another Memorandum For. A "Guidance Memorandum" put out at NMPC warns against making commitments over the phone.

DEPARTMENT OF THE NAVY
NAVAL MILITARY PERSONNEL COMMAND
WASHINGTON, D.C. 20370

IN REPLY REFER TO

8 FEB 1984

COMMANDER, NAVAL MILITARY PERSONNEL COMMAND GUIDANCE MEMORANDUM 3-84

Subj: COMMUNICATIONS WITH OUR CONSTITUENTS

1. Too frequently, correspondence crossing my desk indicates that someone within NMPC has reportedly made a commitment to an individual or provided advice in a telephone conversation that has become difficult to support in terms of current policy. Sometimes the cause may be a sympathetic desire to make a situation more acceptable to a constituent; sometimes a misconception can arise when the individual "hears what he/she wants to hear." When we try to reconstruct what was meant as well as said, there is often no record. It has happened to all of us. In any case, our credibility, if not integrity, can be severely damaged. It is my intention that neither we as individuals nor NMPC as a command be open to questions of credibility. We must be honest and perceived as being honest.

2. As a policy matter, you should avoid verbal commitments or statements of unpublished policy unless they are immediately followed up in writing. I realize that we are in a customer-service business and that a lot of our work is done by phone; however, when we are asked, "Why did I fail for selection?" or other questions that may relate to policy, the best approach is to be polite and helpful while getting the necessary information, but to inform your constituent that you will research the problem and respond in writing. By no means give an answer from off the "top of your head." A copy of the written communication must be retained in your file or be filed in the constituent's record for future reference.

David L. Harlow

DAVID L. HARLOW
Commander, Naval Military
Personnel Command

Distribution:
Department Directors
Special Assistants

Directives

> Review your directives often. I made a policy of reviewing all my instructions within nine months of coming aboard, and in one case I was able to cut them down to a *fifth* their original size. Once they had been made manageable in this way, I could insist my people knew what was in them.
>
> —Captain, USN

Written directives—instructions and notices in the Navy, orders and bulletins in the Marine Corps—are even more vital in the armed services than in other big organizations because sailors and Marines transfer from one outfit to another so often. But if directives are too dense, too long, or too complicated, they will not be read, and your people will "fly by the seat of their pants" instead of looking to the directives for guidance.

"If you want to change things for the better of the Navy, *put it in an instruction*. In part, this is for pass-down-the-line purposes, and in part to make it formal aboard ship (or it will be lost). But also, by putting it in writing you move it up, and give it the force of law. You emphasize it and preserve it for the next generation. Make it clear, and make it stand alone. The problem that was around as the genesis of the instruction will be completely forgotten three years hence—but will occur again!"—Commander

Unfortunately, a great many naval directives *are* verbose and very hard to read. One simple example will illustrate the problems with current directive writing. The following passage, the purpose paragraph from a sample instruction, was taken from a guide on how to write instructions and notices. This paragraph should have been an outstanding example of how to start off a directive. Instead, it is an example of how *not* to begin:

> Purpose. To produce forth a guide by which originators may formulate instructions and notices following the provisions of references (a) and (b). This instruction covers the procedures that originators will carry out in writing directives in the Navy Directives System.

What's wrong with this paragraph?

- Both sentences say the same thing.
- Extra words abound, even within the sentences:
  - "the provisions of" could be omitted in the first sentence without loss.
  - "in the Navy Directives System" could be omitted in the second.
- Big words obscure simple ideas:
  - "To produce forth a guide" is an awkward way to say "to guide."
  - "formulate" is officialese for "write."
- In sum, all four lines could be condensed to *eight simple words*:

> Purpose: To guide originators in writing directives.

In other ways, too, directives are often poorly written. As a result, either they are not read at all or they are not fully understood. Thus they do not govern action as they should. But there are ways to improve.

The Navy Notice and the Marine Corps Bulletin

The Navy notice and the Marine Corps bulletin are distinct among directives in having *short-term authority*. Navy notices, for example, cannot remain in effect for longer than a year, and most last six months or less. Because of their relative impermanence, they are best used for one-time reports, temporary procedures, or short-term information. Otherwise, they have the same force as Navy instructions and Marine Corps orders. Below is a sample Navy notice that discusses how to write clear and usable directives.

USS EXAMPLE (DDG 14)
FLEET POST OFFICE
NEW YORK 09501

EXAMPLENOTE 5215
10 Jan 89
Canc: 28 FEB 89

USS EXAMPLE NOTICE 5215

From: Commanding Officer, USS EXAMPLE

Subj: HOW TO WRITE DIRECTIVES

Ref: (a) SECNAVINST 5215.1C—Directives Issuance System
(b) MCO P5215.1—Marine Corps Directives System
(c) Chap. 10 of OPNAVINST 3120.32B—"Unit Directives System"

1. Purpose: To guide writers in composing directives (Navy instructions and notices, Marine Corps orders and bulletins) that will be *read and understood*. Writing so they will be *read at all* is the greatest challenge.

2. Action: Here is brief guidance.

a. **Smother "Motherhood."** The reason so many directives are not read, or not read carefully, is that they take so long to get to the point. *Omit* most "Background," "Discussion," and "Policy" paragraphs.

b. **Proceed as soon as possible to "Action."** Experienced naval personnel read a directive in pretty much the same way: first they glance at the "Purpose" paragraph, and then they skip to "Action," even if this means skipping several *pages* of the directive. Condense most of your directives so that "Action" follows as soon after "Purpose" as possible.

c. **Designate Responsibilities by Individual.** In the "Action" paragraph, itemize exactly what each individual must do. Readers will take notice if they see specific responsibilities assigned to them.

d. **Use Inventive Paragraph Headings.** The only two paragraphs required for *all* directives are those for purpose and action. Standard paragraph headings like "Objectives," "Scope," and so on are not necessarily helpful. On the other hand, using more pointed titles (as illustrated here) can sometimes help the reader along.

e. **Get Attention by Using Typographic Techniques.** Nothing in references (a), (b), or (c) prohibits you from using modern typographic techniques, especially **bold face** and underlining, but also perhaps ALL CAPS or *italics*. Used sparingly, these techniques can also help you get the vital points across.

A. T. MAHAN

The Navy Instruction and the Marine Corps Order

"Great discipline is required in writing instructions and notices. People often get hoisted by their own petard. They keep putting the paper out—then failing to do what they have told themselves to do!"—Navy Captain

Differing from notices and bulletins, instructions and orders are relatively *long-term*. They have continuing reference value or require continuing action. Since these directives are relatively permanent (more often revised than canceled or superseded), they govern most major administrative efforts within naval commands. If we don't write them well, our units, programs, and communities will suffer.

Again, as in the case of notices and bulletins, drafting a good "Action" paragraph is the central skill. "Discussion should be brief; Action is the key; and action must be indicated by *job title* or *billet*," as a commander pointed out. Learn to draft brief and effective instructions or orders; start by reading the sample Navy instruction below.

USS EXAMPLE (DDG 14)
FLEET POST OFFICE
NEW YORK 09501

EXAMPLEINST 5215.2
03:REA
10 Jan 89

USS EXAMPLE INSTRUCTION 5215.2

From: Commanding Officer, USS EXAMPLE

Subj: WRITING THE "ACTION" PARAGRAPH AS A "TASKING" DEVICE

1. Purpose. To guide instruction writers in composing the "Action" sections of directives: the best course is to *allocate each task to a specific billet*.

2. Rationale. Specifying detailed assignments to individuals in a directive (as in the "Action" paragraph below) does several things:

a. **It gets the attention of readers**, who will learn to look for their responsibilities in the "Action" paragraph. A three-page instruction suddenly becomes readable if, in effect, all you have to read is the "Purpose" statement and one "Action" paragraph directed specifically at you.

b. **It makes drafters do all the vital spadework**. Assigning specific tasking by billet forces a writer to articulate general principles into specific responsibilities. It helps our people to think through and specify in full detail how policies or programs will be made to work.

3. Action. Take action as outlined below:

a. The **Executive Officer** will ensure that all shipboard directives embody "tasking" sections by billet, as appropriate to their content.

b. **Department Heads** will supervise the training of their junior people in writing directives with good "tasking" paragraphs.

c. The **Training Officer** will prepare lesson plans on directive writing, to feature "tasking" procedures prominently, and will furnish such materials to those conducting training.

d. **All writers of directives** will specify in the "Action" paragraphs of their directives specifically *who* (by billet title) is responsible for exactly *what* and, if appropriate, *when*, *where*, *why*, and *how*.

D. G. FARRAGUT

Distribution:
List 1, Case A

On Revising Directives

"You have to take TYCOM guidance, and lots of message input, and then make it workable *here*. Moreover, you not only have to make sure your ship complies with the instruction, but you have to write it so your E-5s and E-6s understand it."—Lieutenant Commander, on writing instructions on a surface ship

Most of your work will be *revising* directives; only 25 percent of the time do you actually write new ones. Even if you must draft a completely new directive, you can often find an old one on a similar topic to guide you. As a Marine lieutenant colonel commented, "When you have to put out a new directive, find parallel orders and plagiarize from them, keeping the format." Similarly, a Navy commander suggested that you "plagiarize where you can. Someone else probably already wrote a similar directive. So go find it, change the names, and use it."

While altering an existing document for your purpose—by changing, adding, or deleting details—*also work to revise for readability*. Here's what a DOD Executive Writing Course suggests:

An Academic Exercise?

Everything in the notice shown below, once issued at the Naval Academy, is "by the book." Clearly, sometimes you might have to throw the book away. . . .

COMDTMIDNNOTE 5000
19 January 1999

COMDTMIDN NOTICE 5000

Subj: Cancellation of Commandant of Midshipmen Notice

1. Purpose. To cancel Commandant of Midshipmen Notice.

2. Action. Cancel the following Commandant of Midshipmen Notice which has fulfilled its purpose:

a. COMDTMIDN NOTICE 5000 of 9 January 1999 (Subj: Planned absence of Commodore ____, USN).

3. Cancellation. When the above action has been taken.

A. C. T. OFFICER
Acting

Distribution:
C-2

1. **Shorten the document as much as possible**.
2. **Write specific subjects**. "Request for Two Parking Spaces" is more helpful than "Parking Spaces."
3. **Put the action up front**.
4. **Use the pronoun *you*, stated or implied**. As much as possible, talk directly to your audience. As the Correspondence Manual advises, "look for opportunities to talk directly to a user." Instead of: *Personnel who are moving this summer are advised to contact the housing office early*, say *If you are moving this summer, contact the housing office early.*
5. **Rely on active verbs in the present tense**. Don't rely on the *must be*s, *will*s, and *will be*s of passive and future verbs. Instead of *All safes must be checked. Each safe dial will be spun by the duty officer*, say *You must check all safes. Spin each safe's dial as part of your inspection.*
6. **Keep lists parallel**. The rhythm of parallelism sets up expectations that make reading easy. A common violation of parallelism is switching from active instructions to passive ones. The sentences that begin parts 1–5 of this series would lose their parallelism if, for example, *Put the action up front* appeared as a passive: *Action should be placed at the front.*

These steps will help ensure the directive you're laboring on *will begin to govern action* instead of just providing window dressing for an inspection.

The Correspondence Manual (p. 1-29) has an example of an excellent revision to a directive that does most of what is outlined above.

Excerpts from Clear, Readable Battle Orders

A special kind of directive is a set of battle orders. Obviously, it is *extremely* important that these be written well. The CO who wrote the battle orders from which these excerpts are taken not only took care with his writing, but he then discussed his orders with each division on his ship to make sure his points got across.

6. COMMANDING OFFICER'S PHILOSOPHIES FOR FIGHTING THE SHIP. The following are a compendium of my battle philosophies.

a. EXPECT A "COME AS YOU ARE WAR." In spite of the best advance warnings, in spite of the best logistics support, in spite of any preparations we might make, in spite of the promise of high technology, we will never have everything we need when we need it. Our goal, therefore, is simple: BE READY TO FIGHT TODAY. You must take every step to ensure personnel and equipment readiness. Continual quality training, inspecting, sampling, and questioning will ensure we can fight at any time.

b. BE PREPARED TO FIGHT FROM CONDITION III. The highly structured refresher training evolutions that start from Condition I, a condition to which we've become accustomed, are now history. It is absolutely impossible to maintain a GQ posture for any length of time. We must be prepared to maintain a Condition II or III watch for extended periods. This being the case, you must work with all department heads to ensure that your watch sections are trained, rested, and properly rotated.

c. BE READY TO COUNTER GUERRILLA WARFARE AT SEA. . . . A relatively new scenario of naval warfare has evolved, one involving guerrilla warfare at sea. This new dimension of naval warfare now includes renegade nations supporting fanatical terrorists. The weapons of these misfits include suicide planes and vessels loaded with high explosives, high-speed launches carrying powerful, armor-piercing munitions, and a bevy of aircraft, conventional warships, and deadly antiship missiles. Many of these craft will not follow expected attack or launch profiles. Rather, they may appear as friendlies or as members of a fishing fleet approaching our ship as "interested observers."

The point is that we must be prepared to fight unconventional naval warfare; we must be prepared to recognize a potentially dangerous situation; and finally WE MUST ACT IN THE INTEREST OF SELF DEFENSE. *If it appears dangerous, it is! If your gut feeling tells you it stinks . . . it does!* We must be ready to counter the modern-day naval guerrillas. . . .

—From Battle Orders of USS CONNOLE, FF 1056.
Used by permission of Commander Kenneth P. Weinberg.

It's much harder to write the one-page for the four-star than the 10-page original document.

—Navy Captain

3

Staff Writing

General Guidance on Staff Work

Three aspects of staff writing deserve special consideration: the audience, the purpose, and the person writing. Let's take the writer first.

The Staff Member New to a Staff

Many service members reporting to a staff for the first time express frustration with their new duties. Often they come to a staff after one or more operational tours—indeed, many Navy officers first report to staff duty as *commanders* or *captains*. Whatever their ranks, most have had little preparation for the kind of writing they now have to do. And many have a difficult time getting up to speed.

One reason for this "staffer's shock" is the greater formality that may be required, especially on larger staffs. For example, although the Marine Corps has many standard formats for staff documents (in FMFM 3-1 and elsewhere), these formats are sometimes ignored in the field. Informal procedures often take over—a few notes appended to a letter sent forward for signature, or a brief phone call that takes the place of writing. At major staffs, however, you can't succeed with informality.

"Keep a file of what you write. It took me six months to a year to learn to be a staff officer—in the meantime, I *lived* by the documents and papers I'd written over the years."—Marine Colonel at MCDEC Quantico

For example, when a Marine lieutenant colonel first reported to Headquarters, Marine Corps, he found that, hard as he tried, he couldn't get anyone to pay any attention to the *content* of what he wrote until he got the *format* right—the format of a point paper, a position paper, a briefing memo, and so on. Since he had never run into the need for briefing on paper before, he found this situation highly frustrating.

Others have had similar experiences. Navy writers have long operated by finding an old document of the kind they now have to write and copying that. Yet such an approach is hardly optimal and does nothing to give a person the larger picture of good staff work.

For many new staffers, the greatest difficulty is the writing itself. Indeed, if you're going to get anything accomplished on a staff, you'll have to do it at least in part by the written word. To many, this requirement will seem a major dilemma. One senior Pentagon staffer commented on his sure-fire way of thwarting any upstart staff officer. When someone new on the staff came to him (as new people invariably did) with the standard suggestion on how to completely turn procedures upside down to "improve" them, he would simply mumble, "Sounds good; just *put it in writing*, and we'll take a look at it." Through long experience, he knew he would hear nothing further about the suggestion.

Besides the writing, some new people have been puzzled by the mysterious process of "chopping" or coordinating staff work. Others (especially 0–5s and 0–6s) are upset when they realize that they will be doing things juniors had done for them in their previous commands. At the Pentagon, such factors as small offices, few yeomen or secretaries, and even small desks irritate many newly assigned officers.

So the situation is frustrating for many a new staffer. Just as frustrating is trying to understand the circumstances of the person for whom the new staffer will be working.

The Situation of the Boss

On a staff there may be many audiences, but most important are the audiences empowered to make decisions. Of course, there are many decision makers, even several layers of them. They are typically highly knowledgeable but also very busy individuals, people capable of absorbing facts and making decisions quickly. Consider the situation of one of the top officials at OPNAV, the Vice Chief of Naval Operations, as described in 1987 by Captain (now Rear Admiral) W. A. Owens, who was the VCNO's executive assistant.

The Vice Chief had no time to himself—*literally* no time. He attended 8–10 hours of briefings or meetings—or preparations for such meetings, or preparation for speeches, etc.—on each of the five regular days in a week. These meetings left some *400 packages of paperwork* requiring action per week, most of them one-inch thick. All of them had to be handled after regular working hours. When could he handle the paper? The Vice Chief began at 0630 on Saturday. . . .

Other top officials have similar schedules. Army General Donn A. Starry once made the same point in a memo to his staff:

> In a week, about 110 staff actions show up in my in-box. I could handle this in a week if all I did was work on the in-box. Yet about 70% of my time in the headquarters goes not to the in-box but to briefings. I could handle that dilemma, too—by listening to briefings and thinking about staff papers at the

same time. I don't. Most of the information I need is in the field. Much of my time must go there. In February, for example, I was here six days.

Within those six days, add 15–20 office calls, a dozen or so visitors, seven social engagements, two or three ceremonies, and 32 phone calls. These are the realities.

—Cited in Better Naval Writing, OPNAV 09B-P1-84, p. C-2.

Clearly, any staff writer must work to be brief—but let the former EA for the Vice Chief make the point. Figure 3.1 is the memorandum that introduced the short "Guide to OPNAV Writing," put together in May 1987. His memorandum is a good discussion of what the ability of a staff writer should be. We'll discuss techniques a bit later on.

One other subject belongs in this introductory section—a comment on the basic mission of the staffer.

The Basic Purpose of Staff Work

When discussing purpose, you should remember the dictum, "Staffs exist to serve command." But how does that idea relate to writing? What should be the end result of the action officer's work? Purely and simply, on most staffs, and especially shore staffs, the major result must be good "staff actions," that is, effective directives, correspondence, plans, and other written documents that are signed out by the top level of the command.

Let's take OPNAV as an example. According to senior action officers there, the ultimate aim of all OPNAV work is legislation and support for the Navy. Consequently, what counts the most there is *what comes out the top,* that is, what documents are signed by the Chief of Naval Operations, or the Vice Chief, or one of the Deputy Chiefs. Almost everything an action officer does (phone calls, staff legwork, briefings prepared or attended, briefing packages put together, paperwork revised and proofed) should contribute to this primary end, *to what decision makers sign off* or otherwise effect. Otherwise, all your painstaking work has *no real impact.*

"Young officers aren't taught to think beyond the immediate command. A key element in being a real staff officer is to learn to think bigger: 'How should the boss be using his presence and authority to influence *the Navy as a whole?*' "—Captain, CO of a training command

The situation on a fleet staff differs somewhat. There the goals are much more oriented toward operational requirements than policy and legislation. Clearly, fleet staff members must often focus much of their time on *liaison,* or on helping to keep the ships or aircraft or other equipment in their command operational. Naturally, in all this liaison work, messages are the written documents that predominate.

Liaison, of course, is also important on shore staffs, though more often conducted by phone, memo, or letter than by message. Such liaison can be a way of helping the boss even if it does not prepare the way for or help to implement written decisions. For one thing, it keeps lines of communication open; for another, it helps to gain support for the decision maker. In other words, being *right* is not always enough; you must also be *supported.*

Still, liaison effort is almost always secondary to the primary need to support the boss's decision making. This priority becomes more and more evident as you climb the ladder of staffs in the chain of command. The higher you go and the larger the staff, the more the balance shifts away

Figure 3.1 Guidance on Staff Writing. A memo introduces a helpful pamphlet on staff writing at OPNAV.

MEMORANDUM FOR THE OPNAV WRITER

Subj: A PLEA FOR YOUR PITY

1. This book was written for each of you, whether action officer, secretary, administrator, officer, enlisted, or civilian. No matter how diverse your individual jobs may be, you share with each other, and with me, a common purpose. We are all here to do the staff work that supports those at the top: SECNAV, CNO, VCNO, and, tacitly, the DCNOs and DMSOs.

2. We outnumber them many times over! There are far more people doing the writing than there are doing the reading. That is why each of you must do your part to ensure the product you write, type, or edit for their eventual use is the most concise, decisive, and technically correct package it can possibly be. While it may take you an extra hour in preparation time to trim away the fat, it is an hour far better spent at your level than at theirs.

3. On a typical day, several of these individuals may return to their offices at 1730 from a full day of meetings and briefings. When many of you are already halfway home, they are just beginning the stack of "hot" correspondence requiring immediate attention. With luck, they will finish in time to start the stack of "warm" packages. As they work their way through the stack, they are not impressed with expressive literary style or extensive vocabulary. If you have written the great American novel complete with tabs for their reading pleasure in the hope that it will cause your name to be remembered, you may very well find that you get your wish!

4. I ask that you read this guide carefully and keep it at hand while you write. I hope it will help make your task a little easier and that you, in turn, will make it easier on those at the receiving end.

5. Thanks for your help.

W. A. OWENS
Captain, U.S. Navy
Executive Assistant to the
Vice Chief of Naval Operations

from operations and toward policy, and the more a staffer must concentrate on the research, coordination, and especially the paperwork that can *get that policy effected.*

Indeed, one could argue that the larger impact even of fleet support work is always going to lie in the written decisions that one's work has helped the boss to make. A staff must make arrangements with a shipyard or Readiness Support Group to correct many of a ship's problems. Some such problems require brief command actions in the form of simple letters and messages. Others—including such vital staff actions as changing operational tactics or altering ship or aircraft configurations—require complex written staff actions.

Clearly, the difference in staff size and staff nature will determine the degree to which a staffer must direct attention to such policy-making documentation. But in most cases, and especially on large shore staffs, wise staffers will focus their attention on *the documents that come out at the end of the paperwork chain.* These packages are pure or complete staff products, having been so well researched and argued and considered and reviewed—in other words, so well filtered by good minds doing good thinking and research—that they are *clearly and evidently the very best answers* to the problems at hand. If staffers have done this work well, all that commanders have to do is to sign the documents for their decisions to become realities.

Yes, prior research and paperwork and briefings and oral arguments have prepared the way for decisive documents of this sort. And after the fact, the staffer must often put together directives or letters or briefings to implement decisions. Both in formulating arguments leading to a decision and in providing means to carry it out, the staff officer has much more to do than just writing the position paper, letter, memorandum-for, or other critical document at the heart of a staff package. Still, such documents as these are the *end results and goals* of all primary staff work.

The Five Basic Processes of Staff Writing

Good staff writing involves several detailed processes, few of them practiced with anything like the same intensity or detail in the Fleet or Fleet Marine Force as they are on a staff. Mastery of each process is a mark of the effective staff officer, whatever staff you serve on—Navy, Marine Corps, or Joint. Described briefly here, the five basic processes are doing the research, writing the basic document, condensing the writing, assembling action packages, and coordinating one's staff work with other agencies.

Do Thorough Research

A memo or an oral command often initiates staff research. Several hours, days, or even months of work may follow, either on your part alone or in a team effort. Clearly, spending this time well is important. Start by carefully *focusing* your research.

First, consider the problem. Analyze it and restate it if necessary so that it is **clear** and its scope is **well defined**. Much of the difficulty in doing focused research is determining *exactly* what the problem is. Sometimes your tasking will be incomplete and vague. Check widely with authorities and good thinkers to make sure you have the larger picture clear before putting out a Herculean effort. And don't hesitate to redefine your original statement of the problem if you find your first description doesn't fit the facts.

Especially make sure you know exactly what your boss wants. As one former OPNAV staffer commented, "How many times have staff officers busted their bums on a package, only to have the boss say, 'That's not what I asked you to find out'? Ask the boss as many questions as he or she can tolerate when you're given the tasking."

Then **limit your scope** so you don't spend weeks on a problem you can't affect anyway. And make sure the effort you expend is worthwhile. If your problem is ship stability in the North Atlantic, don't spend much time on the free surface effect in the ship's toilet bowls and coffee pots.

Follow this additional advice:

• **Develop (and state) criteria for solutions.** Sometimes the tasking memo or other order that has initiated your staff work will give the criteria for a solution; sometimes they will be obvious. But if you take care to formulate them in writing you will be sure to focus on the particular cruxes of the problem—the meaty, difficult parts.

For example, when giving directions for convoy route planning, a fleet staffer might formulate the following criteria: "Any acceptable convoy route (1) will allow for land-based air cover throughout, (2) will avoid known transit lanes for enemy submarines, (3) will skirt navigational hazards by **X** miles, and (4) will require a maximum of **Y** days and **Z** hours at standard convoy speed."

• **Gather data**, and seek additional data, as necessary, following up leads your first research has suggested. Use all your own wits as well as the collective experience of your co-workers to define the best sources for data.

• **Interpret the data,** with an eye to solutions. Work out the implications of the information you've researched. Organize the information into possible solutions to your problems.

• **Make whatever assumptions you need** to fill in for unattainable facts. Often you won't know all the conditions that might affect the subject of your research in the future. Especially if you're writing contingency plans, but also when doing other research, you'll have to make some assumptions about the future. Find out as much as you can, so you can reduce the need for assumptions to the bare minimum. Then base even those few assumptions on inferences from concrete data. In a scenario involving an aggressor state, for instance, base your assumptions on how the enemy has operated in the past, our demonstrated political and economic constraints, firm information as to geographical and political boundaries, the military capabilities of both sides, etc.

• **Identify and evaluate the alternatives.** Use the criteria you've developed in your evaluation. Remember these classic tests of any proposed answer to a staff problem:

— **Suitability**: *"Will it in fact solve the problem?"* Scores of planners have stumbled because, having designed a weapons platform, discovered a new tactic, or worked out a new system of personnel motivation, they find that *it doesn't solve the problem they faced originally* (and they should have known that shortcoming beforehand).

— **Feasibility:** *"Can it actually be done?"* A brilliant concept is one thing; working it out in practice is another. Do all the spadework to see if a great idea is practicable.

— **Acceptability:** "In the overall picture, *is it worth the cost?"* Many solutions may meet the first two tests, but the question may become one of cost. Cost can be measured in terms of money, equipment (including ships, tanks, or aircraft), lives, or troop morale and energy; it can be measured in moral, social, or political terms as well.

Many a solution will pass one or two of the tests outlined above, but only a solution that definitely passes all three is likely to be rock solid.

Realize that sometimes the answer you come up with will meet all the criteria but won't mesh with the way your boss thinks. At other times, your boss will like it, but his or her superiors won't—it isn't "what they want to hear," as the saying goes. You can't always give superiors answers they will be comfortable with. You should, however, get a feel for the political climate before making recommendations and try to measure the costs of fighting for any particular solution.

• Once you have evaluated the alternatives, **decide on your recommendations**. Here, you should consider some classic advice on "completed staff work," written by an anonymous university administrator. It suggests the importance of a staffer using resourcefulness and daring to come up with forceful recommendations:

> It is so easy to ask the President what to do, and it appears so easy for him to answer. Resist that impulse. You will succumb to it only if you do not know your job. It is your job to tell the President what he ought to do, not to ask him what you ought to do. HE NEEDS ANSWERS, NOT QUESTIONS. Your job is to study, write, restudy and rewrite until you have evolved a single proposed action—the best one of all you have considered. The President merely approves or disapproves. Alternate courses of action are desirable in many cases and should be presented. But you should say which alternative you think is best.
>
> —Cited in Better Naval Writing, OPNAV 09B-P1-84, p. C-1.

"In the Navy, it's important to be as self-sufficient as possible. So in point papers, messages, or CASREPs, always include *what you've done* about the problem. Don't raise any new issue without answering this. Your boss or a shore command is much more likely to help *if you've already started* on the problem."—Lieutenant Commander on a DESRON Staff

In summary, your task is to give your boss the best advice you can, and to formulate as best you can *clear* and *simple* recommendations based on your research.

That's a brief discussion of the basic process of staff research. Listen to colleagues or old hands for good advice beyond that outlined above if you haven't done any staff research before.

Write Up the First Draft—and Have It Reviewed for Substance

Having thoroughly researched the problem and determined the best solutions, you should write up a complete draft of a report. Whatever the format and whatever its stipulated length, the best way to start is by writing up the report thoroughly, recording the problem, assumptions, criteria, evaluation of alternatives, and recommendations as mentioned above. Then you can assess your thought processes and look for holes in both data and logic (often called a "logic check") before you put that logic up for review.

When you have your thoughts in a more or less presentable form, have some of your colleagues review what you've put down. This step is especially important for new staffers. But even old hands who are experienced authors of Pentagon staff work, *Proceedings* articles, and speeches for senior officials depend on reviews by knowledgeable colleagues for feedback. Often such review will prompt you to more reflection and even more research. If that extra work results in a better product, it's usually worth it.

It may be useful on an especially long or complex project to have periodic reviews at early stages, so later effort isn't wasted. In any case, on the basis of all reviews, rethink your concept and reformulate it as needed.

Now Draft the *Good* Memo, Paper, or Report

Logical as your thought process and extensive as your research may be, your document must now go through another stage. Once you've done all your research, decided on the best course of action to recommend, and written up the whole process in logical order and thorough detail, you must then write the *brief* memo or letter or point paper *that will get that action put into effect.*

In others words, having the perfect solution and even laying it out in perfect clarity and detail isn't enough—you must also convince your busy boss to adopt it. At this point in staff work the editing discussed in Chapter 1 comes into heavy play. That is, instead of that 10-page research report that you originally wrote, you need to condense that report into a one-page briefing memo. Why so short? Again, consider the predicament of the boss for whom you write. As General Starry commented, "To work the problems of the central battle within the restrictions of the realities, I need less information. But every piece of the less has to be pure. . . . You need to synthesize, condense, strip out, boil down . . . like a good newspaper editor."

How do you boil it down? Condensing your ideas can be difficult, but good editing skills can help greatly. Summarized below are some of the most pertinent editing techniques for staff work.

Craft a Good Subject Line

To get the reader's attention from the start, make the subject line as detailed as possible in a few words (just one line, if possible). Write "Eliminating Restrictions in Camp Lejeune Training Areas" rather than just "Training Areas," or "Seabee Participation in Fiji Aid Program" rather than just "Aid for Fiji."

Start Out With Your Main Point

Except in circumstances in which you want to talk a reader into an idea (as in the point-paper format, below) start out with your main point, as advised throughout this text. As the CO of a battleship commented, "Make your bottom line your top line; put your main point up front. Flag officers don't have time to read anything but the very key points." Then put supporting points in *descending order of importance.*

Use Headings

Headings help the reader skim. The longer and more dense the document, the more important the headings. Note that putting the main point first is not as important on one-page as on longer documents if headings guide the reader quickly to all the key information.

Remember the Advice on Writing Abstracts or Executive Summaries

Found in chapter 8, these classic summarizing techniques can be especially useful in highlighting the key results of experiments, surveys, investigations, or other research projects.

Make Use of Tabs and Annexes

Tabs and annexes organize essential material that won't fit on the one-page briefing memo. Highlight important passages within that extra material.

Use Concise Sentences and Short Paragraphs

Follow the advice on Naval Writing Standards in the first chapter of the Correspondence Manual (briefly recapitulated in chapter 1 of this book): suspect wordiness in everything you write. Write in active voice, and avoid rambling qualifiers, legalese, doublings, superfluous and pretentious words, and other prose-expanding habits.

Of course, you'll make sure that you have selected the best format and adhered to it. This chapter later describes and exemplifies most of the major formats for staff work.

Put a Correspondence Folder Together

Having written the briefing memo, letter, point paper, or other documents that the particular problem requires, you must assemble the correspondence package. Gather together all the paperwork pertinent to any staff action: the document to be signed or approved, the briefing memo, and all necessary explanatory material.

The size of this package will depend in part on the amount of your research. Remember to preface a big package with a one-page briefing memo (referencing many tabs and appendixes). That's better than requir-

"A so-so paper that is technically correct will frequently get signed off, but a paper that needs to be returned for a typo invites a closer look and additional corrections of every kind."—Guide to OPNAV Writing

ing your reader to plow through page after page before getting to the main point.

Pay special care to putting the folder together well. No matter how well you write, your boss will probably send your package back to you if you haven't included the basic references (or excerpts from them), or if you haven't made the required number of copies, used the right forms, etc. *This package must be technically correct in every detail.*

Figure 3.2 shows the Naval Military Personnel Command's standard briefing folder. It resembles the format used on many major staffs. Lower echelon commands will not need quite as elaborate a folder, and since the Pentagon's "blue blazers" and HQMC's "routing sheets" are seldom used outside Washington, D.C., a local staff briefing memo could take on a different appearance from any of these documents. The NMPC sample folder is useful as a comprehensive guide, but you should still become thoroughly familiar with the briefing folders used on your own staff.

Coordinate: Learn How to Get Paperwork Through the Top

Finally, there is an art to routing and negotiating a package through a major staff. No matter how good the research is, how pointed and cogent the writing has been, and how technically correct your correspondence package is, you will accomplish nothing if you don't send that package to the right people, in the right order, for the right kind of comments or reviews.

Realize that at big commands (like OPNAV and HQMC), the boss will look for the coordination signatures or "chops" first, before signing. Without the right chops, the substance will be meaningless; the package will be returned to you, unsigned. On the other hand, if all the chops are done, the package may be signed and sent on immediately.

Here are a few pointers on good coordination, drawn from interviews with various Navy and Marine Corps authorities and from the Correspondence Manual:

Consider Who Should Sign the Briefing Memo

The briefing memo accompanies a document through coordination. If the matter is very important, the boss had better sign the memo.

Decide Who Needs to Coordinate

Some staff members must see your package before you have it signed, and others can be informed afterward. If unsure whose chops to obtain, ask an experienced co-worker or consult an organization manual. Many commands have desktop guides that spell out the required coordination. A large staff will often have an office designated to review your chops before your package goes to the boss. Seek out this office and use it regularly to learn all the nuances of "chop chains."

Figure 3.2 Correspondence Folder. The Naval Military Personnel Command issues helpful guidance on correspondence folders.

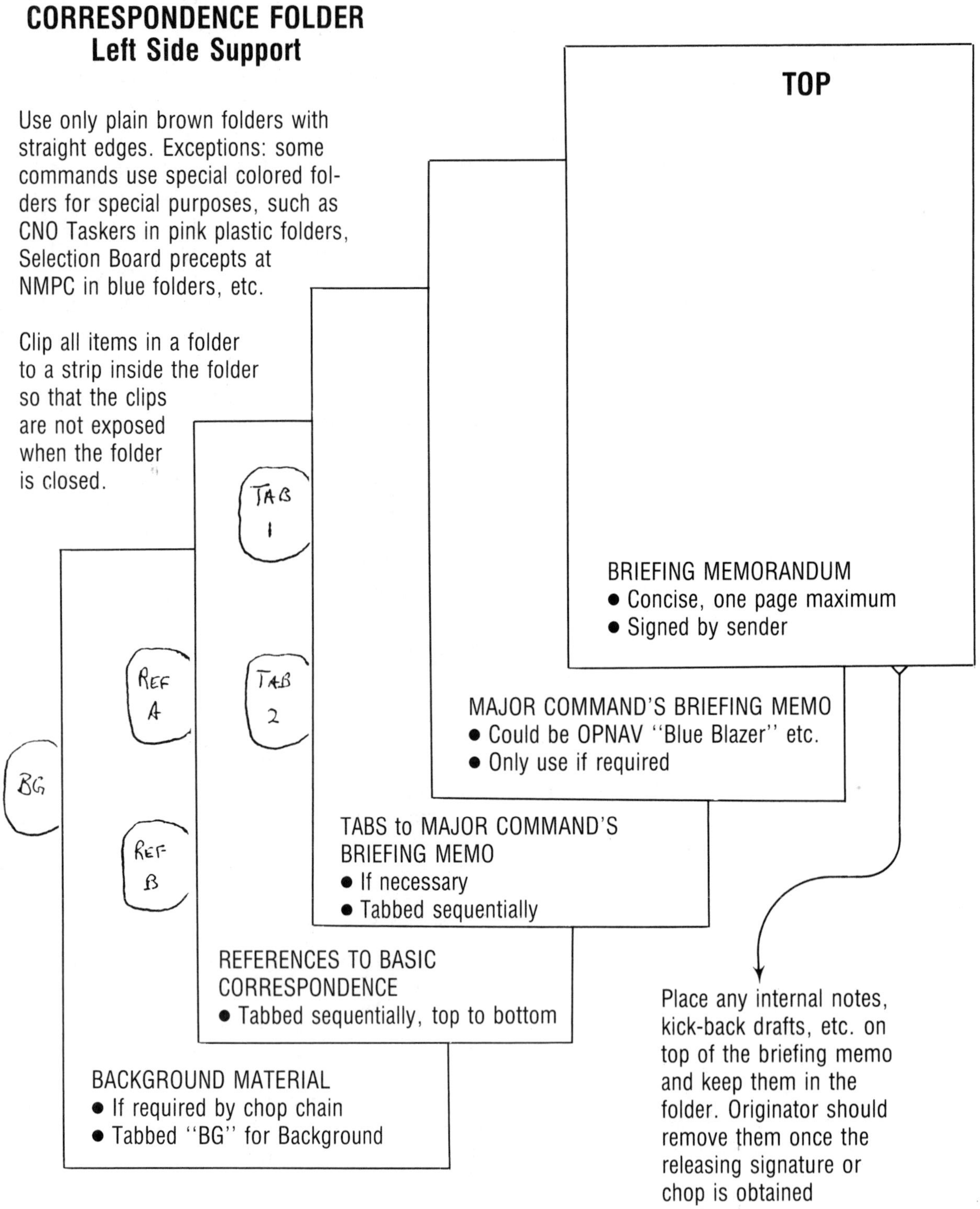
CORRESPONDENCE FOLDER
Left Side Support
Use only plain brown folders with straight edges. Exceptions: some commands use special colored folders for special purposes, such as CNO Taskers in pink plastic folders, Selection Board precepts at NMPC in blue folders, etc.
Clip all items in a folder to a strip inside the folder so that the clips are not exposed when the folder is closed.
TOP
BRIEFING MEMORANDUM
• Concise, one page maximum
• Signed by sender
MAJOR COMMAND'S BRIEFING MEMO
• Could be OPNAV "Blue Blazer" etc.
• Only use if required
TABS to MAJOR COMMAND'S BRIEFING MEMO
• If necessary
• Tabbed sequentially
REFERENCES TO BASIC CORRESPONDENCE
• Tabbed sequentially, top to bottom
BACKGROUND MATERIAL
• If required by chop chain
• Tabbed "BG" for Background
TAB 1
TAB 2
REF A
REF B
BG
Place any internal notes, kick-back drafts, etc. on top of the briefing memo and keep them in the folder. Originator should remove them once the releasing signature or chop is obtained

Figure 3.2 *(continued)*

CORRESPONDENCE FOLDER
Right Side Support

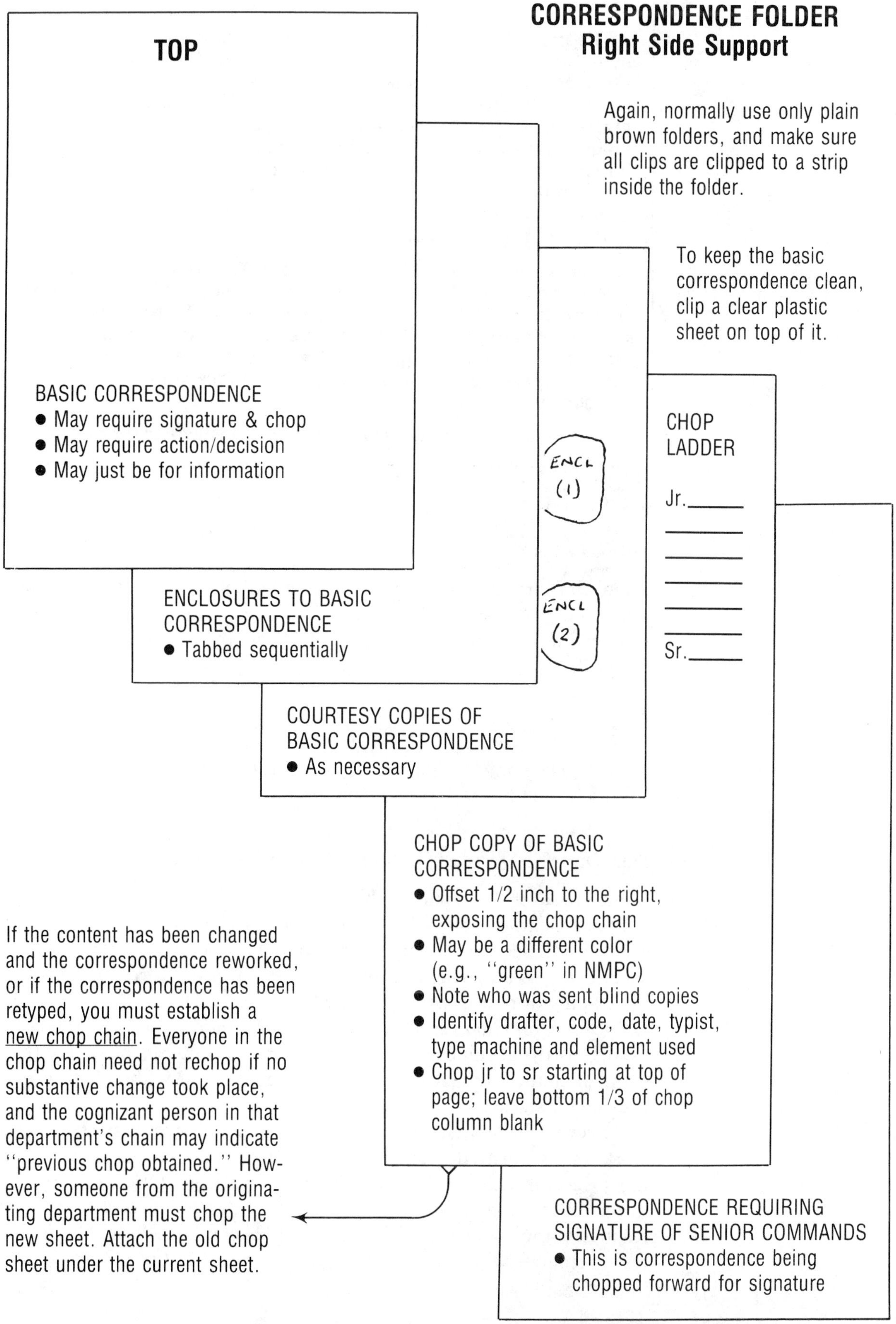
TOP
BASIC CORRESPONDENCE
• May require signature & chop
• May require action/decision
• May just be for information
ENCLOSURES TO BASIC CORRESPONDENCE
• Tabbed sequentially
ENCL (1)
ENCL (2)
COURTESY COPIES OF BASIC CORRESPONDENCE
• As necessary
CHOP LADDER
Jr.
Sr.
CHOP COPY OF BASIC CORRESPONDENCE
• Offset 1/2 inch to the right, exposing the chop chain
• May be a different color (e.g., "green" in NMPC)
• Note who was sent blind copies
• Identify drafter, code, date, typist, type machine and element used
• Chop jr to sr starting at top of page; leave bottom 1/3 of chop column blank
CORRESPONDENCE REQUIRING SIGNATURE OF SENIOR COMMANDS
• This is correspondence being chopped forward for signature

Again, normally use only plain brown folders, and make sure all clips are clipped to a strip inside the folder.

To keep the basic correspondence clean, clip a clear plastic sheet on top of it.

If the content has been changed and the correspondence reworked, or if the correspondence has been retyped, you must establish a new chop chain. Everyone in the chop chain need not rechop if no substantive change took place, and the cognizant person in that department's chain may indicate "previous chop obtained." However, someone from the originating department must chop the new sheet. Attach the old chop sheet under the current sheet.

Too Many Cookes

The greatest danger of staff work is the "too many cooks" syndrome. A great idea, a novel recommendation, or a forceful piece of writing gets neutered in the bureaucracy. Thus, some forms of communication to the boss don't lend themselves to staff work very well. Speechwriting is a perfect example. I learned early at SECNAV that you can't write a speech by committee. The PAO had his agenda, the EA had his, CHINFO threw in his two cents, and before long we had a loose, stream-of-consciousness speech that was forty minutes long and didn't say anything.

This is "office politics" in all its glory. The new staff officer should be warned about its sometimes unpleasant realities, and how to survive it. For one thing, get clear on who really needs to see the stuff you put together. *Work to shorten the pipeline.* Get the right person to give you the okay, and then *modify the chop chain* so your stuff is seen only by those very few who absolutely must see it.

—Lieutenant, former speechwriter for SECNAV

Establish Your Own Infrastructure

Establish contacts in other offices in your building to whom you can talk about your packages. Find out to whom you can send material, and learn who might shepherd your package through their shop in a hurry, if need be.

Vary Coordination by Reference to the Particular Matter at Issue

Consider chopping by phone if the matter is brief and routine. If revisions are likely, you might want to coordinate in the drafting stage.

Plan Out a Strategy for Getting Chops on Very Important Issues

There are several possible methods.

The *sequential chop* is the customary method. In this case, you simply send a folder sequentially from office to office, indicating on the routing sheet who gets the folder and in what order. Eventually, the last office on the chain will return it to your office.

The *shotgun chop* can be useful if time is short. In this method you "shotgun" the document folder to many offices simultaneously and then summarize the responses on a briefing sheet to preface the package as it goes up for signature.

"Type a document and it won't get changed so much in the routing. It also looks more professional."
—Lieutenant on a DESRON staff

However, the shotgun chop can be a two-edged sword, creating extra work. In a sequential chop chain, each succeeding office gets to review the preceding chops before acting on the package. Often this review mitigates or tempers suggested revisions. With a shotgun chop, writers respond without any knowledge of the inputs of other offices. The drafter must reconcile all responses before going forward and may have to get a

The Law of the Chops

Back in the 1950s a Navy lieutenant new to OPNAV was advised by an old hand on how to get a staff paper through the gauntlet without changes. "The trick is to fill up the briefing sheet with initials, no matter whose they are," said the old hand. "Develop a critical mass of chops. If four people initial it, it will get through. The higher-ups want to be reassured that the proposal has strong support. The initials prove that support—it doesn't matter whose—use your staff buddies."

A couple of years later the old hand ran into the lieutenant again, and asked him whether his advice had proved true. "It worked perfectly," the lieutenant replied. "I got signatures from all sorts of people on my Blue Blazers. Like you said, things went right through without a change.

"As a matter of fact, one time it worked *too* well. I worked on a message that was unusually long and complicated, so it necessarily had a very long chop list, and lots of initials. For a while, the message dropped from view. Then one day I had a call. 'Admiral Burke would like to see you.' This was something new. I went down the hall, to CNO's office, and was immediately ushered into the presence of Arleigh Burke himself. I saw my message on his desk. 'Young man,' Burke addressed me, 'I've been around here a long time. It's my experience that if this many people agree on anything, either the subject is of no importance, or you are all trying to do someone in. Which is it? I'd like to know.' "

—Contributed by Captain Frank Snyder (Retired), Naval War College

"re-chop" from one or more people. It isn't good staff work to send a batch of conflicting responses forward, letting the boss iron out the differences.

There is at least one other method of getting chops. If you are *very* short on time, you can sometimes *hand carry* a package through offices personally (indicating to all individuals the material specifically pertinent to them). This way, you can keep superfluous changes to a minimum and often get a document through the process very expeditiously.

Remember Who Has What Responsibility for Coordination

As the Correspondence Manual points out, the originator is responsible for deciding who should coordinate, for resolving major differences, for having retyping done, and for providing copies of the signed correspondence to coordinators who request them. Coordinators, on the other hand, must review the packages on time, date and initial the file copies or coordination forms, and also provide written explanations of nonconcurrences.

Other Resources for Getting Up to Speed on a Staff

Your predecessor may give you a turnover file, but what you do on your own might make you effective weeks earlier than you otherwise would be.

Learn Staff Code Numbering

The larger the staff, the more frequently the offices are referred to by number rather than by the name of the occupant. This numbering is subject to some standardization. In the Marine Corps as in the Army, for instance, when the commander is a general officer, staff organization follows this pattern:

G-1: Personnel
G-2: Intelligence
G-3: Operations and Plans
G-4: Logistics

If the commander is a colonel or below, the codes are S-1, S-2, S-3, and S-4.

In the Navy, a standard division once was as follows:

N-1: Administration and Personnel
N-2: Intelligence
N-3: Operations and Plans
N-4: Logistics
N-5: Communications

However, if Operations and Plans were separate organizations, then N-3 was Operations, N-5 was Plans, and N-6 Communications. These codes will still hold true for some Navy staffs, but there is some variation from one Navy command to another.

The short codes for commander and assistants are still pretty common:

00—Commander
01—Deputy, Chief of Staff, or Executive Officer, with other deputies coded 02, 03, 04, and so on
001—Flag Lieutenant and Aide
002—Flag Secretary and Aide

Often the number "9" designates a Deputy or Vice Chief, as in the following:

00—Chief
09—Vice Chief
051—Division Director
0519—Deputy Division Director

Some small commands prefer to use initials derived from an office or officer's title. One Marine air base, for example, uses the following system:
M—Manpower
ADJ—Adjutant

O—Operations
PAO—Public Affairs Officer
SJA—Staff Judge Advocate
T—Training and Education

Beyond these general guidelines, the best advice is to become very familiar with your particular staff's coding system as described in its organization chart, beginning with your own immediate office, and then branching out. Then stand by to come about: any staff's particular coding (like its staff organization) is likely to change overnight.

Make a Turnover File

Even if your predecessor hands you a turnover file, you can probably enhance it. Be sure it includes:

- your job description, and those of your immediate associates.
- the local organization and regulation manual.
- an organization chart of your own command.
- organization charts of commands to whom your command reports.
- phone books of your own command and of those you must often call, with space for you to add important numbers.
- examples of point papers, briefing memos, executive summaries, letters, and messages that your command has recently approved and issued.
- any available instructions on how the command does paperwork, to include:
  - — a locally written Chapter 11 of the Correspondence Manual, if it exists;
  - — a local Desktop Guide, if one exists;
  - — instructions on the specific briefing-memo format used;
  - — guidelines on putting the local briefing folder together;
  - — local instructions on other formats, if any;
  - — any available guidance on the current commander's preferred style.

"The staff knew so much more of war than I did that they refused to learn from me of the strange conditions in which Arab irregulars had to act; and I could not be bothered to set up a kindergarten of the imagination for their benefit."—T. E. Lawrence, *Seven Pillars of Wisdom*

Make Sure You Have These Standard References at Hand

- the Correspondence Manual
- the pamphlet "Just Plain English"
- a good college dictionary (*not* a paperback)
- perhaps a college grammar handbook
- a thesaurus
- the Standard Navy Distribution List (SNDL)
- the Plain Language Address Directory (PLAD)
- the instructions and notices file, to include
  - — the Directives Manual
  - — evaluation and fitness report instructions
  - — other important instructions
- an old copy of the DOD Phone Directory—highly useful for obtaining office codes, titles, and phone numbers. (The very limited supply

of *new* copies of this sought-after directory should stay in DOD offices.)

- a copy of Maj. Gen. Perry M. Smith, USAF, Retired, *Assignment: Pentagon; The Insider's Guide to the Potomac Puzzle Palace* (Washington: Pergamon-Brassey's, 1989). This text is especially useful if you're being assigned to a staff in Washington, D.C., but is useful in some respects for all staffers.

Read as Much of the Past Year's Correspondence as You Can

Take some extra time (after working hours, if need be) to get familiar with the activities of your office in the past. Review past correspondence, message traffic, old briefing folders, and other such documents. They will give you insight into current issues, peak periods of office operation, common contracts outside your office, personalities and opinions of key players, the boss's buzzwords, etc.

"You'll often find staff officers put down your proposals by saying, 'The admiral wants this' or 'The admiral won't do that,' attributing opinions to the admiral that you might suspect really aren't those of the admiral. There's an easy way to handle that problem. Just ask the staffer to *put the admiral's desires in writing*—and then watch the staffer back off."
—Captain, Naval Reserve

If you prepare this way, you'll take less time to adapt to your new job, and sometimes you'll know more than those already at work. One young Navy lieutenant (jg) was assigned collateral duty as legal officer on joining a ship. His XO counseled him never to show up at the XO's office on a legal matter without the pertinent references *in hand*. Very quickly he found that some officers he dealt with would not know the regulations but would try to bluster their way through an issue as if they did. Having the reference on hand gave him absolutely sure footing in such circumstances.

This experience taught him to get his act together before he went to a senior on any issue; the habit served him well when he was later assigned to a staff.

Typical Staff Documents

The following section gives descriptions and examples of several kinds of documents used on a typical Navy or Marine Corps staff. Other kinds of staff writing—letters, memos, the memorandum-for, instructions and notices, and so on—are discussed elsewhere in this text. The next few pages cover:

The Briefing Memo
The Correspondence Folder
The Point Paper
The Talking Paper
The Trip Report
Lessons Learned
The Plan of Action and Milestones
The POM Issue Paper

One other, a most venerable staff document, deserves special comment. The *staff study* is very seldom written anymore in the Navy, and the Marine Corps already has excellent guidance available. The staff study's format, however, does provide an excellent description of how to go about studying a major problem on a staff. Anyone who may be required to use it, or who just might be interested in how to conduct thorough staff research, can refer to several good sources:

- the staff study format found in NWP 11 (Naval Operational Planning);
- the very brief discussion of a staff study in Armed Forces Staff College Pub 1 ("Joint Staff Officer's Guide");
- the very thorough and well-exemplified treatment of a staff study found in MCI 7702 (Marine Corps Institute's "Professional Communications" course publication).

The Briefing Memo

> Naval officers are trained not to leave any stone unturned—but that's only half the job. The other half is boiling it down to one page on a briefing memo.
>
> —Navy Captain

At the senior officer level, a good route sheet or briefing memo is invaluable.—Marine Corps Colonel

In OPNAV a briefing memo is called a "blue blazer"; in HQMC, paperwork usually moves by a "routing sheet." Joint commands use many names, including "decision paper" and "summary sheet." But whatever the name, the ability to write a good one is an essential ability for any staffer, whether officer, senior enlisted, or civilian. Here's some guidance on how to put one together.

SUBJECT:

WRITING THE BRIEFING MEMO

ISSUE: A briefing memo is an explanation sheet. It's a piece of paper that explains any letter, memorandum, instruction, or other document that needs to be signed by the boss and issued. You can also use it to brief the boss even when there is no outgoing correspondence.

RECOMMENDATION: Use the briefing memo to give a brief history of the package, with supporting and explanatory remarks. Specifically,

— Keep your typewritten memo to one page.
— Use headings to guide the reader, like those on this page—vary as needed.
— Make sure one of those headings is "Recommendation," "Summary," or "Action," so the boss can find the bottom line quickly.
— Write in brief, logically ordered bullets.
— Neatly paper clip the briefing memo to the left side of a folder, across from the document to be signed.

The Length of Briefing Memos—Two Opinions

A favorite response will be that your topic can't be explained in one page. I know of no issue that can't be laid out in one page, or in a 15–20 minute briefing.—Navy Captain, EA for VCNO

Branch heads at OPNAV know that the CNO won't read three pages. So by the time a briefing memo gets to CNO, its information value is limited. Some things simply can't be covered at this length. Recently I got a message drafted for me asking SURFLANT for $20,000 for joiner doors, this in an austere budget climate. It simply had to be written with all the background information or it had no chance of getting approved.—Navy Captain, Commodore of a DESRON

BACKGROUND: Wherever used, the briefing memo has the function of

— explaining what you're proposing and why.
— discussing any rejected alternatives.
— addressing why the package is late, if it is.

But don't use it to

— duplicate what is in the proposed correspondence.
— just make the recommendation "Sign the attached correspondence."

COORDINATION: Ensure you obtain all necessary chops (reviews). Mention the important coordination you have obtained, if not clear from elsewhere in the memo or correspondence. For instance: "The proposed response was coordinated with 04B, and it was chopped by NMPC-9."

Signature:	Office Code & Phone:	Date:
Action Officer, LCDR, USN	03A/x5-5555	30 NOV 90

The Correspondence Folder

Correspondence folders are vital tools for doing staff work. While the structure of these folders varies slightly from command to command, all such folders serve to (1) collect all the important documentation regarding any particular staff action in one place, and (2) organize all relevant documents and information in a standard, usable order. For example, you normally clip the letter, memorandum-for, message, or other document to be signed on the right side of the folder, and any briefing memo explaining that document on the left. Tabs, appendixes, and other supporting documentation go behind these surface documents.

Again, the folder illustrated in Figure 3.2 on pp. 94–95 is based on the Naval Military Personnel Command's organization of the correspondence folder; most major naval commands use a similar structure.

The Point Paper

> I had to consolidate point papers for ships in a squadron—one of the hardest writing tasks I've had aboard ship. I learned that you need to know lots of extra information about the topic in case the boss asks for it, but all that extra dope doesn't have to be in the point paper.
>
> —Navy Lieutenant

Point papers are good ways to press forward recommendations in a direct and objective way. Instead of writing a letter or other document for signature and then attempting to persuade seniors to buy your approach, you can write a point paper seeking a decision and wait to implement what your boss decides. As one Navy captain remarked, "With the point paper you create a grenade with the pin out, but without requiring anyone in the chain to sign it. It's an excellent way to direct things."

Point papers are used widely in many contexts, and there are various formats—each of which can be effective. In most you are trying to talk your audience into something, so often (unlike a briefing memo or many other staff action papers) you can leave the recommendation till last. As long as you *keep the point paper to one page* and *use clear headings*, the audience can skim the document and find your "bottom line" very quickly. Here's a brief discussion of the point paper's format and use.

Rank/Name/Branch
Staff Code/Phone Number
12 Dec 90

SUBJECT: USE OF POINT PAPERS

PROBLEM/ BACKGROUND: Point papers are a good means of stating background, ideas, and recommendations in a relatively formal way for the consideration of the command. Use a point paper primarily to direct the attention of seniors to an issue or problem, and to seek a decision.

You can also use a point paper to bring up issues for discussion in conferences, to help develop policy, to help resolve differences between offices, and to prepare senior officers for appearances before important bodies, such as congressional committees.

DISCUSSION: 1. Some offices stipulate the format, but others allow you to vary format as necessary to suit a particular case. One possible format is illustrated on this page; below are two other popular formats:

PROBLEM	TOPIC
DISCUSSION	REQUIREMENT
RECOMMENDATIONS	DISCUSSION
	SOLUTION

2. Follow this guidance for writing point papers:
— Keep to one page in most cases; use tabs for additional material.
— Include options if useful, and pros and cons of each.
— Be factual and objective.
— Keep the language simple. Explain all technical terms or acronyms the first time you use them.
— Don't make the point paper so detailed that significant points are lost in minutiae.
— Ensure the point paper stands on its own.

STATUS: If your paper concerns an issue already being discussed in an organization, a "status" paragraph can be useful to point out where it is, who is acting on it, what the hang-ups are, when it will move, etc.

RECOMMENDATION: State recommended actions. Be specific and brief, stating who, when, where, how much, etc. Avoid broad, nonspecific recommendations. List a series of options, if desirable, but always make your choice clear among them.

Below is an example of a point paper prepared aboard ship for use at a conference at an operational staff. You will probably be able to locate good examples at your own command.

Point Paper for COMCARDIV STAFF

ORIG: USS CARRIER
DRAFTER: LCDR R. ENGINEER
DATE: 2 DEC 87

SEA/SHORE DUTY ROTATION FOR NONNUCLEAR-TRAINED MACHINIST'S MATES

PROBLEM

Sea-duty obligation for E-7 through E-9 machinist's mates has been increased to 60 months.

DISCUSSION

1. For the second time in less than three years, the sea-tour length for nonnuclear machinist's mates has been increased. The total extension has been 24 months. As a result:

a. Shore-tour planning has been superceded because detailers and career counselors do not have an accurate list of options to discuss.

b. Family planning in regard to PCS moves, retirement options, and future education plans for children is in jeopardy due to uncertainty about career options.

c. Personal career planning—to stay in or get out—is being affected: many senior qualified personnel are choosing to leave the service.

2. Personnel on board USS CARRIER are confronting a sea tour with not just one or two six-month-plus deployments, but possibly three. For senior enlisted, the options are limited—either retire or deploy. Prior to this extension policy, some had decided to stay in and contribute at a shore facility that could use their technical expertise and knowledge.

RECOMMENDATIONS

1. On a case-by-case basis, review the sea/shore rotation dates of all senior machinist's mates. Send men whose shore-tour length (two years) has been fulfilled back to sea to relieve those men whose tours have been extended.

2. Reestablish SRB for machinist's mates at a level that will support the required retention level. Many predicted the current problem when SRB was reduced several years ago.

The Talking Paper

Another staff document similar to a point paper is a talking paper, so named because you usually prepare it for someone to use while "talking," that is, while speaking in informal circumstances. These circumstances might be interviews with visiting officials, informal talks to groups, visits with the media, etc. *Keep the talking paper brief and simple.* Further guidance appears below.

Originator's Name
Code/Phone #
Date prepared

TALKING PAPER

Subj: HOW TO WRITE A TALKING PAPER

ISSUE

- Specify in the "Issue" or "Background" section

— The name of the official for whom this paper has been prepared, the name of the meeting, etc.
— The event or situation that has brought this issue up now.
— Any other brief background information needed.

TALKING POINTS

- Use this outline as a memory aid in a meeting, or as an informal agenda. Also use it as a tickler to prepare seniors for meetings with important officials, such as senior Navy or Marine Corps officials or members of Congress.

- Include the key facts in whatever format is most useful. Change headings as required; include a "Recommendation" section, if needed.

- Be concise—normally keep it to one page. Use bullet style. Single space, but double-space between bullets. Indent subordinate points.

- Say what to avoid talking about, as well as what to talk about. Also note, if needed, who has been involved and concurs or does not concur.

- Mark classification (and paragraph classification) as required.

- Marine Corps format differs slightly. See HqO P5000.1 for format, and MCI 7702 for unofficial format with example.

Here is an example of a talking paper, adapted from a talking paper once prepared in NMPC.

TALKING PAPER

CDR S. F. Housing
OP-999H/#5-4321
13 April 1982

ISSUE

- Shortfall in Military Family Housing (MFH) at Lajes, Azores

BACKGROUND

- This paper was prepared at OP-99's request, in response to an inquiry by Assistant Secretary of the Navy (Logistics). This issue may come up in a meeting between OP-99 and the Secretary next Tuesday, April 17.

TALKING POINTS

- MFH assets at Azores are owned and managed by the Air Force.
- Navy owns no housing there.

- Average waiting time for personnel to get into housing is 8 to 10 months.
- Figures relevant to MFH at Azores:
  - — Total requirement (Air Force and Navy families)—900
  - — Total of 392 Air Force & Navy personnel are on the housing waiting list
  - — Current assets—182 units
  - — Programmed for construction:
    - — FY 83 ---------------- 150 units (approved)
    - — FY 84 ---------------- 150 units
    - — FY 86 ---------------- 100 units

COORDINATION SUMMARY

- USAF point of contact is LtCol D. A. Quarters at 1-2345, who provided some of the above information.

The Trip Report

> Trip reports can have the benefit of keeping the boss informed. Also use them to make your case, and to inform the boss of impending action on which you need support—a sort of "preparatory fire."
>
> —Marine Colonel

A trip report can be an important and very useful document, not the meaningless paper exercise that it sometimes becomes. As a Navy captain remarked, "It's not worthwhile reading trip reports that list the lectures you heard. Trip reports seem to be used to account for your time—but no one cares about that. Give a sense of what you are discovering." Or, as a Marine lieutenant colonel commented, "Don't just say 'I came, I saw this, I talked to so-and-so'; *make recommendations.*"

Ideally, trip reports will be worked into a long-range command strategy, a strategy that will have had a point in sending you to the meeting in the first place. The commanding officer of a Navy training command, for example, had this strategy:

> I send my people to get things to happen at meetings, not just to listen. If we're not playing, we're not going.
>
> So the trip report isn't a drill—it is the end of the trip, the reason you went. It becomes a management tool that (through its recommendations) has an impact or gets things done, either in the Navy at large or at home in your own command.

As this captain suggests, many staff members who attend meetings are unprepared to contribute significantly to the proceedings. A *pretrip report* that requires staffers to outline their reasons for the trip, the people who will be there, the business they will conduct, and any controversial topics they expect to arise can help staff members learn to regard conferences as *means to an end,* or as opportunities to make things happen. After such formal preparation, a *posttrip* report (like the example below) can be a way to report recommendations for action and changes in policy, as well as to relay new information.

Whatever your command's strategy, remember to keep a sense of priority as you pen your final report. As with many other staff documents, make a habit of *putting the vital points up front*—at least on the first page—or they simply won't be read. Leave for appendixes such peripheral material as topics covered at the conference and lists of speakers. Follow a format like the one shown below.

15 March 1989

From: Senior Officer or Officers Who Made the Trip
To: Commanding Officer—via the Chain of Command

Subj: TRIP REPORT TO MEETING, CONFERENCE, ASSIST VISIT, ETC.

Encl: (1) Agenda or itinerary
(2) List of attendees
(3) Minutes or other enclosures as pertinent

1. Trip Purpose: Record the objective of the trip you took. Why was the meeting held, and why did staff members go? What did they expect to get out of it? Whom did they expect to influence, and why?

2. Highlights: Comment in bullet format on such matters as
- Whether the organizers achieved their aims.
- What major decisions participants made and what new information they issued.
- What milestone status on projects, proposals, etc., participants reported.
- Whether you achieved your objective in taking the trip.

3. Unresolved Issues: Report here
- Newly discovered problem areas.
- Unresolved issues, including their current status.

4. Action Items or Recommendations: Note in this section
- What items were assigned to your command for action.
- Anything else you committed your office or boss to.
- What recommendations you have regarding ways of doing business, new developments or projects, etc.

5. Opinions and Impressions: In this closing paragraph, comment on such matters as the overall success of the trip, developments in other areas, ideas about what the future holds, etc.

Very Respectfully,

S. OFFICER
LCDR USN

As an example, here is a trip report written by the operations officer at the Fleet Anti-Submarine Training Center, Atlantic, to his commanding officer about a recent meeting. The report does very well in giving the CO a sense of what the issues are and where things are headed.

MEMORANDUM 9 December 1987

From: N3
To: CO
Via: XO

Subj: TRIP REPORT FOR 14A6 UPGRADE MEETING, 2 DECEMBER 1987

Encl: (1) Agenda
(2) List of Attendees

1. Trip Purpose. To review 14A6 upgrade program progress.

2. Highlights.
— Various areas were briefed per agenda with one exception: no one briefed EW since EWC Britton was not present.
— Milestones are being met, in general. Hard spots are in paragraph 3.
— NAVSEA estimates hardware will start arriving mid-January.
— HP 9020 will be replaced by HP 825 as central computer; more power.

3. Unresolved Issues.
— Passive acoustic system. Several options are being pursued:
— SYSCOM training system developed for P-3 operators.
— SONALYSTS system, which is a spin-off of ASWETA (no raw grams). Our position is: we want grams, but if not achievable in prototype, we will settle for processed data with grams to follow later. FLEASWTRACENLANT will not pick a system; we will only give our requirements.
— EW. OP-392C says he has arranged with EW detailer for EWC Britton to be ordered to CARON via CNSL. He would be TAD here during that period to work on the OTX system. If that plan falls through, an industry system that also meets our needs can be ready in time.

4. Action Items. None for Fleet ASW, but our active involvement now includes:
— Working with EDO to get up a prototype work-up. Already started.
— Reviewing the manual for the SYSCOM gram trainer to see if it meets our needs.
— Briefing. Joe McCartney attended and briefed CLF science advisor, Al Densinbacker. Subsequently, Densinbacker briefed CAPT Gionet who asked to be briefed fully on the program. I agreed to do so this Friday at 1530.

5. Opinions and Impressions.
— I like PADS myself but don't want to dictate which system to use.

When asked, we'll give our opinions on which system can do better/worse.

Very respectfully,

C. F. GORE
CDR USN

Lessons Learned

Lessons learned are naval problem summaries. Widely used on both operational commands and staffs, lessons learned report on difficulties in recent operations, exercises, inspections, and many other evolutions. These papers usually report on problems that *have already been solved,* a solution being recorded along with each particular problem. (For problems that still *need solving,* staffers typically compose point papers and then follow them up with POA&Ms, briefing packages, proposed revisions to directives, etc.)

We record lessons learned both to keep present commanders informed and to guide personnel in the future. Not only might someone forget from one evolution to the next, but given the rapidity of personnel transfers (or wartime casualties), the next month's or next year's evolution will often see different personnel in key positions. These new people will badly need guidance to rely on and will not want to start from scratch.

One wide use of lessons learned during peacetime is to record problems solved during Fleet or Fleet Marine Force exercises, as in "Red Flag Lessons Learned," "Exercise Alpine Charger 86 Lessons Learned," etc. But we write lessons learned on many occasions other than exercises—after major inspections or after standard training evolutions, for example. In such cases, their purpose is to guide those who must prepare for the next INSURV, OPPE, REFTRA, or whatever.

Further, a ship or unit "chopping" into a new operational area (a destroyer reporting to the Persian Gulf, for instance) will often receive from the ship or unit it is relieving an after-action report itemizing lessons learned. In this instance, the document would fit into the standard naval relieving ceremony.

Very comprehensive lessons learned are often written on major naval events, to discuss strategy, tactics, successful employment of new weapons systems, and the like. For a good ten-page example of one of these studies, see the "Lessons Learned on The Falklands War," pp. 279–289 in former Secretary of the Navy John F. Lehman, Jr.'s book *Command of the Seas* (New York: Charles Scribner's Sons, 1988). Lehman himself drew on two *book-length* lessons-learned studies for his discussion.

Write lessons learned often—whenever specific experience has taught something you (or someone at your ship or station) may need to know in the future. Make sure to incorporate these documents into your turnover file. Whatever the topic, remember not to talk just about what went wrong; also discuss what went right. Sound procedures, reasonable rules not to bend, planning ahead that proved right on target—all this information is as important as "problem-solved" commentary.

The example below is one of many lessons learned drawn up following a Marine Corps Reserve exercise. It follows a widely used format, first describing the background, then presenting a brief discussion, and then making a recommendation.

Lesson Learned

TOPIC: Problems Involving Communications Security

BACKGROUND: Drawing on the exercise plan and additional guidance received during prebriefing, units employed communications-security procedures (mainly shackling) from Day 1 of the exercise.

DISCUSSION: Such employment of communications security is doing more harm than good. During the exercise, grids were coded or decoded incorrectly, important messages were delayed because of coding and decoding requirements, CEOIs were not where they were needed, aircraft were on the wrong frequencies, etc.

RECOMMENDATION: For a short Reserve exercise, we should waive shackling. It is invariably done improperly, wastes time, confuses personnel, and therefore delays other training objectives. In addition, on D-day the enemy is likely to know exactly where you are, and shackling your grid coordinates from a known position allows him to break your code.

Another good example of lessons learned is the SURFLANT document (in memo-for-record format) reproduced as Figure 3.3. The author was officer in charge of the 1987 SURFLANT change of command. He recorded his lessons learned so that future changes of command will also go well.

The Plan of Action and Milestones (POA&M)

The Plan of Action and Milestones (POA&M) is a planning document used widely throughout the Navy and Marine Corps. It is exactly what its name suggests. It is a plan of (1) **what steps have to be taken** to complete a project, inspection, or other evolution, and (2) **mileposts for each step.** Virtually any organizational activity can formulate a POA&M, but it is especially appropriate in cases where responsibility for action involves many different departments.

POA&Ms are perhaps most widely used in the surface Navy, both on staffs and on ships. Staffs use POA&Ms for instituting new programs or getting initiatives off the ground. Ships use POA&Ms to guide preparations for a myriad of inspections (NTPIs, OPPEs, Supply Management Inspections, etc.) and to schedule the correction of discrepancies after

Figure 3-3 Lessons Learned. Here are lessons learned in the form of a memo for record.

DEPARTMENT OF THE NAVY

COMMANDER NAVAL SURFACE FORCE
UNITED STATES ATLANTIC FLEET
NORFOLK, VIRGINIA 23511-6292

5 January 1988

MEMORANDUM FOR THE RECORD

Via: (1) N3
(2) 002
(3) 02

Subj: CHANGE OF COMMAND 1987 LESSONS LEARNED

1. This memorandum addresses the planning for and execution of the 1987 COMNAVSURFLANT Change of Command. In general, it was a successful effort; areas that required more than routine effort will be emphasized.

2. As background, a successor to VADM ________ was not known until very late in the game. The same was true of the actual date for the change. As a consequence, specific planning was delayed until about four weeks prior to the event. This time compression had the greatest effect in the expected areas: invitations printing/mailing, program printing, etc. VADM ________ was frocked after the programs were printed, which necessitated printing them again - SHENANDOAH did it in three days.

3. Specific responsibilities were assigned by COMNAVSURFLANTNOTE. Three TEMDU officers were assigned to the project and were able to devote almost full time to it, which blurred some lines of responsibility. This minor disadvantage was outweighed by the clear advantage of full-time help.

4. The "hard" areas included:

- Communications: Although ultimately resolved, a lack of hand-held comms was an issue. Need to resolve early, identify requirements, and get the radios as soon as possible.

- Portable comms didn't work well from LP-1.

- Don't depend solely on NAVSTA to provide hand-held comms. Task one of the Groups early to provide units from ships' assets.

- Ceremony timing: The "ceremony" was scheduled to start at 1000, which meant that the CNO arrived at 0959. This meant that the principals arrived sometime before that, causing the forward brow to be secured in preparation.

- Flag officers attending a 1000 event will arrive at 0955. Some did and had to use the after brow.

- Philosophical question. Does the "ceremony" start with the benediction, or when the principals arrive?

- The issue should be broached next time.

Figure 3.3 *(continued)*

Subj: CHANGE OF COMMAND 1987 LESSONS LEARNED

- VIP transportation: N7 handled this perfectly, but it took a major effort.

- It's a moving target, but identify VIPs who need transportation, then add five and order that number of cars.

- Ask for a list of escort officers from the staff (ACOSs) early. One per car per run, basically.

- Drivers were staff CPOs - trained by N7 - worked well. Lots of practice runs help.

- Attention to minute detail required in this area. Fertile ground for OMIGODs.

- VIPs (aside from principals/principals' families) were out-of-town flags who flew in for the day.

- Standard change-of-command items: Don't overlook mundane items such as UNITREP, releasing signatures, security badges, etc.

- Reception: Nail down as early as possible. Provide options. Sensitive issue - personal money involved. No government funds should be expended on solely reception items. N7 will explain.

- Uniform Issues: Make the uniform requirements clear for every event and then get the word out.

5. Expect full cooperation in the overall effort. Navy Regs and the Protocol Manual provide lots of guidance as questions arise. Start as early as possible.

Very respectfully,

Commander, USN, N00X

inspections. You can also use POA&Ms to schedule change-of-command ceremonies and to plan deployments and training exercises.

The POA&M is very simple in concept and appearance. Usually published in an instruction or other official directive, the basic plan consists of a schedule of action to be taken, and a designation of the cognizant official for each action. In print the document usually consists of three columns, labeled Action Item, Action Individual, and Due Date, these three columns simply designating *what* needs to be done, *who* has to do it, and by *when*.

This simplicity may be misleading. Besides taking care to be accurate, you must be very thoughtful and farsighted to make the plan a workable document, one that makes allowance for other unit evolutions that may affect the plan. Even after you design it, you cannot regard it as having been set in concrete. As one officer on a DESRON staff commented, "The POA&M never happens as you schedule it. Crises are always coming up to interfere with it." You need to revise it often. Indeed, good as it is in concept, a POA&M will be absolutely useless in practice unless you check progress frequently, identify and overcome obstacles, and hold people to the stipulated deadlines. Without such rigorous management, the POA&M will simply be ignored.

POA&Ms have special value for commanders, who can gauge the command's progress toward a goal simply by glancing at the chart of goals and accomplishments it comprises. Because a superior will often judge a department's or division's progress by looking at a POA&M, you can put yourself on report by being less than farsighted in working one up. Make sure you have a reasonable chance to complete any tasking before you assign yourself responsibility to do it. Have the same consideration for your subordinates when giving them responsibilities. In short, *formulate this plan with discretion,* and *evaluate it with understanding.*

In summary, when composing the POA&M,

Do:

- Be very detailed with assignments. Separate complex activities into a number of individual steps.
- Assign responsibility for each step by billet or code to *one specific individual.*
- Assign reasonable due dates.
- Update the plan periodically, adjusting the dates and responsibilities according to changes in schedule, available personnel, etc.

Don't:

- Formulate a POA&M for a period longer than one year. The longer the time and the greater the detail, the more unwieldy the plan becomes. It is likely to become meaningless if stretched too far into the future.

Here is a POA&M used aboard a surface ship for scheduling the qualification of Enlisted Surface Warfare Specialists (ESWSs). POA&Ms

on staffs are often more complex (sometimes they have many sections), but otherwise are usually very similar.

POA&M for ESWS QUALIFICATION

Milestones. PREBLE has established two weeks before outchop as the deadline for 100 percent ESWS qualification of eligible petty officers. Adhere to the following schedule in accomplishing that objective:

Action Item	*COG*	*Due NLT*
a. Promulgate list of Chiefs/POs aboard	XO	01 May
b. Revise Monthly PQS reports to track ESWS quals and progress toward	XO	01 May
c. Conduct review of ship's program, and establish reporting requirements	CO	15 May
d. Promulgate updated ESWS Qualifiers list	XO	15 May
e. Develop timeline that reflects time remaining vs. number of qualification points completed, in order to qualify no later than 15 October	XO	15 May
f. Develop bank of 500 questions for use in ESWS qualification exam. Publish question list for crew's review	SMCS	01 Jun
g. Commence review of ship's program and ship's qualifications	SMCS	15 Jul
h. Identify individuals who have not made acceptable progress, and report delinquents to XO	CO/XO	01 Aug
i. Establish after-hours schedule of instruction for delinquent personnel, and promulgate sked to crew	SMCS	01 Aug
j. Review ship's program and status of crew's qualifications	CO/XO	15 Aug 31 Aug 15 Sep 30 Sep 15 Oct

The POM Issue Paper

The *Program Objective Memorandum* (POM) is an annual input to the *Five Year Defense Plan* (FYDP). They are both part of the *Planning, Programming, and Budgeting System* (PPBS), and they help build the Department of Defense budget each year. If you're put off by this kind of language, just remember that bureaucratese and unfamiliar acronyms introduced into your own documents also drive your readers crazy. We have to live with POM, FYDP, PPBS, and many other budgeting acronyms

(MPN, RPN, OMN&R, etc.)—don't introduce any more than are necessary into the process yourself.

The Navy and the Marine Corps prepare separate POMs for the Defense Plan. While the most critical writing of "POM issue papers" or "POM issues" takes place at major commands, preliminary requests for funds are also often written in the form of POM issues. Hence, a great many officers, senior enlisted, and civilian government employees get involved in writing, rewriting, or combining these documents.

What are the keys for good writing here? One command gave these instructions to its personnel: "The quality of the issue papers is the key to getting the message across. They must be *soundly based, fully developed*, and *correctly stated* to receive full support and consideration." Where the formats for POM issue papers will vary, principles like those above cannot be overemphasized. Basing our discussion on a standard Navy format, let's take the three principles one at a time.

Do Sound Research

First, of course, any program or proposal must be "soundly based." Whether a paper proposes adding civilian guards to replace Marine Corps security forces, expanding manning at intermediate maintenance activities to increase torpedo production, or providing automated teller machines aboard ships, the reasons for doing so must be absolutely sound. You must know all the regulations involving the issue, make reasonable inferences, and scout out the essential *contexts* of the issue too.

Make especially sure to get the dollars and figures right. As a civilian expert in the POM process pointed out, "Proposals go through even if the rationale is not especially strong. But they are *destroyed* by inconsistent numbers and dollars." The budgeting process is a long one; by the time an issue paper reaches OPNAV or HQMC, it is likely to be very time-sensitive. The officials at the service headquarters assembling the Navy or Marine Corps POMs have little time to call the originating command to check figures or correct omissions in the data.

On the other hand, poor data will sometimes have an even worse consequence: the project will receive funding, but some technicality or legal problem that the originator didn't notice will prohibit the Navy or Marine Corps from pursuing the program. As another civilian expert in OPNAV commented (from long experience), "It's terribly frustrating to put money where it can't be used." So make every effort to do sound, thorough research.

Develop Your Proposal Fully

It is one thing to have a good idea or an excellent rationale. It's another matter to elaborate that idea completely into all the parts of a POM issue paper. You must fully develop not only the basic statement of the issue and the background but all the alternatives too.

Stating the basic **Issue and Background**, what monies you're requesting and why, would seem easy enough. But too often this section is not done

Quite a Capability

Often, because of statutory restrictions, slow paperwork, and a multitude of other restrictions, there will be problems using funds that are already in the Navy's budget. Still, an officer was rather startled one day when he came across the following statement in an OPNAV point paper:

> **XXX Program Manager is extremely capable of spending money *now* . . . up to $3 million if available.**

well. As a senior official in POM Development commented, there are far too many POM issues that are hard to use at headquarters simply because the basic explanation is unclear—the writer hasn't explained what the service will be buying and exactly what the service will do with what is bought. Be sure to give very specific and clear information. Another official involved in the budgeting process commented, "You tend to put money where you know *for sure* what it's going for—because you know you have to defend it before the big boys."

The **Alternatives** section is next in importance. When officials at HQMC or OPNAV (or, beyond that, at NAVCOMPT, OSD, or in the House and Senate and White House) are faced with hard choices on what to try to fund under a limited ceiling, they will often want to jockey back and forth, funding a bit less of this and a bit more of that. Do your best to give them alternatives by which they can at least partially fund a program. Three or four alternatives are not too many to set before decision makers. Make it clear in your **Evaluation of Alternatives** which alternative is preferable, and state as precisely as you can the positive and negative implications of each.

Both a clear statement of the alternatives and an incisive evaluation of each one can be crucial. Of course, as mentioned before, the **Funding** figures should be complete and accurate. The **Offsets/Economies** section (however that topic is titled in your format) has become increasingly important recently. The latter section, of course, is set aside for defining how a program might *save* money, if at all, or in what ways it might "offset" or compensate for the price tag of an otherwise expensive program. You can also use it to identify ways in which a command proposes to pay for a new project or program—sometimes by using funds currently available from another area.

Many POM issue papers glossed over this area in the past, just listing vague statements such as "Quality of life and retention will improve" or "Expensive facilities will be protected." But more and more, in eras of decreased availability of government funds, if you don't detail monies from your own program to pay for what you're asking, you are unlikely to have the issued approved. In the words of a POM expert, "Today, if you don't list specific offsets, you're asking for the world."

Of course, this issue can be very dicey. If, to fund one project, you list another item in your own program that can be cut, you might find that not only has the first program been left unfunded, but the offset funds have also disappeared. All the more reason, then, to get the basic argument right and to estimate carefully all the political, economic, military, and other repercussions of what you put down on paper.

Manpower Implications is usually one of the final sections; a consideration of the personnel requirements is vital to an overall assessment of each alternative. List numbers of officers, enlisted, and civilians, new training requirements, and so on.

State Your Argument Well

Consider all the principles of good writing in your actual composition of the issue paper—chief among them brevity, writing for a general audience, and making every sentence count.

Be as Brief as Possible

You don't have to limit the POM issue to a page, but if you write more than two (not counting the "Resource Detail Sheet"—a table of figures accompanying a POM issue) your issue is unlikely to get a thorough reading anywhere. Strive to strike the medium between writing so little that the issue and justification are not clear, and writing so much that a harried manager won't have the patience to read through it all. While putting forth the best argument possible, be careful not to sound like a debator summing up a case with all the flourishes of classical rhetoric. In the POM process, crisp, factual paragraphs studded at key points with impressive dollars and other figures will usually convey the best impression.

Write in short sentences and short paragraphs. Bulky paragraphs of technically dense material—and, unfortunately, much POM material is *very* dense—discourage careful reading.

Write for a General Audience

You can usually be sure that the varied audience you speak to will know nowhere near as much as you do about the issue. Be careful not to use unfamiliar technical or financial terminology as you explain your proposal. Also *use as few acronyms as possible,* and explain the ones you do use.

Be as Specific and Hard-Hitting as You Can

Especially in the "Background" and "Evaluation of Alternatives" areas (sometimes known as the "Justification" and "Impact" statements), you must get your reader's attention, explain clearly what you require, and *rivet home* the argument and impact. The "Evaluation of Alternatives" section or "Impact" statement is probably the most important section that you will write. As a Marine Corps POM official commented, the "Impact" statement is "the real 'meat and potatoes' of the POM initiative."

An Example of a POM Issue Paper

Figure 3.4 is a CINCLANTFLT POM Issue Paper on "Asbestos Insulation Removal" (used by permission). It outlines the proposal clearly, cites pertinent messages and surveys, and not only suggests alternatives but makes clear a "projected payback period." (Note: The "Priority" line is at first left blank, to be filled in later by decision makers juggling the competing proposals.)

Figure 3.4 POM Issue Paper. This sample budget document clarifies both the specific issue's background and the Navy's alternatives in this case.

POM-88 ISSUE PAPER

TITLE: ASBESTOS INSULATION REMOVAL

CLAIMANT: CINCLANTFLT DATE: 1 NOV 85

CINCLANTFLT POC: CDR CODE: N94 PHONE: A/V 564-6138

OPNAV RESOURCE SPONSOR: LCDR CODE: OP-22 PHONE: A/V 222-1984

ISSUE: Asbestos insulation removal at Naval Submarine Base, New London.

PRIORITY:

BACKGROUND: The central steam distribution system at SUBASE New London consists of approximately six miles of piping in trenches insulated with molded asbestos. The insulation is deteriorating. Asbestos is recognized as a major health hazard and poses a serious health threat to personnel when asbestos fibers are dislodged (such as through deterioration), become airborne, and are inhaled. SUBASE maintenance personnel access the asbestos area daily, and in accordance with OPNAVINST 5100.23B and COMNAVSEASYSCOM 082019Z FEB 85, all personnel are required to wear disposable protective clothing and respirators while in an asbestos area. The Naval Submarine Medical Center, Industrial Hygiene Branch, has conducted surveys in 1982 and 1985 and declared that "conditions have worsened regarding asbestos steam pipe insulation" in 1985 over the 1982 survey and "recommends a priority be placed on a project to remove the asbestos debris and replace asbestos insulation in the trenches and tunnels." Fiberglass is recommended to replace the asbestos.

ALTERNATIVES:

Alt I: Do not reinsulate the steam lines with fiberglass insulation. Maintain asbestos health hazard and continue to incur costs of protective gear.

Alt II: Contract for removal and replacement of asbestos insulation.

Alt III: Hire in-house work team of six personnel to systematically remove and replace the asbestos insulation over a two-year period. The specialized equipment required is already owned by the government.

EVALUATION OF ALTERNATIVES:

Alt I: Costs for protective gear and lost productive time (suiting up/down) will continue to be about $60K/year. Asbestos will remain a hazard.

Alt II: Asbestos will be removed. However, extensive design effort would be required to prepare bid specifications since the steam system is not well documented (due to the age of the system). Construction contract is estimated at $2M for replacement of asbestos.

Alt III: In-house personnel would accomplish removal and replacement at a cost of $300K/year. Payback from current method of purchasing protective gear would be 10 years.

Figure 3.4 *(continued)*

FUNDING RELATIVE TO THE FYDP:

	FY 86	FY 87	FY 88	FY 89	FY 90	FY 91	FY 92
Alt I: NAVCOMPT BUDGET	60	60	60	60	60	60	60
Alt II:			+2000				
Alt III:			+300	+300			

OFFSETS/ECONOMIES: Reduced risk of asbestos hazard. Reduced operational costs and increased productive time. Projected payback period is 10 years.

MANPOWER IMPLICATIONS:

Alt III: 1 WG 3610-10 Insulators (billet seq. code - 07632 Billet Occupation Code - FYH)
1 WG 4749-7 Maintenance Worker (BSC - 07634, BOC - FYH)
4 WG 3502-3 Laborers (BSC - 07636, BOC - FYH) Base Pay - $101K, Fringe - $13K, Hazard Pay - $9K, Total - $123K, Materials - $177K/year

Manpower Serial #________________

In the operational Navy, we spend an enormous amount of time writing messages. On the AIRPAC staff, 90 percent of what I wrote was message traffic.

—Navy Commander, Aviator

4

Naval Messages

Because of geographic separation, naval commands write and receive a great many naval messages. Officers in the operational Navy probably write more naval messages than they write anything else. For many reasons, those messages are very important. Ships could not receive or respond to orders without them—quick reaction to emergencies throughout the world depends almost entirely on telegraphic messages. Staffs must communicate with underway units on administrative as well as operational matters in great part by message. Efficient coordination of ships' repairs and the ordering of supplies, ordnance, or spare parts for vessels, embarked aviation squadrons, and embarked or deployed Marine units also must often go by messages. These are just a few of the important purposes that naval messages serve.

One less obvious but equally important aspect of naval messages also relates to geographic separation. When people cannot see your ship or unit, your reputation depends upon what they do see most often—your messages. As a destroyer's CO explained, "On a ship, the reputation of your command to the outside world comes through your message traffic, primarily. What your superiors and others see on a day-to-day basis are messages from your command, and what they think about your command is what they read." Messages that take time to comprehend, that omit crucial information, or that violate protocol or procedure will sour the image of your command—probably much more so than messages in the nonnaval services.

Writing messages well, of course, means much more than just the technical matters of getting all the characters in the right blocks. Although such matters carry weight, more weighty yet are such subjects as what gets said, to whom, from whom, and why. In other words, the *content* is much more important than the *form*, and, as always, the basic communication situation is the first thing to be understood.

The Naval Message—Section by Section

This chapter proceeds by discussing each major section of a nonformatted or "GENADMIN" naval message. Appropriately, the first section of a naval message brings up that key element we have discussed several times before—the audience. The first section of a message is the message *address*.

The Address: Get It Right, and Get it *Politic*

Send it to the Right People

Obviously, writing a top-notch and timely message does no good if you don't send it to the right people. Improper addressing of messages is a major problem in the Fleet. Never merely copy addresses from past messages or just mirror the addresses on the message you're answering. Instead, get a strong grasp of command relationships, and address all who *really need to know*.

Who really does need to know? You'll quickly discover that there is much more than just technical accuracy to addressing messages—there are also "political" aspects to this skill. You need to have a good grasp of how significantly messages differ from letters in their routing and in who reads them.

Realize Who Will Read your Message, and Why

To begin with, aboard ship *perhaps 90 percent of incoming messages are read by commanding officers*. Moreover, on a ship or operational staff, all officers and many chiefs will also read the messages (omitting some routine messages, which may not get placed on the message board). In contrast, COs afloat do not see anywhere near so many letters as messages. Typically, only the executive officer and the letters' action officers see incoming letters, and very few people read all the regular mail.

And then *flag officers* read message boards avidly. If you accidentally add COMNAVAIRLANT to your message as an INFO addee, COMNAVAIRLANT himself (the admiral) will probably read your message. So when addressing your message, not only do you want to make sure that everyone who is supposed to see the message gets it, and that you have listed all the required ACTION or INFO addressees. You must also be sensitive about who (from your CO's point of view) should *not* see it. Young command duty officers have probably been called on the carpet more often because of whom they addressed a message *to* than for what they actually said in it.

On a former skipper's advice: "He told me, 'There is a tone that can be used in a message, a quality of junior talking to a senior, up the chain. Remember, we're the littlest frigate in the Navy, so don't forget to say please and thank you.' The difference was immediately evident in the way people responded to the ship."—Lieutenant Commander

Figure 4-1 PERSONAL FOR. When deployed, a commodore sent a series of policy messages like this one to his commanders, using the PERSONAL FOR format. Note: This message is in pre-GENADMIN format.

JOINT MESSAGEFORM

SECURITY CLASSIFICATION: UNCLASSIFIED

PAGE	DTG/RELEASER TIME: DATE-TIME	MONTH	YR	PRECEDENCE: ACT	INFO	CLASS	SPECAT	LMF	CIC	ORIG/MSG IDENT
X 01 OF	021430Z	SEP	86	RR		UUUU				2451430

BOOK | MESSAGE HANDLING INSTRUCTIONS

FROM: COMCRUDESGRU EIGHT

TO: CRUDESGRU EIGHT

UNCLAS PERSONAL FOR UNIT COMMANDERS AND COMMANDING OFFICERS FROM BOORDA //N00000//

SUBJ: CCDG-8 CDR's MSG 001

1. THIS IS FIRST OF A SERIES OF POLICY MSGS WHILE I'M CCDG-8. MOST WILL GO TO ALL COMMODORES AND CO'S. A FEW WILL BE FOR SPECIFIC ADDEES (I.E. BB/CG CO'S, DESRONS, ETC). THESE MSGS ARE TURNOVER ITEMS SO WE'LL WORK OUT SOME EASY WAY TO LET YOU KNOW WHAT YOU OUGHT TO HAVE. THESE WILL BE "PERSONALS" SO THAT YOU CAN DETERMINE WHAT, IF ANYTHING, YOU WANT TO DO ABOUT SUBJECTS DISCUSSED. FEEL FREE TO SHARE THESE MSGS WITH ANYBODY/EVERYBODY BUT DON'T FEEL THAT IS REQUIRED. I'M ONLY INTERESTED IN RESULTS. I WON'T PULL PUNCHES; LANGUAGE WILL BE STRAIGHTFORWARD. IF YOU DON'T UNDERSTAND, ASK. NO TRIVIAL ISSUES WILL BE DISCUSSED AND I'M EXPECTING EFFECTIVE ACTION IF ACTION IS REQUIRED. THE TONE MAY TEND TO BE NEGATIVE. I'M FAR FROM NEGATIVE ABOUT THE STATE OF THINGS IN TODAY'S NAVY OR GROUP EIGHT. I'M NOT GOING TO WASTE TIME BY USING THIS FORUM TO DISCUSS ALL THE THINGS THAT ARE GOING WELL - NEITHER OF US HAS TIME FOR THAT. WE WILL USE OTHER WAYS TO PROVIDE EACH OTHER WITH WARM FUZZY FEELINGS.

DISTR:

DRAFTER TYPED NAME, TITLE, OFFICE SYMBOL, PHONE

SPECIAL INSTRUCTIONS: JRL//

RELEASER — TYPED NAME, TITLE, OFFICE SYMBOL AND PHONE: RADM BOORDA, USN, 00

SIGNATURE

SECURITY CLASSIFICATION: UNCLASSIFIED

DATE TIME GROUP: 021430Z SEP 86

DD FORM 1 MAR 79 173/2 *(OCR)* PREVIOUS EDITION IS OBSOLETE S/N 0102-LF-000-1735 ☆ U.S. GPO: 1988-208-529

One Navy ship nearing port in the Northern Pacific began conducting a helo operation to get the mail off the ship expeditiously. In the process a fifteen-pound bag was accidentally blown over the side and sank. The official responsible for the mail—the chief petty officer who was mail clerk—drafted the required message about the loss of the mail sack and put down, as INFO addees, CINCPACFLT, COMNAVAIRPAC, and the embarked flag. Soon the Captain summoned the mail clerk. "Who's required to get this message?" the Captain asked. "The mail office," responded the chief. "How about these other addressees? Why are they here?" "Well, the flag had some mail in that bag," replied the chief. "How about the others?" "Just general information," said the chief. *"Then don't send it to them,"* replied the Captain.

The Captain knew the admirals whose commands were listed as INFO addees in that message would probably read each message personally, and he made a policy of not reporting mishaps to anyone except those with a specific need to know. Obviously, we all have a moral and legal obligation to inform our seniors and those affected of significant mishaps. However, this Captain knew that "what people know of your command is what they read," and neither he nor any other alert commanding officer wants every detail of the command's activities spread out unselectively in front of seniors.

"Realize that part of the decision as to whether to send things by mail, message, or otherwise (hand-carried, flashing light, etc.) is because of timeliness; part is because of bulk; and part of it is *to get the elephants involved.*"—LDO, Admin Officer on a Carrier

Sometimes a CO with *use* the fact that the admiral reads every message. Occasionally a commander will send a message to one organization (the ACTION addressee) to get a heavy-hitter at another organization (an INFO addressee) involved. Sending a message INFO to an admiral is a common way to try to get action taken, especially if the activity responsible for action hasn't responded to the originator's problem.

This book takes no stance on either the efficacy or morality of such a practice, but simply points out another reason to be extremely careful about where you send a message. *Know the consequences* of your addressal of messages. As an LDO on a carrier commented, "Don't get the elephants involved *by chance.*"

Remember Protocol

Besides misaddressals, originators can also displease by forgetting simple rules of naval courtesy. Separate action from information addees first, but then within either group, list addees by proper protocol: highest echelons before lower, then by alphabetical order within echelons. Again, remember that all correspondence out of a command is a direct reflection on that command—and this principle is especially true of messages, which have such potentially wide and senior audiences.

Of course, observe protocol not only in the address element but throughout the message. Remember the assumptions that go with certain usages. "Juniors never 'ADTAKE' seniors" is one familiar piece of naval advice; another is that "seniors *direct* attention while juniors *request* or *invite* attention to an issue or problem."

Protocol Rather Overdone?

U.S.S. WASP, 4th Rate

At Sea: Lat:–30–09′N.,
Long:–88–41′W.

June 29, 1904.

Sir:—

1. *I have the honor to report* that on the 27th instant, at about 6:30 P.M., while the "Wasp" was proceeding through the thirty-two mile long narrow dredged channel . . . she sheered out of the channel and ran on to the soft mud flats to the Eastward of the Cut.

....

3. The vessel was not injured in the slightest degree. . . .

Be Consistent with Plain Language Addresses

As NTP 3 points out, the use of automated message-processing systems has made consistency in format and spelling of Plain Language Addresses (PLAs) critical. If you want the message to get to its destination on time, don't rely on memory. Instead, look up all military-wide standard addresses in the *Message Address Directory*; USN PLAD 1 is the naval section of that publication. Here is further specific guidance:

Spell out numbers in Plain Language Addresses:
- 1–19 as one word: EIGHT or ELEVEN or THIRTEEN, etc.
- 20 and up as: COMDESRON FIVE ZERO or TASK FORCE NINE FIVE PT THREE, etc.

Spell out letter designations phonetically:
- FAIRECONRON ONE DET ALFA

Use no punctuation within each Plain Language Address:
- Use PT for period, DASH for hyphen, etc.

Specify Office Codes in the Addresses of Naval Shore Activities

Navy shore commands are often much bigger than ships, and their decision-making processes are much less centralized. So NTP 3 now requires that we spell out office codes in the Plain Language Addresses (PLAs) of all Navy shore activities. As chapter 5 of that publication now states, at least one office code is required per addressee, and more than one is both allowed and, in many cases, desirable. If you list more than one code at the end of any PLA, the first one listed should designate the "Action" office.

Of course, familiarity with the ordinary responsibilities of such shipboard departments as CIC, OPS, ENG, and WEPS does not necessarily help us understand what offices make decisions at a shore command. If you do not know the office responsible for the subject of your message, use the letters JJJ (following the PLA and enclosed by double slants) in place of the unknown code. Having used //JJJ// for any addressee once, however, take note of the code of the shore command that responds to your message, and address that code in subsequent messages or other correspondence.

The Subject Line: Make It a Title, Not Just a Routing Device

The subject line as title helps key the reader to the main issue in the message, gets the reader's attention, and aids a reader in skimming messages for what is pertinent to the reader's own area of concern. Composing a good subject line takes some care.

Remembering the Correspondence Manual's excellent advice, use the subject line to *avoid mystery stories*: announcing the topic in the subject line prepares the reader for what is to come and helps to get the right people to read the message.

Note that the main purpose of a subject line is *not* to aid in message routing, although it may help. The subject line is only one of many parts of a message (such as the SSIC, flag words, AIGs, and so on) that communications personnel key on to decide where to route the message aboard ship or within a particular command. Since the subject line is primarily a title, use it as a title, *making it as pertinent and descriptive as possible.*

Write

RECOMMENDED CHANGES IN SQUADRON MESSAGE HANDLING

instead of MESSAGE HANDLING

Write

DECISION ON BAQ ENTITLEMENT FOR MEMBER MARRIED TO MEMBER

instead of BAQ ENTITLEMENT

If a message were titled just DAMAGE CONTROL rather than DAMAGE CONTROL LESSONS LEARNED FROM FIGHTING THE STARK FIRES, it would clearly have fewer readers, and maybe not the most important ones.

Descriptive titles will also help anyone who is searching through files to find the right message quickly—and, of course, such titles will help those service members who have to route a message within a large command. Naturally, there are some subjects that don't require more than perfunctory titles. Also, in most cases, a subject line longer than a line or two will just slow the reader down.

The References: As Much as Possible, *Make the Message Stand Alone*

Besides helping to make all previously nonformatted messages machine-readable, the GENADMIN format incorporated in the May 1990 change to NTP 3 introduced a significant change in how messages refer to or cite past communications. In the past, one would cite pertinent references at the beginning of the message and then often summarize them in the message's opening paragraph. The new format requires that a drafter organize all references into formatted message sets. It also allows a drafter to comment on any individual reference in an AMPN line, or to comment on all references in a short NARR section that precedes the essential message text.

Since this new procedure keeps most comment on the references from interfering with the message proper (which is now the RMKS section of the GENADMIN message), this change is a step forward. However, such a methodology as is outlined in NTP 3(H) might seem to suggest detailed reference to past messages is always desirable. That is not necessarily the case. Indeed, research done for this text suggests that the whole issue of referencing past messages and other communication is a vexed issue. Why? That requires a bit of explanation.

The Past

At one time, Radio aboard ship (the Comm Center at a shore station) was something like a library. Communications files there were so complete and handy that, by going up to Radio, a reader could readily find all the past files on a particular subject. Moreover, Radio regularly distributed copies of each message to a number of offices. As a message drafter, you could count on an addressee already having much background to a subject on hand. You knew the reader could look up the references in desktop files or quickly run to Radio to find the preceding correspondence if it was hard to find in the office or stateroom.

True, requiring a reader to page through all the past references was in most cases a somewhat inefficient way of working. But it was relatively dependable.

The Present

Now, with tightened security rules, sharply limited distribution, and requirements to destroy files earlier, depending on references is neither efficient *nor* dependable.

Radio and the local Comm Center regularly make only one extra copy of a message—the one for the action officer. And they keep most messages for only a couple of months. As a result, although a ship or station may have received all the references in a message once before, neither Radio nor the Comm Center is likely to have all older messages now. Unless the action officer can lay hands on that original copy in the correspondence file, the reference simply may not be available. Under these circumstances, drafting messages that depend on information in prior message traffic is a sure recipe for delay, retransmittal requests, and misunderstandings. The lesson? *Make your message stand alone* as much as possible.

"We list far too many references in our messages. Radio gets rid of a message after 30 days; if the action officer didn't keep one on file, no one will have it. In the old days, with 90-day files, we could go get a past message. Now we can't. *Make your message stand alone.*"—Lieutenant Commander, former CO

Referencing and Summarizing Prior Messages—The Pros

Do the current rules mean we shouldn't reference prior messages at all? Yes and no. Referencing past messages and summarizing their import in an AMPN line or short NARR paragraph (standard GENADMIN procedures) can sometimes serve important purposes.

To start with, if a message coming into a staff requires action from higher than the ordinary action officer, then besides preparing the recommended response to that message, the action officer on the staff usually has to prepare a briefing memo for the admiral. A message that summarizes all pertinent references cuts the action officer's time spent preparing the briefing memo.

Besides saving the action officer on the other end the potentially big headache of searching for the references (that search can sometimes take half a day—as an LDO remarked, "I can't guarantee the guy on the other end will be able to find the crucial reference—even if it's *from him*"), another reason for summarizing the background for the addressee's action officer or commander is that such a summary helps readers get a good feel for the context. It helps them to see what you are asking or arguing and encourages them to proceed to an immediate decision. If you don't handily bring all relevant information to bear right there in the message itself but instead depend on the addressee's looking up the references, the decision maker may want to look up all the past message traffic on the subject, read it all carefully, and think about it a while before proceeding to a decision.

Using this same line of reasoning, you can occasionally use a summary of the relevant past messages to "prompt the witness." If your addressees have to go back and read several detailed messages on a subject, they may come up with a different conclusion than you have (especially on a complex subject). But if you summarize the past references, you can make sure that nothing essential (from your point of view) is overlooked. Thus, your summaries can make it much more likely for the addressees to agree with you. For them to disagree formally, they have to go to the extra effort of looking up and reading all the references themselves.

Referencing Past Messages—The Cons

"Write and read your messages as your seniors will usually read them—with no knowledge of the situation other than what you will tell them."
—Admiral, skipper of a Surface Action Group

There's another side to this issue, however. For one thing, a commander giving an order seldom needs to cite all the references—often the commander simply says, "Do it," and, except for making clear exactly what is wanted and why, has no need to refer to the past *at all*. The commander is establishing a new procedure, thereby cleaning the slate.

For another thing, both the listing of past references and their summarizing have often gone much too far. A summary has become for many message drafters a habit or crutch, clogging up message traffic with unnecessary volume and encouraging skimming. *There has to be a specific usefulness to the summary* and a real need for the past references; using references is not just a drill to go through.

Clearly, much past referencing has not been helpful. Because of the requirement to refer to each reference somewhere in the message (originally an attempt to *cut down* on unnecessary references), we often find paragraphs like this one:

REF A WAS RESPONDED TO BY REF B DELINEATING THE PROBLEMS WITH EXPANSION OF THE SUB-COST CENTER ORGANIZATION WITHIN THE G-3'S COST CENTER UNDER CURRENT DATA PROCESSING CONSTRAINTS. SUBSEQUENTLY, REF C WAS RECEIVED REQUESTING EXPANSION OF TRAINING AS A SEPARATE SUB-COST CENTER UNDER THE G-3. REF D RAISED THE SAME ISSUES AS REF A WHICH HAD BEEN ANSWERED BY REF B AND REF E WAS FOLLOW-UP TO REF D.

Before writing such a paragraph, ask yourself this question: *Do the addressees really need to know how negotiations have proceeded on this topic*? If not, is there any other major reason for going into such detail? Often, the answer to both these questions is no.

Yes, summarizing all the relevant correspondence on an issue may be important for a senior command—each message may direct action on a certain aspect of the problem, and if so, all commands affected should have a complete file. Months may pass before the appropriate superior puts all those messages together into a comprehensive instruction.

But for many messages, just giving the *general* background is enough without extensive reference to past correspondence.

A Solution

Three conclusions seem reasonable, a three-step decision chain, as it were.

First, since the general background is often enough by itself, see if "CNO HAS REQUESTED . . ." or "PREVIOUS COMMUNICATION HAS SPELLED OUT REQUIREMENTS FOR . . ." can effectively replace "REF A WAS RESPONDED TO BY REF B WHICH CANCELED REF C," etc.

Second, if you believe a summary either necessary or helpful, do your best to reference as few messages as possible and to make any summary as brief as you can. Strive above all to keep in mind the needs of the action officer you're writing to.

Third, in almost all cases, be sure to put the main point up front, in the very first paragraph. The change to GENADMIN format has made that possible in almost all cases.

The Text: Get to the Main Point Quickly

Chief among concerns having to do with the text is the need to get started right—if you do, the rest of the message tends to fall together nicely.

Jump Right in with the Action

How do you get to the main point quickly? Sometimes your addressees just need to know the *action required or requested*, with specifics in later paragraphs after a general announcement in the first. In this case, an effective opening paragraph is simple and to the point. For example:

RMKS/1. EFFECTIVE IMMEDIATELY DO NOT PROCESS PARTIAL PAYMENTS ON PREPAID RESUBMISSION INVOICES. PROCESS THE EXACT AMOUNT LISTED ON THE PITR.

This message opening informs the reader immediately of the basic action required; the reader may at leisure review the specific details found in subsequent paragraphs.

On other occasions, an effective opening makes a simple, direct reference to a prior message that made a tasking or a request:

IAW REF A, FEEDBACK ON RELIABILITY OF ORDNANCE TEST EQUIPMENT FOLLOWS.

—or—

THE USNTPS PREPARATORY CURRICULUM REQUESTED BY REF A IS APPROVED.

These openings are effective because they are clear and immediately grasped. The reader knows exactly what is to follow.

Use the CAP Formula for Opening Summaries

Sometimes giving the reader a brief context for what follows is important. For this purpose, use a paragraph modeled after the CAP formula, that is,

Context—specific **A**spect focused on—message's **P**oint

As an example, the following opening paragraph gives brief context and focus, and then gets to the main point quickly, leaving details to follow in subsequent paragraphs:

Context:	1. PLANS FOR CHANGE OF COMMAND ON 30 DECEMBER INCLUDE A RECEPTION FOR APPROX 700 IN HANGAR BAY OF USS IWO JIMA.
Aspect:	AUGMENT OF IWO JIMA FOOD SERVICE PERSONNEL IS NECESSARY TO ASSIST IN FOOD PREPARATION/SERVICE.
Point:	UNITS WILL RESPOND AS OUTLINED BELOW.

Such an opening prepares those with action obligations for the details that follow and gives a brief executive summary to others who can either stop there or read further for information. Whatever their needs, all readers have gotten the *gist* of the message and have not had to wait several paragraphs to discover what on earth the writer is getting at.

Remember: except on long, detailed messages, you'll usually have no standard paragraph headings such as "Purpose," "Background," and "Action" that help the reader to skim. Clearly, then, *briefing the whole matter* in the first lines is even more important in messages than in other kinds of naval writing.

The Text: Other Guidance

Of Course, Use Telegraphic Style . . .

- Do not waste words. Leave out unnecessary adjectives, adverbs, prepositions, and most articles (a, an, the).
- **Use the imperative voice** liberally. Instead of WE REQUEST THAT, say, REQUEST; instead of YOU SHOULD CONTACT MR. HERBERT, say, CONTACT MR. HERBERT.
- **Use small words instead of big ones** where the sense is the same. Leave out words used only for the rhythm or aesthetic quality of a sentence.

"Keep your messages short; *you lose* if you write more than a page."—CO of a Comm Center

Revised by use of standard rules for message brevity, the following paragraph from a Military Sealift Command letter can be put into brief and clear message style. The letter, with wordy expressions *italicized,* reads:

In order to eliminate *any* delay in *the* ammunition loading *operations, we* request *that, if possible,* you correct all deficiencies prior *to your ship's* arrival *at* Naval Weapons Station, Concord. *In the event* you do not have sufficient crew *members* on board *to accomplish this work, you are hereby authorized to* employ *the services of a* commercial contractor to correct *these* deficiencies.

The message reads:

TO AVOID DELAY IN LOADING AMMO, RQST YOU CORRECT ALL DEFICIENCIES PRIOR ARRIVAL NWS CONCORD. IF TOO FEW CREW ON BOARD, YOU MAY HIRE COMMERCIAL CONTRACTOR TO CORRECT DEFICIENCIES.

. . . But Beware of False Economy

- **Never sacrifice clarity for brevity.** Word a message so that it clearly expresses the meaning that the drafter desires to convey.
- **Be sparing with punctuation,** but **use it where necessary** for clarity or emphasis.
- **Don't customarily omit little verbs** (*is, are, was,* etc.). They don't cost much in transmission time, and often their omission leads to confusion.
- **Abbreviate where useful** with standard, well-understood abbreviations, but **don't overdo it.** Sometimes words have to be spelled out or the transmission time saved will be much less than the time readers spend trying to decode or correctly construe unfamiliar abbreviations.

"Be most concerned with communication, not length. Make it freestanding, so that someone who knows nothing of the subject can get the point."—Captain

You can find a list of abbreviations that commonly appear in messages in the Handbook at the end of this book. That list is unofficial and incomplete, but the abbreviations listed do reflect widespread fleet usage.

Try Using One Governing Statement

Consider reworking longer messages so that, as in "bullet" format, a series of statements or questions falls under one governing statement. By using this method and by making a few other astute changes, a Marine colonel shortened the text of the following message (in pre-GENADMIN format) by one-half. The message originally read:

FROM: USNA ANNAPOLIS MD
TO: CG FIRST MARBGDE HAWAII
BT
UNCLAS //1531//
SUBJ: MARINE SUMMER OPTION CRUISE
A. PHONCON USNA MAJ WHITE/FIRST MARBGDE CAPT PALANCIA OF 10 FEB 83
1. REF (A) REQ THAT ALL REQUESTS FOR INFORMATION CONCERNING THE MARINE OPTION CRUISE BE SUB BY MSG.
2. IAW REF A, THE FOLLOWING INFO REQ.
A. IT IS DESIRED THAT THE MIDSHIPMEN BE ALLOWED TO EAT IN THE ENLISTED DINING FACILITY: WHAT PAPERWORK IS NECESSARY?
B. WHAT IS THE TOTAL NUMBER OF MIDSHIPMEN THAT THE BRIGADE CAN HANDLE? IS ADEQUATE BOQ SPACE AVAILABLE FOR THIS NUMBER?
C. DURING THE SUMMER OF 1982, A SCUBA TRAINING PROGRAM WAS OFFERED IN THE LATE AFTERNOON. CAN THE PROGRAM BE OFFERED IN 1983?
D. IT IS NOT DESIRED (FOR FINANCIAL REASONS) THAT THE MIDSHIPMEN MISS ANY MEALS. CAN "C" RATIONS BE PURCHASED THROUGH THE BRIGADE TO PREVENT MISSED MEALS?
E. IS IT POSSIBLE TO PROVIDE A STANDARD WELCOME ABOARD PACKAGE FOR EACH MIDSHIPMAN WHO PARTICIPATES IN THE PROGRAM?
F. CAN THE MIDSHIPMEN GET THEIR AVIATION PHYSIOLOGY TESTING COMPLETED IN HAWAII?
G. SEVERAL OF THE MIDSHIPMEN ARE AIRBORNE QUALIFIED. WILL THERE BE AN OPPORTUNITY FOR THEM TO JUMP WHILE THEY ARE WITH THE BRIGADE?
3. MAJ WHITE IS CURRENTLY SCHEDULED TO ARRIVE IN HAWAII ON 4 MARCH. HE WILL BE AVAILABLE UNTIL 11 MARCH TO ACCOMPLISH ANY COORDINATION NECESSARY FOR THIS PROGRAM. CAN HE MEET WITH THE BRIGADE LIAISON OFFICER DURING THIS TIME?

The revised message reads:

FM USNA ANNAPOLIS MD
TO CG FIRST MARBGDE HAWAII
BT
UNCLAS //NO1531//
SUBJ: MARINE SUMMER OPTION CRUISE ← Eliminated unneeded "Reference A" and all subsequent references to it.
1. MAJ WHITE, USNA LIAISON OFCR FOR MARINE SUMMER OPTION CRUISE, WILL BE IN HAWAII 4-11 MAR TO COORDINATE WITH 1ST BDE REGARDING THIS PROGRAM. REQUEST HE MEET WITH BDE LIAISON OFCR AT THIS TIME TO DETERMINE IF MIDSHIPMEN CAN:
A. BE BILLETED IN BOQ? HOW MANY? ← Combined separate questions in lines A–G into one question with seven parts
B. EAT IN ENLISTED MESS?
C. BE FED ALL MEALS? (C-RATIONS

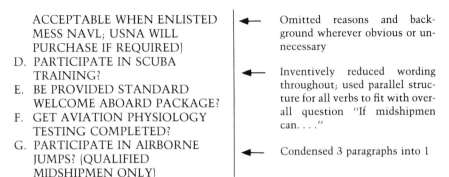

ACCEPTABLE WHEN ENLISTED MESS NAVL; USNA WILL PURCHASE IF REQUIRED)
D. PARTICIPATE IN SCUBA TRAINING?
E. BE PROVIDED STANDARD WELCOME ABOARD PACKAGE?
F. GET AVIATION PHYSIOLOGY TESTING COMPLETED?
G. PARTICIPATE IN AIRBORNE JUMPS? (QUALIFIED MIDSHIPMEN ONLY)

BT

← Omitted reasons and background wherever obvious or unnecessary

← Inventively reduced wording throughout; used parallel structure for all verbs to fit with overall question "If midshipmen can. . . ."

← Condensed 3 paragraphs into 1

—contributed by Colonel C. E. McDaniel, USMC, Retired

Specify the Format for the Reply in Tasking Messages

Tasking people to do work for you is an art. A DESRON staff officer outlined a technique for tasking ships to send information to the squadron. He said that to get good input, you should be sure to specify the following:

- **All applicable references** (usually messages)—and sometimes you have to actually send the references too.
- **A date** to respond by, the date selected so you can collate all information and draft a response to your superior by your due date.
- **A format** that helps you work with the data, that is, a format specifying both what data you want *and* in what order.
- **Specific units of measurement required,** for if you don't specify, they'll send you a general answer and then you'll have to go back again to ask for more.
- **A point of contact** at your location, including a phone number.

Here's part of a message that shows an effective tasking, along with a typical response to that tasking. Note that the tasking message specifies both *the order* and *the kind* of information required. (For abbreviations used below, see "Standard Message Abbreviations" in the Handbook section.)

3. TO DETERMINE SCOPE OF SUPPORT REPLACEMENT/REPAIR INITIATIVES RQRD ON ABOVE CRITICAL TEST EQUIPMENT, REQ YOU PROVIDE SPECIFIC COMMENTS/FEEDBACK AS FOL NLT 30 OCT 87:
   A. TYPE OF ORDNANCE TEST EQUIPMENT (TS-147 OR MK 368)
      (1) EQUIPMENT RELIABILITY
      (2) EQUIPMENT MAINTAINABILITY (AVG TIME RQRD FOR REPAIR OR CALIBRATION AND CAL RQMTS)
      (3) DOCUMENTATION AVAILABILITY (TECH MANUALS, APL SUPPORT)
      (4) RECOMMENDATIONS FOR IMPROVEMENT

The following would be a good response:

1. IRT REF A, FOL FEEDBACK PROVIDED:
   A. ORDNANCE TEST EQUIPMENT TS-147
      (1) TS-147 OPERATIONAL APPROX HALF THE TIME.

(2) INPORT CONUS, CAL/RPR TAKES UP TO 120 DAYS. ANNUAL CAL/RPR CAN BE DONE CONUS ONLY.
(3) TW-147 NOT COSAL OR APL SUPPORTED AND AVAIL OF RPR PARTS LIMITED. TECH MANUAL OUTDATED AND GIVES LITTLE TROUBLESHOOTING GUIDANCE.
(4) RCMD REPLACE TS-147 WITH TS-145.
B. ORDNANCE TEST EQUIPMENT MK 363 MOD 3/4 MEST SET
(1) MEST SET ONBD VERY RELIABLE WITH ALMOST ZERO DOWN TIME.
(2) MK 363 RQRS ANNUAL CAL WITH AVG TIME APPROX ONE WEEK. RPRS DONE CONUS.
(3) ONBD TECHMAN OUTDATED, DOES NOT REFLECT EQPT CHANGES, OFFERS LITTLE USEFUL TROUBLESHOOTING GUIDANCE, NOT COSAL SUPPORTED.
(4) RCMD INSTITUTE COSAL SUPPORT AND UPDATE TECHMAN.

A Last Word

Of course, besides learning prose-cutting techniques, abbreviations, etc., there is at least one other method of keeping costs down and the circuits clear. Limit all electrical transmissions to urgent official business that other means cannot satisfactorily handle. Use mail or telephone whenever possible *in place of* naval messages.

Checklist for Composing Standard Naval Messages

Radiomen and Communication Centers have checklists to help you double-check the technical details of message writing and message handling. This checklist has a different intent: it is formulated to help you get the right points across.

- Have you included all necessary ACTION addees? INFO addees?
- Should you omit any addressees?
- Within respective categories, are addressees listed according to protocol?
- Have you included office codes for any Navy shore activity PLAs?
- Have you included the pertinent references?
- Can you do without any references?
- Is there any correspondence needed for understanding this message that addressees do not hold? If so, have you summarized it or sent it along?
- Will the subject line adequately identify the subject to all readers?
- Have you assigned the appropriate precedence?
- Is the classification proper, and have you followed all proper procedures for classification?
- Does the main point appear in the first paragraph of the message text?
- Consider the commands and officials receiving this message—will they all understand it? Do you need to add or clarify any statements?
- Can you eliminate explanations nobody needs?
- Consider the words carefully; if each one cost you a dollar, would you include all those you have written?

"The toughest thing is to write short. But it's amazing how concise you can be when writing a naval message if you're forced to print, by hand, on one sheet of paper."—Captain

Figure 4.2 Message Guidance. This message outlines general guidance on DD Form 173s.

JOINT MESSAGEFORM	SECURITY CLASSIFICATION UNCLASSIFIED

PAGE	DTG/RELEASER TIME DATE-TIME	MONTH	YR	PRECEDENCE ACT	INFO	CLASS	SPECAT	LMF	CIC	ORIG/MSG IDENT
01 OF 01				RR	RR	UUUU				2421005

BOOK	MESSAGE HANDLING INSTRUCTIONS
	ADMIN

FROM: TEXT AUTHOR//N3//

TO: NAVAL PERSONNEL//JJJ//

MARINE CORPS PERSONNEL//JJJ//

CIVILIAN PERSONNEL IN DEPARTMENT OF THE NAVY//JJJ//

UNCLAS //N02319//

SUBJ USE OF DD FORM 173

MSGID/GENADMIN/TEXT AUTHOR//

RMKS/1. MSG PREPARATION GUIDANCE IS COMPLEX AND THIS SUMMARY IS INADEQUATE BUT RQMTS BELOW APPLY TO ALL DD FORM 173'S:

A. USE ONLY UPPER-CASE TYPE. DO NOT UNDERLINE ANY PART OF MSG.

B. DOUBLE-SPACE ALL LINES. USE NO MORE THAN 69 CHARACTERS, INCL SPACES, ON ANY LINE; USE MAX OF 55 CHARACTERS/LINE IN ADDRESS BLOCK. TYPE 20 LINES OF ADDEES/TEXT PER PAGE: LESS OK ON LAST PAGE.

C. INDENT AS NECESSARY FOR GRAPHIC CLARITY (TO 20 SPACES/LINE).

D. USE ALMOST ANY STANDARD PUNCT IN TEXT TO U.S. ADDEES, BUT ONLY SLANT, DOUBLE SLANT, HYPHEN & APOS IN ADDRESS ELEMENT.

E. FILL OUT BLOCKS AS ON THIS MSG FOR FIRST PAGE. ON CONTINUATION PAGES, LEAVE BOTTOM BLANK EXCEPT FOR RELEASER'S INITIALS.

2. DO NOT PREPARE MSGS UNTIL COMPLETELY FAMILIAR WITH PROCEDURES.

DISTR:
N3

DRAFTER TYPED NAME, TITLE, OFFICE SYMBOL, PHONE	SPECIAL INSTRUCTIONS
J.S. DRAFTER, EA, X2222 8-28-90	
RELEASER — TYPED NAME, TITLE, OFFICE SYMBOL AND PHONE: R.J. RELEASER, 01, X5555	
SIGNATURE: R. J. Releaser	SECURITY CLASSIFICATION UNCLASSIFIED / DATE TIME GROUP

DD FORM 1 MAR 79 173/2 (OCR) S/N 0102-LF-000-1735 ☆ U.S. GPO: 1988-208-529

> **The Usefulness of Ambiguity**
>
> **In the early 60's a Captain (D) led his Mediterranean Destroyer Flotilla into the Black Sea, where he soon sighted a squadron of Russian Cruisers closing his flotilla at high speed.**
>
> ***From leading Russian Cruiser (by light)***
>
> **WHAT ARE YOU DOING IN THE BLACK SEA.**
>
> **Turmoil ensued amongst the Staff on the flotilla-leader's bridge while signal logs were sent for and Diplomatic Clearance discussed. At last Captain (D) raised an elegant hand for silence, and said quietly to the Signalman,**
>
> ***Reply:***
>
> **TWENTY-ONE KNOTS.**
>
> **—From Captain Jack Broome. *Make Another Signal.* London: William Kimber, 1973, 248.**

• Could you condense the message substantially by changing the format?

• On the other hand, have you stressed clarity over brevity? Is the message understandable? Are all abbreviations standard and clear?

• Is the paragraphing logical?

• Can you use indentation or headings to good effect?

• Will anything in this particular message or the way it is written give the command a bad image?

• Have you included all the essential—but only the essential—information?

• Has everyone seen this message who should see it before it goes out?

• Does this information really have to go by message?

• Will the CO release this message?

On Formatted Messages: The CASREP

> When writing a CASREP, put yourself in the place of the person who reads it. Ask, "What would I want to know if I were getting this report?"
>
> —Chief Electronics Technician

Besides standard naval messages in GENADMIN or other specified formats, naval communicators use a variety of fully "formatted" messages—MOVREPS, UNITREPS, LOGREQS, and many others. Formatted messages are designed to ensure all of a specific kind of crucial information—such as ship's movement, logistic requirements, etc.—gets from a ship to multiple audiences regularly and efficiently.

By filing a MOVREP, a communicator won't have to reinvent the wheel when announcing the ship is getting underway—something each ship does dozens of times during a year. The addressees are standardized so the communicator won't forget anyone who ought to know this information. Typically, the formatted message must go to a great many addressees.

You might think that writing formatted messages would just be filling in the blanks. But mere bits of information can never communicate everything we mean, so throughout formatted messages we find "Amplication" (AMPN) lines and "Narrative" (NARR) and "Remarks" (RMKS) sections, which call for good, brief naval prose. Take, for example, one of the most critical of all naval messages in the surface Navy, a form also important to submarines and aviation units, the CASREP.

Writing CASREP Remarks

You need a remarks section in a CASREP because no amount of formatted information can convey the exact technical information required to fix the casualty. Especially on surface ships, the exact impact of a specific casualty on a ship's operations and the difficulty of fixing the problem will vary widely from vessel to vessel, even among identical ship types.

Leading petty officers, chiefs, and officers at all levels may have to write or revise CASREPs. On some ships, division officers write the whole CASREP even though they often don't have specific technical expertise on the particular equipment involved. No matter who does the basic draft, COs and XOs give intense scrutiny to the remarks section (checking for pertinence, completeness, and brevity too) before a CASREP leaves the ship. For many reasons, writing a CASREP is a *high-priority item* at most commands.

"We have to compose the REMARKS and AMPLICATION sections with great care because our admiral reads every one of them. Politics plays a part: we have to work it so as not to slap the tender in the face, because we need their assistance, nor can we make ourselves look bad."—Lieutenant on a DD

Write Your CASREP Remarks for a Multiple Audience

Who will read your CASREP? A great number of people at many commands. Some of them will be experts in the particular technical area involved, but most of them probably will not be. Your "RMKS" section must serve both expert and nonexpert audiences. Solve this dilemma by following three procedures. First, use **headings and indentations** in the RMKS section to help the reader. Second, pen an **executive summary** at the beginning of the section for your operational commanders and other "generalists." Third, follow the summary with a **technical description** composed for the technical expert.

Use Headings and Indentations

Just as they help the reader find a way through any notice, instruction, or technical report, typographical features can help the reader find crucial information in a glance at a CASREP. NTP-3 allows indentation in naval messages when it will increase readability or clarity. The free-form nature of RMKS and AMPN sections also allows for the use of headings.

Write an Executive Summary for Commanders and Nonexperts

Suppose you serve as an officer aboard a combatant. Your commodore (along with other superiors) will want to know the ship or submarine's exact condition so as to know how to employ her, and whether her full war-fighting capability is available. The commodore and fleet commanders will need to know when she'll be completely ready again, if and where she'll have to go for repairs, what they might do to expedite the process, and so on.

Experience suggests a ship's operational commander will immediately look at the following areas of the CASREP, skimming the rest:

"Make sure you comment on the impact of the casualty on the command schedule—what you won't be able to do next week, what problems the casualty will present in the ship's sked. The admiral himself won't pick up the impact necessarily just by being told the specific casualty; the staff might not either; but the ship will certainly know. And the admiral *goes up the wall* if not told."—Commander, XO of a DD

- the name of the ship
- the specific equipment CASREPed—all in the formatted portion
- the C-rating
- the summary portion of the remarks.

Obviously, your summary is very important. A tested procedure is to begin by carefully describing *the exact nature and extent of the casualty.* Write this description for a general Navy reader, not a technical expert. After this description, discuss the casualty's *impact* on the ship's immediate and near-future operational, exercise, or inspection schedule. Then speak to the *mission degradation,* that is, the effect of the casualty on the ship's ability to carry out primary and secondary missions.

Operational and administrative commanders may have issued specific requirements (C-ratings, etc.) as to what you must cover in these areas. If not, by your remembering to write for the informational needs of commanders, and by your keeping your remarks general enough that all of them can get the gist, both captain and chief will be able to grasp the *big picture* immediately. As NWP 10-1-10 (the basic CASREP publication) points out,

> When attempting to determine whether additional or operational information should be included, consider the ISIC and senior operational commanders, whose only knowledge about the casualty, its impact on unit readiness, and assistance required, normally comes from information contained in the CASREP message. (4–25)

Also remember in each initial and update CASREP to include a short statement of the current status of the casualty (4–24).

Follow the Summary with a Technical Description for the Experts

"It's always better if you can do the research, rather than the repair facility. It's not as important to them as it is to you; and it will speed up the process if the chief on the other end doesn't have to punch the pubs for every detail."—Former chief, LDO Lieutenant (junior grade)

The technical description must supply the technical staff on the beach with enough detailed information that they can start the repair process in motion, sometimes well before the ship returns to port.

The ultimate readers will be personnel with technical expertise on the specific equipment CASREPed. These experts will usually work at a repair facility—a SIMA, a MOTU, a tender, or perhaps a readiness support group—and will arrange for parts, organize technical assistance, and act as the control point for all services. They will need detailed and specific technical information with which to begin.

Do not, however, be *obscure* in this description. A duty officer or chief on the squadron or group staff must often get the repair process started, and neither of these people will necessarily be an expert in the specific area of the casualty. For example, the chief who reads the CASREP may be a chief electronics technician, and the casualty may be to a piece of engineering equipment he or she has never seen. Nevertheless, this reader may have to interpret the message and initiate action in response to the CASREP without expert assistance, especially if the message comes in on a holiday or a weekend.

So although the technical description should detail all the vital specifics, it should include as little jargon and technical obscurity as possible.

Be Very Careful about the Details

Recently a chief on a naval supply ship learned just how vital specific details could be. Deciding he was obliged to do a CASREP, he looked at the specific piece of equipment in front of him, called it a "motor generator" on the CASREP form (the name everyone aboard ship customarily gave the equipment), and reported the number he found in front of him.

The Navy Supply System, however, called only the *bottom* part of the equipment a "motor generator"; the equipment that fitted on the top had another name and different stock number. It would be like requiring a *lamp* to be called, for repair purposes, a *lamp* and a *lamp shade.* As a result, the contractor assigned the repair said, "We can't go further with the repair; we haven't been contracted to work on the top part." The confusion cost the Navy an extra $2,000 and several days to straighten out.

Give the Repair Facility Enough Information

"Accuracy in the APLs is especially critical. We have six different FF 1052s; the same valve for each ship might have been made by six different companies. Some engineers will put 88 and their SSN in the blank—but the wrong company's valve simply won't work! And a bad APL is a really big problem for an RSG, because we begin researching long before the ship pulls in!"—Commander of a Readiness Support Group

If a ship is in its home port, completeness may not be crucial; a phone call can clear up questions pretty quickly. But if the ship is underway or at another port, the facility vitally needs *complete* information. Any need to query you by message because you didn't put in enough detail could result in a substantial delay in the repair—perhaps two to four days, according to a median estimate. A senior chief at a SIMA estimated that *50 percent of the time,* there's not enough data in the CASREP.

The Navy's general need to reduce fleet message traffic sometimes conflicts with the needs of the shore-based technical staff to get detailed answers for fixing vital equipment. Only experience will tell you how much is too much information.

One lieutenant wondered why the shore facility was advising him by message how to troubleshoot a type of equipment having a different voltage than the CASREPed equipment aboard his ship. Only later did he find out that the executive officer had cut out the specific voltage he had listed in the CASREP before it left the ship, in order to shorten the message's length.

Think twice before cutting out details.

Poor CASREP Remarks

Here's the REMARKS section of a CASREP from a ship away from her homeport. The duty officer on the staff who received the CASREP says that as soon as he read it he knew SURFLANT would call. Sure enough, they did. But before that, the chief staff officer had already hit the roof. Why? See the duty officer's comments annotated below (the underlines have been added for clarity).

RMKS/MK 42 MOD 9 5″ 54 ELECTRICAL SYSTEM NOT FUNCTIONING. NO IMPACT ON CURRENT OPERATIONS. REDUCES SHIP'S AAW AND ASUW CAPABILITIES. CASUALTY TO ELECTRICALLY DAMAGED SOLENOIDS THAT CONTROL CARRIER AND LOADER DRUM VALVE BLOCK ASSEMBLIES. SOLENOIDS ON ORDER PRIOR TO CASREP CONDITION. SHIP'S SKED: ENRT NEWPORT RI 23 JAN; IPT NEWPORT 25 JAN-26 JAN; IPT PHILADELPHIA 29 JAN-15 FEB.//

← Too generic—is it completely down?

← Far too nonspecific: how?

← So why did they CASREP now?

We don't know from this what happened or how it happened. Did the technician break it? Was it bad PMS? We can assume some things, but he doesn't tell us or SURFLANT enough, for operational purposes or for repair.

Good CASREP Remarks

Below is the REMARKS section of a different CASREP, this one cited by the same duty officer as an excellent message. It affords a clear and concise summary, vital operational information, and a fully detailed technical description of the problem. See the duty officer's comments noted below (again, the underlines have been added and would not be in the actual message).

RMKS/CASUALTY: MK 53 ATTACK CONSOLE WILL NOT POSITION KEEP THEREFORE WILL NOT UPDATE-PREDICT TARGET COURSE AND SPEED. MK 53 AC WILL ACCEPT NDT FROM ALL SONAR UNITS. MANUAL INPUT OF TARGET COURSE AND SPEED CAN BE USED FOR ASROC-TORP FIRINGS. IMPACT: MAJOR IMPACT ON INSURV TO BE CONDUCTED WEEK OF 29 FEBRUARY.

Identifies both the specific casualty and the ship's continuing capability, thus clarifying the exact scope of the casualty.

← The Opn'l Cdr will probably realize this on his own, but the ship makes sure of it.

MISSION DEGRADATION: MINOR IMPACT ON ASW MISSION AREA.
TECHNICAL DESCRIPTION: 12A1A4A15 MG2 (MOTOR-GENERATOR) HAS SAT INPUT BUT HAS INSUFFICIENT TORQUE TO TURN CLUTCH CM3 WHEN CLUTCH IS ENERGIZED. STRAY VOLTAGES HAVE BEEN INTERMITTENT AND BELIEVED TO BE RELATED TO CAUSE OF CASUALTY. WHEN "GOING INTO CONTACT" OR WHEN NDT FROM SONAR THE CLUTCH ENGAGES MOTOR BUT IMMEDIATELY SEIZES DUE TO INSUFFICIENT TORQUE STATED ABOVE, THEN BY PULLING RELAY K1 OR "COMING OUT OF CONTACT" THE CLUTCH DISENGAGES AND SYSTEM WILL PK UNTIL NEXT NDT OR WHEN GOING BACK INTO CONTACT. SIMA NEWPORT R-5 ASSISTED IN TROUBLESHOOTING. CASUALTY DISCOVERED WHILE TROUBLESHOOTING TIMING CIRCUITRY FOR CONSTANT 7 SECOND FLASH. REQ TECH ASSIST TO DETERMINE WHERE STRAY VOLTAGES ARE COMING FROM.
SHIP'S SCHEDULE: 25 FEB ISE (PRE-INSURV); 25 FEB-7 MAR INPORT.

Tells Opn'l Cdr the ship can live with the casualty; she can do an ASW operation if needed.

Identifying particular components as it does, this technical description describes the problem in detail. As a result, the repair agency may be able to troubleshoot the problem by message.

This tells the staff that the problem is beyond SIMA's scope. It also shows that the ship is doing its best to be on top of things, already getting what help it can.

Additional detail that may help the repair agency identify the problem.

CASREP Remarks with Indentations for Readability

NTP-3 authorizes indentation (up to twenty spaces) in messages where it will aid graphic clarity. It does so here, breaking up long two-blocked material into readable (and skimmable) chunks. Consider using indentation in all long RMKS or AMPL sections of formatted messages.

RMKS/CASUALTY: MK 53 ATTACK
  CONSOLE WILL NOT POSITION
  KEEP THEREFORE WILL NOT
  UPDATE-PREDICT TARGET COURSE
  AND SPEED. MK 53 AC WILL
  ACCEPT NDT FROM ALL SONAR
  UNITS. MANUAL INPUT OF TARGET
  COURSE AND SPEED CAN BE USED
  FOR ASROC-TORP FIRINGS.
IMPACT: MAJOR IMPACT ON INSURV
  TO BE CONDUCTED WEEK OF 29
  FEBRUARY.
MISSION DEGRADATION: MINOR
  IMPACT ON ASW MISSION AREA.

Executive Summary

TECHNICAL DESCRIPTION: 12A1A4A15 MG2 (MOTOR-GENERATOR) HAS SAT INPUT BUT HAS INSUFFICIENT TORQUE TO TURN CLUTCH CM3 WHEN CLUTCH IS ENERGIZED. STRAY VOLTAGES HAVE BEEN INTERMITTENT AND BELIEVED TO BE RELATED TO CAUSE OF CASUALTY. WHEN "GOING INTO CONTACT" OR WHEN NDT FROM SONAR THE CLUTCH ENGAGES MOTOR BUT IMMEDIATELY SEIZES DUE TO INSUFFICIENT TORQUE STATED ABOVE, THEN BY PULLING RELAY K1 OR "COMING OUT OF CONTACT" THE CLUTCH DISENGAGES AND SYSTEM WILL PK UNTIL NEXT NDT OR WHEN GOING BACK INTO CONTACT. SIMA NEWPORT R-5 ASSISTED IN TROUBLESHOOTING. CASUALTY DISCOVERED WHILE TROUBLESHOOTING TIMING CIRCUITRY FOR CONSTANT 7 SECOND FLASH. REQ TECH ASSIST TO DETERMINE WHERE STRAY VOLTAGES ARE COMING FROM.

Technical Description

SHIP'S SCHEDULE: 25 FEB ISE (PRE-INSURV); 25 FEB–7 MAR INPORT.

You have to get through to a guy at 1800 who has been reading all day, is tired of it, but is still doggedly trying to form a picture.

—Navy Captain, just returned from a Selection Board

5

Performance Evaluations

Few documents are read as avidly as Navy enlisted evaluations, Navy officer fitness reports, and Marine Corps fitness reports. Various audiences read these documents very differently. When writing such evaluations, you must understand whom you are writing to and what your readers' uses of the evaluations are likely to be. There are *three main audiences* for performance evaluations; we'll discuss each one of them below.

However, while much of what follows pertains to evaluation writing in general, almost all the specific references are to the Navy rather than to the Marine Corps. In 1986 the Marine Corps published the very thorough "User's Guide—How to Write a Fitness Report" (NAVMC 2794), and the Marine Corps Institute put out a "Performance Evaluation System Handbook." Both these guidebooks amplify and reinforce Marine Corps Order P1610.7C, which governs the USMC Performance Evaluation System.

The "User's Guide," in particular, has proved so helpful to Marines of all grades in composing Marine Corps fitness reports that additional specific instruction on the subject in this text does not seem warranted. Non-Marines should know that Marine Corps write-ups are usually much shorter than Navy ones, having to fit into about ten lines on a page; that Marine documents typically use a very abbreviated, entirely sentence-fragment style; and that Marine seniors do *not* customarily provide copies of fitness reports to the person being evaluated. For further information, see the three documents mentioned above—or talk to a knowledgeable Marine.

Three Audiences for Navy Performance Evaluations

Deciding which *audience* you're addressing when writing Navy evals and fitreps is very important—for at least three potential groups will read Navy performance evaluations.

The Navy Selection Board as Audience

The most critical audience for Navy enlisted evaluations and fitness reports is the Navy selection board in Washington, D.C. This group of people is under considerable stress to do a very hard job in a very short time. They have little patience for documents that beat around the bush. They have several other unusual characteristics.

A Promotion Board's Predicament

A recent E8/E9 board met for six weeks; 50 people served on the board. They reviewed 25,000 records, and each of those records was reviewed by at least two "briefers," sometimes three. So each board member read at least 1,000 records over those six weeks—an average of some *30 records per day*—besides spending time briefing, being briefed by others, and voting. With maybe 10–12 minutes to spend on any one record, board members simply have no time to dwell on any one report. Under these constraints, a board member simply can't pull out details if they are packed in dense paragraphs, undistinguished by underlining or other graphics, and two-blocked to the top and bottom of each page.

Officer boards are similarly beset. However, where enlisted boards typically review only the five or so most recent evals in a service record, officer briefers will typically review *all* the fitness reports in a jacket. Take the record of a commander going up for captain as an example. Such a record will fill at least one and one-half microfiche cards and include perhaps *30 fitreps*. On any count, that's simply *an enormous amount of reading* for any particular board member.

Besides these time constraints—which warn against burying vital points in the middle of a report when a briefer expects them to be at the end, and other such cluttering—you should keep in mind another feature of a selection board. That feature is the breadth of its makeup.

Who's on the Board?

Although boards vary in composition depending on the level (mainly E-8s and E-9s on an E-7 board; Navy captains on a commander's board, etc.), the important point is that a line selection board is typically a mixed group. A line officer's selection board, for instance, is composed of all line communities (aviation, surface, subs, etc.). Similarly with a chief's board: many different rates are represented. Even though a chief's board may separate into smaller panels of similar ratings for some deliberations, still, any one of those panels may not contain two members of the same rating.

Even in a restricted-line board, you can't expect each member to know the finer points of any particular job. All the board members will understand warfare-fighting capabilities, leadership, directing, individual effort, etc., but they certainly won't care whether it was "Number 5" or "Number 7 BQA-8 Hydrophone" that the petty officer you are writing about repaired. By using *generic* terms—"directed the replacement of a self-noise hydrophone"—you can make an evaluation easier to read *and* easier to evaluate. In all cases, you must learn to write for a mixed audience.

What Are They Looking For?

Realize that board members are looking for several different kinds of comments in a write-up. They must pick up a great deal of specific information, including not only whether you're recommending the individual for advancement and any specific future duty, but also what Navy schools he has completed, what qualifications she has achieved, who has profited from his or her performance, etc.

Then board members must determine whether the write-up manifests *qualities* important in a chief or officer. Besides demanding leadership and supervisory abilities, a chief's board will also diligently look for such qualities as initiative, education, and the habit of volunteering, for example. Specific accomplishments can suggest the candidate has these qualities, but you should also speak explicitly to the qualities themselves.

A good reviewer will look back at the evaluations to get a holistic or whole-person feeling for the service member. Here's where the ability of a writer to describe a person comes into play. Writing about fitness reports, one Navy captain comments, "The key problem . . . is that people write too much about the job and too little about the officer. Pick out personal characteristics and write about them. Tell who this man really is: his loyalty, his charisma, his intellectual capacity."

The point is that in an evaluation a selection board is looking for many different topics: detailed evidence of strong accomplishment; discussion of various personal qualities; specific recommendations for promotion and future jobs; and a good general *feel* for the person being evaluated.

Your Own Command as Audience

The selection board is only one (although the most important) audience for an evaluation or fitness report. An enlisted eval has yet another public audience, one much closer to home. Your own commend will use enlisted evaluations widely, as will any new command to which an enlisted service member reports.

When a new division officer, department head, or leading chief reports aboard a ship or unit, one of the first things he or she may do is to read key enlisted service records. Similarly, when enlisted men or women report aboard a new duty station with records in hand, their department heads, division officers and chiefs are all likely to read the evals in those records to find out the qualities of the people they're receiving. That will help them assign the new people where they will be most productive.

These are all official functions of the enlisted evaluation. In addition, an evaluation directly affects whether an enlisted person is allowed to reenlist or not. Whenever reenlistment rates are up and the Navy can begin to be selective about who to keep, the required recommendation for or against retention becomes increasingly important. You should give as much care to writing evals on weaker performers as on stronger ones. If a middling seaman or petty officer has shown any potential at all, you should discuss that potential and carefully modulate the recommendation for retention. "Recommended for retention" is not a throwaway line any more.

Other audiences at your ship or station are just as public, though less official. Several people in the chain of command—the leading petty officer, division officer, department head, XO, and CO—are initial audiences for a performance evaluation. Each one of these people may learn from the report and may form his or her opinions of the person evaluated from what you say even in a rough draft.

Despite the command's best attempts to keep these reports confidential, they may not always remain so. A petty officer may lay the copy of the evaluation you just gave him down in the workplace, and soon his whole work center may know how you rated him—as well as anything you may have said about *them* in his report. All the more reason to use discretion in what you write.

Informally, officers too may see the remarks sections of locally prepared fitness reports other than their own. For example, two junior officers may compare notes to try to understand the nuances of what their senior is saying about them. A few officers in the chain will see subordinates' reports (and will often form impressions of the individuals involved) when fitness reports are being written, reviewed, and processed. Beyond such incidental viewing, officer reports have no official audience at the local command, for Navy fitness reports are not kept for any local use (only the reporting officer keeps a copy).

The Service Member as Audience

Finally, you are almost always writing the report for at least one more audience—the person being evaluated. Normally, in the Navy (not as often in the Marine Corps) the senior shows the evaluation or fitness report to the person being evaluated just before submitting it, and sometimes must get a signature to verify the sighting. Often this session is occasion for formal counseling between senior and junior. Specifically, Navy rules require you to show evaluations to every enlisted person and to officers of paygrades 0–1 to 0–4. In fact, most more senior officers see theirs as well.

"Why should you have to know the secret, hidden buzzwords to know what the guy above you thinks of you? *Be honest* in your conferences with your junior people."—Lieutenant Commander, CO of an MSO

For two reasons, what you say in the remarks section is vitally important to the person being evaluated: (1) obviously, the remarks section may have critical effect on this person's selecting or nonselecting for a higher rate or rank; but (2) this evaluation constitutes, as one officer put it, a "psychic paycheck" for all the effort the person has done for the command. So there is a strong tendency when composing the remarks *to write to the subordinate rather than to the selection board,* or to try somehow to write to both.

This dual audience is in part responsible for the inflated grades and also for the inflated language that are so prevalent on modern performance evaluations. Even if a subordinate's performance has been mediocre or worse, a superior is often reluctant to alienate the person being evaluated, for harsh criticism could be personally uncomfortable for the superior and could also result in a decline in the subordinate's performance. Even with a good performer, the fact that he or she will see the report you draft may sway you in the wrong direction. That is, because a sailor is still working for you, and because you will be confronting that person personally with this piece of paper, you often may want to put *too much information* or *the wrong kind of information* into the report.

As one officer put it, "The member needs to know how he or she's doing in order to improve and to get that needed pat on the back for good performance. So the writer needs to acknowledge jobs and include detail that selection boards may not score or score highly." Given this tendency, it is no wonder that some selection board members think the bullets are just "fodder—they're for the member, to make him feel good about what he's done. I never look at the bullets, but concentrate on other points," says a Navy captain. However, that feeling is by no means universal; other officers tend to concentrate *more* on the bullets because of the inflation problem. As another veteran of many boards put it, "In the crunch, I concentrate on the bullets, *to see just what this officer has done* to merit promotion."

Overall, probably the best advice is to find other ways than the write-up to give an extra pat on the back, that "psychic paycheck." Don't counsel your people only when handing out the report, once a year or so. Instead, try to make your discussion of evaluations fit into an ongoing counseling process. Otherwise, as the CO of a destroyer commented, "The evaluation can be a kind of psychological bomb. Nothing is worse for a ratee than when he's surprised by a fitrep or eval. How many times have you heard, 'And I thought you were satisfied with my performance!'?"

"You feel obliged as the senior to put all you can in a fitrep, for a great part of your relation to your junior officer is in what you say there. But the vital part is for an officer to screen and/or select."—Commander

Whatever the subordinate's reaction, the superior's primary responsibility is to the Navy. As one commander commented, "Of course you want the guy to feel good. Still, don't write a thousand bullets—it's unfair to the briefer." Instead, write all evaluations and fitness reports chiefly *with the selection board in mind.*

Six Principles for Writing Navy Performance Evaluations

Many have offered advice on how to compose the write-up so as to get the selection board's attention. What follows is some of the best of this advice.*

1. Place Vital Points in Strategic Places

Follow the long-standing tradition of placing the most important points in the strategic places—at the beginning and at the end. These placements, having become familiar over time, help the reader find the vital facts quickly and help to make the overall evaluation very clear.

Set the tone of the report with an attention-getting *opening statement*, an overall judgment of the person you're evaluating. The opening paragraph must be eye-catching if it is to alert the selection board member, who has to search through bewildering columns and files on a microfiche screen and review hundreds of reports in a very few days, to the special quality of this particular individual.

Besides the overall judgment in the first paragraph, the *last paragraph* should include summary judgments and recommendations. For example, Navy fitness reports normally make recommendations for department head, XO, and CO in this paragraph. Other important recommendations—for the individual's logical next billets, for special jobs, for schools, and so on—are also appropriate here. Of course, the promotion recommendation is usually kept for the very last line. (An attention getter of late is to put the overall recommendation in the top rather than the last line of the report, a technique that can also be effective.) See the separate sections on evaluations and fitness reports for other comments about recommendations.

"To get the selection board's attention, you need a 'show stopper' for a real winner. But don't write them all like that. The tendency is to write top comments about everybody!"—Captain

As for *the middle*: supporting information in old-style fitness-report writing often appeared in order of primary duty, collateral assignments, qualifications achieved, leadership, watchstanding, etc. However, the shortened length of modern reports and bulleted style have rendered this formula pretty impracticable. Certainly you must address performance in primary and collateral duties, attainment of qualifications, and the critical issues of leadership and supervisory abilities somewhere in the report, but very few standard assumptions apply anymore as to exactly how you should organize these comments.

*Besides the section that follows, official guidance appears in NAVMILPERSCOMINST 1616.1 (on Navy enlisted evaluations,) NAVMILPERSCOMINST 1611.1 (on Navy fitness reports), and Marine Corps Order P1610.7 (on Marine Corps fitness reports). George Haering's article "Fitness Report Finesse" from the January 1980 U.S. Naval Institute *Proceedings* (pp. 34–38) is must reading for anyone preparing Navy fitness reports, while those concerned with the vexing problem of inflation in Navy, Coast Guard, and Marine Corps performance evaluations should consult the series "Fitness Reports" in the August, September, and November issues of the 1987 *Proceedings*, respectively. Of course much specific guidance on Navy and Marine Corps performance evaluations, fitness reports, and award write-ups (including a myriad of examples) appears in civilian guidebooks available in most Navy exchanges.

One solid piece of advice, however, is that the most impressive accomplishment should be the first "bullet"; don't bury vital information in the middle of a long list of bullets, or in the midst of a dense paragraph, or else the reader may never pick it up.

***Remember*: Selection Board members can't (and don't) read every word; if your report is to be effective, it must be brief and to the point. What information you do include must be the most pertinent information.**

2. Make Use of Formatting Techniques

If the person you're writing to has only a few seconds to read, important comments have to stand out. You can emphasize them by

* beginning with headings;
* using bullets (like this);
* adding special graphics, such as <u>underlining</u>, **bold-face**, occasional ALL CAPS (if the write-up is in lower case), maybe even *italics* or other special type;
* and making effective use of paragraphing, spacing,

  and white space.

The use of *white space* is particularly effective in write-ups. One line set off by itself is instantly clear. *Bullets* marking out specific accomplishments, *graphic devices* used sparingly but placed tellingly (including differing sizes of type), and perhaps *headings* to alert the reader to the special quality of this particular service member all greatly improve the readability of reports that would otherwise be choked with denseness of type.

Remember also to use *lower case for the write-ups* instead of the OCR all capitals required on the front page of the report. Lower case is easier and more pleasant to read, and research indicates that reading lower case takes about 12 percent less time than all caps. (Punctuation is often hard to pick out in all caps. Also, underlining and other graphic marks for emphasis stand out more clearly in lower-case print.)

Of course, designing reports well in terms of format requires some education of yeomen/personnelmen or civilian secretaries, as well as a commitment on the part of reporting officials to see through each seemingly minor aspect of a report from the first draft to the final product. But the effect will be worth the effort if what you say catches the eye of the screening officer on a selection board, someone often bleary eyed from reading prose that all sounds the same after a while.

3. Cite Specific Accomplishments

Supreme among the assets of a report writer's skills has to be, now as ever, an able use of *specifics*. In every service, and for officer or enlisted, all the literature on performance evaluations cites specific evidence as crucial to the report's success. Particularly when format begins to be overworked, and style becomes an obsession (bullets aren't everything!), readers and honest writers will fall back on one chief stay: *what did this person actually do* that suggests potential and promotability? On this subject we'll spell out several guidelines.

Use Quantitative Terms

Quantitative measurements are often particularly clear cut. How many personnel did the officer in question supervise? How many dollars did she manage? Did she save a substantial amount? What was the grade on the latest administrative inspection? What were the scores on the recent REFTRA?

Similarly for enlisted: How many enlisted shipped over in this leading petty officer's department? What RFI rate did he attain for the cruise? How many spaces were repaired and repainted under his direction? And so on. Figures, numbers, percentages, dollars, ratios, grades—whatever you can quantify might conceivably be meaningful to a selection board sweating hard to judge one person against another fairly. Figures are graphic and hard to dispute and sometimes seem to be more objective than descriptive statements. Seek them and make use of them, within reason, and with good knowledge of their likely effect.

Fill the Report with Particular Accomplishments

Details regarding nonquantifiable achievements are equally useful and usually more plentiful. Did this officer qualify as OOD and CDO all on the same deployment? Say so. Did that enlisted attain his ESWS overnight? Say that. Accomplishments affecting the primary mission are perhaps most significant, and the variations of actual achievements beggar description. Combat experience, participation in major fleet exercises, and hazardous duty illustrating leadership talents obviously comprise major subjects for a report, as do important qualifications attained.

"Give us your opinion, but then give us the data to back it up. Don't *just* generalize. If a chief prepared the division for a super inspection, what were the inspection results? And if you tell us percentages, tell us percentages *of what*. To improve retention 50 percent is fine, but that doesn't mean much if you improved retention from one to two in a department of one hundred."—Former Selection Board Member

But don't omit mentioning such particulars as awards, voluntary additional duty, and selections to special assignments or service schools, even if some of these achievements will show up elsewhere in the service record. If you also put them in an evaluation, they'll be highlighted in both places, and you'll be doubly sure a selection board will notice them. Moreover, the accumulation of several such accomplishments in the space of a year or six months can sometimes take a reader's breath away.

Written or oral commendations from outside the command should also find a place. If someone highly praised the person you're evaluating, tell the readers who did the praising and for what. Also, rather than stating, "This program received high praise from senior officers," specify *which* senior officers, either by billet or by name or sometimes by both. On the other hand, random praise from members of an inspection team could translate to "Fleet Training Group, San Diego, commented . . ." or " 'This is the cleanest galley in the fleet' according to Environmental Preventive Maintenance Unit, Norfolk." And so on.

Quotations from flag officers, squadron commanders, or other like authorities can be most effective. In the eyes of board members numb with reading volumes of extravagant praise, quotations not only constitute additional evidence of excellence but, because they come from outside observers, they also add objectivity to laudatory comments.

Back up Superlatives with Evidence

"We need the meat—not only what you think of him or her, but *what exactly* has the officer or chief done?"—Navy Commander, just back from a selection board

Adjectives without supporting details are weak, so *support the accolades with facts.* There's a world of difference between saying, "This junior officer is an excellent writer," and pointing out, "He's so good a writer that I had him draft all the award nominations, budget justifications, and fitness reports we had to do this last quarter aboard ship."

On the other hand, bullets recording facts without accolades can be equally uninformative. A reader often wants to know not only *what* but also *how* the member did. A comment on an officer assigned to NMPC such as "She supervised the writing of five precepts for the convening of selection boards" leaves up in the air whether the precepts were any good or not. But to say of an officer, "He prepared extensive correspondence for SECNAV's signature, all of which was signed without change," suggests the quality was very high.

***Remember*: To prepare for writing reports, commanding officers should have their subordinates maintain ongoing tickler files on their own accomplishments so that the brag sheets they submit are as complete and timely as possible.**

4. Master the Use of Adjectives and Other Qualifiers

So long as supporting details back up overall judgments, carefully chosen adjectives and adverbs—terms known by everyone, not just by a tiny group of lexicographers—can greatly strengthen the overall judgment. Most people are aware of the criticality of adjectives and adverbs in the recommendation for promotion—the difference between "she is recommended for promotion" and "she is *most strongly* recommended for *early* promotion" is decisive.

However, modifiers can be used in many places other than the promotion recommendation, and to diminish as well as to build up. Consider the case of an officer who was made personnel officer so that "his daily efforts could be supervised and evaluated." After six months the officer received another evaluation, a report that contained the following bright words of praise:

> In this assignment he has been able to handle most routine office work satisfactorily.

"Most"—not all; "routine"—nothing out of the ordinary; and "office work"—neither management nor leadership nor even physical labor, apparently. As for "satisfactorily": given the current inflationary climate, the word "satisfactorily" itself used in an evaluation will often be interpreted as a warning signal. Clearly, when carefully chosen, adjectives and adverbs can have *great effect,* for better or for worse.

5. Write for the Generalist Reader, Not for the Expert

Board members come from all communities. For chiefs' boards, some members are officers, but most are E-8s and E-9s from a great variety of rates and every major community (aviation, surface, and subs). The two board members who brief a record may have general knowledge of the area of a service member's expertise but are not necessarily of the same rate.

So write in a way that a *generally* well-rounded career naval officer or senior enlisted person can understand what you're saying. Don't use jargon; avoid abbreviations that are not known Navy-wide. Don't depend on the reader's knowing all the ordinary measures of success on your platform or in your workplace. Provide standards if needed: "Achieved a 98 percent test-bench availability against a Navy average of 87 percent." Beware, too, of sending subtle messages based on your assumptions that everyone knows what's important—readers simply may not pick up your message.

Finally, while the eval or fitrep should not be a mere job description, still, you may have to describe out-of-the-way billets a bit so that readers can justly appreciate job performance. For example, the Navy publication *Perspective* once argued of shore billets, "It is more meaningful to read about a division officer with 30 troops, a $200,000 budget and four buildings to maintain than to see only the words 'Division Officer.' " You can usually work critical facts about the job right into the write-up, often preceding a specific comment, like this: "Responsible for 450 personnel and $3.5 million consumable OPTAR, she. . . ." Such very brief job descriptions are vital for lesser-known specialties or subspecialties, officer and enlisted.

6. Make Sure the Report Paints a Good Picture of You, the Writer

Of course, some individuals establish wide reputation; even disregarding reputation, one of the board members is more and more likely to know the person who wrote a report the smaller the group being evaluated and the higher the rank. The point here is that the *report itself establishes an image of its writer*, often as memorably as a person's bearing or manner of dress.

A CO's pride in his own command may come through in his mentioning special features of his unit's activities, its engagement in combat, fleet exercises, unit awards, or unique duty assignments. Sometimes fitness reports overdo these comments, so that the author sounds very self-interested and turns the reader off. As one recent member of a screening board commented, "What I saw way too much of were glowing comments about 'my ship' and 'myself.' " Eliciting a negative reaction doesn't help anyone.

However, when used primarily to add luster to a service member's performance rather than yourself, trumpeting the command's achievements can make the individual and the commander *both* sound good. Take, for instance, this comment from a Navy lieutenant's fitrep:

Three Captains Comment on Credibility

***Navy captain, aviator*: "Watch recommending someone for something he's not ready for. If he's just promoted to commander, and hasn't even been a squadron's XO yet, don't put him up for captain tomorrow. Instead, say 'He's on the fast track to command.' You need to protect your own credibility."**

***Navy captain, just back from heading an E8/E9 Selection Board*: "One CO had 25 chiefs, and rated them all 4.0—but then also ranked them from 1 to 25! Our impression? The 25th chief out of 25 really was probably not very good, but the CO was afraid to confront him with less than a 4.0. As you can imagine, that CO's opinion didn't carry much weight with us.**

"On the other hand, another CO had four chiefs, and gave them all 3.8s, but also gave them each outstanding comments and comparative rankings. Our impression? Tough grader. These chiefs did very well indeed, especially the top one or two."

***Navy captain, on his way to his fifth command*: "I wrote to the board about an officer who had been passed over. I had already blown his horn in fitness reports, and I had also had another ship since he served under me, so now I spoke of my own background. I said, "I've had command of three ships, and I've had twelve officers as department heads. He was in the top three of those who should be XOs. Clearly, he's in a select group.' On the next board, this officer sailed through."**

> By keeping attuned to the needs of his men, he *shows outstanding leadership*. His personal involvement in the NIMITZ retention program resulted in a 63 percent first-term retention rate for his department, and directly contributed to NIMITZ's winning of the COMNAVAIRLANT Silver Anchor Award for retention excellence.

By using the command's award as evidence for the individual's leadership, the commander sounds principally concerned for the individual rather than himself, and this leadership trait enhances the author's credibility.

Such concern for the service member stands out if the writer seems to know the person he's reporting on and the situation that person is in. The writer displays this awareness not only by mentioning details of the subordinate's job performance and personal facts, but sometimes by making recommendations as to career progression. A male line officer who is knowledgeable enough to mention the likely next step for staff or women officers sounds like a leader who cares about his people; that is, he seems to be somebody worth listening to.

Needless to say, any errors, incompleteness, lack of neatness, or other evidence of inattention to detail can adversely affect the basic credibility of the report writer.

Applying the Principles

Sample Navy Fitness Reports

To illustrate some of the principles just discussed, I present here two actual fitness report write-ups of a few years ago. They were written on the same competent officer by different COs three years apart. Differing so widely in effect as they do, these write-ups suggest some of the differences attention to the principles of fitness report writing can make.

The third example is a rewrite of the second report to reflect modern "bullet" format.

Comments on the Ensign Report

First, the write-up in Figure 5.1 neglects format (underlining, bulleting, spacing) and audience. It has only the one paragraph, and a nonunified one at that; the report seems to be a set of sentences written in response to a checklist and then spliced together into the form of a paragraph. The writer provides insufficient information on the duties of a quota control officer, offers the selection board no way to compare this officer to her contemporaries, and makes no recommendations for future billets. The report just gets started, and then it stops. Its format, organization, and concern for the audience are all second-rate.

Second, this report has only two concrete details—the officer's pursuit of a master's and her augmentation into the regular Navy. Nary a specific detail about job performance, but only extremely broad and therefore rather meaningless statements: "Demonstrates excellent management, leadership, and administrative ability" (that covers all the bases; what else is there to say?). Without any data to back them up, these hackneyed phrases, and the other positive but equally general statements—"ensures the highest degree of accuracy in all tasks"; "as Staff Duty Officer, displays exceptional resourcefulness and judgment"—carry very little weight.

Other statements in this ensign report reduce the impact even of the vague praise we've seen so far: Is she "responsive to guidance from seniors" because she *needs* guidance? And does she only *strive* but *not succeed* at introducing new quota control measures? As a rule, when readers might interpret a statement in more than one way, they will, especially board members diligently trying to judge between so many high ratings and glowing adjectives, and wondering whether some of this praise is tongue-in-cheek.

Similarly, the last two lines, probably meant to be strong, are actually weak. "Qualified for positions of increased responsibility" is a stock cliché, which actually means very little (isn't *everybody* so qualified?). And the lack of adjectives surrounding "recommended for promotion" (not *early* promotion, not *highly* or *strongly* recommended) leaves the thrust very weak.

Figure 5.1 An Ensign's Fitness Report. The drafter of this fitness report seems to have spent little time with it.

21. EMPLOYMENT OF COMMAND (Continued)

28. DUTIES ASSIGNED (Continued)

88. COMMENTS. Particularly comment upon the officer's overall leadership ability, personal traits not listed on the reverse side, and estimated or actual performance in combat. Include comments pertaining to unique skills and distinctions that may be important to career development and future assignment. A mark in boxes with an asterisk (*) indicates adversity and supporting comments are required.

Ensign ________ is an outstanding naval officer. Demonstrates excellent management, leadership, and administrative ability in assignment as assistant quota control officer. Responsive to guidance from seniors, strives to introduce new and innovative approaches in quota control. Ensures the highest degree of accuracy in all tasks. Particularly noteworthy for her friendly outgoing personality which contributes to harmony and high morale among associates. Pursuing off-duty course of instruction leading to a Masters in education. As Staff Duty Officer, displays exceptional resourcefulness and judgment. Recently augmented USN, clearly qualified for positions of increased responsibility. Recommended for promotion.

One might wonder for a moment if the author's intent is actually positive in this report, or whether he means instead to damn by faint praise. Using faint praise instead of honest criticism is sometimes done, though it is a risky practice (the message may not get through to the selection board) and is dishonest as well (for the writer does not say what he or she means). However, in the particular fitness report we are looking at, innuendo does not seem the author's intention.

Finally, despite the fact that the report's lack of details means the board members cannot judge the ensign's performance for themselves but must rely solely on the reporting officer's say-so, this reporting official makes a relatively poor impression of himself. He shows no detailed knowledge of his ratee's performance. Moreover, his stock phrases, sentence fragments, and laundry-list organization offer an unfavorable portrait of the author's verbal inventory.

Overall, this report seems hurried, the product of a few moments' effort, which even a mediocre officer, let alone the "outstanding" one offered here, hardly deserves. You say, "So what—she's just an ensign; she's got time to improve." But have you looked at any ensign fitness reports lately? Or seen the figures for augmentation?

Comments on the Lieutenant Report

Figure 5.2, although not perfect, is superior to the first in almost every category.

First, as for format, although this writer does not use bullets (we'll get to that topic shortly), he does use underlining occasionally and writes in short and competent paragraphs. Perhaps he could have underlined even more (especially the recommendation for promotion in the last paragraph) or selected other key items such as "the very top officer recruiter" and "140% increase in productivity" for greater emphasis.

But the write-up covers all the vital points without burying details too badly or running on much too long, except perhaps in the long paragraph on "Leads Coordinator," which does slow the reader down. That particular paragraph seems to be aimed more at explaining the recruiting concept than at demonstrating the rated officer's performance. Except for this explanation, the writer does reasonably well at including helpful information on the command and the job to give the selection board needed context. The write-up is thorough without running over one page, so that all details are visible at a glance.

As for substance, this report is dense with specifics. Besides the composite rating "very top officer recruiter" in the first sentence, the report also lists percentages: "140% productivity increase" and command productivity increase of "115% over FY80." The writer mentions awards ("two gold wreaths") and award nominations, and frames very specific recommendations for promotion and additional assignments. The word picture is relatively strong too, with phrases such as "corner-stone," "superlative rapport," and "meticulous follow-up" spicing the narrative. These terms are not the most memorable, perhaps, but they are relatively forceful.

Figure 5.2 A Lieutenant's Fitness Report. This report was written about the same officer as was Figure 5.1, but makes a much better impression. (It could make an even better impression; see Figure 5.3.)

88. COMMENTS. Particularly comment upon the officer's overall leadership ability, personal traits not listed on the reverse side, and estimated or actual performance in combat. Include comments pertaining to unique skills and distinctions that may be important to career development and future assignment. A mark in boxes with an asterisk (*) indicates adversity and supporting comments are required.

LT ________ is a dedicated professional and an extremely determined officer whose exceptional performance has distinguished her as the very top officer recruiter in my command.

As the ______________ Program Manager, LT ________ is primarily responsible for recruiting a goal of 32 Surface Warfare, Supply, and women officers. Having to conduct her work throughout the largest geographical recruiting district in the nation is a formidable challenge. LT ________ manages five officers, one enlisted person, and one civilian. LT ________ has developed advertisement, initiated direct mail campaigns, and visited numerous college campuses in Alaska, Montana, Northern Idaho, and Washington to create the necessary responses for her programs.

Her superlative rapport with people, complete understanding of Navy opportunities, and meticulous follow-up have already resulted in a 140% productivity increase in the first quarter of FY 81 over the entirety of FY 80 recruiting efforts for the same programs.

LT ________'s commitment to the total mission accomplishment far surpasses her assigned programs. Her collateral duty assignments have consistently been on time and well prepared. I consider LT ________ to be the "cornerstone" of the officer recruiting team because of her concern and direct support for all officer candidate programs and, in particular, the Nuclear Power, Nurse, and Aviation efforts. The management of her resources and personal time has been so expert that LT ________ additionally volunteered to develop the concept of an officer LEADS coordinator. This position, designed to assist all officer recruiters, prescreens and classifies responses from locally prepared classified advertising, national advertising, and enlisted referral leads and simultaneously schedules preliminary tests and interviews. The results are a standardized sound management program for the suspect/prospect card filing system, follow-up on advertising leads, and immediate feedback for enlisted referral leads. Although only in its inception, the "LEADS coordinator" concept has already had positive impact upon the structure and function of the officer recruiting department.

LT ________'s superlative performance is a major reason that current command productivity in all officer programs has risen 115% over FY 80. LT ________ has been awarded two Gold Wreaths for recruiting excellence, was nominated both as the FY 80 "Recruiter of the Year" for Navy Recruiting Area _____ (CNRA__) and the CNRA__ Officer Recruiter of the Quarter for first quarter FY 81. She also received a Meritorious Unit Citation for being a member of the most productive recruiting team since the inception of the All Volunteer Force.

LT ________ is extremely conscious of her physical fitness and has developed a regular, rigorous maintenance program. Additionally, LT ________ has demonstrated a keen civic awareness through her participation in a local nursing home's "Friend-to-Friend" program, providing friendship to elderly people.

LT ________'s outstanding management and leadership ability demonstrates a superior potential for upward mobility. LT _______ is most strongly recommended for accelerated promotion to lieutenant commander and assignment as an Executive Officer of a recruiting district, or an Officer-in-Charge of a major recruiting district "A" station. LT _______ is also considered highly qualified for selection to the Junior Officer Course at the Naval War College.

Only a few of the comments are unclear. The comment on physical fitness—"extremely conscious of her physical fitness"—may mean she takes care of herself, or it might be construed to mean that she is worried about fitness and knows she has to get into shape! Toward the end, when the author says "Lt ___ is also considered," you wonder, considered by whom? Using first person in that last paragraph would make the evaluation a little clearer and a bit stronger too. Otherwise, the terminology is fine.

Finally, consider the issue of credibility—the picture the report paints of its author. This report suggests that the officer writing it knows his recruiting work and is proud of it. This commander connects the lieutenant's fitness to his own command's performance and to Navy-wide recruiting success as well, thus not only praising the lieutenant's worth by association with a good unit but showing a natural and commendatory pride in his own outfit. Although perhaps a bit less articulate than it could be, the report manifests the author's attention to detail, concern for his subordinates, and solid professionalism.

In only one major respect is the report not all it could be. The report is written in paragraphs of small type and two-blocked to tops and sides of the page. If anything, the author probably put *too much information* in the report, for it is relatively hard to read (and would be even harder on a microfiche reader). Once you have good data down on paper, remember to revise for readability. See Figure 5.3, rewritten by an expert.

Comments on the Reformatted Lieutenant Report

This report differs from the preceding one primarily in format and selection of details. Without changing the overall judgment, writing style, or specific details noted (except by omission and a bit of rewriting), the report has been made much more readable by:

- writing in "bullet" format;
- using underlining and strategic bold face;
- shortening the report by omitting less important details, tightening up the prose, and so on;
- adding a heading for the report, and using large type for the recommendations.

The board member can now get the essential story by reading the beginning headlines, the closing recommendations, and the bold-faced and underlined material in between. The board member can peruse the other material for reinforcement.

There are several other effective formatting techniques. Another officer just back from a board mentioned he planned to get a "script" typewriter element because he had found that print was much easier to read. Be guided by your experience and that of former board members as to the best formatting styles.

Figure 5.3 Lieutenant's Fitness Report, Rewritten. Here is an expert's rewrite of Figure 5.2.

88 COMMENTS Particularly comment upon the officer's overall leadership ability personal traits not listed on the reverse side and estimated or actual performance in combat Include comments pertaining to unique skills and distinctions that may be important to career development and future assignment. A mark in boxes with an asterisk (*) indicates adversity and supporting comments are required.

LT _____ IS MY TOP OFFICER RECRUITER

LT _____ is a dedicated professional and extremely determined officer. As a Program Manager, LT _____ manages five officers, one enlisted, and one civilian, and is responsible for recruiting a goal of 32 Surface Warfare, Supply, and Women Officers. By outstanding efforts in the last reporting period, LT _____:

- Attained a 140% productivity increase in the 1st Qtr of FY 81 over the entirety of FY 80 recruiting efforts for her programs.
- Contributed greatly to the 115% increase in command productivity over 1980.
- Earned award of two Gold Wreaths for recruiting excellence.
- Always presented her collateral duty assignments on time and well prepared.
- Volunteered to develop a major new managerial concept for the command.
- Developed astute advertisements, initiated excellent mail campaigns, and visited numerous college campuses to promote her programs.
- Manifested keen civic awareness through dedicated involvement in the community. Personally, maintained excellent physical fitness.
- Won nomination as the FY 80 "Recruiter of the Year" for Navy Recruiting Area X, and the CNRA-X Officer Recruiter of the Qtr for 1st Qtr, FY 81.

By her superlative rapport with people, complete grasp of Navy opportunities, and meticulous follow-up, LT _____ has proved **the best of 15 officer recruiters** at this command. She is most strongly recommended for:

- **The Junior Officer Course** at the Naval War College
- **Executive Officer of a Recruiting District,** or

  OINC of a Major "A" Station
- **EARLY PROMOTION TO LIEUTENANT COMMANDER**

Further Guidance on Writing Fitness Reports

> An opening paragraph, two or three bullets on why the guy was good, a closing paragraph ending with what wickets he needed next and the recommendation—that's all I had time to read!
>
> —Navy Captain, on his selection board experience

We can approach fitness-report writing from several other angles. To start with, presented below are examples of stronger and weaker comments in fitness report write-ups, with annotations based on the principles outlined earlier in this chapter. Note that *a commander may intend to write weakly*—to leave out a hard-hitting beginning, to write "job description" bullets (saying what was done, but not saying whether it was done well or not), or to leave the strong adjectives out of a promotion recommendation. Any of these nuances may be used to convince a briefer that a write-up lacks evidence or warmth of support.

Such an approach is a problematic option, at best. There are usually better ways of sending your messages, the main problem with "writing weakly" being that board members may not perceive your intent. Based on his experience with heading a selection board in Washington, D.C., a Navy captain commented: "Don't 'damn by faint praise,' don't 'send signals.' The board may not pick up your nuance. *You've* got the information; *you* make the decision. Don't make the board member have to pull a judgment out of thin air."

Fitness reports, like enlisted evaluations and award justifications, usually fall into three basic parts. An opening paragraph (often just a sentence or two) introduces the service member and the overall judgment; bullets follow, reporting on specific accomplishments; and a final short paragraph summarizes and adds recommendations. (As shown in several examples in this text, sometimes a *headline* can be used to preface the whole report, but it would be in addition to the three sections mentioned here.) Whatever the pattern, *what you say* is the crucial issue, whether in openers–bullets–closing paragraphs, as shown below, or in some other organization.

Opening Statements

John ____ is the best Executive Officer in Submarines. *[A startling opening. Requires top-notch support.]*

LCDR ____ is a hard-driving submariner who has gained sound professional maturity in his executive officer tour and is now ready for command at sea. *[Solid opening—for someone apparently not of the very top quality or only now coming on line. Others, presumably, were ready even* <u>before</u> *their XO tour. So, at least, many fitreps claim.]*

LT ____'s performance in all areas has been *outstanding*. He is ranked *one of the top three* lieutenants aboard CARL VINSON in a field of over thirty officers in his competitive category. *[Including an informal rank-*

ing can help a "1 of 1" departure report; this ranking helps out by including not just "top three" but "top three" out of how many.]

CDR ___ reported aboard a ship that, upon its return from deployment, was self-satisfied but not proud. Spirited and professional performance was not the ship's strong point; discipline and positive leadership by example were weak. He immediately took charge and began implementing high quality standards of professional workmanship, supervision, and management. His approach emphasized thoughtful planning, thorough training, attention to detail, basic tenets of military smartness and discipline, and aggressive identification and correction of substandard conditions of performance throughout [and so on]. *[This beginning forces you to read endlessly through a very dense report to find out how the commander actually did. He seems to have started well, but what were the results?]*

Dynamic, resourceful, industrious officer, Number 3 of 21 top-notch lieutenants. The margin between LT ___ and the top two lieutenants is slight and largely a factor of seniority and time aboard. Clearly at his present pace he's *destined for the Number One Ticket. [This commentary adds strength to an already impressive ranking. However, the command must make sure the next report follows this prediction up, or his falling back later may hurt him more than these comments help.]*

LCDR ___ reported to GRIDLEY well prepared for the task at hand. His attitude, depth of knowledge, and experience are more than adequate, but most impressive are his drive and capacity for work. He has made, in a short period, a significant impact on the way this ship and her crew do business. *[Hard to judge. "Well prepared" and "more than adequate" are very faint praise in a fitrep and might be interpreted as negative signals. Perhaps this author is just using an understated style—but such a style is risky in a fitness report.]*

Ensign ___'s performance has been unsatisfactory. His inept management, complete lack of understanding of basic leadership skills, and inability to set work priorities led to steadily declining job performance, recurring personnel conflicts, low morale, and organizational chaos in his department. *[No ambiguity here.]*

Until he placed himself in an unauthorized absence status, missed ship's movement, and was issued Technical Arrest orders, Ensign ___ was. . . . *[The rest of the fitrep explained the circumstances and recommended against promotion.]*

Bullets Describing Officer Accomplishments

Bullets Needing Improvement

- Qualified as TAO. *[But how long did it take, and how did he perform? Either the drafter or the officer needs to improve.]*
- Scored 92.6 at Vieques in October. *[The briefer may not know Vieques, nor the kind of test or exercise that was conducted there.]*
- She has supervised the writing of five precepts for the convening of selection boards. *[Yes, but were they any good?]*

• Was officer in charge of the ship's firing squad during a most impressive burial at sea. *[But no credit is given specifically to him—apparently he was just there.]*

• Thoughtful author. Submitted article to Approach on "The LSO's Role in Safety." *[But did Approach publish it?]*

• Lieutenant ___ substantially enhanced office morale by orchestrating and acquiring approval for a plan to obtain new office furniture in order to better utilize available space. *[Very weak, without additional explanation. He got a plan approved? Just approved, not carried out? To get new office furniture?]*

• He is a strict disciplinarian whose emphasis on the military aspects of the naval service have struck a responsive note with the most self-disciplined and most valuable elements in the crew. *[A peculiar statement—what about the ordinary sailors, one wants to ask?]*

High-Quality Bullets

• Tireless effort resulted in achievement and maintenance of an 87 percent two-way Link 11 (NTDS) rate. Cited by COMCARGRU SIX (RADM ___) for outstanding Link 11 availability in FLEETEX 2-86. *[The percentage may not mean anything to a nonspecialist, but citations from a flag are always impressive.]*

• He was a superb TAO in the Persian Gulf—an unbeatable accomplishment on this Aegis-class ship. *[Ship type and location clarify the degree of success.]*

• Planned and conducted 55 safe, successful Unreps. Outstanding seamanship and department morale highlighted all Unreps; most occurred at night during an Indian Ocean cruise that included a stretch of 111 days at sea. *[Discussion of circumstances enhances the quality of the achievement.]*

• Prepared extensive correspondence for SECNAV's signature, all of which was signed without change. *[The last phrase suggests the importance and high quality of the work.]*

• In 3M, the XO produced results. 97.7 percent is the ship's 3M numerical grade, the highest ever assigned by these inspectors. *[Gives numerical results and explains their excellence.]*

• Because of the extensive cross-training he initiated, a five-day work stoppage by Philippine Nationals had absolutely no adverse effect on communications services for the fleet, despite his site's extreme isolation. *[Explanation of unusual circumstances illuminates the achievement.]*

• Stands outstanding submerged OOD watches, an exceptional accomplishment as an ensign. *[Rank is obviously very important here.]*

• His foresight in installing boat engine preheaters, along with a meticulous maintenance program, made EL PASO boats the most reliable in the task force, performing flawlessly in subzero weather. *[Excellent specifics, especially the conditions in which the ship operated.]*

• The driving force behind VS-28's embarked ready room rehab. The squadron was cited by CO, CV-59 (Capt ___), for having the "Showcase of FORRESTAL." *[Good use of memorable quote in an otherwise forgettable line.]*

• The only lieutenant of 70 on board who is qualified as an Assistant Command Duty Officer. He routinely stands an impressive watch. *[One out of 70 is tops anywhere.]*

A Sample of Closings

Promote ___ now and assign him to command at sea. He is totally competitive on one of the Navy's fastest tracks. *[The "totally competitive" line seems very strong, but it does suggest on second look that he may not be the fastest of the fast—just competitive, not superior.]*

LT ___ is a superb naval officer who should be given only the most challenging assignments. I specifically recommend him as an admiral's aide and for assignment as weapons officer in Trident. He is recommended for immediate promotion to lieutenant commander. *[Specific recommendations clarify the level of the commander's support.]*

LT ___ is a prime candidate for PG School in telecommunications. *Give this officer major responsibility* as soon as possible. She's ready to handle an XO job. If none is readily available, she'll make an unbeatable department head. She has my highest recommendation for early promotion to lieutenant commander. *[Specifics aid the recommendation, and specifying the next wicket an officer is ready for may be vital.]*

Top performer in truly demanding position. Dedicated to nothing less than total success. Ready for any position afloat or ashore of increased responsibility. Most strongly recommended for accelerated promotion to lieutenant commander. *[Lack of specific recommendations weakens this closing somewhat, despite the apparently strong support, for the writer gives no indication of the special strengths of this officer.]*

I am most fortunate to have this intelligent, hard-charging officer as one of my department heads. He stands even now as number three of eight URL LCDRs and in the top 5 of 25 LCDRs of all categories. He is most strongly recommended for command of a PHM and early promotion to commander. *[Such very specific breakouts are very helpful to the promotion board.]*

Making a Good Fitrep Better

Having discussed the parts of a fitrep, we should see once more how the parts should fit together. Figure 5.4 is a fitness report written on a hard-charging surface line officer in 1981, written in the style then common. Following the critique, Figure 5.5 presents a suggested revision in modern fitness-report style.

Critique of the LCDR Report

Stretching from side to side and top to bottom of the sheet as it does, the original LCDR report seems to be composed to pack in as much information as possible into a limited space. However, its one massive paragraph of over 40 lines—in all caps, with no underlining, and even typed on top of the instructions—is virtually unreadable. Harassed board members then as now would have had great difficulty in picking out vital

Figure 5.4 A Lieutenant Commander's Fitness Report. There's far too much in this report; if we *read less*, we would appreciate this officer's performance more.

88. COMMENTS. Particularly comment upon the officer's overall leadership ability, personal traits not listed on the reverse side, and estimated or actual performance in combat. Include comments pertaining to unique skills and distinctions that may be important to career development and future assignment. A mark in boxes with an asterisk (*) indicates adversity and supporting comments are required.

LCDR ______'S PERFORMANCE HAS BEEN, WITHOUT EXCEPTION, OUTSTANDING. AS ENGINEER OFFICER, LCDR ______ HAS DISPLAYED SUPERB LEADERSHIP SKILLS. ALTHOUGH TOUGH AND DEMANDING OF HIS PERSONNEL WHERE MATTERS OF MATERIAL READINESS, GOOD ENGINEERING PRACTICES AND SAFETY ARE INVOLVED, LCDR ______ IS OBVIOUSLY CONCERNED WITH THE WELL-BEING OF EACH MAN IN HIS DEPARTMENT. HIS PERCEPTIVE INSIGHT INTO PERSONAL MOTIVATION ENABLES HIM TO OBTAIN THE UTMOST IN WORK PERFORMANCE WHILE MAINTAINING DEPARTMENTAL MORALE AT A HIGH LEVEL. AS A PROFESSIONAL ENGINEER LCDR ______ IS UNSURPASSED. HIS INDEPTH KNOWLEDGE OF ALL FACETS OF THE OPERATION AND MAINTENANCE OF THIS COMPLEX 1200 PSI STEAM PLANT, COUPLED WITH HIS ABILITY TO QUICKLY AND ACCURATELY DIAGNOSE MATERIAL CASUALTIES HAVE ENABLED ____ TO MEET ALL HER COMMITMENTS SAFELY AND ON TIME. THESE COMMITMENTS INCLUDE THREE MAJOR EXERCISES AND THE FIRST FOUR MONTHS OF AN EIGHT-MONTH INDIAN OCEAN/PERSIAN GULF DEPLOYMENT. IN FULFILLING HIS DUTIES AS SENIOR WATCH OFFICER, LCDR ______ SKILLFULLY EVALUATES THE STRENGTHS AND WEAKNESSES OF EACH OFFICER WATCHSTANDER, BUILDING WATCH SECTIONS TO ENSURE THE MAXIMUM CAPABILITY IS ACHIEVED ON EACH WATCH TEAM. LCDR ______'S RECORD OF ACHIEVEMENT DURING THIS REPORTING PERIOD IS NOTEWORTHY. SERVING AS SHIPWIDE COORDINATOR FOR ____'S INSURV INSPECTION, LCDR ______'S CAREFUL PLANNING AND ATTENTION TO THE MYRIAD INTRICACIES OF THIS EXHAUSTIVE INSPECION RESULTED IN THE SHIP'S HAVING FEW MISSION DISCREPANCIES, AND NONE IN ENGINEERING. IN THE ANNUAL 3-M INSPECTION THE ENGINEERING DEPARTMENT DID EXTREMELY WELL WITH THE DAMAGE CONTROL WORK CENTER, ER09, RECORDING A CONFIDENCE FACTOR OF 100 PER CENT, A RARE OCCURRENCE IN FLEET UNITS. CHOSEN AS THE SHIP'S COORDINATOR FOR THE VISIT OF THE VICE PREMIER OF THE PEOPLES REPUBLIC OF CHINA, LCDR ______ CARRIED OUT THIS RESPONSIBILITY IN SUCH A MANNER THAT THE VICE PREMIER ACKNOWLEDGED HIS VISIT TO ____ AS THE HIGH POINT OF HIS VISIT TO THE SAN DIEGO AREA. THIS REPORTING PERIOD ALSO SAW ____ AWARDED ITS SECOND CONSECUTIVE ENGINEERING "E" AND DAMAGE CONTROL "DC," ADDITIONAL EXAMPLES OF THE STANDARDS OF ENGINEERING EXCELLENCE THAT LCDR ______ HAS ESTABLISHED. DURING THE LAST TEN MONTHS, LCDR ______ MANAGED THREE REPAIR AVAILABILITIES, TWO PRIOR TO DEPLOYMENT AND ONE AT SHIP REPAIR FACILITY, SUBIC BAY, THE LATTER CUT FROM ELEVEN TO SIX DAYS. THAT ____ OBTAINED ALL MAJOR WORK REQUESTED ON TIME WAS IN LARGE MEASURE DUE TO LCDR ______'S ABILITY TO OBTAIN THE UTMOST IN PERFORMANCE FROM DIVERSE MAINTENANCE ORGANIZATIONS, KNOWING TO THE LAST INCH HOW FAR OUTSIDE REPAIR ACTIVITIES CAN BE PUSHED WHILE STILL MAINTAINING ____'S SUPERIOR WATERFRONT REPUTATION. LCDR ______ BRINGS TO HIS WATCHSTANDING DUTIES THE SAME SUPERB PREPARATION AND PERFORMANCE AS HE DOES TO HIS PRIMARY DUTY. HIS KNOWLEDGE OF SHIP AND FORCE CAPABILITIES AS WELL AS THOSE OF POTENTIAL ENEMIES HAS BEEN AMPLY DEMONSTRATED IN HIS PERFORMANCE AS FORCE ANTIAIR WARFARE COMMANDER (ALFA WHISKEY) FOR THE RANGER BATTLE GROUP AND FOR THE COMBATANT FORCES OPERATING WITHIN THE PERSIAN GULF. HE HAS MADE SIGNIFICANT CONTRIBUTIONS TO THE DEVELOPMENT OF VECTOR LOGIC APPROACH TO THE TACTICAL EMPLOYMENT OF COMBAT AIR PATROL. LCDR ______ ALSO ACHIEVED THE DIFFICULT QUALIFICATIONS OF ENGINEERING OFFICER OF THE WATCH AND TACTICAL ACTION OFFICER DURING THIS PERIOD. LCDR ______'S THOROUGH KNOWLEDGE OF SHIPHANDLING TECHNIQUES COUPLED WITH HIS WELL DEVELOPED "SEAMAN'S EYE" ENABLE ME TO PLACE TOTAL TRUST AND CONFIDENCE IN HIS ABILITY TO CONN THIS SHIP IN THE MOST DIFFICULT MANEUVERING SITUATIONS. LCDR ______ IS TRULY A "HEAD AND SHOULDERS" OFFICER WHOSE ABILITIES SHOULD CONTINUE TO BE DEMONSTRATED IN POSITIONS OF INCREASED RESPONSIBILITY INCLUDING ASSIGNMENT TO COMMAND OF A SURFACE COMBATANT. HE HAS MY STRONGEST RECOMMENDATION FOR PROMOTION TO COMMANDER AT THE EARLIEST OPPORTUNITY.

I HAVE GRADED EACH OF MY DEPARTMENT HEADS AT THE HIGHEST POSSIBLE LEVEL IN EVALUATING THEIR MISSION CONTRIBUTION. I CANNOT DO OTHERWISE AND ADEQUATELY REFLECT THEIR SUPERB PERFORMANCE WHEN COMPARED WITH OTHER OFFICERS OF SIMILAR GRADE WHO ARE SERVING IN LESS DEMANDING BILLETS.

details, or indeed in reading the report at all. Further specific criticism follows.

Organization

The *organization* of the report into duty areas—primary duty, senior watch officer, collateral duties, watch standing, shiphandling, etc.—is a once-standard one. But since this organization is not clarified by paragraphing, underlining, or other typography, a reader cannot skim efficiently. Remember that just as you need not cover every single feature of any individual's performance in an evaluation, so you need not discuss every possible area of responsibility. Yes, it would be damaging to omit comments on the primary duty or on leadership. Beyond that, what to omit is much less clear.

Details

The *details* about this officer are impressive. He ensured that the ship met all commitments in an extraordinarily high tempo period, guided her very successfully through various important inspections, won the ship an engineering "E" and a damage control "DC," and managed superb availabilities, to say nothing of his collateral work. Yet all these accomplishments are run together in the write-up and are hard to pick up.

The Writing

The *writing* itself is not bad—although the writer does use doublings a great deal, commenting on "trust and confidence" when "trust" will do, etc. See for example the early sentence: "His indepth [should be in-depth] knowledge of all facets of the *operation and maintenance* of this complex 1200 PSI Steam plant, coupled with his ability to *quickly and accurately* diagnose material casualties have enabled ___ to meet all her commitments *safely and on time*." True, the individual terms in these doublings have distinct meanings, but such repetition dilutes the overall effect; almost every sentence in the report contains a doubling of one sort or another.

Other Comments

Finally, in his attempt to overwhelm the reader, the writer gives board members information they already know, further diluting the actual achievements. Do you really need to tell the commanders and captains on promotion boards that an INSURV is an "exhaustive" inspection with "myriad intricacies," that a 1200-psi steam plant is "complex," or that an "E" designation is an example of "engineering excellence"?

A Suggested Revision

Figure 5.5 is a revision that attempts to make clear the special nature of the officer's performance. It retains all the vital accomplishments but formats the report and condenses the discussion so that crucial facts are not only *included* but are likely *to be picked up by the reviewer*.

Figure 5.5 Lieutenant Commander's Report, Rewritten. Here is an expert rewrite of Figure 5.4.

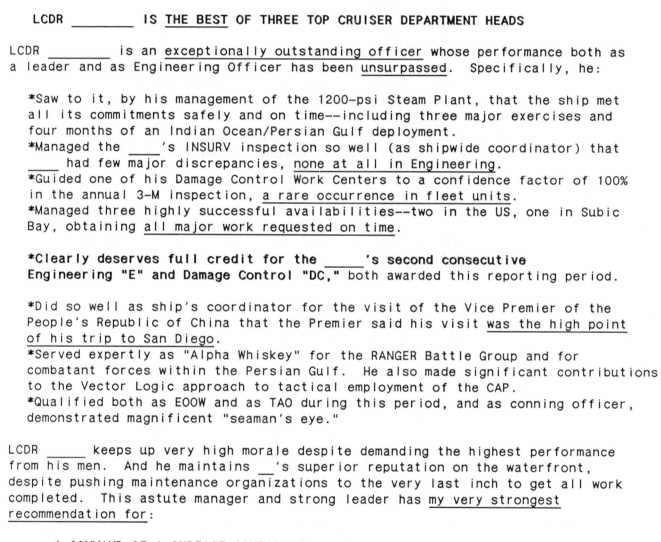

88. COMMENTS. Particularly comment upon the officer's overall leadership ability, personal traits not listed on the reverse side, and estimated or actual performance in combat. Include comments pertaining to unique skills and distinctions that may be important to career development and future assignment. A mark in boxes with an asterisk (*) indicates adversity and supporting comments are required.

LCDR ________ IS THE BEST OF THREE TOP CRUISER DEPARTMENT HEADS

LCDR ________ is an exceptionally outstanding officer whose performance both as a leader and as Engineering Officer has been unsurpassed. Specifically, he:

*Saw to it, by his management of the 1200-psi Steam Plant, that the ship met all its commitments safely and on time--including three major exercises and four months of an Indian Ocean/Persian Gulf deployment.
*Managed the ____'s INSURV inspection so well (as shipwide coordinator) that ____ had few major discrepancies, none at all in Engineering.
*Guided one of his Damage Control Work Centers to a confidence factor of 100% in the annual 3-M inspection, a rare occurrence in fleet units.
*Managed three highly successful availabilities--two in the US, one in Subic Bay, obtaining all major work requested on time.

***Clearly deserves full credit for the _____'s second consecutive Engineering "E" and Damage Control "DC,"** both awarded this reporting period.

*Did so well as ship's coordinator for the visit of the Vice Premier of the People's Republic of China that the Premier said his visit was the high point of his trip to San Diego.
*Served expertly as "Alpha Whiskey" for the RANGER Battle Group and for combatant forces within the Persian Gulf. He also made significant contributions to the Vector Logic approach to tactical employment of the CAP.
*Qualified both as EOOW and as TAO during this period, and as conning officer, demonstrated magnificent "seaman's eye."

LCDR _____ keeps up very high morale despite demanding the highest performance from his men. And he maintains __'s superior reputation on the waterfront, despite pushing maintenance organizations to the very last inch to get all work completed. This astute manager and strong leader has my very strongest recommendation for:

* COMMAND OF A SURFACE COMBATANT
* EARLY PROMOTION TO COMMANDER

Checklist for Fitness Report Write-Ups

The following comments are meant for a drafter to review before, during, or after writing the comments section of a fitness report. A checklist for an enlisted evaluation would be very similar.

Writing Style

* Will the opening statement catch the attention of the selection board member dazed by reading report after report? Should it? (A good guide: did this officer attract *your* attention during the reporting period?)
* Did you support generalities with specifics?
* Can you describe any important achievements more effectively?
* Are the adjectives appropriate? Strong enough? Too strong? Too numerous?
* Have you crowded the report with stock superlatives that will put the reader to sleep? Did you intend to?
* Is everything clear? Could a reader misinterpret any comments?
* Have you damned by faint praise unintentionally?

Content

* Did you include, if pertinent:
  combat time
  major fleet exercises
  awards and award nominations
  oral atta-boys
  written compliments
  service schools attended
  hazardous duty
  qualifications obtained
  extra civilian schooling
  community activity
* Does the report describe the officer's specific duties in enough detail? In too much detail? Did you include the kind and number of personnel supervised?
* Have you identified any special skills or unusual talents of this particular officer? Did you describe his or her personal qualities adequately?
* Did you record the employment of the command, if noteworthy?
* Have you dealt with this officer's leadership in a prominent way?

Format

* Is the report appealing to the eye? Is the formatting effective? Is there too much or too little underlining?
* Did you use bullets? Do they mainly emphasize specific accomplishments? Are they parallel in structure?

* Can the reader pick out the vital judgments in the report at a glance?

Report Recommendations

* Does the promotion recommendation stand out on the form (usually in the last line, underlined)? Does the write-up support the recommendation?
* Have you made other recommendations, if appropriate? (War College, specific billets, recommendation for command if at senior level, etc.)
* Should you try, by adding explanatory remarks in the recommendation section, to soften any possible setback to this officer caused by a low comparative ranking? (See Haering's "Fitness Report Finesse" in the January 1980 *Proceedings* for an explanation.)

Internal and External Comparisons

* Do the write-up and the marks agree? Do you explain major marking deviations to the right or left on the front page in the write-up? Also, if you marked "early promotion" on the front, do you repeat it in the comments?
* Are there inconsistencies from paragraph to paragraph in this report?
* How about changes from your last report on this officer to this one? How will those reports sound, read one right after the other? What could a reader construe any differences to mean?
* Check especially your previous recommendations on this officer. Did you recommend for command or early promotion before, but not now? If you altered your recommendation, how will this change appear to readers?
* How does this write-up compare with the other officers' write-ups you are drafting at the same time? Are they sufficiently differentiated? Can you justify the distinctions you make between the officers you are reporting upon?

Also

* Try setting this report aside for 24 hours before doing a final revision.

Finally

* Can you live with what you've said in this report?

Some Things Fitrep Writers Should *Not* Do

According to the captain who headed a recent selection board, some fitrep writers had badly hurt those they were writing up. They had done so by such errors as the following:

- **Evaluating three different officers 1 of 3 even though they were in the same competitive category in the same reporting period.**
- **Copying paragraphs right out of a commercial fitrep guide, paragraphs that selection board members recognized.**
- **Commonly including negative comments even on top performers, forgetting that in the "crunch" zone, board members are looking for what might *detract* from an officer, that is, some reason *not* to select.**
- **Failing to take the time to read the final versions of their write-ups. In one report seen by the board, because of paragraphs transferred wholesale from one evaluation to another by word processor, three different officers' names appeared in the same write-up.**

Points on Navy Enlisted Evaluations

The key question to ask yourself after writing an evaluation is this: how well did I transmit the special qualities that separate this person out?

—Navy Captain

Probably two major differences distinguish Navy enlisted evaluations from Navy officer fitness reports. (1) The evaluations are kept in the service record aboard ship or station; therefore, an enlisted person's superiors can review the last few on the spot. In contrast, once signed, a fitness report is filed in the officer's service record in Washington, D.C. (and a newly reported CO is not to read prior fitness reports on the vessel's or unit's officers). (2) Chiefs' selection boards use a complex rating-sheet and numbering system that requires board members to rate each person's performance *numerically* in several particular areas, these ratings based on information gathered mostly from the write-ups. The only form comparable for officers' boards is the Officer Summary Sheet, which is primarily a sketch of numerical ratings and has little to do with the write-ups.

As a result of this numerical scoring system, the enlisted evaluation write-up differs from a fitness report in being a bit more specifics oriented. If you don't cover most areas mentioned on rating sheets by adducing *specific accomplishments* in those areas—such items as "volunteer work," "initiative," and "community involvement," as well as the standard and vital "leadership," "managerial ability," etc.—you may be hurting the person you're evaluating.

Otherwise, however, the techniques are pretty much the same. Yes, the blocks are a bit different, and obviously you should mention different kinds of particulars in an enlisted person's than in an officer's write-up. But in general, *opening statements, lots of bullets describing specifics,* and *closing recommendations* are as characteristic of the best modern evaluations as they are of the best modern fitness reports. All the other principles discussed at the beginning of this chapter apply similarly.

Strong and Weak Bullets in Enlisted Evaluations

Writing effective bullets is an important skill. Here are some bullets for evals written on Navy enlisted men and women—first some weaker examples, and then some stronger ones. Remember, reviewers often look for nuances in report writing—so be careful not to damn by faint praise unintentionally.

These Bullets Don't Say Very Much

• Instrumental in GLOVER's successful TYCOM 3/M inspection. *[Just "instrumental"? What did he do, and how successful was the inspection?]*

• Supervised numerous unconventional foreign refuelings with NATO forces in Northern Europe. *[But <u>how did he do</u> in the supervision?]*

• Member of Engineering Casualty Control Team. *[Just a job description.]*

• Reviews all AC&R logs and effects corrective action. *[Another job description—no help.]*

• Her training program was singled out in a successful command inspection as one of the two best training programs audited. *[Top two <u>out of how many?</u> And who singled it out?]*

"Remember that you are trying in most cases to write for impact—impact on the CPO selection board, for example. FACTS, FACTS, FACTS! Navy guys are tough, and too much "flowery" language conveys the idea that there is no hardness to the ratee. 'Hit hard, and hit fast.' Then get out—if there's nothing more to say, don't waste a paragraph on trivia that dilutes all the 'hard' stuff you did put in."—Navy Captain

These Bullets Seem Relatively Impressive

• He was hot work coordinator for CVN 69 (approximately 200 jobs daily) without an incident. *[Numerical data help indicate the magnitude of the accomplishment.]*

• During REFTRA at Flag Officer Sea Training at Portland, UK, he consistently impressed Royal Navy observers with his vitality, skill, and uncommon ability to control the situation, regardless of its complexity. *[Impressing the Royal Navy is strong—it would be stronger yet with quotes or citations.]*

• BTC (SW) ____'s detailed preparations earned high praise from board inspectors during the INSURV and resulted in a superb engineering performance, including full-power turns and emergency crash-back achievement on the first try. *[Again, good specifics.]*

• Service-oriented performance while assigned TAD to the MDMAA contributed greatly to the ship's selection as the FY 88 Ney Award Winner. *[Connecting performance to the ship's selection makes this service significant.]*

• In spite of counseling, BM3 ___ has not demonstrated the motivation or manual dexterity needed to learn his rate in such areas as boom handling and cargo hatch captain. *[Specifics help substantiate weak performance too.]*

• During this period, GROTON received the following awards, due in no small part to RMCM ___'s efforts and leadership: CINCPACFLT Golden Anchor for best retention by a submarine in the Pacific Fleet in 1984, COMSUBPAC Engineering E, Damage Control DC, and Communications C. *[Drafter awards credit for these accomplishments to the master chief.]*

• He demonstrated superior capabilities as an S-3A acoustic sensor operator against Soviet nuclear/diesel submarines as well as allied ASW targets. *[Operating well against the potential enemy is a very strong credit.]*

Making a Good Eval Better

Figure 5.6 is an actual enlisted evaluation on a superb petty officer (since deceased). This package serves as an interesting example of how changes in format, in wording, and in selection of detail—principles mentioned above—can make an evaluation fully reveal to a harried board member the excellence of its subject.

Critique of the YN1 Report

This report is very thorough. It is filled with details, some of which are very striking, and attempts to do justice to a truly outstanding petty officer. *It's a good rough draft.* However, in the inflationary climate of the past few years, what it does not do well jeopardizes its intent and makes uncertain whether this truly fine sailor will be picked up for chief petty officer.

Overall Problems

Some problems strike you immediately. The narrative is typed in all caps and two-blocked from side to side and pretty nearly top to bottom of the page, with only a few paragraph markings and no "bullets." This format inhibits readability. The extensive doublings in the prose—"subordinates and superiors," "ship's correspondence and internal routing," "pay and allowances"—add to the denseness. Occasional grammatical errors and typos (like commas taken for periods) are less important problems.

The Beginning

Block 55 leaves unclear whether YN1 Stanko received a COMSIXTHFLT letter of commendation and was also selected petty officer of the quarter, or got a COMSIXTHFLT letter for being the ship's honoree, or exactly what commendations he did get. Besides that problem, the personal achievements here are hard to pick out because they're sandwiched between the *ship's* employment and the *ship's* Battle "E."

As for Block 56, the opening is a forgettable line—you can imagine that virtually *all* competitive YN1s "continue to impress." The sailor's

Figure 5.6 Evaluation on a top-notch Yeoman. A draft evaluation on an outstanding Yeoman First Class records many impressive details.

OCR TYPING FONT NOT REQUIRED FOR COMPLETION OF THIS SIDE

50 MEMBER'S LAST NAME, INITIALS	51 SSN	PERIOD OF REPORT
STANKO, R E		52 From 01DEC83 53 To 30NOV84

54 DUTIES AND RESPONSIBILITIES

ASSIGNED AS LEADING PETTY OFFICER OF XP01 DIVISION, AND SHIPS SECRETARY. STANDS DUTY MASTER-AT-ARMS AND DUTY ADMIN INPORT. QUALIFIED TO STAND OFFICER OF THE DECK (INPORT)

55 SPECIAL ACHIEVEMENTS DEPLOYED TO NORTH ATLANTIC (UNITED EFFORT/TEAMWORK '84) 14FEB-28APR84. RECEIVED NAVY UNIT COMMENDATION FOR EASTERN MEDITERRANEAN DEPLOYMENT (MARG 2-83), MAY-DEC '83 AND COMSIXTHFLT LETTER OF COMMENDATION SELECTED PETTY OFFICER OF THE QUARTER, SEP84. RECEIVED NAVY EXPEDITIONARY MEDAL, BATTLE "E".

56 EVALUATION COMMENTS

☆U.S. Government Printing Office: 1988—505-007/67128 2-1

YN1 STANKO HAS CONTINUED TO IMPRESS SUBORDINATES AND SUPERIORS ALIKE WITH AN INTIMATE KNOWLEDGE OF HIS RATING AND UNPARALLELED DEDICATION. AS SHIP"S SECRETARY, HE IS UNUSUALLY METICULOUS. HIS UNCOMPROMISINGLY HIGH STANDARDS AND CLOSE ATTENTION TO DETAIL HAS ENSURED THE NEATNESS, ACCURACY AND TIMELINESS OF OFFICERS' FITNESS REPORTS AND ALL FACETS OF SHIP'S CORRESPONDENCE AND INTERNAL ROUTING. HE HAS WORKED CLOSELY WITH SHIP'S PERSONNEL TO MAINTAIN THE ACCURACY OF SERVICE RECORDS, AND HAS ASSISTED NUMEROUS MEMBERS OF THE WARDROOM IN SUBMITTING CAREER-RELATED CORRESPONDENCE SUCH AS DUTY PREFERENCE CARDS AND REQUESTS FOR AUGMENTATION, CHANGE OF DESIGNATOR, ETC. IN ADDITION, PETTY OFFICER STANKO MAINTAINS A CLOSE RELATIONSHIP WITH HIS COUNTERPARTS IN THE SHIP'S DISBURSING DEPARTMENT TO RESOLVE EXPEDITIOUSLY PROBLEMS RELATED TO PAY AND ALLOWANCES.

YN1 STANKO IS TOTALLY COMMITTED TO THE CONCEPT OF "SERVICE TO THE CREW", AND HAS INSTILLED A SIMILAR ATTITUDE IN HIS SUBORDINATES. AN EXAMPLE OF HIS DEDICATION TO HIS SHIPMATES IS HIS VIRTUALLY SINGLE-HANDED VERIFICATION AND REVISION OF DEERS INPUT FOR ALL PERSONNEL, A GARGANTUAN TASK. BLESSED OF AN UNUSUALLY CONGENIAL PERSONALITY, YN1 STANKO RELATES EASILY TO ALL PERSONNEL, BOTH OFFICER AND ENLISTED. HIS GOOD-HUMORED DIPLOMACY HAS SMOOTHED OVER MANY A DIFFICULT SITUATION. HE HAS HAD NOTEWORTHY SUCCESS WORKING WITH JUNIOR PERSONNEL: UNDER HIS SUPERVISION, THREE INEXPERIENCED YNSNs WERE PROMOTED TO THIRD CLASS, A SIGNIFICANT ACHIEVEMENT CONSIDERING THE LIMITED ADVANCEMENT OPPORTUNITIES CURRENTLY AFFORDED YEOMEN. A FIRM BUT COMPASSIONATE LEADER, HIGHLY RESPECTED BY HIS MEN, YN1 STANKO IS NOTICEABLY FAIR TO ALL PERSONNEL, AND ACTIVELY SUPPORTS THE NAVY'S EQUAL OPPORTUNITY PROGRAM. POPULARLY KNOWN AS "FATHER STANKO", BECAUSE OF HIS EFFORTS AS CATHOLIC LAY READER. HIS "PASTORAL COUNSELING" HAS AIDED MANY A TROUBLED SAILOR.

IN ADDITION TO SUSTAINED GROWTH IN HIS PROFESSIONAL AREAS, YN1 STANKO REMAINS ACTIVE IN A MYRIAD OF OUTSIDE ACTIVITIES, BOTH ON AND OFF THE SHIP. HE IS A VALUED MEMBER OF HIS LOCAL PARISH (AND FREQUENT VOLUNTEER WORKER). HAVING ALREADY COMPLETED ESWS QUALIFICATION, PETTY OFFICER STANKO BROADENED HIS KNOWLEDGE OF SURFACE WARFARE BY VOLUNTARILY STANDING JOOD WATCHES DURING THE SHIP'S NORTH ATLANTIC DEPLOYMENT.

POSSESSED OF SUPERIOR COMMUNICATIONS SKILLS AND OUTSTANDING MILITARY BEARING AND APPEARANCE, YN1 STANKO RANKS NUMBER ONE OF THIRTY-THREE E6s ABOARD SHIP. THE ONLY FIRST CLASS AFFORDED DUTY SECTION LEADER STATUS, HE IS PRESIDENT OF THE FIRST CLASS MESS, AND WAS RECENTLY NAMED PETTY OFFICER OF THE QUARTER. THIS DEDICATED, HIGHLY MOTIVATED PERFORMER IS STRONGLY RECOMMENDED FOR RETENTION AND IMMEDIATE ADVANCEMENT TO CHIEF PETTY OFFICER.

(BLOCK 39 "JUSTIFICATION")

WERE IT NOT FOR HIS TIME SPENT IN THE RESERVE FLEET, THIS SUPERB INDIVIDUAL WOULD ALREADY BE AN E-7. HE IS THE EPITOME OF THE 4.0 SAILOR, AND RICHLY DESERVES THE HONORS HE HAS BEEN ACCORDED AS WELL AS ADVANCEMENT TO CHIEF PETTY OFFICER.

extremely impressive ranking—that he is the *very top* first class petty officer *out of thirty-three* aboard ship—doesn't show up until the very end (and even then it lacks the emphasis of underlining or bold face).

THE MIDDLE

The middle paragraphs include many striking accomplishments and some telling personal description. You get far more of a sense of personality from this write-up than from most enlisted evaluations. All these good details are likely to be skimmed or overlooked entirely, however, because they are hidden in the midst of long, dense paragraphs in the middle of the eval.

THE CONCLUSION

The last paragraph has *very strong* specifics. He's #1 of 33, the only first class who is a duty section leader, president of the first-class mess, and petty officer of the quarter—they certainly don't appear to be just the usual palaver for the selection board (especially when seen in light of the wonderful personality sketched in paragraph 3). On the other hand, the commonplace ending—"strongly recommended for retention and immediate advancement to Chief Petty Officer"—doesn't do justice to the exceptional sailor sketched elsewhere in the report. (Note: The "Justification" section shown at the end was required when this report was drafted. That section has since been judged redundant and is no longer required.)

SUMMARY

Many excellent specifics fill this evaluation—probably too many. Few briefers would have the time to read this dense an evaluation word for word. If we *read less*, we might *appreciate YN1 Stanko more*. In addition, to make the evaluation fully worthy of its subject, the drafter should have used formatting to help us pick out the fine facts. He should have made Stanko's top-notch quality clear to us *from the very first line* of Block 56. And he should have created special language for the very end of the evaluation to frame and spotlight the special quality of this magnificent sailor.

Another Try

Figure 5.7 is a revision, crafted to help the board member perceive the exceptionally fine quality of this particular sailor.

On Submitting the "Brag Sheet"

As input for an evaluation, an enlisted person should use the official brag sheet, or whatever form the local command may have prepared. An officer may have to list bullets on a smooth piece of paper, or adapt the fitness report input sheet. In either case, the subordinate should take some time to *compose several carefully crafted bullets* that the drafter can use or adapt for the actual report.

Figure 5.7 Rewrite of the YN1's Eval. Here an expert has revised Figure 5.6 into modern "bullet" format.

OCR TYPING FONT NOT REQUIRED FOR COMPLETION OF THIS SIDE

50 MEMBER'S LAST NAME, INITIALS	51 SSN	PERIOD OF REPORT
STANKO, R. E.		52 From 01 Dec 83 53 To 30 Nov 84

54 DUTIES AND RESPONSIBILITIES

Leading Petty Officer of XP01 Division, and **Ship's Secretary**. Stands Duty Master-at-Arms and Duty Admin in port. Qualified to stand Officer of the Deck (In Port). Qualified as ESWS; voluntarily stands JOOD (Underway).

55 SPECIAL ACHIEVEMENTS **Received COMSIXTHFLT Letter of Commendation and was selected Petty Officer of the Quarter, Sep/84**. Ship deployed to North Atlantic Feb-Apr 84; received NUC for Eastern Med Deployment, May-Dec 83.; Battle "E," etc.

56 EVALUATION COMMENTS

☆U.S. Government Printing Office: 1988—505-007/67128 2-1

YN1 STANKO <u>RANKS #1 out of 33 FIRST CLASS PETTY OFFICERS</u>

HE HAS SUPERIOR LEADERSHIP TALENTS:

- **Is already recognized for his chief's qualities. He is the only E6 given duty section leader status aboard.**
- Provides good-humored diplomacy to all ranks with the aid of his unusually congenial personality. His "pastoral counseling" as Catholic Lay Reader has aided many a sailor; aboard ship, he is popularly known as **"Father Stanko."**
- **Has trained three inexperienced YNSNs superbly**. They passed their exams and were advanced in the first increment, <u>highly significant</u> in view of recent advancement stats for YNs.

HE IS AN OUTSTANDING, GREATLY DEDICATED YEOMAN:

- Is absolutely committed to "service to the crew." Ensured neatness, accuracy, and timeliness in fitreps, and in all facets of ship's correspondence.
- **Almost single-handedly** verified and revised DEERS input for all personnel aboard ship, **a gargantuan task**.
- Provided outstanding assistance to ship's officers in submitting augmentation and change-of-designator requests, duty preference cards, etc.
- Helped greatly to resolve pay/allowance problems quickly through his close relationships with his counterparts in the ship's Disbursing Department.

HE IS ALSO A FINE SEAMAN AND CITIZEN:

- **Volunteered** for a myriad of outside activities, on and off the ship. A valued member of his local parish, and frequent volunteer worker.
- **Voluntarily stood JOOD watches** during the ship's North Atlantic deployment, using the ESWS qualification he had gained last cruise.

SUMMARY: A superior communicator with superb bearing and appearance, besides being **ranked #1 of 33 First Class Petty Officers aboard**, YN1 Stanko is **President of the First Class Mess**, and was recently named Petty Officer of the Quarter (of 200 petty officers aboard). **<u>Promote this dedicated sailor immediately, even if only one YN1 in the Navy can be made a chief</u>**.

Remember, your boss may not be aware of everything you've been doing. Try to give the boss more than enough bullets to fill the middle part of the write-up. This way the boss can be selective and put in only the *most important* items—as the brag sheet says, including information you submit is "discretionary on the part of the reporting senior."

The more care you take, the better—you will help your senior out in the drafting. If you give your senior a set of bullets complete with all the important dates, figures, percentages, numbers, SSN, etc., then your boss will be more likely to include some form of the bullets in the write-up. By your careful spadework, he or she will have a ready example of the good quality of your work and, from having a smaller workload, may also be in a better mood when writing.

A Painless Method of Compiling a Brag Sheet

One Navy commander has a blank piece of paper under his blotter. On this sheet, whenever he finishes a task, he writes down a brief description of what he has done. He always writes it down—because he knows a fitness report will be due in August, and he'll need a brag sheet for it.

When the time for the fitrep comes, he writes and submits a bullet apiece on each of his major activities or groups of activities. In this way, the CO has a rough draft of the middle of the report, and all he has to write up from scratch are the opener and closing. The CO can spend the most time where he or she ought to, in crafting and fine-tuning those *vital* parts.

An Example of a Completed Brag Sheet

Figure 5.8 is a brag sheet that a sharp first class aviation boatswain's mate assigned to an Aviation Intermediate Maintenance Department aboard a carrier might have written for his division officer. As best he can, the writer crafts his accomplishments in each area in bullets that the division officer might insert right into the write-up, as is. He crosses out those headings that don't apply and adds other appropriate information, as needed.

Command-Specific Input Sheets

Some commands may prefer to prepare their own brag sheets. In this way, a command can solicit the best possible input for the evals (the brag sheet helping individuals to brainstorm about their accomplishments), but it can also *set an agenda for its troops*. If the command introduces a form and insists people adhere to it, the form will tend to encourage behavior in the areas listed.

If you prepare such an input sheet, keep in mind the Navy's needs as well as your own command's requirements. Forms designed for enlisted personnel should reflect the enlisted "work sheets" that selection boards

Figure 5.8 Individual Input. Here a petty officer describes what he has done in a form adaptable for an evaluation.

ENLISTED PERFORMANCE EVALUATION REPORT – INDIVIDUAL INPUT
NAVPERS 1616/21 (8-76)
S/N 0106-LF-016-1705

DATE PREPARED	DEPARTMENT
15 October 1987	AIMD

NAME (*last, first, middle*)	RATE	PRESENT SHIP OR STATION
JONES, JOHN P.	AB1	USS CARL VINSON

THE SUBMISSION OF THIS FORM IS A MEANS OF ENSURING THAT YOUR PERSONAL ACCOMPLISHMENTS, ACHIEVEMENTS AND CREDITABLE ACTIVITY, DURING THE CURRENT REPORTING PERIOD, ARE BROUGHT TO THE ATTENTION OF YOUR REPORTING SENIOR, THROUGH THE CHAIN OF COMMAND.

1. IN-RATE AND NORMAL DUTY QUALIFICATIONS ACHIEVED:

* Completed 3-M System Coordinator PQS (NAVEDTRA 43241-D);
* Completed Damage Control Petty Officer PQS (NAVEDTRA 43119-5Q1)

2. SPECIAL QUALIFICATIONS ACHIEVED:

[None this reporting period.]

3. IN RATE PROFESSIONAL DEVELOPMENT:

* Planned and successfully coordinated the complete rework of over 200 pieces of ship's equipment during the SRA.

4. OTHER EDUCATIONAL AND TRAINING ACCOMPLISHMENTS:

* Qualified 75% of newly assigned personnel in 3-M PQS in less than 3 months, where the standard is 6;
* As supervisor of 20 personnel in Damage Control/3-M Maintenance Functions, contributed to the final Surface 3-M grade of 95.1%.

5. VOLUNTARY NAVY RELATED CIVIC AND COMMUNITY SUPPORT ACTIVITY:

* Voluntarily raised $500 among departmental personnel in local charity campaign to help orphaned children, a 50% increase from last year.

6. ~~OTHER CIVIC AND COMMUNITY SUPPORT ACTIVITY:~~ CONTRIBUTIONS TO DEPARTMENT'S MISSION:

* Supported 225 flight hours per day during the recent cruise.
* Contributed to Dept's achievement of "zero lost sorties caused by lack of support equipment" during 11 months of operation through October 87.

7. COMMENDATORY CORRESPONDENCE RECEIVED DURING THIS REPORT PERIOD

* Received the Navy Achievement Medal for outstanding accomplishment during recent WESTPAC Deployment.

8. OTHER ACHIEVEMENTS, ACCOMPLISHMENTS, AND SIGNIFICANT EVENTS ACTIONS:

* Contributed to a zero major discrepancy grade during the COMFAIRWESTPAC Mid-Cruise corrosion-control inspection.
* Supervised the complete rehabilitation of 5 office spaces, 5 shop spaces, and 3 berthing compartments, all on schedule, all with outstanding results.

NOTE: THE USE OF THE INFORMATION PROVIDED BY THE RATEE IS DISCRETIONARY ON THE PART OF THE REPORTING SENIOR. UPON COMPLETION OF THE EVALUATION REPORT, THIS FORM SHALL BE RETURNED TO THE RATEE.

★U.S.GPO:1986-0-726-006/41572

typically use. And forms for officer input should solicit information vital for officer selection boards.

Telling Your Boss How to Write Your Report

A topic closely connected to brag sheets is telling your boss the kinds of things you need included on your evaluation. This input is especially important when you're working ashore or working for someone in a community different from your own. Your boss may not know the key accomplishments and recommendations that are vital to someone in your career field, and if you don't fill the boss in, no one else is likely to. Some officers have learned this the hard way: "Sometimes you have to educate your superior," a commander remarked, "especially if he's in another community or service. In Army reports, for example, it was once common to say of an officer, 'He is physically fit and combat ready.' But that didn't help a naval officer up before a Navy selection board."

On having subordinates "write their own" fitness report: "It's unfair to require a junior both (1) to be in sackcloth and ashes, and at the same time (2) to put his own destiny forward in a breathtaking fitness report."—Captain

Whether you're a Navy chief working for an Air Force colonel, a Marine serving in a Navy command, or *any* service member working for a civilian, you may need to educate your boss. Making your needs known could also be important if you're a naval aviator serving on a ship with a SWO captain; that captain may not know the key tickets you need to punch in the VS or VA community. Female service members would be wise to remind their superiors what kinds of billets they need recommendations for. By tactful memos, by short letters transmitting your eval or fitrep input, or by some other means, do your best to inform your superior of the realities of your particular specialty.

Some Last Words on Evals and Fitreps

Use the Strength of Clear Prose—Not Fragments—in Openers and Closings

The "bullet" style certainly has helped us read and write effective evaluations, but it makes intense use of sentence fragments and you can carry them too far. Without specifics to embellish them, successive fragments often sound like a checklist. The lines printed below from the closing paragraph of an E-5's evaluation sound like the writer just thumbed through a "phrases for performance evaluation" guide to make sure every possible comment got into the evaluation.

DEDICATED PROFESSIONAL. VIGOROUSLY SEEKS INCREASED RESPONSIBILITY. ABLY IDENTIFIES AND SOLVES PROBLEMS. TIMELY COMPLETION OF TASKS. DISPLAYS POSITIVE ATTITUDE. SETS THE EXAMPLE FOR JUNIOR PERSONNEL. WEARS UNIFORM WITH PRIDE. APPEARANCE SHARP AND NEAT. EXCELLENT COMMAND OF THE ENGLISH LANGUAGE. FULLY SUPPORTS EQUAL OPPORTUNITY.

Resembling as it does a mere list of desired attributes, this paragraph offers no picture at all of the person himself. The same phrases could appear on almost anybody's evaluation.

In general, reserve the fragments for hard-hitting bullets in the middle section. Especially on fitness reports, *make use of the potential descriptiveness of complete sentences* in the beginning paragraph and in the critical closing remarks. Those sentences can help you make the fine distinctions you often need to make in the opening and closing lines.

Don't Overuse Graphic Techniques

Just as the language tends to lose its full descriptive power when you limit yourself to phrases rather than sentences, remember that graphic emphasis also loses its effect when you emphasize *everything*. Here's a bullet that suffers from too much underlining and capitalization:

- Demonstrated INITIATIVE and KNOWLEDGE IN DATA PROCESSING resulting in a REVISED PROCEDURE for SUPPLY MANAGEMENT that SAVED this command $10,000.

As you can imagine, a whole report styled in this manner would give the reader absolutely no help in sorting out the really significant details. Yet in many a report seen by selection boards, *over half the words* are underlined.

Keep Track of the State of Your Record

Every day, NMPC receives, literally, a *pallet of paper*—some 50,000 pieces of paper per day. Sorting it alone is a major task. As a result, something critical to your record can easily get misrouted or misfiled. So do what you can to make sure your own record is up to date. *Review the microfiche copy of your record* that NMPC will send out to you upon written request, at no charge. This personal record review is the best quality control on your record that NMPC has.

"Take care when writing about your lesser performers, too. About ten years ago, NMPC began to look at E-5s and E-6s whose performance was down. Individuals judged to be poor performers are often put in a probationary status. Although some may get discharged from the Navy, more often, those judged subpar performers will not be allowed to reenlist, which obviously *ends the Navy career of an individual.* To make their decisions, these performance review boards will look carefully at the evaluation remarks—so your comments may be crucial here as well."—Commander

Keep Track of Selection Board Practice

One is wise to take every opportunity to talk to those who have served on selection boards, especially recent boards, for the context changes gradually from one year to the next. Keep in touch with this primary audience for all the evaluations or fitness reports you may write. Actually, the best way to learn is to serve on a selection board personally. No matter how much they thought they knew beforehand, new board members consistently report how actual board service opened their eyes. But few junior service members have a chance to serve on a board. Second best, and also good, is to keep talking to former board members and form a picture that way.

What Good Evaluation Writers Do

Here are a few characteristics shared by *good writers* of fitness reports and enlisted evals. Each time they write, they

- **Consistently draw a word picture that unmistakably characterizes *this particular individual*, simply refusing to copy lines from other reports or depend on "canned" language for the key writing in the evaluation.**
- **Use graphic and formatting techniques to excellent effect, never making the hard-pressed board member search the screen to find buried information.**
- **Support generalizations with specifics: they give board members facts, numbers, and percentages—but give figures along with the percentages, too. In short, they *tell the truth, then let the reader judge.***
- **Select the key points from among all data—they don't use everything!**
- **Only use negative comments in serious problem cases (knowing their damaging effects, in the current climate).**
- **Know their people so well that they can (and do) recommend specific future billets and schools.**
- **Match the write-up with the marks, but also enhance their credibility as demanding graders by showing a spread in their marks, and a similar gradation in their write-ups.**

Finally—What's the Best Use of Report-Writing Guides?

Resist the temptation to copy sentences or paragraphs from evaluations written on other personnel or published in performance evaluation–writing guides. Board members have seen those guides too: "Hey, I saw this paragraph in that eval-writing guide," was a remark often heard on a recent E-7 board. Copying the guides usually hurts the person you're evaluating, for it suggests the writer is lazy and the report's picture of the ratee is not authentic.

Report-writing guides are valuable because they give a sense of the kind of writing that is being done, of the possibilities of prose, of ways to phrase recommendations, and of current uses of graphics and formatting. They may help a writer form a sense of audience, helping to indicate what kinds of comments board members are looking for. Lists of suggested words and phrases that such texts often include may sometimes help a drafter get through a writer's block or find the exact word he or she is groping for.

But the best way to use such a book (including the examples in *this* book) is to *page through it* for context and ideas, then

SHUT THE BOOK

and compose the best report possible **on this particular individual.**

The problem with writing an award nomination is how to use one piece of paper to convince a reader totally unaware of an individual's performance, the difficulties of the job, or any peculiar circumstances of the command that the award you're recommending is merited.

—Senior Civil Servant in OPNAV

6

Awards and Commendations

Awards and letters of commendation help build morale on a ship or in a unit. They can hurt morale too if the paperwork snarls and people who should get commendations don't get them, or if the paperwork becomes too burdensome on those who have to write up the awards. Of course, whoever proposes the award must follow the guidance in the Navy and Marine Corps Awards Manual (SECNAVINST 1650.1 series) and in amplifying local instructions. Beyond that, what's most important is to master the *two kinds of writing* involved in award nominations.

An award package beyond the level of letters of commendation or appreciation normally consists of two documents: a write-up or summary of action (also known as the justification), and the citation. You might ask, why two documents? Both describe the actions of an individual and also commend that person. Couldn't one piece of paper do the work of two?

In fact, one major command recently dropped the justification portion and directed its subordinate commands to submit only the citation, but then three months later reversed that decision. That reversal is not surprising. Despite the similarity of the two documents, they have one crucial difference: they serve two very different audiences. The summary of action sheet is written for those who must approve the award, while the citation is aimed at the service member, shipmates, family, and friends. These two audiences have much different needs and levels of understanding. To write one document for both groups usually serves neither group well.

The Justification

The audience for the justification is one or more award boards. It is important to know the way such boards use a justification.

Remember the Audience: The Awards Board

The justification will first go to a board of officers at your own command. If this board approves the nomination, and if the captain of a ship or squadron or a Marine Corps battalion commander does not have authorization to sign the proposed award personally, the package will be forwarded further up the chain of command to whoever does. Thus, the award must often go through two or more committees of approval—a local board first, then to the commodore or higher. Certainly few members of the higher board will know the nominee. Even if the nomination goes just to a local board for approval, several board members may not know the nominee well, and they will look to the justification comments to prove the service member merits recognition. Even those who know the individuals you're recommending will not know everything about them.

In addition, board members will customarily *read the whole document,* not just skim it. Unlike a Navy or Marine Corps selection board, this group will have a comparatively limited number of nominees to consider, and only one evaluative write-up per person. They will not, like selection boards, have to read from 5 to 30 evaluation comments on every single individual (a quantity that guarantees skimming). So awards board members will have time to read the *whole* summary of action.

This difference is profound. Looking for patterns under severe time pressure, selection board briefers focus on numerical ratings and the opening and closing comments in evaluations before them, and then, if they need to, will scan the actual accomplishments. In contrast, an awards board *will normally turn immediately to the accomplishments,* to see if this person's actions or services merit the recommended award.

Pay Special Attention to the *Middle* of the Justification

The space on the summary of action form (the back of SECNAV Form 1650/3) is about the same as the space for Navy evaluation or fitness report comments—that is, most of a 8.5" by 11" sheet. One is wise to begin this summary (like an evaluation) with a tone-setting opening statement and to conclude with a summary or convincing close. However, the adjectives typically used at the end of an eval or fitrep—"most strongly recommended," "my highest possible recommendation," etc.—are not as standardized in award justifications as in performance evaluations, and these phrases don't count for as much either. Instead, the board member usually focuses on the details found in the middle portion, or on *just what this person did* that might be worthy of special recognition.

Normally bullet format is appropriate for the write-up, as it is with evaluations. Indeed, you may want to borrow some of the bullet descriptions from the individual's fitrep or eval for the write-up (if any are on hand). Some of them will serve as good starting points, at least; you don't need to reinvent the wheel with every new piece of paper. In many respects the stress in evaluation write-ups and award justifications is the same: superior performance. However, besides differences in the period covered or the exact events discussed, the aims of the two kinds of documents differ subtly. The performance evaluation focuses on *potential for the future*; the award nomination on *how exceptional the past service has been.*

Rather than having to decide whether this particular first class should take on a chief's responsibilities, or this 0-5 should be made an 0-6, the awards board will be deciding whether their past accomplishments merit public recognition. Also, as too many awards cheapen any single one of them, an awards board always has standards to uphold. As a result, the board will be looking mainly to decide *the level* of the award, and usually whether to lower it from what you've recommended—only a few award nominations are bumped up.

So besides describing the accomplishments very clearly and quantifying or objectifying them in some way, in the write-up you should repeatedly *imply comparisons with the norm* and show how this particular service has been *consistently above it.*

Follow This Advice, Too

When writing for the awards board, you may assume knowledge of standard abbreviations, common terms, and even specialized terminology because the members will usually be seniors in the same chain of command and generally familiar with what their subordinates do. If the nominee had very unusual duties, you should explain those duties briefly, to make clear the nominee's special impact. The higher up the line the award package has to go for approval, the greater the need to explain unfamiliar achievements.

Length? Normally, except for very high awards or awards for valor (about which the Awards Manual has special rules), the write-up should fit on the form, with no continuations. On the other hand, several squadron and ship commanders suggest you write *at least 8–10 short bullets* per write-up, or the achievements may not come across as very strong.

How to go about the writing? Here are a few pointers.

Avoid

- generalities,
- a "job description" approach,
- excess superlatives (they tend to obscure the basis for the award).

Pursue

- an objective summary,
- specific examples,
- explicit comparisons with the standard or norm.

Stated in other terms, you should **recount specific details or achievements**, as in the following examples:

- Personally authored three TACFACTS including "S-3A Radar Offset Mining," "Acoustic Tripwire," and "Viking Chainsaw," articles lauded by seniors in the chain of command.

or

- Repaired a function generator, part of the CAT IIID test station vital to the bench operation, saving the Navy $3,800 in replacement parts and avoiding long test-bench downtime.

or

- Established effective management programs to monitor the processing of over 14,000 demands per month and the reconciliation of over 18,000 outstanding system requisitions.

And then make sure you **use quotes or other laudatory citations**:

- Was cited by COMCARDIV ONE for "extremely sound judgment and tact."

or

- The equipment was characterized by inspectors as "the best Basic Point Defense Missile System we've ever seen."

Finally, **specify comparisons** or **improvements** that the individual has made:

- Made major reductions in the error rate on fitness reports, from the traditional 35–40 percent error rate to 15–20 percent.

or

- Reduced the average time per service call from 4.6 hours to 3.5 hours in FY 87, reducing costs by 25 percent.

or

- Developed new techniques for torpedo overhaul, techniques that resulted in a 60 percent increase in torpedo production, significantly expanding the total number of available weapons for the Atlantic Fleet.

Figure 6.1 is an example of a good summary of action justifying a proposed Navy Commendation Medal. This medal is meant to be an "end-of-tour" award for a first class dental technician after a long tour of duty ashore.

As a brief summary of the advice on writing award justifications outlined above, below is another summary of action, this one a totally *fictional* justification written about a young lieutenant who supposedly writes awards justifications well. (Of course, we all know that the Navy and Marine Corps hand out awards for such qualities as leadership, organizational ability, heroism, and mission contribution, rather than for writing. However, if anyone did get an award just for writing, a good summary of action might look like the following.)

26. Summary of Action.

Lieutenant Craftsman has composed many superb award justifications during his tour as administrative officer from 15 January 1988 to 20 February 1990. In writing such justifications, he

- Always remembers to say how well the member performed, not just what he or she did (doesn't compose mere job descriptions);

Figure 6.1 A Summary of Action for an Award Nomination. Taken together, the bullets in this write-up document impressive performance.

OPNAV 1650/3 (Rev. 3-76) BACK
S/N 0107-LF-016-5015

INSTRUCTIONS

1. Before completing this form see SECNAVIST 1650.IE.
   a. Para 121 and 122 explain the preparation and submission of a recommendation.
   b. Chapter 2 contains the criteria for each award.
2. Insure all blanks are filled in and the form is dated.
3. The Summary of Action *(Item 25)* is required in all cases in addition to an attached proposed citation. *(double space)*
4. This form should be forwarded directly to the authority authorized to approve the award recommended or to the appropriate Fleet/Force CINC *(whichever is lower in the chain of command)*.

25. SUMMARY OF ACTION

Petty Officer Ortega's performance as Leading Petty Officer, Dental Equipment Repair Division, and as technical advisor for the Management Information System at Naval Dental Clinic, New Orleans merits recognition by award of the Navy Commendation Medal. His specific accomplishments from 15 May 1983 to 15 April 1988 include the following:

* Developed an accountable repair-parts inventory-control system, eliminating loss and duplication while decreasing equipment downtime.

* Established a tracking plan for Dental Equipment Work Orders that reduced trouble call response from eight days to three.

* Wrote and instituted a comprehensive user maintenance guide for equipment with a value of two million dollars.

* Initiated a reliable dental equipment replacement program to eliminate obsolete high maintenance items.

* Designed a Special Project for construction of a new dental equipment repair shop and renovation of existing Finance/Supply spaces, a project planned for FY 88 completion at a cost of approximately $100,000.

* Provided fleet dental departments with the best possible service available through constant contact with each individual ship.

* Voluntarily provided self-help installation of dental equipment of the local Dental Clinic Annex, an effort that saved the command $12,800.

* Used his computer skills to write programs for inventory and reporting of 1100 pieces of equipment, working long hours after the normal work day to complete this project.

* Wrote a supply inventory control program that reduced the supply maintenance time required by eighteen man-hours per month.

* Volunteered his time after hours to instruct supply personnel in computer operations and programming, which insured the continued development of an important computer users group. He also gave of his time and expertise in many similar circumstances.

Petty Officer Ortega's actions as a sailor and as a professional have contributed immensely to the command mission and will serve as keystones for future dental equipment repairmen. He is most enthusiastically recommended for the Navy Commendation Medal.

☆U.S. Government Printing Office: 1981—703-100/8638 2-1

- Specifies figures, dollars, or percentages when these numbers clarify the special magnitude of the service member's achievement;
- Makes explicit comparisons with the standard or norm, showing how the performance has conspicuously surpassed that normally expected of the individual's rank/rate and time in service;
- Delineates specific improvements the service member has brought about by comparing the results of the service members work with what went before;
- Cites praise from commanders and other authorities whenever possible, quoting the actual words used where those words shed light on the individual's performance;
- Takes special care to highlight personal initiative, voluntary work, and service beyond the call of duty;
- Remembers to cite several specific examples of the individual's performance (including names, dates, and places), giving the readers a good general feel for this individual's unique accomplishments;
- Always ensures the level of award is appropriate for service rendered and that the justification supports the recommended level of the award.

Truthful and objective, Lieutenant Craftsman takes care to delete excess superlatives and never writes just to snow the awards board. Rather, he makes sure to manifest, as well as possible, the actual achievements of the recommended individual. For the consistent care he takes, the clarity of his written justifications, and his success in helping board members recognize truly superior service (and only that), Lieutenant Craftsman clearly merits the Navy Wordsmith Award.

A Case Study: The Guantanamo Bay Training Group Case

To further exemplify the process of justification writing and to show something of its typical context too, here is a case study involving an actual award nomination. We've changed the name of the officer involved, but not the basic circumstances. The case study's subject is how to enhance a write-up, *just by remembering what made the achievement so special.*

The Situation

A commander at the Fleet Training Group in Guantanamo Bay told one of the lieutenants to write himself up for a Navy Commendation Medal.

For many reasons, having your subordinate write his or her own award nomination is not a good idea. Not only can it encourage self-justification and, therefore, prove awkward for a fittingly humble service member, but it also suggests that the superior really doesn't know enough (or care enough) to do the recommendation personally. Moreover, it can ultimately prove disappointing to the person you're recommending, as many

On Writing Your Own Award—An Opinion

I have some strong opinions on "writing up your own award." Absolutely, positively, never, never! Every award should be a surprise; the intended recipient should be completely blind to the whole process.

Consider it this way. "Hey, Joe, you're a good guy, how about writing yourself up for the Medal of Honor? I don't really know all of what you've been doing 'cause I'm too busy flapping about other stuff or playing golf [to pay attention to you], but you deserve a medal. Don't worry, I'll make sure you get taken care of."

Later: "Gee, Joe, I guess you're really disappointed about that letter of commendation you got from the admiral after we had discussed getting you a nice medal. Well, maybe they just didn't read between the lines enough. We sent in your write-up pretty much unchanged because we figured you had the best view on what you did. Well, don't worry, it's fitreps and not medals that count, anyway."

Now how does the guy feel? If he had never known what he was being considered for, he wouldn't have been disappointed. Awards are often downgraded, so if you don't tell him he's being put in for a Navy Comm, he won't be upset that he got only a Navy Achievement Medal.

Evaluations are different. The guy will see those in the final form. Here too I never ask my people to write their own, for many of the same reasons outlined above, but I do ask them for inputs, preferably in the form of bullets I can use directly. If the guy wants to write the whole thing, great; but since I sign it, I will edit it—it's never a straight shot from him to signature, even if I just change the "happys" to "glads."

—Navy Commander

award nominations are disapproved or downgraded after being submitted. Not least in importance, having a subordinate write up his or her own flies directly in the face of official policy as outlined in the Awards Manual, which says not to disclose recommendations for awards either to the recommended individual or to the next of kin.

This particular story, however, concerns the lieutenant who was asked, not the commander doing the asking. Faced with this request, and believing his service had indeed merited the award (though feeling a good deal of awkwardness about it all), he went ahead and typed up the cover sheet, and then composed a summary of action and citation. The summary of action he turned in appears as Figure 6.2.

Believing himself worthy, and having written up his achievements in such a way, Lieutenant North was greatly surprised when he heard later that he would receive a Navy Achievement Medal while another lieutenant, who in his opinion had not done nearly as much, would receive a Navy Commendation Medal. His command's administrative officer later informed him that his write-up simply had not been strong enough.

Figure 6.2 Summary of Action for an Award that Got Downgraded. Not all Lieutenant North's achievements got into this summary.

OPNAV 1650/3 (Rev. 3-76) BACK
S/N 0107-LF-016-5015

INSTRUCTIONS

1. Before completing this form see SECNAVIST 1650.IE.
   a. Para 121 and 122 explain the preparation and submission of a recommendation.
   b. Chapter 2 contains the criteria for each award.
2. Insure all blanks are filled in and the form is dated.
3. The Summary of Action *(Item 25)* is required in all cases in addition to an attached proposed citation. *(double space)*
4. This form should be forwarded directly to the authority authorized to approve the award recommended or to the appropriate Fleet/Force CINC *(whichever is lower in the chain of command)*.

25. SUMMARY OF ACTION

During the period from 30 July 1985 to 31 July 1987 Lieutenant North consistently performed his demanding duties as Gas Turbine Branch Head in an exceptional and outstanding manner. As the senior gas turbine engineer at Fleet Training Group, he was responsible for the Propulsion Systems training on all LANTFLT gas turbine units conducting refresher or shakedown training. Volunteering for the additional responsibilities of command Reserve Training Coordinator, he aggressively pursued a set of initiatives enhancing the utilization of assigned reservists. Lieutenant North's success in this area was evidenced by numerous laudatory remarks and comments by members of the reserve force as well as representatives of COMNAV-SURFRESFOR and COMTRALANT. Specific accomplishments during this tour include:

--Supervised the engineering training of 32 LANTFLT gas-turbine ships

--Qualified as Senior Engineering Instructor for DD 963/DDG 993/CG 47-class ships

--Performed duties as Training Liaison Officer on seven LANTFLT ships, receiving numerous letters of appreciation from commanding officers

--Designated Master Training Specialist

--Oversaw the development of Instructor Professional Qualification Standards (PQS) for the Gas Turbine Branch that then became the model for the development of Instructor PQS for all other branches of FLETRAGRU

--Represented Fleet Training Group at the 1986 and 1987 CINCLANTFLT PEB conferences

--Managed the training program for 246 selected reservists performing ACDUTRA at FLETRAGRU

--Researched, organized, and updated mobilization plans and requirements

--Planned, organized, and conducted two successful Reserve Training Conferences for FLETRAGRU reserve detachment commanding officers

"But I just told them what I did," was his reply, "and they know many of these jobs themselves, how important they are. Besides that, the other fellow hyped his collateral duty, and I purposely played down mine—I didn't want it to overshadow the gas turbine engineering work."

Despite Lieutenant North's feelings, judging only by the justification, the board might have been right. Many aspects of the lieutenant's accomplishments, factors that explained the quality or magnitude of his performance, had failed to come out in the write-up. (This deficiency turned out to have been especially important, since on the day the awards board met, no one from his own department could attend the board.)

Later, Lieutenant North recalled that the commander had asked for his input during a heavy work period; Lieutenant North had had no time to set the write-up aside for two to three days and revise it. He had put it together at home, at night, and hadn't revised it after that; he was in the midst of a heavy ship-riding schedule at work. Had he had time to work on it again—and he would have *found* the time, had it been for someone other than himself—the board's vote might have been different.

With some assistance from an expert writer, Lieutenant North sat down much later and considered ways in which he might have clarified the special quality of his work. Below is a detailed commentary as to how, by explaining his varied achievements, he could have substantially improved the write-up.

Discussion of Lieutenant North's Award Write-Up

INTRODUCTION

The introduction in the write-up does little to set the tone for the whole report, includes some unhelpful standard navalese—"pursued a set of initiatives enhancing the utilization of"—and is too long. Readers of justifications tend to be impatient with long paragraphs of introduction, and the subject does not justify the length of the introduction since every item it brings up also appears later in the bullets.

ACCOMPLISHMENTS

The set of accomplishments is the key section of the justification comments. Lieutenant North's effort is not especially well formatted, and it could use some <u>underlining</u> or **bold-facing** for emphasis. But it does use bullet format, puts the bullets in proper parallel grammatical structure, and makes no errors. The key issue is **what is said**. Let's go through it line by line.

- "Supervised the engineering training of 32 LANTFLT gas-turbine ships." This phrase is simply a "job description," and a very skimpy one at that. Yes, the board members probably have a general idea of what these duties involve. But most of them will have no idea of all the specifics and, more importantly, will not appreciate *how well* he performed the job. In a sense, Lieutenant North lost out from the beginning by failing to describe in any detail at all *how well* he performed his primary duty.
- "Qualified as Senior Engineering Instructor for DD 963/DDG 993/CG 47-class ships." The interview revealed that this qualifica-

tion was not a requirement but a voluntary achievement on Lieutenant North's part. Again, the vital aim of award write-ups is to show unusual, "head and shoulders" behavior, so you must take full advantage of opportunities like this one. The following revision is both truthful and persuasive:

At his own initiative, and even though his billet did not require it, he qualified as Senior Engineering Instructor for DD 963/DDG 993/CG 47-class ships. Moreover, he qualified in only four months, rather than the usual eight.

- "Performed duties as Training Liaison Officer on seven LANTFLT ships, receiving numerous letters of appreciation from commanding officers." We are left in the dark as to what those duties were, how difficult, and, again, how well performed. The write-up does tell us he received commendations for them. How much to elaborate on these duties is a judgment call, but *at the very least* he might have named the ships whose COs wrote letters of appreciation. If he could name three or four specific vessels and even cite key lines from those letters, this phrase wouldn't be a throwaway line (as it almost is now) but a strong justification.
- "Designated Master Training Specialist." Lieutenant North assumed that the board knew what this entailed. After all, the same board that approved awards also approved designations, and several months earlier it had approved his. But he forgot that the specific accomplishments that caused them to approve this designation *then* were not spelled out in writing *now* before the board. Moreover, by not elaborating on what this designation meant, he lost the opportunity to keep the wagon train moving—to show *in every accomplishment* how superior his performance has been. He could have added significant details, summing up with something like this statement:

For these achievements he was singled out as an expert in training and earned the designation "Master Training Specialist."

- "Oversaw the development of Instructor Personal Qualification Standards (PQS) for the Gas Turbine Branch which then became the model for the development of Instructor PQS for all other branches of FLETRAGRU." Lieutenant North reports that he had worked some time on this particular sentence, to see that the value of this achievement came through. And certainly, this is the best sentence in all the summary of action. It indicates that here, at least, Lieutenant North forges ahead and sets the standards for the whole group. Still, the interview with Lieutenant North revealed that the circumstances were even more impressive, as suggested in the changes below:

. . . which the group commander personally judged so superior as to make them models for the development of Instructor PQS for all other branches of FLETRAGRU.

- "Represented Fleet Training Group at the 1986 and 1987 CINCLANTFLT PEB conferences." Again, remember to say *how*, or you've just penned another job description. Additional detail, gleaned from the interview, clarifies the accomplishment here:

Represented the Fleet Training Group superbly at the 1986 and 1987 CINC-LANTFLT PEB conferences, despite being the only 0-3 among 0-4s, 0-5s and 0-6s.

- "Served as Officer in Charge of Training Readiness Team sent to the Dominican Republic." This statement needs more specifics—why he was sent, to begin with. The details added below (discovered in the interview) showcase senior officers' confidence in this officer's soundness of judgment.

. . . sent to the Dominican Republic to evaluate the condition of one of the Republic's patrol boats and its readiness to go through FLETRAGRU training. His assessment that the boat was "unsafe to steam" and his list of recommended improvements were accepted in full by the Dominican Navy and immediately implemented by FLETRAGRU."

- "Managed the training program for 246 selected reservists performing ACDUTRA at FLETRAGRU," etc., to the end. The lieutenant thought, on reflection, that he could have expanded the reserve program management by itself into many more bullets. As originally written, it simply does not support strong medal recognition. That he managed a training program for reservists, did some research, and "successfully" ran two conferences doesn't say an awful lot. The reported laudatory comments mentioned in the introduction (which the readers have probably forgotten by the time they read this far) are much too vague to impress. He could have done a great deal here; let a revision to the final sentence suffice:

Single-handedly planned, organized, and conducted two highly successful Reserve Training Conferences for 50 reserve unit commanding officers and training officers, 0-3 to 0-6. In total charge of every aspect of the conferences, LT North earned highly laudatory comments not only from the reservists themselves but also from representatives of COMNAVSURFRESFOR and COMTRALANT.

CONCLUSION

Although summary comments are not as important in award nominations as they are in fitreps and evals, a strong conclusion can help board members decide what to think about what they have just read. A board may interpret the omission of that conclusion as the command's "sending a signal," because it is so seldom done. Here's a possible concluding statement:

In summary, LT North's service to FLETRAGRU has been highlighted by superb technical knowledge, the utmost of professionalism, and tireless effort. His achievements have always been so far above the norm as to be characteristic of officers far more senior than he. His truly exceptional service would be most fittingly recognized by award of the Navy Commendation Medal.

Of course, not all of the above would fit in a page-long justification statement, but having developed the subject in such a thorough way, you would have more than enough to put together a most impressive justification. With such improvements further cut and crafted to fit the write-up sheet, Figure 6.3 presents a fully descriptive version of the write-up.

Figure 6.3 A Revised Summary of Action. This summary revises and upgrades Figure 6.2 by adding key information, structuring it so as to catch the eye.

OPNAV 1650/3 (Rev. 3-76) BACK
S/N 0107-LF-016-5015

INSTRUCTIONS

1. Before completing this form see SECNAVIST 1650.IE.
   a. Para 121 and 122 explain the preparation and submission of a recommendation.
   b. Chapter 2 contains the criteria for each award.
2. Insure all blanks are filled in and the form is dated.
3. The Summary of Action *(Ite 25)* is required in all cases in addition to an attached proposed cita...n. *(double space)*
4. This form should be forwarded directly to the authority authorized to approve the award recommended or to the appropriate Fleet/Force CINC *(whichever is lower in the chain of command)*.

25. SUMMARY OF ACTION

During the period 30 July 1985 to 31 July 1987, Lieutenant North consistently distinguished himself in his primary duty as Gas Turbine Branch Head, and also performed exceptionally in a wide variety of collateral and voluntary duties. In this work he:

• Supervised superbly all the engineering training of 32 LANTFLT gas-turbine ships, from each ship's Day*1 Safety Check to its final OPPE Certification.

• Qualified as Senior Engineering Instructor for DD 963/DDG 993/CG 47 class ships although not required by his billet, qualifying in just 4 months rather than the usual 8.

• Performed duties as Training Liaison Officer on seven LANTFLT ships, receiving LOAs from the COs of the COMTE DE GRASSE (DD 974), STUMP (DD 978), and PREBLE (DDG 46).

• Oversaw the development of Instructor PQS for the Gas Turbine Branch. The group commander made this training package the model for all other branches of FLETRAGRU.

• Represented FLETRAGRU superbly at the 1986 and 1987 CINCLANTFLT PEB conferences.

• Served as OINC of the Training Readiness Team sent to the Dominican Republic to evaluate the readiness of a patrol boat to undergo FLETRAGRU training. His assessment that the boat was "unsafe to steam" and his list of recommended improvements were accepted in full by the Dominican Navy and immediately implemented by FLETRAGRU.

• Single-handedly planned, organized, and conducted two highly successful Reserve Training Conferences for 50 reserve unit officers, O-3 to O-6. For this voluntary duty, LT North earned highly laudatory comments not only from the reservists themselves, but from representatives of both COMNAVSURFRESFOR and COMTRALANT.

• Was designated "Master Training Specialist" by board action for excellence in training.

In summary, LT North's service to FLETRAGRU has been highlighted by superb technical knowledge, the utmost of professionalism, and tireless effort. His truly exceptional service would be most fittingly recognized by award of the Navy Commendation Medal.

☆U.S. Government Printing Office: 1981—703-100/8638 2-1

One Final Comment

What about the morality of this "enhancement"—should we really be tooting our own horns like this? Couldn't this rewriting be seen as promoting slick verbal skills when we ought to be getting rid of inflated language, not promoting it?

One answer, at least for award writing, is that awards by their very nature reward superior performance—and the description of the events should mirror such superior quality. But ideally, as suggested above, *the facts themselves* will impress readers and listeners. The words, when well used, serve primarily as windows through which the readers can glimpse the real achievement. Fortunately, because it puts the accomplishments center stage, bullet format has decreased the importance of mere verbal skills.

Of course, inflation can still be a problem. Command initiative is vital here, both in toning down comments when necessary and in deciding who deserves awards in the first place. In any case, the proof of good award nominations and of the writing of nominations is in their moral *effects*.

If the process succeeds, and by means of the writing it singles out *actual merit*, the best performers are then receiving support and recognition. Their morale improves because they see that you reward the good work they do. Others around them, acknowledging the justice of the awards, tend to emulate the behavior that you've so highly commended.

On the other hand, if the recipient does *not* really merit the award, if the truth has taken a back seat to politics or cronyism or just self-centered campaigning (including inflating your own or another's achievements in type)—then morale disintegrates. The commanding officer of a destroyer, on returning from a deployment, complained to his commodore that he hadn't received an award while the skipper of a ship that had gone aground during that same deployment had gotten one. So the commodore gave him an award. But all the destroyer's officers knew the circumstances, and also knew that the skipper had honored few of the crew. As a result, the occasion of the ship's award ceremony—held strictly to hand out that one medal to the Captain—was not a positive one.

The Citation

Write the Citation for a Non-Navy Audience

The citation's audience is very different from the justification's. While the nominee and shipmates will listen to the citation at an awards ceremony, other listeners may include children, spouses, other relatives, and friends, many of whom will have little or no naval background. So use very few abbreviations and no acronyms; leave out technical jargon; make the citation so clear that it can *stand alone*, without requiring an expert to explain the details. As you draft the citation, imagine a civilian relative or friend listening as you commend the awardee, and try to speak to *that* person.

Since it has to be short (usually 15 lines or less, according to the Awards Manual), the best idea is to focus on two or three major accomplishments. Normally the exact wording of the beginning and end is specified. The creativity comes in the middle of this document, in giving the readers a sense of the *real accomplishment*.

Keep the attention of this lay audience by citing a few impressive details. As best you can, write so almost anyone can appreciate some major aspects, at least, of what the Marine or sailor has done.

Don't Try to Impress with Language

One of the chief mistakes citation writers make is to try to impress with language, by using lots of pretentious adjectives and bureaucratese. The write-up should be relatively *formal*, yes—but formal doesn't mean *deadly*. Do we really want to put family members to sleep by telling them how their loved one "initiated and implemented" something? Or "developed, coordinated, and executed" something else, even if he or she did it in "an exemplary and professional manner?" Doublings (and triplings!) are the special sins of citation writers. Be on the lookout for tiresome, long-winded, and pretentious ("boiler-plated") phrases such as:

— paragon of success
— pinnacle of recruiting quality and proficiency
— highlighted the culmination of
— in a timely manner
— coordinated the planning to upgrade
— was instrumental in the preparation and revision of
— the driving force in the implementation of
— to maximize utilization of available assets
— initiating and implementing an efficient, effective, and accountable organization to gain the necessary visibility and control during . . .
— contributed materially to the success
— had a profound influence on the efficiency and effectiveness of

This list is literally endless.

By using fresh and natural language, make your statement crisp, to the point, and hard-hitting. Keep to the facts, and as much as possible *let the facts impress by themselves* rather than requiring the crutch of adjectives and adverbs.

Follow These Dos and Don'ts

Don't use jargon, be overly technical, or use abbreviations that will be unfamiliar to a civilian. Don't write statements like:

- Performed timely recalibration of the MK 113 MOD 9 FCS.
- Corrected several difficult problems in the MK3 MOD 7 Ships Inertial Navigation System (SINS) and the AN/URN-20 TACAN, and

completely overhauled and tested all 40 SINS aircraft alignment output terminals.

- Performed superbly through a Middle East Deployment, SRA, Operational Propulsion Plant Examinations, NTPI, DNSI, Command Inspection, and INSURV. (Instead, write "Performed superbly during a six-month deployment to the Middle East and several major ship inspections.")

And Don't specify items only of interest to those at your duty station. They won't care that you repaired "NR 1 High-Pressure Air Dehydrator, Numbers 1 and 2 High-Pressure Air Compressor, NR 2 Distilling Plant Heater Condenser, NR 2 Sewage Plant Incinerator," and so on.

Do follow the guidelines in the following checklist:

- Be specific enough to get across some sense of what the individual has actually achieved.
- Make all details interesting and intelligible for a civilian audience.
- Write the first sentence exactly as specified in the Awards Manual for the particular type or level of award.
- Vary sentence style—don't always begin with the subject.
- Write the entire citation in the simple past tense ("improved," not "has improved"; "was responsible," not "has been responsible").
- Always use the third person, i.e., "he" or "she" rather than "you" (this rule differs from some letters of commendation/appreciation).
- Use the individual's name only in the heading, the second sentence, and the last sentence of the citation.
- Make certain the spelling of the full name is correct, including, "Jr.," "III," etc., as needed.
- Spell out the rank or rate. (See Awards Manual and local instructions for further guidance on "Petty Officer Smith" rather than "Petty Officer Second Class Smith," etc.)
- Capitalize the entirety of any ship's name, and use a ship's designation in parentheses the first time (no hyphen between ship and number), i.e., USS MISSOURI (BB 63).
- Make sure all ship and command names and numbers are exactly right.
- Read the basic instruction, the Navy and Marine Corps Awards Manual (SECNAVINST 1650.1), and follow the format found there.
- Find and follow the guidance of the local command, the type commander, or any other relevant authority.

Finally, Remember All Those You're Talking to—and *For How Long*

The citation, beyond almost any other kind of Navy writing, is an eminently public document. In addition to friends and family members, you are also speaking in the citation both to the service member you're honoring—who will appreciate accuracy—and to shipmates of that service member. The latter will also appreciate their shipmate's genuine accomplishments but will notice when you're stretching the facts.

Moreover, the citation will have a very long life. Think of it framed, and gracing the wall of the service member's office or home for years. Then write it so it's worthy of such a place.

For Example

Below are two good citations, good because they are specific and because the achievements narrated are understandable and impressive. The first (based on an example in a Marine Corps instruction) is meant to be a citation for a Navy Achievement Medal. In this case, the medal would be given out for a single noteworthy accomplishment.

The Secretary of the Navy takes pleasure in presenting a Gold Star in Lieu of the Second NAVY ACHIEVEMENT MEDAL to

SERGEANT JONATHAN ARTHUR BROWN
UNITED STATES MARINE CORPS

for service as set forth in the following
CITATION:

"For professional achievement in the superior performance of his duties while serving as Battalion Armorer, 3d Combat Engineer Battalion, 2d Marine Division, Fleet Marine Force, Atlantic, from 11 March 1981 through 8 July 1982. During this period Sergeant BROWN devised an improved system of field firing for the M-60 machine gun, which made it possible to employ the inexpensive .22-caliber round instead of the much more expensive 7.62-mm standard ammunition. His inventiveness resulted in the savings of $.05 per round of ammunition expended, with an overall annual savings of $105,000 at the parent command alone. Service-wide adoption is being considered and would result in an impressive cost reduction for training ammunition throughout the Department of Defense. Sergeant BROWN's exceptional professional ability, initiative, and inventiveness have reflected great credit upon himself, the Marine Corps, and the United States Naval Service."

For the Secretary of the Navy

As a second example, the citation below graced a Navy Commendation Medal to the Navy dental technician whose justification appears as Figure 6.1. This medal was an end-of-tour award, and so the citation touches on just a few of the petty officer's many important accomplishments.

The Secretary of the Navy takes pleasure in presenting the NAVY COMMENDATION MEDAL to

RONALD L. ORTEGA
DENTAL TECHNICIAN FIRST CLASS

for service as set forth in the following
CITATION:

"For meritorious service while serving as the Leading Petty Officer, Dental Equipment Repair Division, and as Management Information System technical advisor at Naval Dental Clinic, New Orleans, Louisiana, from 15 May 1983 to 15 April 1988. Petty Officer Ortega consistently provided dental equipment repair services of the very highest quality to commands throughout the New Orleans area. Among many other accomplishments, he used his expertise in computers to develop an unprecedented tracking system for a two-million-dollar equipment inventory, and he reduced supply maintenance time by eighteen work hours per month. His volunteered technical expertise saved the command $12,800 on a project to modernize a dental facility, and he successfully promoted the building of a dental equipment repair shop. Petty Officer Ortega's exceptional achievements and total devotion to duty reflected credit upon himself and were in keeping with the highest traditions of the United States Naval Service."

For the Secretary of the Navy

The Letter & the Certificate of Commendation

Navy letters of commendation (LOCs) and Marine Corps certificates of commendation, although not personal decorations, do often carry with them material benefits. They can add to the multiple for selection through E-6, and enlisted selection boards often take them into account, especially if flag officers sign them. So they carry weight in advancement proceedings, in addition to simply being valued as expressions of approval.

Two Different Formats and Styles

The format and, to a degree, the style of letters of commendation vary. Sometimes they are on official parchment complete with seal, command's heading, and other graphics. At other times, they are in standard-letter format. When formalized, they usually resemble award citations—you write them in the third person and past tense and use specified openings and conclusions. Below is an example of a formal citation from a flag officer:

COMMANDER SUBMARINE FORCE
UNITED STATES ATLANTIC FLEET

The Commander Submarine Force, U.S. Atlantic Fleet
takes pleasure in commending
MACHINIST'S MATE FIRST CLASS
FREDERICK R. SUNDER, III
UNITED STATES NAVY
for service as set forth in the following
CITATION

"For professional achievement in the superior performance of his duties while serving as Assistant Shift Officer in Charge of the Steam Generator Inspection Team in USS TENDER (AS 99) from May to October 1988. Petty Officer SUNDER consistently performed his demanding duties in a highly professional manner. As a direct result of his painstaking technical supervision, TENDER inspected and repaired the primary sides of two steam generators on board USS ATTACK (SSN 999), a tended unit of Commander Submarine Squadron UMPTEEN. Because of his tireless efforts, this complex task was completed five days ahead of schedule, considerably below the projected cost, and without mishap. Petty Officer SUNDER's exceptional professional abilities, initiative, and loyal devotion to duty reflect great credit upon himself and the United States Naval Service."

[Signed]
Vice Admiral, U.S. Navy
Commander Submarine Force
U.S. Atlantic Fleet

This document (when printed on parchment with seal, Submarine Force Insignia, etc.) is appropriate for formal presentation. The write-up presents Sunder's repair of the generators clearly and impressively.

Write the Formal Letter of Commendation Just Like an Award Citation

When writing these formal documents, follow the same guidance given earlier about award citations: write to a lay audience; avoid hackneyed phrases; describe clearly a few specific, impressive accomplishments; and forgo all jargon and acronyms. Your command may decide to present this letter at meritorious mast or on another formal occasion with friends and family present. Do your best to get across a sense of *the actual achievement.*

Figure 6.4 An Informal Letter of Commendation. An officer in charge commends a sailor freshly and naturally.

DEPARTMENT OF THE NAVY
U. S. NAVY PERSONNEL SUPPORT ACTIVITY DETACHMENT
MISAWA, JAPAN
APO SAN FRANCISCO 96519-0006

1650
Ser 00/841
30 Sep 87

From: Officer in Charge, U.S. Navy Personnel Support Activity Detachment, Misawa
To: PN1 ______ _. _________, USN

Subj: LETTER OF COMMENDATION

1. With great pleasure I commend you on your selection as U.S. Navy Personnel Support Activity Detachment, Misawa's Sailor of the Quarter from 1 July to 30 September 1987.

2. The professional and personal traits that have led to your distinction are numerous. Above all, you have managed busy, pressure-filled days with maturity and grace, and used quieter times to find innovative ways to improve efficiency. As the man "on the front line," you often provide the first impression customers develop about PERSUPPDET Misawa. Customers consistently comment on their appreciation for your outstanding courtesy and patience, and their respect for your professional advice, information, and quick actions on their behalf. Your attention to detail is daily evident in the reports and messages you prepare without discrepancies. You have shown great initiative in designing new ways to improve reporting procedures and keep communication flowing well within the detachment.

3. Your unflagging professionalism has been an inspiration to us all. Well done!

J. GARZONE

Be More Personable in Informal Letters of Commendation

To be somewhat more personal and expressive, commanders will often loosen formality just a bit in such letters by using the second person, "you," and by varying from strict past tense.

The officer who wrote the letter in Figure 6.4 commends the sailor on his selection as sailor of the quarter. The details she cites are subtle ones, harder to "objectify" than many other achievements, yet they can be very important to a "customer-oriented" military unit. The activities commended here are not all in the past; the use of past perfect and some present tense suggests the sailor's good works are still going on.

Figure 6.5 A Letter of Appreciation. This brief letter does well at praising a team of Marines.

DEPARTMENT OF THE NAVY

COMMANDER NAVAL SURFACE FORCE
UNITED STATES ATLANTIC FLEET
NORFOLK, VIRGINIA 23511-6292

1650
Ser 00W/00193
11 Jan 88

From: Commander, Naval Surface Force, U.S. Atlantic Fleet
To: Commanding Officer, Marine Corps Security Force Battalion
Via: Commander, Naval Base Norfolk

Subj: LETTER OF APPRECIATION

1. The performance of the saluting battery during the COMNAVSURFLANT Change of Command ceremony on 30 December 1987 was marked by cooperation and professionalism. The battery's performance and crisp military bearing made this group perfect representatives of the Marine Corps during this important ceremony. Many remarks were made on their impressive performance.

2. Please convey to Corporal ________ and the battery a job well done.

The Letter of Appreciation

Writing a letter of appreciation (LOA) is a way to express thanks, and sometimes to call another commander's attention to the good job his or her people have done for you. The letter carries with it no points, multipliers, or other helps to advancement, nothing but simple thanks and good will.

The Correspondence Manual gives some good advice on how to write such a letter. It begins by quoting this line from an LOA: "AD1 John Smith did a superb job during our recent engine change." Then the Correspondence Manual goes on to comment: "This is the first sentence of a thank-you letter to Smith's supervisor. Notice that it avoids a slow buildup. The second paragraph described Smith's long hours, careful trouble-shooting, and determined search for parts. The last paragraph read, 'Please thank AD1 Smith for all his extra effort.' This three-paragraph formula will keep your thank-you letters short, detailed, and focused on the person being praised."

We'll show two examples, which vary only slightly from this pattern. Each is effective in its own way. Figure 6.5, to the commanding officer of a Marine Corps corporal and his men, probably didn't take much time to write, but it does its job smartly—as smartly as the performance of the battery that it commends.

The letter below tells an airman—an AMEAN is an aviation structural mechanic equipment airman—that the commanding officer himself took notice of the airman's good work. Written to a junior enlisted man at a very impressionable period of his naval career, the letter is likely to spur him on to more work of the same and even higher quality. Although the letter is very formal, the commander's sincerity still comes through.

1650
00/150
24 NOV 87

From: Commanding Officer, Attack Squadron THREE ZERO FOUR
To: AMEAN Jeffery Grant, USNR, 549-49-6017

Subj: LETTER OF APPRECIATION

1. On 6 October 1987, while performing a routine turnaround inspection, you discovered a three-inch structural crack in the starboard wheel well of aircraft 407. You promptly reported it to maintenance control, which grounded the aircraft for an in-depth inspection.

2. While the crack was not considered a safety-of-flight structural defect, you exercised sound professional judgment in reporting it. Had this discrepancy been more severe, your sharp eyes and attention to detail might have prevented a mishap.

3. Maintenance men of your caliber are crucial to the safety of naval aviation. Your very commendable action was in keeping with the best of Firebird spirit and the highest standards of maintenance professionals. Thank you for a job well done.

D. R. KESTLY

As with other letters of thanks (see the section on thank-you letters in chapter 2), you should strive to be genuine in an LOA and avoid the appearance of writing just because you feel you ought to. For the very reason that a naval letter of appreciation usually carries no institutional reward, it will mean little unless the recipient perceives it as conveying sincere thanks.

Naval Contests

To end this chapter, let's look for a moment at a related area—special awards that the naval services have established, both for individuals and units. While we have no space here to discuss unit awards, we can look at a good example of a nomination for an individual award.

The kind of writing recommended above for standard naval awards—*clear writing* pointed by *strong evidence*—works here too. The nomination presented below is especially well written. The accomplishments are clearly described and most impressive, so impressive that the officer recommended won the Vice Admiral Batchelder Award for that year (in the "small ship" competitive category). Winning the award was due both to the lieutenant's performance and to that of the outstanding writer who drafted the nomination.

The nomination's author commented that he purposely touched on several different areas of accomplishment, to show the nominee's well-roundedness. This approach also helped him to avoid technical jargon that would have slowed the reader down. While impressive details stud the recommendation, the author leaves the most stunning accomplishment for the very end.

LT R___'s performance of duty, leadership, and overall support of this command have been extraordinary. His individual contribution to the supply and operational readiness of this fast attack nuclear submarine has been superlative. Significant specific items highlighting his performance are below:

- Completed an extensive 15-month Integrated Logistics Overhaul (ILO), including significant combat system and nuclear propulsion plant configuration changes. He backloaded the ship's repair parts in only three weeks with a 99+ percent validity.
- Took personal charge of identifying and correcting potential supply support problems as the ship neared the end of overhaul, particularly ensuring COSAL support of several significant ship's systems. In conjunction with this effort, he personally ensured that the entire ship was stowed exactly per plan—an accomplishment unmatched in the Pacific Fleet.
- Prepared, opened, and operated the ship's galley at an extraordinarily high level of efficiency, despite frequent short-fuse demands of shift-work to support major overhaul events and a severe shortage of mess management specialists.
- Completed Supply Corps Officer Submarine qualifications, an intensive, demanding, and rigorous professional milestone.
- Established a highly effective training program for both MS and SK Divisions and the ship's RPPOs. Additionally, he provided quality supply input to officer training.
- As the ship's most proficient and professional Diving Officer of the Watch, was assigned to conduct the first dive after overhaul and the first dive to test depth. His performance during these most significant postoverhaul tests was superb.
- Worked diligently to achieve the NAVSEA 08 requirement of 100 percent nuclear (Q) COSAL on board to support the extensive nuclear reactor critical test program. In particular, he achieved this goal without any need to transfer material from any other activities.

LT R___ is clearly a most effective and professional Supply Officer. His exceptional work is best measured by the results of the ship's most recent COMSUBPAC Supply Management Inspection: a perfect score of EIGHT OUTSTANDING GRADES, an achievement unmatched in many years. He clearly merits selection for the Vice Admiral Batchelder Award.

The best ideas in the world are worthless if you can't communicate them.

—Speechwriter for SECNAV

7

Speaking and Briefing

Few professions need effective speakers as vitally as the military. The reason is partly the military's emphasis on leadership. In so many forums—a leading petty officer's speaking to the people at quarters, a young officer's addressing his or her first unit, a commander's briefing of a combat mission—the ability to speak effectively is vital both to mission and morale.

Superiors must speak to their troops in greatly varied circumstances, from such informal settings as speaking to the crew on the public address system to formal occasions like awards presentations, promotion ceremonies, and changes of commands. In all these cases a commander can make a pronounced effect simply by good verbal presentation. Disraeli said, "Men govern with words." A service member makes a good start at the talent of leadership simply by learning to speak effectively.

Somewhat less obvious is the need for good speakers on staffs. Some senior staff people are highly visible—those who must make the case for military appropriations before Congress, for example. Clearly, their presentations can have wide-reaching effects, both in getting support for specific programs and in giving the naval services a good or bad image. As a former Marine Corps Commandant, General Robert H. Barrow, once commented,

> If you are testifying before Congress on Capitol Hill, if you speak to the senators or the congressmen effectively . . . they conclude that the Marine Corps has good leadership at the top because of the way you come across to them. They think, "This guy must be a good leader because I asked him tough questions and he was forceful and straightforward and forthrightly gave me those answers." On the other hand, if you go out and mumble around, they may never say it, but somehow deep in them they think, "Is that guy a Marine? Is that what Marines are like?"
>
> —*Naval Leadership: Voices of Experience*, Annapolis: Naval Institute Press, 1987, p. 60.

But besides such public spokesmen, there are untold myriads on staffs who must brief their superiors daily. They must prepare informational briefings, decision briefings, reports on deployments, and briefs on the state of a command, to name just a few important occasions. If they don't do all these jobs well, the Navy and Marine Corps suffer, either from not having crucial programs approved or simply from not functioning well as armed services.

"Of 15–20 memos I wrote for CNO, two or three were successful in being persuasive. A visit or a phone call or an in-person contact of some kind is the best way to persuade—it has much more effect than writing. You can put a note on the bottom of a written document—'I'd like to talk to you about this.' Face-to-face, before or after he reads it—that's the best way to persuade."—Commander, speechwriter for CNO

Service members (especially commanders) must also learn how to speak to the public, including local community leaders and the news media, to name just two likely public audiences. To an important extent, the ability of senior Navy and Marine Corps officers to communicate to the public the need for a strong national defense helps determine the national will.

Clearly, in all of these areas, verbal facility can be crucial.

Yet, important as it is, we pay far too little attention to the ability to speak well. College educations usually ignore it, for example, and officer accession programs often give it little more than lip service. If you're prudent, you'll recognize the omission and take steps to enhance your speaking ability. Here are some principles to help you begin.

Speaking in the Military

General Guidance

When you speak as a military representative, the first matters you should attend to are physical—your personal appearance, general assurance, stance, gestures, and eye contact. All of these factors can affect the delivery of your talk, its effectiveness, and your own feelings about speaking.

Be Smart in Personal Appearance

Make sure your uniform and overall appearance are top-notch. The standard sprucing up is even more important than usual. You'll be the center of attention of a whole group for several minutes, not, as in a personnel inspection, for just a few seconds in front of one inspecting officer. A cleaned and pressed uniform, haircut, shined shoes, straight name tag, and bright rather than faded ribbons—we naturally expect any military representative to look sharp in all these ways.

Knowing you look sharp can help you think sharply too, or at least keep you from getting sidetracked. Worrying that you really need a new pair of shoes can drain your confidence. You don't need any more distractions than are already present in any speech situation.

Speaking with Confidence

"We think we got what we thought we were required to come up with. . . ."

—from the remarks of a student leader in a recent Navy course

Be Confident—and *Never Apologize*

Almost everyone is nervous before giving a speech, even when long accustomed to speaking in public. But remember, no matter how nervous you feel, often none of your listeners can tell that you're nervous just by looking at you. Even if your voice quavers a bit, people in the audience will often simply ignore it, thinking you speak that way normally. Whatever you do, *never apologize* for being nervous or in any other way draw overt attention to your heightened emotions. Doing so will make the audience aware of your feelings and perhaps begin to make them feel uncomfortable, and their uneasiness in turn will upset your own confidence.

Anyway, your nervousness will usually die down as you get into your talk. So adopt a pose of confidence even if you don't feel very confident at the moment. Don't talk in a mumble or whisper, but speak in a strong voice, and enunciate clearly—a little extra enunciation will make all the words clear and will add decisiveness to your tone. Make sure the back row can hear you. Even ask if the audience can hear you there.

There's another reason for not apologizing for your nervousness or for what you have to say: an apology can make your audience lose faith in you or lose interest. As a former speechwriter for the Secretary of the Navy commented, "No speech should ever be self-editorialized. Comments such as 'I really don't know what to say,' 'This is dry stuff so I'll keep it brief,' and 'Thanks for bearing with me' *drastically undermine your effectiveness* as a speaker. Do your best, and let the audience be the judge of the quality of your remarks."

In this officer's experience, even senior naval officials were, unfortunately, prone to begin speaking by shedding doubt on the importance of what they were about to say. "I know it's late and you're cold, and so I won't be long . . . ," began one speaker at a ceremony held outdoors. After that kind of a beginning, a listener starts trying to remember where the car is in the parking lot.

Stand Straight

Your physical presence—beginning with your stance—can affect both the way you think of yourself and the way the audience receives you. We have all become annoyed with speakers who shift from one foot to the other, or look down at the floor, or play with the keys in their pockets throughout a talk. We feel embarrassed for them because we know they must be feeling embarrassed themselves—or why not stand straight and talk to *us*?

That's a good question. Again, why not at least *act as if* you're confident? Even just pretending to be at ease will help the confidence come. Confidence, direction, leadership are central virtues of naval service—so try those habits on. For a starter, stand square on both feet, facing the audience—not rigidly, but with two feet on the floor. Stand erect, and don't lean on the lectern. And stand still. Don't cross your legs or shift back and forth on them.

Make Natural Gestures

Don't fuss with your hands, but use them instead to gesture with. Unless you're trained as an actor, don't plan out the gestures you use, but just let your hands float up naturally to enhance your talk. Gesture a bit more broadly if your audience is large.

If you don't feel natural gesturing, leave your hands at your sides or lay them on the lectern, if you're speaking from one (don't grip it tightly, however). Don't jingle change in your pockets, constantly smooth your hair, grip your opposite arm awkwardly, or make other nervous gestures. Normally, place your notes on the lectern rather than hold them (it's too easy to play with papers in your hands). If you have to hold the notes, use one or more 5 × 7 note cards rather than pages, which can rattle in nervous hands, communicating nervousness to the audience and rattling yourself in the process.

Make Eye Contact

"The ability to speak well, like the ability to write well, will get a junior officer noticed faster than almost anything else."—Navy Lieutenant, Speechwriter for SECNAV

Look up from notes or a manuscript frequently, first looking at one part of the audience, then another. Don't stare, of course, and don't look out the window, at the ceiling, or down at the floor either. Meet the eyes of the people in front of you. If you don't (if you bury your head in your notes, for example), your audience will tend to lose interest.

Looking at your audience will also help you pick up how they are taking the speech. Often you'll find one or two people especially well disposed to you, laughing at your jokes, agreeing with your comments, or simply paying very close attention. These people will do lots for your confidence, and you can key on them as you glance around at the audience.

Besides the eyes, let your face play a part. There may be natural times in your talk to grin, to look skeptical, to frown, and so on. As a rule, simply smiling as you go about your speech will help you express confidence and tend to ingratiate you with the audience.

Be Expressive

Don't forget your voice, but put some natural expression in your talk. Otherwise, if you sound wooden or bored, your audience may get bored too. Try varying both the pitch and the volume of your voice, and make sure you speak strongly enough. Act interested and concerned—be *enthusiastic*, and your attitude will communicate itself both to your audience and to your own psyche.

Furthermore, don't talk too quickly. Most inexperienced speakers speak too fast, partly from wanting to get through the talk as soon as possible. Remember that the audience needs time to assimilate your argument. Take your time, and don't be afraid to pause occasionally. (Yes, stay within the time allotted—but when you first outline your talk, plan for pauses and asides.) Don't let any pauses come from fumbling with ideas. The uhs and nows and other terms that you might tend to throw in from not really knowing a speech well (usually from lack of practice) will get on the audience's nerves.

Decide on the Degree of Formality

Realize that the degree of formality you adopt in your appearance or style of presentation can affect the whole atmosphere. Formality is an especially important consideration in our business. If you're the boss, dressing up and having your unit remain standing while you speak to them can be effective at times—certainly when giving out an award, for example, and (like Patton before the flag) perhaps at other times as well. On the other hand, rank sometimes interferes with communication. A very senior officer's presence, for example, can be particularly inhibiting. By leaving off his uniform jacket, a commander might be able to foster an informal atmosphere with a unit and have more interaction with the group. Let your circumstances and purposes govern your approach in a particular case.

Remember to modify your approach when speaking to a civilian audience. At the Naval Academy, about half the faculty is civilian. Once, when addressing the whole faculty at the first of the year, a superintendent decided to forgo flags, the opening ceremony, the salutes, the standing at attention—in short, all the formalities, including lectern and notes. Instead, he simply stepped through the stage curtains (with a mike) and began speaking. The civilian faculty perceived him as speaking *with* the audience, rather than *down* to them. At an institution where rank inevitably plays a great part, this gesture on the behalf of the military superintendent to the civilian faculty was a much-noticed and welcome change of pace. It enhanced rather than inhibited communications (and at no real cost to the dignity of the institution, either).

Learn Other Ways to Warm the Audience to You

On many occasions, lightening up your tone can be useful. Find some way to "break down that invisible wall between you and the audience," as one speech expert put it. Humor is one method: telling a joke or two can be very effective in making the audience more receptive, or putting them on your side. A joke is usually most effective toward the beginning of your talk—to establish rapport early. Remember to use good taste, be kind (watch sarcasm or ridicule), and learn to laugh at yourself.

You can overuse humor, of course, and it may not fit all occasions. Another excellent approach (again, usually for the beginning of a speech) is to recognize one or more members of the audience or, in formal settings, to acknowledge those on the dais with you. Try saying a word or two about an audience member in a supportive way. By mentioning that person's views or deeds in your own speech context, you figuratively put the both of you on the same side of an issue. The idea is to try to convince the audience in a subtle way that you are all really soul mates, thus making them more receptive to the points you'll make later on.

Practice!

The way to build confidence and learn is to practice, and to do so *repeatedly* and *out loud.* Don't just give your speech in your head, or you may skip over the hardest parts and then have difficulty expressing them in the actual talk. Whether you plan to speak from a manuscript or from notes, run through the speech out loud a few times in private, perhaps in front of a mirror, or into a tape recorder, or both.

If you can find a friend or colleagues to listen to you, practice in front of a live audience. This way you'll be able to practice looking up at someone and speaking so you'll be heard. If your colleague can offer pointers—if you choose someone who is knowledgeable in speaking and helpfully critical—that practice will help even more. Often naval staffs will "murder board" a critical briefing before the toughest local audience they can assemble. They figure that the tougher the questions they have to face *now,* the better prepared they'll be *later* in front of a target audience of major officials. Such a critique, in which briefers and staffers try to anticipate and practice answering likely questions, can be an outstanding learning experience in its own right.

If you ever have the chance to have yourself videotaped while speaking, take advantage of it. You'll probably feel embarrassed the first time you see yourself giving a speech, but this experience can be absolutely invaluable for your development as a speaker.

"I believe that a leader's effectiveness is measured in three ways: by his acts, by his decisions, and *by what he says.* Why else would plebes be required to memorize famous naval sayings?"—Naval Academy graduate

Best of all, you can take a college course in speech, or you can practice by joining a group that practices public speaking. There are Toastmasters' Clubs at most major bases and sometimes aboard major combatants. There may be a club in the community near where you live. Such a group usually meets once a month or so, and there you'll give short speeches, receive critiques, and also get some good material to read. There's nothing like speaking regularly to a live audience to improve your skills, and such organizations as Toastmasters' offer a very supportive audience. The confidence you build in this informal way can come in handy later, on official occasions.

In short, speaking in public and in the military are both part of the job. They merit sound preparation and skillful execution *just like everything else we do.* Speaking is a skill that you can perfect by knowing its principles and by practicing. Work at it until you can do it well, and quit worrying about whether you're up to it or not.

Recently, a carrier returned from a deployment, and the Captain had to brief his operational commander about the cruise. According to an LDO aboard, the briefing was essentially a test: how well the Captain performed in front of the admiral might determine his future assignments or promotions. The skipper reportedly cloistered himself in his cabin, personally selecting slides, practicing his talk, checking clock time, etc. As the LDO remarked, the Captain had probably never had to prepare such a briefing before. Had he trained to give briefs earlier in his career, with lots of practice and critiques—"and especially if he had seen himself on tape," the LDO pointed out—he would have been much better prepared for this critical performance.

This advice applies to all those who have to go into flag offices at OPNAV, at CINCPACFLT, at FMFLANT, or in any of hundreds of other offices where the future of a service member's program, unit, or personal career might depend on how well he or she performs in a few minutes' formal speaking. Simply stated, in the naval service you can distinguish yourself more from others through communicative skills than almost anything else.

How to Speak: Off the Cuff, From Notes, or From a Manuscript?

Sometimes you'll have to speak on the spur of the moment, without preparation; another, you may be on a formal program in which your audience expects a prepared text. Usually, however, you'll have at least some choice about how fully to write out what you're about to say.

Speaking Impromptu—Off the Cuff

Often, at a conference or morning briefing, the commander will ask you to "give us a rundown" of your program, or your latest staff trip, or your plans for the preinspection procedures. The commander might brief you ten minutes ahead of time on what to cover, or ask you on impulse when noticing you across the table. This unprepared or *impromptu* situation has advantages. No one expects you to be polished in such circumstances, and you'll have no time to get jitters. Obviously you can't prepare much, but you might be able to consider whom you're talking to and what they need and to think out a brief outline.

Practicing such quick reaction is worthwhile. In a lull at a meeting, recollect one of the tough questions you're currently dealing with and practice putting together a quick mental outline to answer a superior's sudden inquiry. This exercise will help pass the time, and it will pay dividends when someone suddenly does put you on the spot.

Speaking from Notes

Using notes is the most common and usually the preferred speech situation. Compared with impromptu speaking, speaking from notes provides more security. On the other hand, using notes allows much more spontaneity than reading from a text. Notes also enable you much more easily than a manuscript does to contract or expand a talk, if you need to.

How to go about it? Write brief notes to yourself on each area of your talk. Jot down a phrase or clause, rather than a full sentence. Then you can fill in the rest of the sentence verbally, in this way adding to your talk's spontaneity. Leave gaps in your notes for filling in details that you know well and can describe easily. You might want to pen in the beginning and ending a bit more fully—these parts of a speech are especially important and deserve more care. Of course you'll want to make fuller notes for less familiar subjects than for topics you know well.

Don't write out notes for every sentence. Know whatever subject you're speaking on well enough that you feel comfortable adding entertaining details between the lines of your notes.

As said before, use note cards—probably 5 × 7 cards—rather than paper (paper rustles). Whether you use cards or pages, print in large letters so you can read more easily. Better yet, *type* your notes, and with as large a typing element or printer font as possible. Indeed, most commands have a special large element or font for this very purpose—ask the yeoman or admin clerk to use it. Make sure to use one side of a page only, and number your notes so you can get them back in order quickly if you drop them.

Reading from a Prepared Manuscript

Of course, reading a manuscript is in some ways the most secure kind of speaking, for every word is spelled out in print, and you can make sure while writing it that you cover all the key points clearly and precisely. However, prepared speeches often lose spontaneity. Read from a manuscript only on very formal occasions, and even then work hard to keep the conversational tone, the freshness, and the audience contact that naturally enliven a talk from notes or an impromptu performance.

How can you keep it lively? Prepare the speech so your sentences are relatively short and simple, for one thing. Look up often, for another. Keep the text short enough so that you can add some spontaneous examples if they occur to you, or so you can add some unrehearsed remarks to explain the points you have made in the text. Such ad-libbing will help keep the audience with you and will add variety to the talk. Finally, don't read too fast; keep the pace slow, sure, and confident.

What to Say—The Substance of Your Talk

What you say will depend on your specific subject. However, you can look into some standard sources for information on general topics. Take the universal military subject of leadership, for example. Whether the occasion be a change of command, an address to a local civic group, or a talk to your own command or division, you need not start from scratch.

You might consult *history* and *tradition*, *literature* and *philosophy*, or *famous sayings*, for instance. All these sources have perennially served military speakers and speechwriters as well as they have politicians. The same can be said for *current events* or *recent military issues*—such topics might well find pertinent reference in a leadership speech. One other great source of effective remarks on leadership is, of course, the treasury of *war stories*, *anecdotes*, and *memorable expressions* that you have encountered personally through your military service.

Below are a just few instances where topics like those discussed above have filled an important place in a naval or military address.

Arguing from Historical Precedent

The fourth goal of American seapower is to be supreme on the sea in order to be supreme on the land. You might recall the historic race for Tunis in World War II, where the Germans moved a quarter of a million troops from France, principally by airlift, into North Africa, but were unable to control the sea in order to supply and re-equip them. The end result was disastrous. On the strategic level, the Germans lost twice: We captured more than 200,000 of their best soldiers when we took Tunis, and we did not have to fight those soldiers when we invaded Normandy two years later. In building our own strategy for the defense of Europe in today's world, we have not forgotten that control of the sea impacts much more than the war at sea.

—Secretary of the Navy James H. Webb, Jr., at the Ninth International Seapower Symposium, Newport, Rhode Island, 28 October 1987, as printed in Vol. 2, No. 58 of *Defense Issues*, under the title "Role of American Seapower," p. 2.

Citing an Acknowledged Authority

. . . naval strength is, I believe, essential to America's national security. To keep peace and deter our enemies, we must be able to defeat them if deterrence fails. As Winston Churchill said of his country in another time, "Nothing in the world, nothing you may think of, or anyone may tell you; no arguments, however specious; no appeals, however seductive, must lead you to abandon that naval superiority on which the life of our country depends."

—Secretary of Defense Caspar W. Weinberger, before the Dallas Council Navy League of the United States, 7 October 1981, as reproduced in NL 102 course booklet, U.S. Naval Academy, 1986, p. 4.

Finding Significance in Recent History

Concerning survivability, just look at this ship [*Nimitz*] which surrounds us with its more than 2000 watertight compartments, designed and constructed to permit this ship to go in harm's way, to accept battle damage, and to continue to fight. It wasn't designed carelessly or recklessly, nor with bigness for bigness' sake in mind. It was designed with survivability in mind.

Let me remind you that in 1969, the USS *Enterprise* had nine 500-pound bombs explode on its flight deck, the equivalent of being hit by six Soviet guided missiles. Not only did *Enterprise* survive, but within several hours—not days or weeks, but several hours—was capable of conducting flight operations.

It is not unimportant to take another lesson from recent history, remembering that in Vietnam we had over 400 aircraft destroyed and 4000 additional aircraft damaged—on the ground—on land bases—while not one single aircraft aboard a carrier was destroyed or damaged by enemy action throughout that conflict. Nor should we soon forget that every airfield constructed in Vietnam was lost in its entirety. Even more dramatically, at least one of them has been turned against us, as the Soviet Union today operates with impunity from the field we built there.

So much for vulnerability.

—Admiral Thomas B. Hayward, CNO, at the change of command of USS *Nimitz* (CVN 68) on 26 February 1982, as printed in the May 1982 issue of *Surface Warfare* under the title "CNO Speaks Out: Why the *Nimitz* Aircraft Carrier," p. 11.

Linking Tradition to Recent Events

Gustavus Conyngham, the namesake of this fine ship which is affectionately called 'Gus Boat,' was captured and placed in a mill prison on his first cruise as skipper of a privateer. An individual who did things with pizzazz and a never-say-die attitude, he quickly escaped and was reassigned to a new command. That same spirit is alive today in Gus Boat, in people like MM3 Finan who volunteered to be lowered into a flooded compartment of the STARK with an electric submersible pump which could not be lowered past battle damage by itself. After the line severed on jagged steel, he remained in the compartment, holding down the pump. This heroic action began the dewatering process that stopped the list and probably prevented the ship from sinking. . . .

—Captain C. K. Kicker, then Commander, Destroyer Squadron Two, at the 14 November 1987 change of command of USS *Conyngham* (DDG 17). Commander David Rose was relieving Captain Don Pollard on this occasion.

Using an Anecdote to Make a Point

But I caution you that the news from the fleet could change. The progress we have made during the first half of this decade now stands in jeopardy. We are at a critical period for our Navy, indeed our nation. Will we maintain what we've built up in the last five years?

While all are eager to find solutions to deficit spending, it makes little sense to seize upon a short-term solution which jeopardizes future national security. I am reminded of the situation the captain of a ship faced at sea one night. He was awakened by the shouts of his duty officer who said, "Captain, the ship is on fire. But don't worry. The resulting flooding will put out the fire." I sometimes wonder that some of these defense budget cuts may put out the deficit fire, but sink our positive defense momentum which took so long to rebuild.

—Admiral Frank B. Kelso, II, USN, CINCLANTFLT, remarks to the Texas Daily Newspaper Association, 25 July 1986, as reproduced in "Navy Excellence: A Story to Tell," a booklet for a seminar at CINCLANTFLT Headquarters, 2 Dec 1986.

Bringing a Sea Story to Bear

Several years ago I was Executive Officer in the diesel submarine TANG, which was the oldest commissioned U.S. submarine at that time. Keeping the boat going was quite a challenge and only a dedicated crew made it possible. In the entire crew, the most energetic and dedicated person was the captain, Carmine Tortora. One night about 3 AM, at the end of one of those grueling days at sea, the boat was surfaced charging batteries and the captain and I were the only two sitting in the wardroom. I asked him point-blank why he worked so hard. What was he after? What was his goal in all this labor? I tell this tale now because I want to borrow his response. I expected he would talk of a life-long goal to reach flag rank, or of a desire for a medal or other recognition of his command tour. That's not what he said, though. I asked him what his goal was and he replied with a simple three-word phrase that sums up to me the best there is in the officer corps. His goal, he said, was "Service with Honor."

I need to borrow Carmine's response to describe Jim Parks' Navy time. . . .

—Captain John Byron in a speech on an LDO's retirement.

Basic Resource Material for Naval Speakers

Besides the classic speech sources mentioned earlier, there are also several good *naval* speech resources. These resources and a few others are outlined below. Usually they don't tell you what to say, but they do provide valuable information. Many of them were designed specifically as resources for speechwriters or for commanders.

- Annual Posture Statements by SECNAV, CNO, CMC. Available in March, annually, following congressional testimony.
- *Soviet Military Power*. Available in March annually. Put out by the Secretary of Defense.
- *Understanding Soviet Naval Developments*. Published by CNO's office (OP-009) about every 2–3 years.
- *The Almanac of Seapower*. Published annually in April by the Navy League of the United States.
- *The Maritime Strategy*. Published by the U.S. Naval Institute, January 1986.
- Sample Speeches. (SECNAV, CNO, CMC, CINCLANTFLT, etc.) Available from PAO or staff speechwriter.
- *Vital Speeches*. A civilian periodical publishing a wealth of speeches and other information, which many naval speechwriters consult for ideas, examples, and ways of writing speeches. Available at libraries.
- *Commanders' Notebook*. Pocketbook compendium of Navy information intended as a source for speech writing, recruiting assistance, etc. Updated yearly by OP-01B4.
- Annual Naval Review issue (usually May), U.S. Naval Institute *Proceedings*. Contains summary articles on many Navy and Marine topics. Includes recent events and much general information, as well as an index to the previous year's *Proceedings* articles.
- *Navy Fact File*. Includes all sorts of unclassified facts on force structure, manpower, etc. Published annually by CHINFO; every PAO has a copy.
- Reference texts like *The Naval Institute Guide to Combat Fleets of the World*, *Jane's Fighting Ships*, etc.
- Quotation Sources:
  — *Bartlett's Familiar Quotations*. John Bartlett, 15th ed. (Little, Brown and Company, 1980).
  — *Dictionary of Military and Naval Quotations*. Robert Debs Heinl, Jr., ed. (Naval Institute Press, 1978).
  — *The Great Thoughts*. George Seldes. (Ballantine Books, 1985).
- Dorothy Sarnoff's *Speech Can Change Your Life* (Dell, 1972). One of the more helpful books about speech writing on the commercial market.

Speaking to the Public—A Checklist

Speaking as a representative of the military to the public can be an outstanding opportunity to help get our Navy and Marine Corps messages across. Such talks can promote excellent public relations and serve many other purposes. Whatever the motive, you should prepare well. Here are some tips about how to prepare, tips drawn from a checklist in "Navy Excellence: A Story to Tell," a booklet put out for a conference held at CINCLANTFLT Headquarters on 2 December 1986.

Accept the Right Speaking Engagement

• Make sure the audience is right. For example, an active-duty service member should not address a partisan political group or any extremist organization; doing so might potentially embarrass yourself and the service. Do not accept an invitation unless you are going to be proud of your association—*in uniform*—with the group.

• Make sure, also, that you want to talk to the audience. (If not, *don't!*) Some factors might influence your decision. For example, have they invited the media? Will there be another speaker besides you? If so, what topic will that speaker address? Be sure you understand exactly why the group invited you and the circumstances of your talking before you accept.

• The local *area* PAO can often provide good advice and put you in touch with local contacts who can tell you more.

Research Your Audience

• Know your audience to tailor your message appropriately. (Local contacts are again the key.) Is this group well defined? What do these people stand for? What interests them? Will any topics or remarks offend them? Will they be a friendly audience? What is their level of knowledge? You should also find out what officials will be there so that you can recognize notable civic leaders in the audience during your introductory remarks.

• Make sure you know whether just any Navy/Marine Corps topic will be of interest, or if they want some specific subject. Also find out what their military interests are. For example, does a local plant produce a weapons system or parts for it? Are local military facilities important to the economy? Discovering such facts might help you tailor your remarks to your audience's interests.

Choose Your Topic Carefully, and Research Your Message

• Tie the topic and message to your direct area of responsibility, past experience, or expertise.

• Flesh out general themes with real-life facts and/or sea stories.

• Get a security policy review, if you need one (see SECNAVINST 5720.44, ch. 4, para. 2). Check all security questions through your PAO.

• Consider whether you can announce something new, some information your audience won't know and might be interested or excited to find out about. If so, work this news into your talk.

Speech Preparation

• As mentioned above, outlines are usually easier to speak from and promote better eye contact than manuscripts. However, some speakers prefer a double- or triple-spaced text, which can be effective if rehearsed and written for oral delivery, i.e., with short sentences.

• With most groups, 20 minutes is the best speech length. If you read from typescript, time yourself reading a page, to get a good estimate as to how much you can get through. Don't try to read too much or too fast, but read slowly, with emphasis.

• Avoid using visual aids in most public speech opportunities. The larger the audience and room, the less effective visual aids can be, and the greater the opportunity for equipment inadequacy. Moreover, your audience's greatest interest will usually be in hearing from *you personally*.

• Make sure you AVOID NAVAL JARGON whenever speaking to the public.

Speech Delivery

- Strive hard for
  - Poise
  - Eye Contact
  - Humor
  - Pointedness
  - Brevity (Tell them what you're going to say—say it—then sit down.)
- Consider whether you should open to questions at the end.

Other Tips

• Arrive early enough to mingle with the hosts *and* audience (this time is a good chance to get names to drop, hear anecdotes, etc.)

• Visit the speaking location ahead of time, or have someone do so for you. Check out the podium, the microphone, the water glass, the cord that you don't want to trip over, and so on.

• Don't drink *before* your speech.

• Don't make public promises or extend invitations to the audience to visit your unit unless you mean it.

• Do thank your hosts.

• Do enjoy yourself—keep smiling.

Tips on Speaking to the Media

In 1987 Atlantic Fleet ships alone hosted more than 200 major news media visits. Clearly, "public speaking" in the sea services reaches far beyond just speaking at an occasional Rotary Club or city council meeting. The ability to deal effectively with the media has become an important qualification for all who aspire to command.

In May 1988 in Norfolk the Navy ran a pilot half-day seminar on dealing with the media for COs and XOs. More recently, the Navy Chief of Information instituted a mobile media training team to assist COs and XOs in the fleet with news media relations. Here's a partial list of some of that team's training tips (as reported by Navy Captain Brent Baker in "The Public Affairs Front" in the September 1988 *Proceedings*, pp. 116–17).

Training Tips for Speaking to Media Representatives

- Do your homework before a media encounter—don't wing it. Homework includes finding background on the issues, the reporters, their typical questions, and on other people who will be part of the story.
- Have an experienced public affairs officer or another knowledgeable individual drill you on questions and answers prior to the interview. Don't just listen to a question and stop, thinking that you'll know how to answer it. Go through the answer thoroughly, both to make sure you know it, and because it may trigger an unexpected follow-up question.
- Decide what points you want to make. Rehearse those points. Learn to take command of the interview, then guide the discussion to your own agenda.
- Limit your discussion to your own "paygrade"—your level and area of responsibility. Also, keep in mind the political context of the discussion. One CO said he would rehearse to deflect political questions, and if he didn't have firsthand knowledge on a subject he would say, "I wasn't involved." The main objective is to have answers you are comfortable with, which requires asking yourself difficult questions in advance to be sure of your reaction when a reporter asks them.
- Speak only "on-the-record" with reporters, unless you have been given other guidance by higher authority and have the advice of a senior public affairs specialist.
- Always remember that you are communicating to the public. Keep answers short and to the point. Avoid military terminology, jargon, and acronyms whenever possible.
- Use examples of your operational experience to stand up to outside experts who have never been in the military or who have outdated experience.
- Relax and enjoy the interview. It will come naturally if you know you are prepared and ready to meet the reporter.

Brief Bibliography on Speaking to the Media

Captain Brent Baker, "The Public Affairs Front," U.S. Naval Institute *Proceedings* (September 1988), 114–17.

Herb Schmertz, *Good-bye to the Low Profile: The Art of Creative Confrontation* (Boston: Little, Brown & Company, 1986).

Clearly, developing expertise in any one area of speaking—military briefing, public speaking, media relations—can only enhance your ability in the others. All the more reason to take every opportunity to learn to speak well.

Using Visual Aids to Get Your Points Across

Visual aids help the audience both follow and retain what you tell them. Often they are useful; sometimes they are indispensable. Flip charts, hardboard charts, slides, overhead transparencies, blackboards or whiteboards, handouts, photos, objects and models—the list is a long one. Consult any speech or technical writing textbook for a comprehensive discussion of the pros and cons of each. Here we discuss what are perhaps the two most common naval visual aids.

Overhead Transparencies or "Viewgraphs"

Perhaps the most versatile and most common visual aid in naval presentations is the overhead transparency, also known as a "viewgraph" or "overhead." The advantages of viewgraphs, which use a simple machine called an "overhead projector," are numerous. You can make transparencies of documents on virtually any copy machine, or you can draw them by hand with a special pen. You can prepare them virtually on the spur of the moment without any loss of quality. There is little limit on the size of audience you can use them with; by adjusting the distance of projector to the screen, you can effectively reach hundreds with this simple device.

"Military briefers are notorious for abusing visual aids. My rule is 'If the picture is worth a thousand words, then use it. If not, keep it off the screen.' "—Navy Lieutenant

The projector typically sits comfortably on a table, often beside the lectern, and you can operate it personally while speaking. You can even cover up a viewgraph with a sheet of paper and reveal only portions at a time, to maintain control of the visual material. To help maintain good eye contact, read right off the transparency or viewgraph as it sits on the projector (rather than turning your back to the audience as you read off the screen). You don't have to dim the lights when using an overhead projector, but you should turn the machine off when not using it to draw all the audience's attention back to the speaker.

On the other hand, you must be very careful to *comment about* the viewgraph, not read it verbatim. One of the biggest complaints about viewgraphs is that speakers *read the whole viewgraph to the audience,* insulting their audience's intelligence. Instead of reading, point out only the key information (perhaps with a pen as a pointer, which will show up in profile on the screen), but let the audience pick up other data for themselves.

Don't have too many viewgraphs—a big stack laid on the table can make your listeners lose their concentration. As a captain in OPNAV commented, "A successful briefer will have five or six viewgraphs, will have thought each one out, and will have written a note to himself about the bottom line he wants the audience to take from it. If you can't summarize it, *cut out* the viewgraph."

Since normal text from a book or typewriter will usually not be readable beyond a few rows, don't submit to the temptation of copying pages out of books or other printed material. Instead, retype the needed information on an ordinary sheet of paper with a large type element, and then copy that sheet. Use bullets framed by lots of white space—remember that the most common fault of transparencies is that they are often too busy or too complex. Pay special attention to the printing. Be sure to make the viewgraph highly professional in appearance. Computer type, of course, can also look good, and computer graphics can greatly expand both the appearance and the range of overhead presentations.

Finally, make sure you check out your equipment *before* your presentation. Fumbling with an unfamiliar overhead projector can shake your confidence and irritate your audience too. Unfortunately, such fumbling occurs far too often. As a civilian at a major naval command commented, "I've wasted an astounding amount of time in my ten years here as officers adjusted projectors and tried to figure out how various overheads worked."

Slides

Thirty-five-mm slides are a standard tool, not only for sessions in which you need to show true reproduction (photos of ships, equipment, or personnel) but also for graphs, charts, diagrams, or just words. Slides are permanent, portable, and versatile; colored slides can enhance visual presentations even further.

On the other hand, slides have distinct disadvantages. They require advance preparation, and you can't shuffle them quickly into a new order without risking a serious disruption to your talk if you get the order wrong or lose a slide somewhere. You must usually darken the room while showing slides, making it easier for the audience to be inattentive. Watch that you don't let a very long series of slides numb the audience's attention.

When you use slides, consider putting them in sequences of no more than six or seven at a time. Use them for specific purposes, and then break away to stimulate the audience. If you're in a darkened room, put light on yourself while showing them, perhaps while standing at a podium. Use a hand-held slide changer, or have someone work the machine for you.

Used selectively, slides can be effective and most impressive.

General Pointers on Using Visual Aids

• Reveal them at the right time during the talk, and hide them or put them away after they no longer serve a purpose. Get the audience to return their attention to you.

• Do your best to face your audience and talk *to them* while discussing a visual aid. Don't "talk to the blackboard"—a common beginner's fault.

• Keep the visual aid simple and readable. Don't put too much on any one viewgraph or slide. And make sure to label each chart or viewgraph appropriately.

• Tell the audience what they're going to see in a slide, chart, diagram, or other visual. Don't expect them to pick out your main point without guidance. Identify the key information.

• On the other hand, never read the entire slide, viewgraph, or chart. Have some respect for the audience's ability to see for themselves the thousand words that are the reason for having a visual in the first place.

• Get out of the visual's way. Stand to the side of the chalkboard or chart when speaking to your audience. Make sure everybody can see the screen clearly.

• Pay special attention to spelling, grammar, punctuation, and numbers on your visuals, including any handouts. Spelling or numerical errors, especially, are immediately apparent—and can be quite embarrassing.

• Work with your visual aid assistant (if any) beforehand, and make sure you have spare bulbs and electricity, besides a projector and screen.

• Finally, don't abuse visual aids. Too often they become a crutch for the speaker who ends up as a mere voice-over for a seemingly endless series of overhead projections.

Giving Military Briefings

Military briefings differ from public speaking in several ways. Typically, military briefings are relatively brief and to the point. Since the audience is a "command audience," briefers don't usually need to use attention-getting devices or to ingratiate themselves with the audience. You seldom need to explain military terms and concepts. When briefings are directive in nature, you have less need to persuade than you would otherwise.

Still, be on your guard. Argument is possible in many more situations than you would expect. In all briefing situations where important differences of opinion might exist, you should *habitually expect opposition and prepare to argue strongly and prove your case definitively.* Usually, you will be briefing an issue or recommendation because you're the expert on the subject. So *prove your expertise* when someone challenges you in a brief.

Know your subject backwards and forwards. Murder board your presentation with as tough an audience as you can get, and be prepared to talk somebody down if that becomes necessary—because sooner or later it will be. You will face challenges no matter how rational you are. As an experienced speechwriter commented, "Nothing is more embarrassing than to have some know-it-all in the back of the room raise a hand and ask a question that succeeds in wrestling control of the subject matter from you."

Occasionally you won't win your case despite all your good preparations because of sudden new developments that completely change the situation you are briefing. But don't let your presentation fall into disarray because you don't know the material well enough, or haven't looked into all the consequences, or are astonished that someone dared to disagree with you.

Military briefings fall into four general types (although they are not necessarily exclusive categories—two or three types may be mixed into one). Navy commands, Marine Corps units, and staffs everywhere make wide use of *staff* briefings, in which various members of a staff typically speak in succession, each on a single area of responsibility. These briefings do not differ much in concept from *informative* briefings, which a single person usually delivers, except that some of the latter can be very formal, especially on major staffs. All of these presentations are primarily informational, rather than persuasive or directive in nature.

Decision briefings, on the other hand, have a specific focus, to present a superior with enough background, information, and focused counseling to enable that superior to make a decision on the spot. Most decision briefings occur on major staffs.

Finally, a *mission* briefing finds its use at operational commands or units—Navy or Marine—about to order an operational mission.

Staff and Informative Briefings

Staff briefings exist to keep the commander and the staff informed. Besides ensuring an exchange of information among staff members, they offer opportunities to announce decisions, issue directives, share information, and give out general guidance. These purposes serve a command's larger goals of unity and coordination.

Many variations of staff briefings exist. One officer may brief the entire staff, or several staff officers might speak in succession. The method and the formality of such a briefing will depend on the size of the staff, the nature of the command, and custom. The executive officer or chief of staff will usually preside and set the agenda, while the commander will normally conclude the briefing. Both officers may take an active part throughout the presentation.

Informative briefings are very similar to staff briefings, although they may be more formal and deal with only one rather than many issues. All informative briefings deal mainly with facts rather than recommendations. A simple, standard speech organization—

- an introduction that announces the topic and orients the listener;
- a body that presents facts in an orderly, objective, clear, and concise way;
- a conclusion that reiterates the main points

—will usually work well. Try to anticipate questions that might arise, and treat most of them in the briefing itself, before the audience asks. Bring along any background information that might help you respond to questions, but know your subject so well that you can respond directly to any reasonable inquiry.

Of course, some commanders will use staff briefings to help them make decisions; in that case, the presentation is really a decision briefing.

Advice on Giving Briefings in OPNAV

OPNAV tongue-twister. Say these words three times quickly:

BRIEF A BRIEFING BRIEFLY.

Now, stop saying it and do it.

Some OPNAV action officers appear to be under the impression that they are being paid by the word. They take what is, at most, a 10-minute brief and stretch it to 45 minutes by the ingenious method of giving detailed, unnecessary background information, and reading—ever so slowly—every word on every slide. They fool nobody, and irritate everybody (all of those who stayed awake, that is).

Those on the receiving end of your briefing are a captive audience. Have pity on them.

- **Don't give more than a brief introduction. On 9 topics out of 10, they don't need details back to Genesis.**
- **Don't insult their intelligence by reading slides to them. They can read silently far more quickly than you can read aloud.**

A few words about the slides themselves:

- **Remember to be brief and clear; use no more than a dozen lines per slide.**
- **Clearly identify the issues & decisions to be made; give a lot of thought to making appropriate recommendations.**
- **Make slides as slides. Don't copy a page from a book.**
- **Use straight English. Phrases are fine.**

Walk your listeners through your slides. What you say should elaborate on what your slides show. And when you are done with everything they need to know (although not everything you want to tell them) . . . stop.

Be responsive to the sensitivities of the "Briefee."

—From "Guide to OPNAV Writing"

Decision Briefings

You will have many occasions to advocate one course of action or another. You'll often be making your case before a superior who has the responsibility for decision. This presentation might be in informal circumstances, perhaps while standing before your boss's desk, or on a very formal occasion, while giving a decision briefing before an officer of flag rank and several members of that officer's staff.

Whatever the circumstances, keep in mind that several factors other than what you actually say will influence the outcome of your briefing:

• **The audience's knowledge and acceptance of you.** Have you or has anyone explained to those you're briefing what your background is or why they should listen to you, if those reasons are not obvious? (Also, do you have the *right rank* to give this briefing?) Might some in the audience be antagonistic to you, to your office, or to your topic for any reason? If so, how should you deal with your opponents? On the other hand, will anyone in the audience help you? How can you best "use" such supporters?

• **Where you give the briefing.** Speaking in your own offices, on your own turf, might be a subtle psychological advantage. Any of several other physical factors might also affect the outcome of your talk, such as whether you brief in a large room or a small one; to a large group, or a very small, private meeting; with the audience sitting around a table or all facing you in theater-type seats; etc. Check with senior staffers on their experience with each choice.

• **The timing of the brief.** Have you given yourself enough time? Will another evolution interrupt? Remember that the time of day (early morning, just before lunch, mid-afternoon, etc.) may influence the mood, attentiveness, or even the wakefulness of your audience.

Below is a proven format for a formal decision brief, with guidance. It is based on the classic staff-study format, as adapted to oral briefing requirements. Alter it as you wish, based on your particular subject matter, the occasion of the brief, and your knowledge of the decision maker.

One Format for a Decision Brief

FORMAT	EXAMPLE
Greeting. Use military courtesy. Address the decision maker and other key persons in the audience. Identify yourself and your organization, if necessary.	Good afternoon, General J____. I'm Colonel M____, the Staff Operations Officer.
Type of Briefing, Classification, Purpose.	This is an unclassified decision briefing.
Subject and Problem. State very briefly the background and present context of the problem at hand.	As you know, one Marine per year is killed in the mine field at Guantanamo Bay, Cuba, and incidents are occurring more frequently. Lately, this problem has attracted congressional attention.
Basic Recommendation. Put your bottom line up front—this is perhaps the most important advice of all. Don't leave your listeners in any doubt as to your basic recommendation. Tell them early, and speak forcefully.	To solve this problem, I recommend that we replace the conventional munitions in the mine fields at the U.S. Naval Base in Guantanamo with FASCAM Munitions.

Detailed Statement of the Problem. If necessary, outline more fully the problem this briefing intends to solve.	Defense of the U.S. Naval Base at Guantanamo Bay has been a significant issue since 1959. Much of the existing barrier relies on antitank and antipersonnel mines. We must emplace and replace these conventional munitions by hand. This process is time consuming and dangerous. . . .
Any Necessary Assumptions. State any assumptions needed to bridge gaps in the data. Make sure they are reasonable, and be prepared to support them if challenged.	We can assume that the political situation will remain the same for the foreseeable future, and that the mine barrier must continue to remain in place. Thus, an improved process to emplace the mines would seem a long-term need.
Facts Bearing on the Problem. State pertinent facts objectively. Present both sides of the issue, even if recommending just one. Research indicates that a high percentage of audience members will lean toward your argument when you present both sides, but just a few when you present only your side. Be sure to cite authorities and relevant supporting opinions.	1. FASCAM munitions now available offer some antipersonnel, antitank capabilities with distinct improvements over conventional land mines. . . . 2. FASCAM munitions can be emplaced by artillery and so offer a significant safety improvement. . . . 3. FASCAM munitions allow for a more flexible response, since they can be fired in reaction to enemy action. . . . 4, 5, 6, etc.
Possible Courses of Action. State major feasible options. Explain the advantages and drawbacks of each, and any potential dangers involved.	1. The major alternative to using FASCAM munitions is the current method, which is to bury mines below ground level by hand, a tedious and dangerous process. With this method we must painstakingly record mine locations and replace each mine before its shelf-life expiration date. . . .

	2. The major advantage of the present system of mine emplacement is cost. Equivalent mine munitions are considerably less costly than FASCAM rounds, and FASCAM will require augmenting the Security Battalion with a 155-mm howitzer battery. . . . 3, 4, 5, etc.
Analysis. Present your conclusions briefly. Mention any concurrences and nonconcurrences.	1. The admittedly significant increases in cost, personnel, and equipment are worthwhile, when weighed against the recurrent loss of life presently incurred in handling conventional mines. The employment of FASCAM will totally eliminate this loss of life. 2. Besides being safer, FASCAM mine fields are more effective, and more flexible. 3. CMC received a brief during a visit to GITMO and liked the idea of FASCAM.
Restated Recommendation. Restate your recommendation, wording it so it requires only approval or disapproval.	We recommend that FASCAM munitions replace the current mines emplaced at Guantanamo Bay.
Opening for Questions. Try to anticipate questions; conduct murder boards if you can. Do your best to have thorough knowledge of the whole issue so you can respond intelligently to questions or arguments.	Are there any questions?

—Example based on instructional material used at Marine Corps Development and Education Command, Quantico, VA.

In some settings, you can expect a decision on the spot. In fact, the flag or flag's staff may have asked for the decision brief for the very purpose of deciding the issue quickly. In that case, you might end your brief by saying, "General, I have completed my presentation, and I am prepared for your decision," or words to that effect. This is standard procedure on some Marine staffs.

But be careful, as a briefer, not to try to force a public decision. If the senior renders no decision immediately, leave the issue at the "recommend" level, and pursue the decision later through staff channels. Note that Navy briefers seldom ask the admiral for a decision so directly as in the statement above. Be guided by staffers experienced with your command's way of operating.

Mission Briefings

Service members deliver mission briefings to Marines, ship drivers, and naval aviators alike as they are about to embark on operational missions either for training or for actual combat. Although such briefings will vary widely in technique, subject, and location, they each have one central aim: to instill the best possible understanding of an impending operation in all participants.

For example, a Marine patrol going out will normally learn of its specific mission through oral orders. Then a mission briefing may provide further specific instructions such as the route of march, what to look for, identification procedures, and so on. The briefing may also afford the Marines a brief explanation of why the patrol is necessary and what it will contribute to the overall mission of the command.

Ships have similar procedures. Key officers and senior enlisted personnel on a destroyer, for instance, might go over to the flagship by high-line or helo for a mission briefing on an impending operation, perhaps an operation involving naval gunfire support, air operations, search and rescue, or a missile shoot. The briefing would include all manner of specifics, from call signs, radio frequencies, and emergency procedures to formations, tactics, and weapons employment. Here too, besides rendering specific plans and details, the briefing officer would usually touch on how the operation fits into larger operational or training objectives.

Naval aviators pay great attention to effective delivery of mission briefings, partly from having to give them so often. One naval school that has developed a strong program of operational briefings and debriefings is the Naval Fighter Weapons School (TOPGUN). Below are excerpts adapted from that school's guidance on mission briefing. Although originally designed to guide those who must brief Navy and Marine Corps fighter squadrons about to fly a tactical exercise, this advice is adaptable to many other situations.

Briefing and Debriefing at TOPGUN

A. Introduction. Tactical flight time will continue to be at a premium in the months and years ahead because of funding constraints and aircraft availability. We must take advantage of every opportunity to refine our aviation skills. Your squadron has made a large investment in OPTAR, TAD funding, and maintenance support to provide for your attendance. It expects a return on the investment. One way you can pay off is by giving professional briefs and debriefs. Comprehensive briefs and debriefs are the cornerstones of an effective squadron training program. While you may not use all these pointers on every sortie, they apply to almost any tactical fighter mission.

B. Preparation. If the first time the briefer has considered the mission is thirty minutes prior to the flight brief, then the briefer has done a disservice to the squadron by not taking full advantage of a valuable training opportunity. Mission planning varies widely, but certain elements are applicable to all missions.

1. As flight leader, have a clear idea of what the mission and/or training objectives are. If the flight leader doesn't have it clear, certainly no one else in the flight will.

2. Start mission planning early—at least the day prior.

3. Involve other members of the flight. This will be no problem if the mission is an air superiority sweep in the Gulf of Sidra but some arm twisting may be required for night max-conserve 2v2s off the coast of Diego Garcia. Make sure all members of the flight arrive at the brief having familiarized themselves with the SOP, mission objectives, operating area, and any other information required to maximize the performance of the aircraft. Anything less is unprofessional.

4. Develop a scenario that will be challenging but within the capabilities of all members of the flight. Don't give a lengthy dissertation on a country's political-military situation, but rather make the situation a detailed framework from which the fighters can make intelligent tactical decisions.

5. Review written material for guidance on tactics, maneuvers, and the threat. Refer to Tactical Manuals, TOPGUN Manuals/Journals, VX-4 Newsletters, etc., for information. Dust off the contingency plans from the last cruise or deployment for reference.

6. Allow for contingencies such as maintenance problems and weather aborts. Plan an alternate mission.

7. Write it down. Putting the brief on paper—either in outline or paragraph form—will help briefers organize their thoughts and make them more familiar with the material. The result will be a smooth brief that is not repetitive and disjointed. If the brief is large and complex, a practice run-through is worth the effort.

C. The Brief. Below are some specific pointers on the brief itself.

1. WHERE. During shore-based operations, it's not too difficult to set aside a briefing/debriefing room—complete with whiteboard, models, and VTR/monitor—that allows for a quiet atmosphere without interruptions. Unfortunately, the reality of shipboard life is such that Navy and Marine Corps squadrons must often conduct their briefs amid the confusion of the all-purpose ready room. The squadron duty officer must ensure minimal interference with a flight that is briefing or debriefing. Try posting a sign on the ready room door that alerts everyone that a brief or debrief is in progress.

2. WHO. The flight leader traditionally conducts the brief. However, briefing can provide valuable training to a less-experienced member of the flight. Naturally, any briefer should have been intimately involved in the planning.

3. WHEN. Most squadrons brief 1–1½ hours prior to man-up, depending on the mission and size of the flight. You'll have enough time to cover all the necessary items—*if you're prepared.* When the squadron is operating in a new locale, you may have to lengthen the brief to cover local course rules and operating areas. *DO NOT SACRIFICE THE TACTICAL PORTION OF THE BRIEF FOR ADMIN ITEMS.*

4. SETTING UP. Here are a few general pointers:

- Be at the squadron early to take care of any last-minute items such as aircraft availability, weather, scheduling changes, etc.
- Set up the briefing room so that everyone has a full view of the briefer, whiteboard, and other briefing aids. Clean the whiteboard of all items not pertaining to the mission. Check that models and colored markers are available. If time constraints prevent whiteboard preparation, have the briefing items photocopied and passed out.
- Start on time! A flight that briefs late will walk late, take off late, etc. It only takes one instance of losing a hop for tardy players to change their ways.
- As briefer, remain standing throughout the brief. This posture makes for better delivery and reinforces the briefer's leadership.
- If you have players who were not involved in the planning, start with a brief overview of the mission.

(The TOPGUN instruction continues with details of the "ADMIN Brief" on take-off times, comm plan, weather and divert procedures, mission and training objectives, etc.; and with details of the "TACTICAL Brief"—the heart of the mission and the set-up of each engagement. Then the instruction goes on to . . .)

5. BRIEFING TECHNIQUES. All of us have our own briefing styles. Note others' effective techniques, and use what works well for you. Here are some suggestions:

- Keep an eye on the clock, and pace yourself during the brief. Allow 10 minutes at the end for questions, crew coordination, and a pit stop prior to man-up.
- Maintain eye contact with the flight members. It will keep them attentive and provide feedback as to whether your points are getting across.
- Ask questions from time to time to keep everyone involved in the brief. They can be rhetorical or specific. However, be careful not to bilge your wingman by playing NATOPS Trivial Pursuit in front of the CO.
- Recap the mission in general terms as a conclusion to the brief, with a review of the training objectives.
- If you complete the brief with time to spare, cover any tactical contingencies/issues that are relevant. As Navy and Marine Corps of-

ficers, we accept the paperwork burden as an unavoidable price to pay to fly high performance fighters. Don't sacrifice a scheduled opportunity to talk tactics just to read the message board, make a phone call, or push papers between the brief and strapping on the jet.

(A section on "Remembering the Flight" comes here, then . . .)

D. The Debrief. The most important consideration about the debrief is to have one! We neglect or gloss over many debriefs because of follow-on missions, lack of space availability, crew rest, or a hundred other reasons. Too often, we lose valuable training/learning because we're not interested enough in conducting a meaningful analysis of the mission. If the mission was so mundane or routine that it doesn't merit a debrief, then the flight lead was negligent in identifying training objectives.

The debrief should not be simply a chronological regurgitation of the mission. It should emphasize analysis and should identify lessons learned for subsequent missions.

The debrief begins as soon as the brief is over. Jot down any point worthy of discussion. After the mission, review your notes and VTR/microcassette to organize your debrief comments. Ask yourself some pertinent questions: Were the mission objectives achieved? How about the training objectives? What mistakes were made? Were the mistakes due to poor planning, briefing, or execution? A few minutes taken to organize your thoughts will dramatically improve the quality, expeditiousness, and professionalism of the debrief.

Follow these additional guidelines:

1. Have the debriefing room set up—whiteboard, colored pens, models, VTR/monitor. Draw notable geographic features of the operating area on the board, with north oriented to the top, and include the position of the sun. In one corner of the board list all the players next to the color of the arrow that will represent them, and list the training objectives as well.

2. Make sure all players attend the debrief, including the controller and the adversaries.

3. The overall debriefer—generally the flight lead—is responsible for maintaining control of the debrief. Emphasize that everyone will have a chance to talk, but only after the debriefer has first addressed the important points.

4. Spend the first few minutes of the debrief covering any ADMIN problems (clearance, line procedures, rendezvous, recovery, etc.). Get these matters out of the way quickly to clear the air for the important TACTICAL debrief.

5. As the debriefer, actively promote an atmosphere that encourages frank discussions without recriminations. See that all participants set aside personal feelings, friendships, and rank as they walk in the door. At TOPGUN we strive to "take the who out of ACM" by recounting engagements in the third person. Instead of, "Here's where I gunned you, Dirt, when you were obviously out of knots and tried a nose-high guns defense," say, "At this point the A-4 achieved a valid gunshot when the F-14 attempted a nose-high guns defense at a low airspeed." Both

examples address the ACM mistake, but the players will accept the lesson more readily in the second case.

6. Solicit inputs from the crowd to keep everyone interested in the analysis. Admit mistakes to maintain credibility, and acknowledge good performance to reinforce the positive. Keep the discussion oriented to the mission objectives and relevant points.

7. Structure the TACTICAL debrief to cover the important points thoroughly. You can address relatively minor points that didn't affect the success of the mission at the end of the debrief, or perhaps not at all.

(The TOPGUN instruction goes on to cover methods of boardwork in drawing fighter engagements and details of the TACTICAL debrief. Finally, . . .)

8. After the TACTICAL debrief, summarize the flight with reference to the training objectives identified in the brief. At TOPGUN we use a "Goods and Others" format. This discussion provides the basis for determining training objectives for subsequent flights.

E. Summary. The trademark of the TOPGUN graduate is being the best briefer and debriefer in the squadron. In the next five weeks, carefully observe the techniques of all the instructors. Select what works the best for your own personal style, and perfect your briefing and debriefing skills. Lessons learned in peacetime training must equip us for the challenging scenarios we can expect in modern aerial warfare. In the final analysis, the aircrew's flying skills will determine success or failure of the mission, no matter how well equipped they might be with weapons, intelligence information, and policy guidance. These aviation skills are a direct function of how well you've briefed, led, and debriefed your aircrews.

—Adapted from NFWS TM B&D 5–88.

Most executive summaries are very disappointing—writers seem unable to recognize the key ideas in their own reports. They allocate space in the executive summary in the same proportion as in the original document, whereas they ought to focus only on the *essential* items, the *results*. Always think to yourself, "I'm likely to lose my readers unless I get their attention *here*."

—Naval War College Professor

8

Technical Reports, Executive Summaries, and Abstracts

Naval personnel must often work with industry, or with reports and other documents prepared by industry. Those doing research at naval labs, naval test centers, or naval schools must help generate technical reports, while others will just have to use them.

Specifically, naval personnel will often encounter technical reports when they work on staffs that monitor military contracts, perhaps while working for an 0-5 or 0-6 project officer or program manager. That officer may have requested an analysis, a proposal, or a progress report of some kind. Perhaps the Navy wants to build a helicopter engine that will operate effectively in deserts. The program manager might have contracted for a report as to what such a design would look like, how reliable the engine would be, and how much it would cost.

In the latter case, the company with the contract would respond with a feasibility report, which Navy officials would use to guide them. The report would first help them decide whether or not to build the engine. Then, having decided to build it, they would use the report to persuade senior officers and other government officials to award them the funds.

If the company with the contract were to do its work well, it would organize the report so everyone could use it intelligently. Who would likely readers be? First, the *technical experts* on the program manager's staff. These engineers, accountants, weapons experts, tacticians, and so forth (some of them military, some civil servants) would be tasked by their boss to examine the design, the engine's capability, and the costs in great detail. Possessing the technical background to understand all kinds of charts, tables, diagrams, and descriptions, they would expect detailed technical explanations.

However, many others who might read this document would not be experts, among them the most important audience—*decision makers.* These readers would probably not understand all the technical parts of the report, nor would they need the detail that experts require. The project manager, for example, might be generally knowledgeable in tactics and weapons systems but would not necessarily be an engineer. This person would need a semitechnical explanation, one emphasizing conclusions and recommendations.

Senior military officials would also need a semitechnical discussion of key, summary information (rather than a highly technical discussion of all the details). So would elected government officials and their staffs. Still, at any point, an official up the line might need to examine—usually by assigning staff members to examine—the specific technical features of the project.

So both highly technical and semitechnical discussion must be present in the same report. Moreover, usually *one document* must satisfy both experts and decision makers. Similarly with the many other kinds of documents needed if the government were to go ahead with the project. Each report would have to address readers with very different backgrounds and needs. Whether a later document were

- a formal proposal by a firm to build the engine;
- a progress report submitted by the contracted firm;
- a research report used in the technical design;
- an instruction manual designed for operators; or
- a final report submitted upon the project's completion,

it would still have to address multiple audiences.

We can't go into each kind of report mentioned above; refer to one or more of the references on technical writing mentioned at the end of this chapter for thorough discussions of various technical writing genres. What we *can* do, however, is to discuss the organizing and summarizing techniques industry has used for decades to satisfy such diverse audiences. In the process, we will mention some of the other naval uses these methods have come to serve.

Organization of Technical Reports

Following are several proven methods of designing technical reports so they reach their multiple audiences (1) with the right kind of information, (2) at the necessary reading level, and (3) with the appropriate detail. (Again, you can apply these methods to a variety of complex naval documents, not just technical reports.)

Present Conclusions Before Rationales

Of course, when investigators have a problem to solve, they typically begin by assessing the problem, then they conduct the investigation or research, and they eventually come to conclusions. Sometimes investigators write up their reports following this same order—with conclusions last.

However, as we've seen before in other contexts, the chronological order of the investigation may be backward to the reader's needs. Just as naval readers habitually glance at the action paragraph of a message before reading the whole message through (sometimes *instead of* reading it through), decision makers typically *look for the conclusions first*. Often they only skim the rest of the report—they don't need to read it all.

So help these readers out. As the Correspondence Manual points out, "Avoid Mystery Stories. . . Put requests before justifications, answers before explanations, conclusions before discussions, summaries before details, and the general before the specific." Here's an example of what this guidance might mean for a standard investigative or research report:

Instead of	Organize This Way
Statement of Problem	Statement of Problem
Procedures	Conclusions & Recommendations
Methodology	Support
Analysis	Methodology
Results	Analysis
Discussion of Results	Results
Conclusions	Discussion of Results
Recommendations	

Sometimes you might have to write your report in a rigidly specified format, and that format may resemble the one on the left above. If not, put the conclusions and recommendations *at the beginning*, to give readers a head start on the vital information

Use Appendixes

Relegate to appendixes material only specialists need. Don't let numbers, designs, and other data overburden the text of the report. Full-length reports, like operation orders, often have many appendixes.

Subdivide into Short Sections with Many Headings and Tabs

You can help the reader immensely by organizing your reports into sections. Use care in carving sections out—don't imitate military phone directories, which so poorly sort and identify information that we can seldom find what we need quickly. Instead, design your sections and headings with *the readers' needs in mind*.

Then add paper or plastic tabs to make sections readily visible. On very long documents, consider adding indexes too.

Use Reviews, Surveys, and Summaries Throughout the Report

Summaries aid everyone. Remember that even those few reviewers who read a report straight through will seldom be able to avoid all interruptions from meetings, office visits, and phone calls while they read. At strategic locations in your text (such as the beginnings or ends of major sections), review topics that you've presented before, and summarize the information that follows after. *Above all,* once you've written the whole report from introduction to the conclusions and recommendations . . .

Carefully Compose an "Executive Summary"

The executive summary is a summary of vital information. See below.

The Executive Summary

Design the executive summary so that by reading it—perhaps along with a couple of other key sections of the report, but not much more—an executive will have enough information to proceed to a decision. Actually, whoever picks up a report with a good executive summary can use it to get a quick feel for the report's contents. But the main purpose of an executive summary is to *provide executives the wherewithal to make decisions.*

The length of an executive summary varies—it may run 20 pages for a book-length document but only a page or two for a 20-page report. Here is a common rule-of-thumb: keep the executive summary *one-tenth the size* of the report it summarizes.

Place an executive summary at the beginning of a report, soon after the title page. One Navy lab makes sure a reader can immediately locate the summary by printing it on blue or green paper. A tab, of course, would serve the same purpose. The point is to set off the summary from the rest of the document because everyone is likely to read this section. The summary identifies *the gist* of the report, its overall import.

You've probably seen an executive summary before, even if you didn't recognize it at the time. A briefing memo for a correspondence package on a staff is a kind of executive summary, for the briefing memo, too, enables a superior to understand the matter at hand quickly without having to page through the whole package. Submarine patrol reports typically begin with executive summaries, for here, also, not everyone needs all the details. When a board convenes in Washington, D.C.—the Retired Personnel Board, for example—an executive summary begins the board's report. And so on.

For an excellent example of an executive summary of a major government report, see the Executive Summary of the Department of Defense Commission report on the Beirut Terrorist Attack. The *Marine Corps Gazette* published this summary in its February 1984 issue (pp. 10–13).

You can construct the executive summary in various ways. What usually sets this document off from other summaries is its emphasis on results, conclusions, and recommendations. Executive summaries differ in how much they discuss background, procedures, and methodology (some treat each of these items briefly, while others don't discuss them at all). But the best of them focus mostly on *what all the factors lead to,* that is,

- what results show;
- what conclusions you can draw;
- what action your audience should take.

Don't try to cover everything in an executive summary, but include only the most essential information. Also, remember not to write the executive summary until you have written the whole report in its final form, or it may not do justice to the actual report.

Here's an example of a relatively formal executive summary. Put together at the Navy Personnel Research and Development Center in San Diego, it attempts to evaluate for Navy managers a dual-career personnel track that the Navy had initiated four years before. Note: since the report is designed primarily for *managers,* the executive summary spends most of its time discussing "Managerial Questions and Answers" and "Recommendations." And for its relatively heavy dependence on the passive voice, see "Passive Voice in Technical Writing," later in this chapter.

"You have one chance to get to the decision makers—emphasize the *key* ideas, the *key* findings."—Naval War College Professor

SUMMARY

Background
In November 1984, the General Unrestricted Line (URL) Officer community instituted the dual-career system, composed of the Specialist Track (ST) and General Track (GT). The ST was designed to meet the Navy's need for specialized skills at the senior-officer level. Approximately 30 percent of General URL lieutenant commanders (LCDRs), or 60 per year group, would be selected for the ST. The remaining 70 percent would advance in the GT, which emphasized leadership billets. The ST represented a break with tradition and thus represented more of a concern to the Navy than the GT.

Problem
Having instituted the dual-career policy, the Navy had little subsequent information on how well it had been received by the officer corps. Without such information, it was difficult to modify the policy or project the numbers of officers who would be selecting each track as they progressed in their carrers.

Objective
The objective of this report is to provide information to career managers and policy makers that will help them decide whether the dual-career track should be retained as is, modified, or dropped.

Approach
The dual-career track decision represented a critical new issue to officers and was examined, along with other decisions, in a questionnaire mailed to General URLs. 1,204 questionnaires were completed and analyzed for this study. In addition, 58 General URLs were interviewed in San Diego

to provide a deeper understanding regarding how officers had reacted to the new policy.

Managerial Questions and Answers

Two questions of interest to career managers and policy makers were examined. What the data showed with respect to these questions is as follows:

1. Do officers consider the Specialist Track to be a viable option?

Officers considered the ST to be an "unknown." If forced to make a choice, most would choose the GT.

For example, close to 40 percent of the officers (LCDRs and below) reported that they were undecided about which track to select. The closer officers are to LCDR (the point at which officers can become specialists), the more likely they are to prefer the GT. For those preferring one track or the other (as opposed to undecided), the following percentages of officers preferred the ST and GT, respectively, for each grade: ensign (73%, 27%), lieutenant junior grade (56%, 44%), lieutenant (45%, 55%), and LCDR (26%, 74%).

LCDRs selecting the ST tended to score lower than those selecting the GT in the following areas:

1. Fitness reports (as recalled by the officers themselves).
2. Satisfaction with past assignments.

In addition, LCDRs were more likely to select the ST, the more they reported they had cut back on their career involvement to meet the needs of their spouses and/or children.

LCDRs were more likely to view the ST as "appealing" the lower they scored in the following areas:

1. Satisfaction with their careers.
2. Satisfaction with the Navy as an organization.
3. Desire to strive for captain.
4. Desire to remain in the Navy beyond the date they were eligible to retire.

2. Do General URLs feel knowledgeable about the dual-career system?

A substantial number of individuals do not feel knowledgeable enough to make effective career decisions.

For example, 78 percent of the officers were unaware that 75 percent of LCDR executive officer and commanding officer 1000-coded shore billets are, according to policy, supposed to be fenced for General URLs. In addition, 54 percent were unaware that individuals are permitted to switch to the Materiel-Professional track from either the ST or GT.

Recommendations

Two overall recommendations resulted from the study:

1. **The Navy should decide whether the ST should be continued**, given the findings of the present study. If the track is continued, then a commitment should be made to further clarify and develop it.

2. **The ST should be reevaluated in 2 years** to determine if some of the current problems have been alleviated and if implementation of the track has progressed satisfactorily.

—Gerry L. Wilcove. "Officer Career Development: General Unrestricted Line Officer Perceptions of the Dual-Career Track." NPRDC TN88-62 (September 1988).

Two Kinds of Abstracts

Another kind of summary device for technical reports is the "abstract," which may preface a report whether or not the report also has an executive summary. The abstract differs from an executive summary primarily in function and audience. That is, where an executive summary is a *synopsis* of a report's conclusions/recommendations and is meant for decision makers, an abstract is a *screening tool* that is usually intended for researchers. Also, where the executive summary is designed so the decision maker can read it *instead of* reading the whole report, the abstract helps a researcher decide whether or not to read the report at all.

Writers compose abstracts for professional articles as well as technical reports. But whatever documents they summarize, abstracts have certain standard features:

- They often include much technical detail in a very condensed and highly technical discussion that a layperson will have trouble following.
- They are typically short—from a couple of sentences to about 300 words (but they still use full sentences, not fragments or bullets).
- They usually are written as one paragraph.
- They don't focus on conclusions or recommendations but either give equal value to every part of a report or concentrate on a project's results, quickly letting the expert reader see the scientific or *technical significance* of the research.

Write each abstract so it makes sense as a separate document. You have two different styles to choose from.

The Informative Abstract

The informative abstract is meant to *reproduce the report in small*, mirroring all its essential features. In fact, some texts recommend that to write such an abstract you should first identify the topic sentence from every major section in the report, and then simply string all these key sentences together, just smoothing out the wording. Others suggest you work from an outline. However you proceed, include in the informative abstract a brief discussion of the background of the research project, its intent, the way you set it up, the procedure you used to carry it out, and the results.

Reading such a summary will tell the researcher whether to order the whole report or not. Here's an example of an informative abstract that a ship research center put out, written in 1987 and entitled, "Smoke Management on FFG 7 Class Ships—An Evaluation of Smoke Removal Diagrams and Procedures on USS CLIFTON SPRAGUE (FFG 16)."

> We performed a series of smoke migration tests on board USS CLIFTON SPRAGUE (FFG 16), at the Philadelphia Naval Shipyard, to validate the FFG 7 class Smoke Removal and Procedures Diagram developed by the Naval Sea Systems Command. These diagrams divided the ship into 23 smoke control zones; three of those zones were tested. A smoke generator designed by the Naval Equipment Training Center was used to release a chemical smoke and to simulate the smoke from a fire. We found that smoke can be confined to the designated zones, but some leakage will occur through cable penetrations and nondogged doors. Removal of smoke was hampered by a local fan controller located within a zone, which is necessary to reset the ventilation system in that zone. Such a fan controller should have a means of being bypassed or should be relocated external to the zone. We were able to de-smoke the test zones within four air exchanges.
>
> — E. Rodriguez and R. Carey, Rept. no. DTNSRDC/SME-87/16, 103 pp., David W. Taylor Naval Ship Research and Development Center, Annapolis, MD.

Clearly, the emphasis here is not on conclusions/recommendations but rather on faithfully representing the whole report. By using this abstract, researchers looking for information either on the FFG 7 class of ship, on smoke migration, on testing smoke removal, or just on the USS *Clifton Sprague* itself might find information enough to decide whether or not to read the whole report.

The Descriptive Abstract

A descriptive abstract simply describes *from an outside point of view* what the report contains. The descriptive abstract is a kind of prose table of contents. It serves the same general purpose as the informative abstract, but rather than reproducing the original report in small (like an informative abstract), the descriptive abstract *describes what the report contains.*

Here's an example of a descriptive abstract for an interim report that the Naval Postgraduate School at Monterey issued in 1987. The report is entitled, "Opportunities for Tropical Cyclone Motion Research in the Northwest Pacific Region" (author Scott A. Sandgathe).

Tropical cyclone track prediction problems in the Northwest Pacific region that need to be researched are reviewed from the perspective of the operational forecaster. This information is provided as background for the upcoming Office of Naval Research field experiment on tropical cyclone motion. A short-term climatology of the frequency and spatial distribution of tropical cyclones is provided. Seven classes of operationally interested track forecast situations are described. Each cyclone from 1982 through 1985 is tabulated in terms of these classes.

Government and industry widely use both descriptive and informative abstracts. The informative abstract is generally more helpful, for it gives a reader more information. However, some kinds of research do not lend themselves easily to informative abstracts. Whichever kind you write, wait to compose the abstract (as you wait to draft your executive summary) until you have completed the final draft of your report. That way, you'll be sure you summarize only what is *actually in* the report.

"Key Words": Abstracts and Computers

Where will an investigator see an abstract? Researchers at a library or lab may see the abstract in a printed collection of abstracts. Now that libraries and researchers are making greater use of computers, a researcher will more likely turn to a computer abstracting service for on-line researching.

If a researcher types in a key word or phrase in one of these computerized indexes, perhaps the term "missile detector radar," then the titles of all the recent articles on such radars will appear on the screen. The researcher can select some of these articles to investigate further, and the computer will put their abstracts on the screen as directed. By reading each abstract, the researcher decides whether or not to order the articles represented. By using telephone or computer links, researchers now have access to technical information from throughout the world.

On the Department of Defense "Report Documentation Page" (DOD Form 1473) that accompanies most formal technical reports used in the military, you'll not only type an abstract, but you'll also fill out a section called "Key Words." List there the terms that best indicate the substance of your report, both the subjects that it addresses directly and others that it touches on significantly. Take some care in selecting terms; don't make them too complex. In some cases, you'll have to conform to a printed list of standard terms.

For example, the documentation page for the article on tropical cyclone motion research (whose abstract appears above) listed "tropical cyclone motion,""tropical meteorology,""tropical cyclone path prediction," and "typhoon motion" as its key words.

Passive Voice in Technical Writing

One other matter is noteworthy in the abstract on tropical cyclone motion reproduced above: it is written in the *passive voice.* Indeed, in that abstract *every sentence is passive,* the main verbs being "are reviewed," "is provided," "is provided," "are described," and "is tabulated." Since this text elsewhere recommends that you avoid the passive voice as a general rule, such heavy dependence on the passive calls for comment.

Passive voice is widespread in technical writing. Why? Perhaps the main reason is that scientists have purposely used passive voice for decades. Instead of stating, "the chemist observed the experiment," scientists have usually written, "the experiment was observed," not only writing in the passive voice, but also omitting all mention of the person doing the observation. The rationale is that (1) normally the results of scientific investigation are much more important than the investigator, and (2) passive verbs make the sentence more "objective."

"Passives are generally weak because they place a mushy emphasis on the thing done rather than on the doer. 'The battle was won by the Marines' is a flabby way of saying, 'The Marines won the battle.' 'I love you' is far more likely to get results than 'You are loved by me.' "—Argus Tresidder, former Professor of English, MCDEC, Quantico

This rationale is only *half* right. Using passive verbs does focus attention on the receiver of a sentence's action. Often the object of the action is more important than the actor and deserves more attention. To say, "The feasibility of ocean surveillance platforms in detecting submarines has repeatedly been demonstrated" focuses attention on that feasibility rather than on who demonstrated it, and that focus may be perfectly appropriate, depending on your purpose.

But realize that such a statement is in no way more objective than a statement that identifies who did the demonstrating. Changing a statement to say *"it was concluded* that low-flying aircraft would not cause mines to detonate" is no more objective than saying *"we concluded* that low-flying aircraft would not cause mines to detonate." The way you write the sentence doesn't change the facts or the objectivity; someone must have drawn the conclusion in either case.

Understanding this concept, modern technical writing experts recommend much less use of the passive voice than they once did. So should you rigorously correct the passive voice in technical documents you have to chop or sign off on? That depends. In circumstances where such rewriting won't make much difference, or where it will be highly controversial (say, where your boss was trained to use the passive voice and deems doing otherwise unprofessional), the improvement probably will not be worth the effort. However, wherever passive voice adversely affects the readability of a document in a major way or when the document is destined to have very high visibility, you should at least put the executive summary into the active voice and perhaps go on to rework the "Conclusions" and "Recommendations" sections as well.

Other Technical Documents

Much of the writing in industry and business is very much like the writing in the naval services—letters, memos, and directives prevail in almost all organizations. While formats and styles differ from firm to firm, and one organization may use full-block style and another semiblock for its letters, a writer can usually recognize a letter anywhere and adapt to the required format quickly.

However, some technical documents differ greatly from standard naval correspondence or staff work. Such documents can be very troublesome for those few naval personnel who have to compose them. Supply officers and others, for example, often have to write "specifications" for contracts. Also involved in the contracting process are "statements of work," which shipboard officers frequently have to write. While on staffs, many naval personnel will have to draft or revise "position descriptions," and then try to get those positions funded. Naval personnel will have to write many other technical documents from time to time.

You may find the office or lab you work with has put out a style guide to help you. If not, seek guidance for writing such documents from knowledgeable professionals, or from standard technical writing texts and sourcebooks such as those listed below.

References on Technical Writing

Charles T. Brusaw, Gerald J. Alred, and Walter E. Oliu, *Handbook of Technical Writing*. New York: St. Martin's, current edition. An encyclopedic dictionary of technical writing terms. Also includes some treatment of grammar, punctuation, and usage and discusses how to write many kinds of reports, illustrations, and layouts. Has an excellent index.

Kenneth W. Houp and Thomas E. Pearsall, *Reporting Technical Information*. New York: Macmillan, current edition. A comprehensive text, covering each major type of technical report. Oriented both for technical and nontechnical readers. Includes a strong discussion of graphics as used in technical reports and a solid chapter on speech.

Marine Corps Historical Center Writing Guide. Washington, D.C.: Marine Corps Historical Center. Revised 1983. For use by historians and others writing about Marine Corps history, including those writing for *Fortitudine*. Major sections on doing historical research, footnoting and writing bibliographies, and preparing maps.

J. C. Mathes and Dwight Stevenson, *Designing Technical Reports: Writing for Audiences in Organizations*. Indianapolis: Bobbs-Merrill, 1976. Another standard text, but primarily designed for engineers. Especially good on how to treat multiple audiences. Oriented toward industry; includes some examples from the field of naval architecture.

Naval War College Research Guide: Style Manual and Security Classification. Newport: U.S. Naval War College, revised annually. Primarily covers research-paper preparation and format, footnotes and bibliography, and security procedures. Mainly for students at the Naval War College.

Report Writing Handbook, Naval Air Test Center Instruction 5213.3. A very detailed guide on how to write reports for NATC; a good example of a lab or test center's style and format guidance.

Patricia A. Robinson, *Fundamentals of Technical Writing*. Boston: Houghton Mifflin Company, 1985. A highly readable discussion of the basics of technical writing. Very good for general introduction to the subject, although not as detailed on specific types of documents as other texts.

Two major technical information sources that defense researchers use widely are abstracting services: NTIS—*National Technical Information Service* (also on disc), and DTIC—*Defense Technical Information Center.* And a major resource for military researchers is the *Air University Index of Military Periodicals,* found in many military libraries.

Unfortunately, the JAG instructions are all written by lawyers, and they terrify the ordinary walk-around guy.

—Retired Navy Captain

9

JAG Manual Investigations

General Background

Introduction

A JAG Manual (JAGMAN) Investigation is basically a *management tool,* a means by which a command can gather the facts needed to make a decision. That decision might concern public or congressional inquiries, loss or compromise of classified material, claims for or against the government, destruction of property, accidents, injuries to personnel, or loss of life. Even minor investigations can have substantial effects.

When doing an investigation, you gather information, express considered opinions, and make careful recommendations that will help a commander (the "convening authority") make intelligent decisions. In some cases, people's careers depend on what appears in a JAGMAN Investigation. These investigations routinely affect medical retirement, disability pay, veterans benefits, and promotion opportunities. In other cases, many thousands of dollars are at issue. As you can see, doing an investigation is a very important responsibility. Conducting one can also teach a person a good deal about command decision making.

The type of investigation covered in this chapter is the *One-Officer Investigation Not Requiring a Hearing* (the label used to be "Informal JAG Manual Investigation"). It is the most common type and the one most often assigned to someone who has never done one before. If you must do one of these investigations, understand several important points.

First, a JAGMAN Investigation will normally become *your primary duty* until you complete it. Second, doing an investigation is an excellent opportunity to get the attention of your commanding officer, for the CO will review and personally endorse your report once you complete it. The CO can ask you to do it over if it isn't as good as he or she thinks it should be. (On the other hand, as investigating officer, you can recommend that the CO enlarge, restrict, or modify the scope of the investigation or change any instruction in the appointing order.) Third, realize that this investigation will usually go on up the line, through your boss's boss and so on, to the Office of the Judge Advocate General. Sometimes the CO will decide the Investigation doesn't need to be forwarded—but normally it will be.

Another point to remember. Should anyone have criticisms along the way, criticisms either of the report you prepare or of your command's way of doing business as reflected in the report, they won't be private. Your boss will hear of them for sure, and possibly many other officers as well. Those critiques could reflect both on you and on your ship or unit.

These investigations are not kept within the military either. Because of the Freedom of Information Act, they are not proprietary information, and virtually anyone can get copies. Not only *can* people get them, but they routinely *do*: the Office of the Judge Advocate General sends out thousands of copies a year. Next of kin, lawyers, reporters, members of Congress—all can request copies (and can almost always get them), and a JAGMAN Investigation involving the death of a service member goes to the next of kin as a matter of course.

"Our problems are that JAGMAN Investigations are usually shuffled off to people with little Navy experience."—JAG Commander

Altogether, then, these investigations have very high potential visibility—probably higher than anything else a junior officer (or senior enlisted person) will write, except perhaps an important message. But even in the case of a message, a junior person would usually just be drafting, not signing it, while that same person *will* sign the JAGMAN Investigation. All these factors—to say nothing of the most important matter of all, to see that justice and truth are served, both for the service member and for the Navy or Marine Corps itself—suggest you should do your very best with this demanding research/writing task.

What follows below is a quick (and, because of space limitations, necessarily incomplete) primer on doing a JAGMAN Investigation. Reading this section will serve as a starting point. *Do not depend on this section alone*, but *go to the official sources*, especially the JAG Manual. Also consult official instructions, chain of command directives, and the other helpful guides that are available (see below). As you'll see, many sources are available to help you both *do* and *write up* this kind of investigation.

References on JAGMAN Investigations

- Article 31, UCMJ.
- Manual of the Judge Advocate General (JAG Manual or JAGMAN). This is of course the standard reference on JAGMAN Investigations, as on many other things.

Of special importance for JAGMAN Investigations are the sections in the JAG Manual on:

— Privacy Act compliance
— the Appointing Order
— the Investigative Report itself
— Line-of-Duty and Misconduct Determinations
— Injury/Disease Warnings
— Article 31 Warnings
— Investigations of Specific Types of Incidents
— Checklists of Various Kinds
— Claims for or against the Government.

- Civil Law Study Guide, Naval Justice School, Newport—for detailed guidance on JAGMAN Investigations. This textbook is for the lawyer, legal officer, and senior officer courses at Newport.
- OPNAVINST 5510.1 series, Security Manual—for JAG guidelines on Classified Material, especially sections 4–5, "JAG Investigations," and Exhibit 4A, "JAG Investigation Checklist on Security Violations."
- MILPERSMAN, Section 4210100—for death cases.
- Checklists and instructions issued by the local JAG officials and various type and administrative commanders.

Note that while galleys of this book were being reviewed, word came that the JAG Manual was undergoing an extensive change, and that a new version would likely be approved before this book's publication. The author reviewed chapter 2 of this revised manual ("Administrative Fact-Finding Bodies"). That review indicated that the revision would not alter the JAGMAN Investigation in substance; changes would mainly affect organization and numbering.

Most of the topics mentioned above were to be found in chapter 2 of the proposed change, a chapter entitled "Administrative Fact-Finding Bodies." Using the table of contents and index of the revised JAG Manual, find the appropriate sections in chapter 2 or elsewhere, and jot their numbers down on the paragraphs of this book as you read it, for future reference.

Preliminary Steps When Assigned a JAGMAN Investigation

Some officers in the fleet and field say that the problem with a JAGMAN is not writing the report but doing the investigating. They argue that the tough part is digging down to the underlying, determining facts of the case. However, those people who review JAGMAN Investigations insist (from having read dozens) that the writing is a big problem too. So we'll look at both tasks. We'll start by discussing what you should do to begin your investigation.

- First, read the whole section on JAGMAN Investigations in this book, for general familiarity. As you do, pay special attention to the various terms and concepts involved.

• Then, read the appointing order very carefully. It is your basic marching order, and it should address your specific investigation. If you don't understand any item in the appointing order, ask the "convening authority" (which is usually your CO or someone acting for the CO) about it. Further, if during your investigation you feel that you should broaden or narrow the scope of the inquiry, or that you need to change any instructions in the appointing order, submit a request (orally or in writing) to the convening authority. Realize too that any single JAGMAN Investigation should cover *only one* incident. If you find you're really investigating two or three separate incidents, report this finding too.

• Get hold of an updated JAG Manual, and review the sections mentioned specifically in the appointing order and those listed under "References," above, especially those sections involving your particular case. For instance, if you must make a line-of-duty/misconduct determination, be sure to review that section of the JAGMAN; if you are investigating a death, review the section on death cases, and so on.

• Take a look at some recently completed JAGMAN Investigations from files at your ship or station. Reading a few will give you more familiarity with what they look like and, perhaps more importantly, what they customarily look *into.* (Be careful with the handling of these investigations; don't let them circulate all over the ship or station.)

• Talk to others aboard your ship or station who have done investigations before or who have been to a naval school on this or related subjects. For example, normally someone aboard will have been to the Legal Officer Course in Newport or San Diego or to the traveling Senior Officer Course for XOs and COs and other senior officers (according to several naval officers, the best naval school they've attended). This officer should be able to give you both practical advice and good written guidance.

However, if this person is also the ship's or station's legal officer, he or she might have to keep a distance from the case. If it goes to mast or trial, this person may be required to get involved in the case later. On top of that possibility, the legal officer will usually have to draft the first endorsement for the CO.

• Find out where the local staff JAG is, or if that officer is not available locally, seek another naval lawyer (perhaps at a local Naval Legal Services Office) who might be able to give you some help. Most staff JAGs are more than willing to discuss with you how to go about an investigation, and later they will be glad to look at a rough draft. Indeed, *some staff JAGs expect you to come visit them first* and then to send them a rough draft before you formally submit your report. Such a review will often save them time later. In addition, poorly done JAGMAN Investigations can affect a staff's (and a staff JAG's) reputation. (Of course, don't communicate with the staff JAG unless your CO first gives consent.)

On the other hand, you should realize that "political" considerations may play here too. You can ask about technical considerations and about specific details, but don't ask the staff JAG how to make sure the investigation gets approved. The staff JAG works for the flag or 0-6 first; potential conflicts of interest may hinder this officer from getting too much involved in your conclusions, recommendations, and so on.

• Don't forget to take counsel from those in your own chain of command, such as the executive officer. JAG officers are not necessarily attuned to the special sensitivities of operational commands or all the intricacies of shipboard situations.

- Whomever you talk to, make sure you get a good feeling for

— where to go for information;
— what to look for;
— whom to talk to;
— what kind and number of questions to ask;
— any available checklists concerning the specific kind of incident you are investigating, beyond those discussed below (see the section "Pointers on Conducting the Investigation");
— when to stop investigating and start writing.

Important Features of Investigations

Privacy Act Statements

As investigating officer, you must ask individuals to sign Privacy Act Statements whenever you request them to disclose private (personal) information about themselves. Such situations, however, are *not* the rule, and *you should avoid unnecessary use of the Privacy Act Statement.*

During an investigation into a loss of funds, for example, if you ask an accountable individual to disclose his or her personal financial status, this disclosure is subject to the Privacy Act. But asking a service member to account for actions when on watch, to recount actions in the course of official duties, or to relate events observed in the course of routine activities is *not* a request for private information and does not require a Privacy Act warning statement. Investigators are often too quick to use the Privacy Act warning, sometimes to the detriment of the investigation. Use this warning statement only when absolutely required.

The requirement for a Privacy Act Statement is spelled out in the JAGMAN, and a format for one can be found in a JAGMAN appendix. Very good formats appear in an appendix to the NJS Civil Law Study Guide and in many local instructions, such as PHIBGRU 2 INST, which shows two forms—one for the person who incurred the injury, and one for a witness.

Social Security Numbers

Watch how you use social security numbers (SSNs). As a rule, *don't solicit SSNs from individuals.* You must have an individual sign a Privacy Act Statement before you ask *personally* for an SSN; otherwise, you are in violation of JAGMAN. On the other hand, if you get the number from a service record, you're using an official source, not personal information. You can use that SSN in the report without a Privacy Act Statement as long as you stipulate in the report that you got the SSN from an official source. *But in most cases, including SSNs in JAGMAN Investigations is simply not necessary.*

Injury/Disease Warnings

Don't ask service members about the origin or aggravation of any *disease* or *injury* or *disability* they have suffered without first advising them of their statutory rights not to make such a statement. Have them sign JAGMAN Warnings that they have read and understood their rights before proceeding with interviews. Again, a proper warning form is in an appendix of the NJS Civil Law Study Guide.

Article 31 Warning

Whenever a person is suspected of committing an offense under the UCMJ, you must advise that person of his or her rights under Article 31, UCMJ, before proceeding with any questions. These so-called "Article 31 Rights" include the right to remain silent, the right to consult with a lawyer, and the right to terminate the interview at any time, as well as the warning that any statements made might be used against that person in trial by court-martial. (A proper warning form is an appendix of the JAG Manual and also in an appendix of the NJS Civil Law Study Guide.)

Line-of-Duty/Misconduct Determinations

Perhaps the most common JAGMAN Investigations are cases of injury and disease. Here a major part of your responsibility is to help your commanding officer make a "line-of-duty/misconduct" determination, that is, to help the chain of command determine (1) if an injury was incurred "in the line of duty" or not, and (2) whether it involved misconduct—two separate determinations. Many rights and benefits (such as eligibility for extension of enlistment, longevity and retirement multipliers, disability pensions, severance pay, and VA benefits) depend on these determinations.

What constitutes "line of duty," and what is "misconduct"? Put briefly, the service presumes you've incurred any injuries or diseases "in the line of duty" unless clear and convincing evidence exists otherwise. What would such evidence be? If a service member incurred an injury as a result of misconduct, while deserting, or while an unauthorized absentee in excess of 24 hours, then the injury might be regarded as "not in the line of duty."

A finding of "misconduct," on the other hand, would come about if an investigation clearly showed that (1) a service member *intentionally* incurred an injury, or (2) that it was "the proximate result of such gross negligence as to demonstrate a reckless disregard of the consequences." These rules are pretty clear, but of course pinning down individual cases can be tricky.

Specific relationships exist between misconduct and line of duty. For example, a determination of misconduct always requires a determination of "not in the line of duty." To put the whole issue simply, the finding must be one of these three:

1. In the line of duty, not due to own misconduct.
2. Not in the line of duty, not due to own misconduct.
3. Not in the line of duty, due to own misconduct.

Consult the JAGMAN section on "Line-of-Duty and Misconduct Determinations." In particular, study the special rules on intoxication, on mental responsibility, and on suicidal acts and gestures to make sure you fully understand these determinations.

You should realize also that a determination of misconduct is *not a punitive measure.* While it may directly affect such compensations as VA benefits, medical retirement, and disability pay, a favorable or unfavorable determination has no binding power on any issue of guilt or innocence in a disciplinary proceeding. Of course, an investigator has the responsibility to draw up specific charges if the investigation suggests they are warranted. But the determinations of "line of duty" and "misconduct" are *administrative* rather than judicial determinations.

Indeed, once having had an injury investigated, a commander may report the LOD/misconduct determination informally by an entry in a health record, on a form 5800/15, or in a letter report. The commander does not have to proceed with a JAGMAN Investigation that will go all the way up the chain to the Office of the Judge Advocate General (OJAG). Many investigators forget this possibility. As a senior judge advocate once remarked:

> My advice to commands/investigating officers is to use the documentation vehicle that requires the least amount of work and that is sufficient to protect the rights of the service member and the interests of the government. I am *not* suggesting that we look for ways to avoid work. What I mean is that you should use health or dental record entries and forms or letter reports (in accordance with JAGMAN) when appropriate. I see too many JAG Manual Investigations that did not need to be done.

See the decision tree on LOD/misconduct reporting in Figure 9.1 for a step-by-step approach to deciding whether a JAGMAN Investigation is actually required.

Relations of Line-of-Duty/Misconduct to Injury, Disease, and Death

Investigation into LOD/misconduct can relate either to *injury, disease,* or *death*—but somewhat differently to each.

Injuries

Rules on *injuries* are pretty clear-cut. You must make an LOD/misconduct determination whenever a service member incurs an injury that might result in a permanent disability, or that results in physical inability to perform duty for a period exceeding 24 hours (as distinguished from hospitalization for evaluation or observation). See the JAGMAN section entitled "When Line-of-Duty/Misconduct Determinations are Required."

Therefore, make sure you have an opinion as to the line-of-duty and misconduct status of each member whose injury caused over 24 hours of lost time, or which might possibly result in a permanent disability. See

Figure 9.1 A Decision Tree on Line-of-Duty/Misconduct Reporting. This decision tree aids an investigating officer in determining what kind of report is required.

Decision Tree --

LOD/MISCONDUCT REPORTING

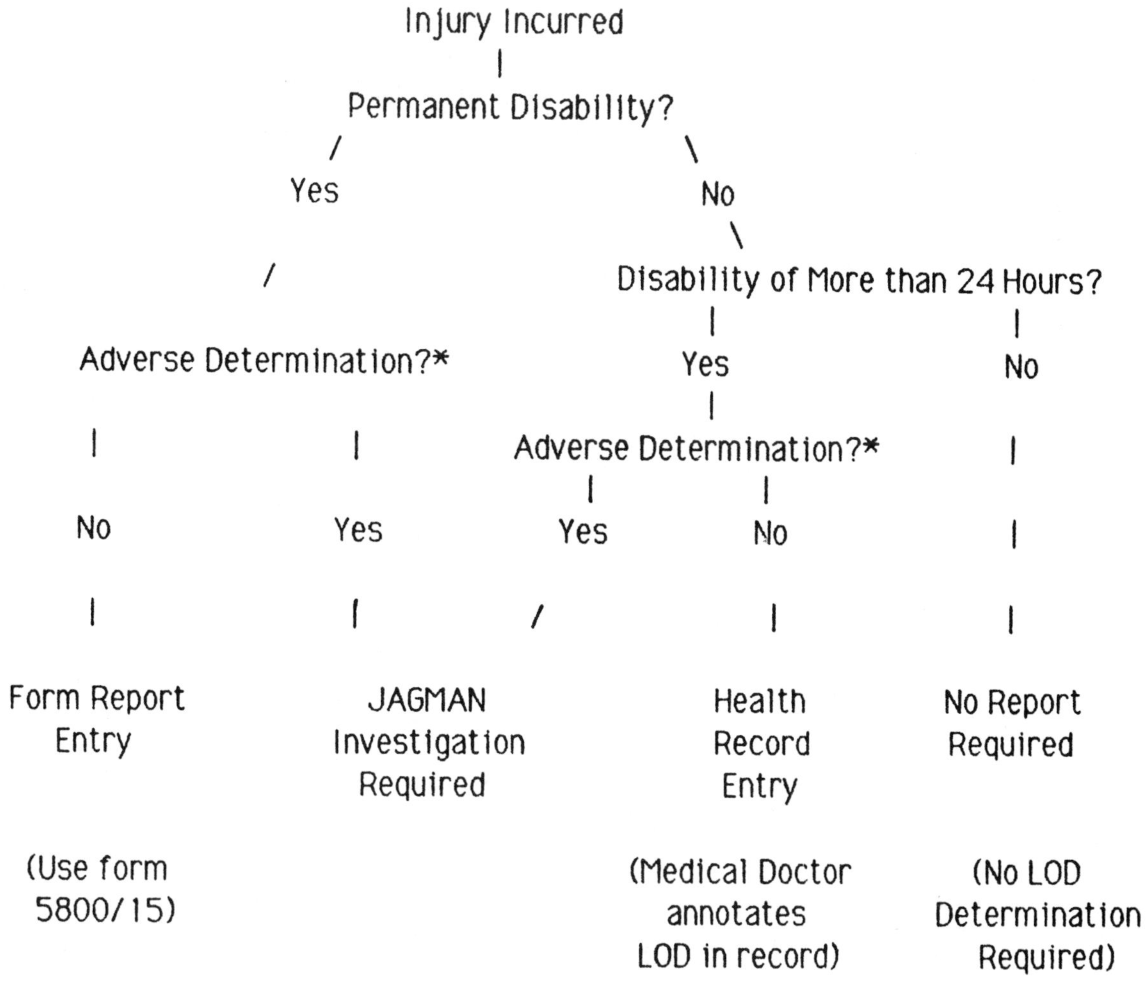

* "Adverse Determination" means the injury was found to have been incurred not in the line of duty, or due to misconduct, or both.

the JAGMAN section on "Relationship between Misconduct and Line-of-Duty." Again, remember that while an LOD/misconduct determination is always required, a JAGMAN Investigation is not. The vehicle for reporting that determination can be a 5800/15 form or a health-record entry rather than a formal investigation.

Diseases

The issue is murkier in the case of diseases. Basically, intentional efforts to contract disease to avoid service or grossly negligent conduct that results in a disabling disease *might* be considered misconduct. Specifically, in the past the service has considered alcohol- or drug-induced disease, venereal disease, and unreasonable refusal of medical or dental treatment that results in disability as misconduct. Other circumstances (such as a service member's intentionally disregarding posted quarantine warnings, with the result that he or she contracts a highly contagious disease) may also require a finding of "Not in the line of duty, due to misconduct." Various parts of the JAGMAN section on LOD/Misconduct apply.

Death

As for death, while a JAGMAN Investigation is required in certain cases of death, an investigator is *never* to express an opinion of the decedent's line-of-duty/misconduct status in such an investigation, for no Navy Department–administered survivor's benefit depends on such a determination. Other agencies have the responsibility to determine whether the decedent's survivors are eligible for benefits.

However, in practice, such determinations as those other agencies (like the Veterans Administration) make will rest at least partly on Department of the Navy documentation. So while you don't explicitly express a line-of-duty/misconduct opinion in the JAGMAN Investigation in a death case, do your best to *develop the facts fully*, to provide others with a basis for such a determination.

General Guidelines for LOD/Misconduct Determinations

The following are guidelines to follow concerning LOD/misconduct determinations. These guidelines are in addition to other guidelines for JAGMAN Investigations.

- Ensure you understand fully line of duty, misconduct, the relationship between these concepts, and all special rules involved.
- Make sure you make a finding of fact as to the leave, liberty, or duty status of any injured person (JAGMAN 0817e).
- See that the investigation clarifies the nature and extent of all injuries, and includes the place, extent, and cause of any hospitalization. Especially ensure that you differentiate periods of alcohol or drug impairment and periods of psychiatric treatment.
- Ensure that you state clearly the *amount of lost work time*, if any, as a finding of fact. If the injured person is still disabled when you submit the report, *include a medical officer's prognosis.*

• Include costs of treatment at civilian and/or military hospitals, if available. (The Navy or Marine Corps can sometimes make a claim—an MCRA claim—against a third party who injures a service member.)

• The convening authority will afford a JAGMAN hearing to any service member who is thought to have been injured or diseased either "not in the line of duty" or "due to his own misconduct" and will append the hearing results as an enclosure to the first endorsement to the investigation. Appropriate hearing forms are in the appendix to the NJS Civil Law Study Guide and in the appendixes to the JAGMAN.

• Fill out a line-of-duty/misconduct checklist as you conduct your investigation. See JAGMAN, Appendix A to the NJS Civil Law Study Guide, or local directives.

Pointers on Conducting the Investigation

Get the Right Checklists

Assemble all the relevant checklists. There are the two standard ones—the first the JAGMAN section on the "Investigative Report," which is an overall guide on doing the investigation; the second the JAGMAN "Checklist for Fact-Finding Bodies," which is a line-of-duty/misconduct checklist. Then there are various special checklists. Several—"aircraft accidents," "vehicle accidents," "explosions," "postal violations," and many more—can be found in the JAGMAN section on "Investigations of Specific Types of Incidents."

There are also locally prepared checklists, some of which deal with events that commonly occur in a particular type of ship or unit, and others that cover standard situations even more thoroughly than the JAG Manual. You should ask about these lists as you talk to your XO, local JAG, and other JAG officers. Indeed, sometimes you will find you are *required* to follow a special checklist. In any case, local lists may help you greatly in figuring out what to look for and in making sure you've researched all the right data. They'll tell you what witnesses to interview and the kinds of documents to seek out, and sometimes they'll suggest physical evidence to look for too.

If a single incident you are investigating involves more than one of the categories specifically listed in the JAG Manual section entitled "Investigations of Specific Types of Incidents," you should go through the checklist *for each category* that is involved. For instance, an investigation of an automobile accident between a Navy vehicle and a civilian resulting in injury to the Navy driver would involve:

— The Checklist for Fact-Finding Bodies, in general;
— The section on Vehicular Accidents; and
— The sections concerning Claims for or against the Government (investigators often overlook claims or potential claims).

Make sure you have covered *all aspects* of the incident you're investigating.

Make Careful Plans Before Interviewing Witnesses

• Have a plan for going about your interviews. Do them in a reasonable order. Again make sure you know what warnings to give (see JAGMAN on warnings and Article 31, UCMJ), and be sure you give them in each case.

• You should ordinarily collect relevant information from all other sources prior to interviewing persons suspected of an offense or improper performance of duty. When the interview begins, make sure you give the proper warning (see above), and afterwards document your warnings.

• Also, for witnesses suspected of an offense or other difficult witnesses, make sure you have done your homework. Research the case as best you can before you see them, write down some questions ahead of time, check with lawyers, and so on. The more complex the case, the more homework you'll want to do before you talk to the key people.

• Conducting interviews in person is best—but for witnesses out of town or otherwise hard to reach, you can conduct telephone or mail interviews (though remember that mail will take a while). For each phone interview, prepare a written memorandum for record. Setting down the substance of the conversation, the time and date it took place, full identification of the interviewees, and any rights or warnings provided.

• Begin an in-person investigation by sitting down with the person, giving out a voluntary statement form, and asking the person to write down all relevant facts surrounding the incident. Then ask specific questions orally if you want to make sure you cover particular points. Work any oral responses into a final draft of the person's statement, and have the individual review the statement as soon as possible.

• When taking a statement from anyone, be sure to phrase it in the actual language of the witness. Try to have the witness sign it, but if the witness cannot or will not, certify it yourself to be an accurate summary or the verbatim transcript of oral statements the witness made.

• Most importantly, be sure the witnesses speak as factually and specifically as possible. Vague statements such as "pretty drunk," "a few beers," and "pretty fast" do not specify events clearly enough to be very helpful. Try to pin the witness down. For example, instead of accepting "pretty drunk," use a series of questions:

— How long did you observe this person?
— How clear was his speech?
— Did you observe him walk?
— What was the condition of his eyes?
— What did he smell like?
— What was he drinking?
— Exactly how much had he drunk?
— Over what period of time? etc.

Look for Relevant Documents and Physical Evidence

General

In general, include whatever of the following may be useful as real or documentary evidence: photographs, records, operating logs, directives, watch lists, pieces of damaged equipment, sketches, military or civilian police accident reports, autopsy reports, hospitalization or clinical records, etc. (although watch out for Privacy Act problems with the latter). The NJS Civil Law Study Guide contains good guidelines for collecting each kind of evidence. Below are a few guidelines for particular types of cases. See the JAGMAN checklists for additional pointers on your specific case. Also see the section "Documents and Enclosures," below, for further guidance on documentary evidence.

Automobile Accidents

"I have had to return several investigations or request by phone that commands provide additional information regarding automobile or personal property insurance. The ability of the government to assert affirmative claims and the information needed to perfect these claims must be explained to investigating officers."
—Senior Judge Advocate

In cases involving an automobile accident, include maps, charts, diagrams, or photographs of an accident scene or of a vehicle or other evidence, as needed. Identify the date and subject matter of any photographs. You can write notes and refer to directions, objects, or elevations, and attach those references to the reverse of the photo, if helpful. Note that photos used as enclosures, like the rest of the investigation, are subject to public release under the Freedom of Information Act. So normally don't include gruesome photos of dead bodies or bloody weapons, beds, floors, and the like.

Claims

If the incident involves possible claims either for or against the Department of the Navy, make sure to include photos of property damage, estimates of value of such damage, and complete information on insurance coverage (name of company, amount of liability, policy number, name and address of local adjustor, owner of vehicle if not the operator, and so on). See the section on claims in the JAGMAN. Also, remember in possible claims cases to include the Attorney Work Product Statement both in the appointing order and in the preliminary statement (see JAGMAN). This statement will often protect the opinions and recommendations in a JAGMAN Investigation from release to the public.

Death

In the case of a death, make sure that the death certificate supports a finding of fact as to the *time* and *cause* of death. (However, don't wait to submit a death investigation beyond the mandatory processing time if you still haven't obtained the death certificate; instead, send the investigation on, noting "death certificate to follow." When the certificate comes, send it on to whoever holds the investigation at the time.)

LOD/Misconduct

In LOD/misconduct cases, *locate and include documentary evidence that substantiates the member's duty status at the time of any injury, disease, or death.* This evidence could be a message report of the member's duty status, certified copies of service record documents, or a written statement from the division officer, platoon leader, personnel officer, or other person authorized to grant liberty or record leave status. *Note*: An unsupported statement by the investigating officer as to the duty status of the individual is not an acceptable substitute for *documentary evidence* of such status.

Don't Combine JAGMAN Investigations with Other Investigations

More than one kind of investigation may go on with respect to any one incident. Make sure your JAGMAN Investigation is completely separate from (and has no reference to) any Aircraft Mishap Investigation Reports, Inspector General Reports, or Medical Quality Assurance Investigations that are under way. Do not include any reference at all to polygraph examinations. Do not make any use of the narrative of any Naval Investigative Service (NIS) investigation that may be going on.

However, you may use the *exhibits* of an NIS investigation in your report. NIS investigators are usually extremely thorough and professional about giving warnings, questioning, and so on. If you know the NIS is talking to someone you would also like to talk to (say, about misconduct), you might go on with other aspects of your investigation, and then ask to see (and use in your report, if pertinent) advance copies of applicable statements by witnesses or like NIS exhibits. This way you might find that part of your work is already done. Of course, you may then have to conduct additional interviews on your own. On this whole subject, see JAGMAN on "Noncombinable Investigations" or "Investigations Required by Other Regulations."

Follow These Additional Guidelines

- Get started quickly. Witnesses will be more likely to be on hand and to have fresh memories, ships or units may still be in the area, and damaged equipment/materials are more apt to be in the same relative position and condition if you get to them quickly.
- Be careful to observe the time limits specified in NAVOP 059/83 and MILPERSMAN 4210100, that is, 30 days to complete an investigation from the investigator's appointment, and 20 days in cases involving death, disappearance, or serious injuries. Any deviation from the 20-day limit in the latter cases requires *advance approval* from the immediate senior who will next review the investigation.
- Be far-seeing, and request any delay as soon as you see a need for one. But try your best to get the investigation done quickly. Some investigations stretch over months because of unforeseen ship movements, TAD, or other such interruptions.

On two different audiences for a JAGMAN Investigation: "There are two dragon's mouths to avoid, and they read the investigation in different ways. The staff JAG, the attorney, looks to see if you followed the regulations, if you jumped through all the hoops. Was the checklist completed, was the specific language used? The flag, on the other hand, looks for readability and the bottom line. And he doesn't appreciate legalese."
—Marine JAG Major

- You may acquire evidence in any reasonable manner, and the formal rules of evidence required for courts-martial do not bind investigating officers. The reason is that a JAGMAN Investigation is purely administrative in nature and not judicial. Its report is strictly advisory, and its opinions are not final determinations nor legal judgments. On the other hand, if investigating officers uncover good evidence for use in criminal actions related to the investigation, you may invalidate the evidence if, in acquiring it, you have ignored rules of evidence. So keep your wits about you here too.
- Remember, the overall purpose of your investigation is to tell a *complete story*, to answer the standard questions who, what, where, when, how, and why. As you go through your investigation, keep brainstorming with these six basic questions in mind until you're sure you've answered them all.
- Realize, of course, that investigations containing sensitive matter must be classified. See OPNAVINST 5510.1 and appropriate sections of the JAGMAN.
- Having considered all the above, begin your investigation.

Writing the JAGMAN Investigation—Section by Section

Since these reports have a stipulated format, the paragraphs below contain a detailed discussion of how to write *each section* of the JAGMAN Investigation. You shouldn't begin writing immediately, however. Instead, first work on grouping the facts. By making use of outlines or note cards, you can work to see the main structures in your material. You can fit all the facts together, separating them from the opinions and recommendations. If you have many facts, you can try different patterns for them.

Focus on the big picture that your report will present, first. Then proceed to paint in all the details, according to the requirements of each individual section of the report, as discussed below. Look to the examples for guidance; although all the personal names included are fictional, the examples have been carefully crafted to resemble actual JAGMAN Investigations.

One other thing. When you read JAGMAN Investigations and other legal writing, you'll notice that writers use the passive voice widely (alongside other legalisms). Normally there is no need to. As much as possible, write in active voice here as in other naval writing.

Subject Line

Subject lines for JAGMAN Investigations differ from other subject lines chiefly in their length; don't be concerned if you need three to five lines to identify the incident thoroughly. Using ALL CAPS, begin with the word "INVESTIGATION," and then go on to cite:

1. The *basic nature* of the incident, i.e., an accident, a collision, etc.;

2. The *identity* of the unit or ship that was involved in the incident, or of the service member who was involved, or both;
3. The *date* the incident occurred or was discovered.

Examples of Subject Lines

Here are three good subject lines. Each of them identifies the *nature* of the incident, the *identity* of the unit or individual involved, and the *date*. (The third example also includes the *location* of the incident, which is occasionally useful.)

Subject: INVESTIGATION INTO THE CIRCUMSTANCES SURROUNDING THE SHORTAGE OF FUNDS IN THE SHIP'S STORE ON BOARD USS COONTZ (DDG 40) WHICH WAS DISCOVERED IN JANUARY 1988

Subject: INVESTIGATION TO INQUIRE INTO THE CIRCUMSTANCES CONNECTED WITH THE PHYSICAL INJURY/ACCIDENT THAT OCCURRED ON 13 FEBRUARY 1987 INVOLVING SERGEANT GEORGE F. W____, USMC

Subject: INVESTIGATION TO INQUIRE INTO THE CIRCUMSTANCES CONNECTED WITH THE COLLISION OF LCM 10-1 AND PRIVATELY OWNED FISHING VESSELS WHICH OCCURRED AT LONG BEACH, CA ON 5 OCTOBER 1987

List of Enclosures

The JAG Manual requires that the Appointing Order be the first enclosure to a JAGMAN Investigation. Beyond that, while a JAGMAN article suggests placing witnesses' statements before other documents in the list of enclosures, commanding officers often insist on using naval-letter format, which requires numbering all documents *in order of their use.* Senior JAG officers recommend you follow your commander's desires on this issue. See the complete JAGMAN Investigation on page 265 for an example of a list of enclosures.

Preliminary Statement

In the preliminary statement you inform the convening authority of the nature of the investigation and of any difficulties you had in complying with the appointing order or in procuring evidence. Also call attention to any other difficulties encountered in this particular investigation. First refer to the appointing order, and then comment on as many of the following as are pertinent:

- the general nature of the investigation
- whether you carried out the appointing order and all other directives of the convening authority (some may prove to be impossible)
- any difficulties encountered, including difficulties in gathering information or in ascertaining a particular fact
- conflicts in evidence, if any, and how you resolved them

- reasons for any delay (you should have requested one earlier, and the written request and approval will be enclosures, but still mention the reasons in the preliminary statement)
- the name and organization of any judge advocate consulted
- whether you have advised persons of various rights, as required
- a note of any refusal by a service member to sign or make a statement concerning disease or injury
- the Attorney Product Work Statement, in investigations that might involve claims
- any other preparatory information necessary for a complete understanding of the case

DO NOT include a synopsis of the facts here—the findings of facts should tell the basic story. DO NOT include opinions or recommendations. DO NOT include your own itinerary for doing the investigation.

Examples of Preliminary Statements

The preliminary statement below explains several of the items mentioned above:

PRELIMINARY STATEMENT

1. Following enclosure (1) and reference (a), a one-officer JAGMAN Investigation was conducted to inquire into the circumstances surrounding a collision between assault craft LCM 10-1 and fishing vessels privately owned by Mr. William A. C____, which occurred at Long Beach, California, on 5 October 1987. All reasonably available relevant evidence was collected. The directives and special requirements articulated in enclosure (1) were met except as noted below:

a. I did not take a statement from Mr. William A. C____ because I was unable to contact him after numerous attempts.

b. There was no evidence of personal injury, and I do not consider it likely that any claim for personal injury will be filed.

c. Two conflicting accounts as to whether LCM 10-1 collided with the pilings or the privately owned fishing vessels appear in witnesses' statements (Enclosures 2, 3, 4, 5, and 7). However, after viewing the physical damage myself along with Commander L. F. J____ (CO of USS ROBERT H. MCCARD, DD 822), I did not accept the account of LCM 10-1 colliding with the pilings as fact.

Most preliminary statements are shorter; the one below specifically mentions the advising of rights:

PRELIMINARY STATEMENT

As directed by enclosure (1) and in accordance with reference (a), a one-officer investigation was conducted to inquire into the circumstances surrounding the damage sustained by SH-3H BUNO 152131 (also described in this report by its MODEX number, 519) on board USS KITTY HAWK at or about 2200, 17 March 1984. There were no difficulties encountered in obtaining evidence or information required to complete the investigation; all parties interviewed provided testimony or cooperated fully in all respects. The investigating officer consulted LCDR Jeffrey A. T____, USN, Command Judge Advocate, USS KITTY HAWK, on several occasions.

Based upon testimony received, AA John R. J____ and AA Earl F. R____ were warned that they might be suspected of dereliction of duty and were advised of their rights under Article 31, UCMJ.

Findings of Fact

In the findings-of-fact section, the investigating officer assembles all pertinent evidence. Strive to present the reviewer with an accurate picture of *exactly what happened*—the specifics as to times, places, and events—in the most logical and clear manner possible.

Although the JAG Manual states that you may group facts into narrative form, most JAG officers find this format cumbersome to work with and recommend that you *list each fact separately*. Once you're sure you have all the facts, assembling the information *chronologically* is usually best; normally a chronological order is more coherent for the reader.

Admittedly more than one series of events may have been taking place simultaneously, and you'll have to adjust by first narrating one series of events and then going back chronologically to describe another. Don't jump around aimlessly, leaving facts in haphazard order, or you will confuse the reader as to exactly what did happen. Do your best to be as coherent as possible. As an 0-5 JAG on a major type command's staff remarked, "I can tell a good investigation if, after reading the findings of fact, I can tell what happened. The biggest problem is that often investigators don't tell a narrative story."

For each finding of fact you must reference an enclosure. However, your treatment should be so clear that the reader doesn't need to look up an enclosure to understand what happened.

Follow these additional guidelines:

- State each fact with definiteness.
- Number each finding of fact, and make sure you support each fact with one or more specified enclosures (one of which might be the observations of the investigating officer).
- Include a specific finding of fact as to the time of any death and cause of the death, supported by a certificate of death or statement by a doctor or medical officer. (Again, don't hold the investigation to wait for the certificate.)
- If a finding of fact is based upon your personal knowledge as investigating officer, provide the basis for your personal knowledge in a signed memo for record.
- Make sure you've questioned all material witnesses. (If not, explain why not in the preliminary statement.)
- Ensure you've included a finding of fact as to the active duty for training, or inactive duty (drill) status for an injured member of the Naval Reserve (see JAGMAN).
- Overall, you will almost never go wrong by putting *too much* information in an investigation—almost always you will go wrong only by *leaving information out*. However, the facts you come up with are chiefly valuable for their inferences. So not all the facts you discover need to go into a report—only the pertinent ones.
- On the other hand, make sure to record the right kinds of data for the kind of investigation at hand—road and visibility conditions in an automobile accident, alertness of the watch team in a collision, etc. Again, *checklists* for each kind of investigation will help you

know exactly what to look for in each case. *Double check these checklists* as you draw up your findings of fact.

Examples of Findings of Fact

Example of a poor Findings of Fact section from a report on a vehicle accident

The excerpt below is representative of reports that *fail to tell a coherent story*. The writer lists facts randomly, showing neither chronological nor logical order, so it's very hard to tell exactly what happened by reading the report. As it turns out, endorsers had to add several additional findings of fact (speed of the vehicles, the speed limit, etc.) to this report.

FINDINGS OF FACT

1. That LCDR W____ did not hold U.S. Government Motor Vehicle Operator's Identification Card (CT-14) in his possession at the time of the accident. (encls (2), (5))
2. That immediately following the accident, the Fort Polk Military Police were notified. (encl (2))
3. That Mrs. Mary J____ was within posted speed limits on Magnolia Avenue. (encl (2))
4. That LCDR W____ did fail to yield right-of-way to westbound traffic on Magnolia Avenue after having made a complete stop on General Lee Boulevard. (encls (2), (5))
5. That LCDR W____ was on official business at the time of the accident. (encls (2), (5))
6. That LCDR W____ holds a valid state driver's license. (encl (2))
7. That LCDR W____ observed pavement markings (stop line) on General Lee Boulevard. (encls (2), (5))
8. That LCDR W____ made a sworn statement to Fort Polk Military Police concerning the accident. (encls (2), (5))

Example of a good Findings of Fact section on an accident

The report below follows rough chronological order and tells a coherent story. When it has to shift from the events to describe one of the drivers and a vehicle, it follows a logical train in that discussion too.

7. That Lance Corporal A____ was involved in a motor vehicle accident at 1600 on 22 March 1988. (encl (6))
8. That the accident occurred on the Elysian Expressway, Shreveport, Louisiana. (encl (6))
9. That Lance Corporal A____ was driving eastbound on the Elysian Expressway when he lost control of his vehicle. (encl (6))
10. That Lance Corporal A____ lost control of his vehicle because of a blowout in a tire on his vehicle. (encls (5), (6), and (8))
11. That the blowout caused the vehicle Lance Corporal A____ was driving to cross the cement median and collide head-on with Ms. J____'s vehicle. (encls (6) and (8))
12. That there were two vehicles in the subject accident. (encl (6))
13. That Lance Corporal A____ was driving a 1976 Ford Mustang bearing Louisiana license plate number 579X203. (encl (6))

14. That the vehicle identification number for the vehicle that Lance Corporal A____ was driving is 4D05V465698. (encl (6))
15. That there is no record that Lance Corporal A____ is the registered owner of the vehicle he was driving. (encl (6))
16. That the Police Officer who investigated the subject accident ran a check on the license plate on Lance Corporal A____'s vehicle to determine if the vehicle was stolen or had any outstanding citation. Officer M____ discovered that the license tag on Lance Corporal A____'s vehicle was assigned to a 1980 Volkswagen Rabbit owned by a Mr. Ralph A. T____. (encl (6))
17. That when questioned by Officer M____, Lance Corporal A____ indicated that he had found the license plate and placed it on his vehicle. (encl (6))
18. That Lance Corporal A____ was cited for a total of six traffic law violations, consisting of no driver's license on person, no brake tag, no proof of liability insurance, switched license plates, no license plate, and no registration papers. (encl (6))

Especially in longer reports, you can divide the findings of fact up into sections that are logically complete in themselves. In a report on damage to an aircraft, damage that occurred while it was being towed about the hangar spaces of an aircraft carrier, for example, the investigating officer divided the findings of fact into these coherent sections:

Environmental Conditions
Personnel Qualifications
Equipment Condition and Documentation
Circumstances Surrounding the Damage

Opinions

Opinions are logical inferences that flow from the findings of fact. List only those opinions required by the appointing order—that is, those required by regulations (such as the various "Line-of-Duty and Misconduct" and "Investigation of Specific Types of Incidents" sections of the JAG Manual)—or opinions naturally pertinent to the case. A good opinions section will seem to flow so naturally from the findings of fact that the opinions seem virtually self-evident.

The biggest mistake made in this section is to begin with preconceived opinions and try to prove them despite evidence to the contrary. Be sure to be open-minded in your investigation, follow where the facts lead, and dig deeply enough to get those *key* facts that bear *significant inferences*.

Beyond those basics,

- Number each opinion separately.
- Support each opinion by explicit reference to one or more findings of fact (abbreviated "FF").
- Don't confuse facts with opinions. (This confusion is unfortunately very common; too often, opinions appear as findings of fact.)
- Remember that you must include an opinion on line-of-duty/misconduct in a case involving injury or disease, but that you never include line-of-duty/misconduct opinions in an investigation into the death of a service member (see the section on LOD/Misconduct, page 247).

Examples of Opinions Sections

The following opinions section is from a Line-of-Duty/Misconduct Investigation; note the reference to specific findings of fact in each opinion.

OPINIONS

1. That, due to the length of LCpl K____'s unauthorized absence prior to his injuries (seven days), his absence materially interfered with the performance of his required military duties. (FF (1), (2), (4))
2. That LCpl K____'s injuries were not sustained in the line of duty. (FF (1), (2), (4))
3. That LCpl K____ was under the influence of alcohol. (FF (6))
4. That the minor injuries received by LCpl K____ during the motor vehicle accident were proximate results of the influence of alcohol and demonstrate a reckless disregard of the consequences. (FF (4), (5), (6))
5. That the minor injuries received by LCpl K____ in the motor vehicle accident were due to his own misconduct. (FF (4), (5), (6))
6. That LCpl K____ handled a firearm in a grossly negligent manner and demonstrated a reckless disregard of the consequences. (FF (6), (8), (9))
7. That LCpl K____ willfully violated a law of the state of North Dakota by assaulting a police officer with a firearm. (FF (9), (15))
8. That the injuries received by LCpl K____ from gunshots were due to his own misconduct. (FF (6), (8), (9), (11), (13), (14), (15))

The following example is from a report on contamination of an enlisted dining facility. Note the clear, conclusive statement of opinions and the use of underlining to point those summary opinions.

OPINIONS

1. During the course of authorized work to remove sealant from the deck tiles of the Enlisted Dining Facility's galley, the Contractor deviated from the approved plan. He introduced an unapproved chemical (muriatic acid), and used that chemical in a careless manner by failing to follow the directions of LT B____ or the labels on the boxes and jugs. Muriatic acid mist spread from the work sites throughout the galley, contaminating and damaging the building and equipment in the building. The Contractor's unapproved use of muriatic acid was the direct cause of the damage. (FF (4), (5), (11), (12), and (15))
2. LT B____ advised the Contractor of at least three precautions to take while using muriatic acid. The boxes and jugs had instructions, precautions, and warnings on their labels. The Contractor failed to heed any of these precautions, precautions that might have prevented the damage or reduced its scope. The Contractor's failure contributed directly to the damage. (FF (6), (8), (13), and (14))
3. The General Provisions of the Construction Contract state, in part, that the Contractor "will repair or restore any damage . . . resulting from . . . failure to exercise reasonable care in the performance of the work." The Contractor poured large quantities of undiluted muriatic acid over large areas of the galley, allowing the mist to damage and contaminate equipment and surfaces throughout the building. The Contractor did not exercise reasonable care in the use of muriatic acid and is responsible to repair or restore any damage. (FF (16) and (18))

Recommendations

Make recommendations *only if the appointing order or the JAG Manual specifically directs you* to do so. These recommendations should flow clearly from the expressed opinions and findings of facts, and they may suggest corrective, disciplinary, or administrative action.

In addition,

- Make your recommendations *as specific as possible.*
- Make sure your recommendations are *reasonable* and *just.*
- See that your recommendations are *practicable,* that is, that *they can be carried out.*
- Realize that your recommendations are not binding on any reviewing authorities; those recommendations will undergo a thorough review. As investigating officer, you won't bear the whole weight of the judgment in any particular case.
- If you recommend punitive charges or letters of reprimand, see the top of page 264 on follow-up documents to prepare.

Examples of Recommendations Section

Recommendations involving personnel

Below is a straightforward, clear section from an automobile accident report:

RECOMMENDATIONS

1. That Petty Officer M____ be the subject of some form of punitive action, either NJP or a Summary Court-Martial.
2. That steps be taken to ensure that Petty Officer M____ completes a safe driver's training course.
3. That Petty Officer M____ be held responsible for all medical expenses incurred as a result of this accident.
4. That Petty Officer M____ be charged lost time for the period of time he was hospitalized at County Hospital.
5. That Petty Officer M____ be processed for administrative separation for misconduct, either for civil conviction (MARCORSEPMAN 6210.7), pattern of misconduct (MARCORSEPMAN 6210.3), or both.

Recommendations for changing procedures

The recommendations below suggest how to avoid another occurrence of a laundry fire such as has just taken place in the ship's laundry.

RECOMMENDATIONS

1. As stated by the Fire Marshal, it does not appear that lint removal every two hours is sufficient to allow proper circulation of air in the dryers. Recommend that NAVEDTRA 414-01-45-81, Chapter 6 be amended to reflect this change. Until this change is made, recommend lint removal be conducted hourly to preclude any further difficulties.
2. Recommend the ship continue to wash and dry laundry in laundry bags, because washing and drying laundry for several hundred personnel without laundry bags could pose a severe accountability problem. When using the open-mesh laundry bags, recommend the following precautions:

a. Do not overload the dryers.
b. Do not place recently dried clothes in nylon bags; avoid concentrating the heat.

3. Recommend that laundry personnel be instructed to keep the dryer thermostats at the recommended level (140–160 degrees). Further, recommend that laundry personnel be required to man the space for a minimum of four hours after the completion of the drying cycle to ensure detection of any other fires of the sort that occurred.
4. Recommend including all the above recommendations in the laundry training program and in the daily operation of the laundry.
5. Recommend no disciplinary action be taken, as apparently no deliberate actions caused the fire.

Documents and Enclosures

Make the written appointing order the first enclosure. Subsequent enclosures should contain all the evidence developed in the investigation, as well as charge sheets and punitive letters of reprimand, if recommended. In addition,

- Make each statement, document, or exhibit a separate enclosure.
- Ensure you've completely identified each document.
- Number the pages of a lengthy enclosure to help the reviewer. This way, you can specifically reference the relevant passage (by page number) in the finding of fact, as in: "15. The Ferguson vehicle was traveling in excess of 50 m.p.h. Enclosure (10), p. 7; Enclosure (14), page 3; Enclosure (15), p. 1." You can also tab and highlight pertinent passages in any enclosure that is particularly bulky.
- If your personal observations provide the basis for any findings of fact, attach as an enclosure a signed, sworn statement of those observations.
- For every witness's statement, consider laying a foundation in that statement, either by preface or in the questions asked, to explain to the reviewer why the witness can speak competently on a particular subject.
- Since handwritten documents are often illegible, have witnesses' statements printed or typed. Whenever possible obtain signed, sworn statements. Sworn statements carry greater weight with readers and reviewers than unsworn statements.
- When you cannot obtain a witness's signature, draft your own summaries of a witness's oral statements. Make sure to sign this summary, certifying it is a valid account or an accurate transcript of the interview, if it is.
- Include as an enclosure the Privacy Act Statement for each party or witness from whom you obtained personal information by direct inquiry. Attach it to the respective witness's statement.
- Include as an enclosure any prior request (and its approval, too) for exceeding time requirements in conducting the investigation.
- Make sure all copies of the report itself and all enclosures are clear and readable.

You may also want to take the following steps:

• Preparing a signed, sworn charge sheet if you recommend punitive action, and including it as an enclosure. This step is part of completed staff work.

• Preparing a punitive letter of reprimand or admonition if you're recommending that the command issue such a letter, and including it as an enclosure. This step also shows completed staff work.

• Preparing a *non*punitive letter of reprimand, if your recommendation is to issue one. You should *not* include this letter in the investigation but forward it separately to the appropriate authority for issuance.

Signature and Security Classification

Sign your report.

Omit classified material unless inclusion is essential. Assign the whole report the classification of the highest classified material in it. Staff Judge Advocates and reviewers will often declassify enclosures and investigations whenever possible; still, some reports will have to remain classified. If yours must be, see that you classify and label *the whole report* appropriately, and ensure that you appropriately classify and label each individual finding of fact, opinion, recommendation, and enclosure. Remember to include the proper downgrading instructions. See OPNAVINST 5510.1.

Addresses and Copies

• Normally address the report to the convening authority (usually the commanding officer). The convening authority will forward the investigation to the Office of the Judge Advocate General (OJAG) (Code 21) via the chain of command. For details as to all addressees, see your convening authority and the JAGMAN sections on "Action by Convening and Reviewing Authorities" and "Disposition of the Record of Proceedings and Copies."

The address of the Office of the Judge Advocate General (Code 21) is 200 Stovall Street, Alexandria, VA 22332-2400.

• Provide original and one copy for OJAG (Code 21). In case of a death or injury investigation, provide original and three copies.

• Provide an *advance copy* directly to OJAG in admiralty cases (Code 11), death cases, or other serious cases, so OJAG will not have to wait for all officers in the chain to act before reviewing the initial findings.

• Provide a copy for each intermediate addressee.

• Make sure that copies to all addressees include all the enclosures.

• Ensure all photocopies are legible and securely fastened.

• Keep a copy for yourself, unless especially sensitive or classified.

Example of a Complete JAGMAN Investigation

Below is a decent example of a complete investigation. All of the names in this example are fictional.

23 February 1988

From: LT Joseph L. Wilson, USNR, XXX-XX-XXXX/2305
To: Commanding Officer, USS Piedmont (AD 17)

Subj: INVESTIGATION TO INQUIRE INTO THE CIRCUMSTANCES SURROUNDING THE FAINTING OF ET2 SYDNEY LEE SAILOR, USN, XXX-XX-XXXX, ON BOARD USS PIEDMONT (AD 17) DURING GENERAL QUARTERS ON OR ABOUT 1415, 10 FEBRUARY 1988

Ref: (a) JAGMAN
(b) OPNAVINST 5100.20C

Encl: (1) Appointing Order dated 20 Feb 88
(2) CIC Watchbill for 7-27 February 1988
(3) Deck log of USS PIEDMONT (AD 17) 701R09 time 1326 to 1427
(4) Statement of ET2 Sydney Sailor, USN
(5) Statement of LT R. B. Rome, USN, Operations Officer, USS PIEDMONT (AD 17) TAO
(6) Statement of ENS E. F. Snyder, USNR
(7) Statement of ENS E. C. Johnson, USN, CIC Officer, USS PIEDMONT (AD 17)
(8) Statement of ET3 V. I. Shirley, USN, JA Phone Talker
(9) Statement of LTJG R. S. Reynolds, USNR
(10) Statement of HMC R. C. Jefferson, USN
(11) Statement of HM2(SW) Y. B. Murfree, USN
(12) Statement of HM2 C. C. Bruce, USN
(13) Statement of LT D. T. Daniel, MC, USNR, Medical Officer, USS PIEDMONT (AD 17)
(14) Medical Department Log Book 0730, 10 February 1988 to 0800, 11 February 1988
(15) SF600 Chronological Record of Medical Care ET2 Sailor on 10 February 1988
(16) NAVMED 6500/1 Report of Heat/Cold Casualty ET2 Sailor

PRELIMINARY STATEMENT

1. Following enclosure (1) and in accordance with references (a) and (b), an informal investigation was conducted to inquire into the circumstances surrounding the fainting of ET2 Sydney Sailor, USN, XXX-XX-XXXX, on board USS PIEDMONT (AD 17) during General Quarters on or about 1415, 10 February 1988. All relevant evidence was collected. The inves-

tigator met all directives and special requirements set out in enclosure (1).

FINDINGS OF FACT

1. On 10 February 1988 ET2 Sydney Lee Sailor, USN, was on active duty and assigned to the USS PIEDMONT (AD 17). (encl (2))

2. On 10 February 1988 the USS PIEDMONT was steaming from Mayport, Florida, to Norfolk, Virginia. (encl (3))

3. On 10 February 1988 ET2 Sailor was standing underway log watch at his General Quarters station in the Combat Information Center. (encls (2) and (4))

4. Ventilation had been secured because of the drill, and CIC was described as "very uncomfortable." (encls (4) and (5))

5. Material condition "Circle William" was improperly set in that the recirc system R-03-43-2, classified "William," was also secured at the time of the incident. (encl (6))

6. ET2 Sailor "became overheated and was perspiring profusely . . . and felt weak and sick. Because of the importance of the drill and because everyone else was uncomfortable . . . [he] was reluctant to take off the MK V gas mask and anti-flash any earlier." (encl (4))

7. ET2 Sailor was instructed by LT Rome to take off his MK V gas mask but became unconscious before being able to do so. (encl (4))

8. ET2 Sailor was caught as he became unconscious and lowered to the deck. His MK V gas mask was removed. (encls (5) and (7))

9. ET3 Shirley, JA phone talker, relayed "Medical emergency in CIC, not a drill" to D.C. Central. Medical emergency was called away on the 1MC at 1411. (encls (2) and (8))

10. When medical emergency was called away, LTJG Reynolds, HMC Jefferson, and HM2(SW) Murfree responded from the Forward Decontamination Station with a stretcher team. LT Daniel, Medical Officer, also responded. (encl (9))

11. ET2 Sailor was lying on the deck, alert and conscious. (encls (9), (10), and (11))

12. ET2 Sailor had his feet elevated and was conscious and responsive when the medical officer arrived at the scene. (encl (13))

13. ET2 Sailor was evaluated for injuries and was able to walk from CIC with some assistance by medical personnel. (encls (9), (10), (12), and (13))

14. ET2 Sailor again lost consciousness at the bottom of the first ladder. He was transported to Medical in a Neil-Robertson stretcher. (encls (9), (10), (11), and (12))

15. ET2 Sailor arrived at sick bay in a Neil-Robertson stretcher at 1415. (encls (14) and (15))

16. ET2 Sailor's vital signs were normal. (encl (15))

17. ET2 Sailor was diagnosed and treated for heat exhaustion, i.e., VASOVAGAL SYNCOPE SECONDARY TO HEAT STRESS. (encl (15))

18. Medical Officer's notes state: "Past medical history unremarkable except that patient states that he and other members of his family have a tendency to 'pass out easily.' " (encls (15) and (16))

19. ET2 Sailor had eaten lunch before General Quarters, had had some nine hours of sleep in the past 24 hours, and had drunk four to five cups of coffee and six glasses of water in the 12 hours prior to his illness. (encl (16))

OPINIONS

1. That ET2 Sailor became unconscious as a result of mild heat exhaustion. (FF (17))

2. That ET2 Sailor was motivated to participate in the drill and would not have fainted if he had spoken up sooner. (FF (6))

3. That the combination of material condition and battle dress probably precipitated the illness, but that ET2 Sailor is prone to fainting and might have fainted as a result of battle dress alone. (FF (4), (5), and (18))

4. That the illness occurred in the line of duty and not as a result of his own misconduct. (FF (3), (6), and (7))

5. That there is no likelihood of permanent or recurring illness or disability as a result of the single episode, and that claims against the government are not warranted. (FF (16–19))

6. That first aid rendered by personnel at the scene was correct, that the medical emergency was promptly and correctly called away, and that medical department response was prompt and correct. (FF (9–15))

RECOMMENDATIONS

1. That ET2 Sailor be counseled not to tax himself to the point of illness during a drill scenario.

2. That supervisory personnel in CIC and the Communications Center ensure that recirc system R-03-43-2 remain energized so long as electrical power is available to the controller.

JOSEPH L. WILSON

What an Investigating Officer Ought to Know about an Endorsement

How will the chain of command review your report? *Thoroughly* and *repeatedly*. That's why you have to be sure that you've done it all as well as you can.

The purpose of an endorsement is to give the reviewer's point of view on the matter under investigation and to make sure that you've followed all technical procedures (e.g., that you've observed all the rights and given the appropriate warnings). In other words, an endorsement is at once a check or review and an opportunity for the reviewing authority (the first of which is usually the commanding officer) to make comments.

The reviewing authority will comment on the soundness of the findings, opinions, and recommendations in the report and will also advise what follow-on actions have been taken in relation to the case. A commanding officer will typically state what recommendations have been approved and acted on, what further steps beyond the recommendations have been taken, what disciplinary action the unit has initiated, and what administrative improvements the command has decided on. The following is an example of an endorsement such as a reviewing authority might make. The names are fictional.

5800
Ser 12/0037
15 SEP 88

FIRST ENDORSEMENT on LT John L. Wilson, USNR, XXX-XX-XXXX/ 1310, ltr dtd 11 SEP 88

From: Commanding Officer, USS ROBERT A. OWENS (DD 827)
To: Commanding Officer, Naval Legal Service Office (Claims Department), U.S. Naval Station, San Diego, California

Subj: INVESTIGATION TO INQUIRE INTO THE CIRCUMSTANCES SURROUNDING OVERSPRAYING OF VEHICLES IN THE VICINITY OF USS ROBERT A. OWENS DURING THE PERIOD OF 10 AUGUST THROUGH 15 AUGUST 1988

1. Readdressed and forwarded.

2. The Deck Department, USS ROBERT A. OWENS, and Port Services, U.S. Naval Station San Diego, did take reasonable precautions to place drivers in the vicinity of the ship on notice of spray-painting operations. Although most claimants knew or should have known about the potential for damage to their vehicles, it is apparent that some vehicles incurred damage after reasonable preventative steps had been taken.

3. Spray painting is a fact of life for Navy ships. This ship must be painted regularly, and the methods of accomplishing this evolution during the month of August were appropriate. In addition, significant efforts were taken to provide information to those who park and work in the vicinity of USS ROBERT A. OWENS.

4. During the period in question the ship was fully engaged in Selected Restricted Availability, which required extensive refurbishing, repairs, and painting. The Availability was the primary mission of all personnel assigned to USS ROBERT A. OWENS at the time.

5. Typical paint overspray consists of a light mist that is normally removed from a vehicle with a rubbing compound and an hour or two of buffing. It was this method that I used successfully on my own black sports car to remove overspray from the same painting operations.

6. Subject to the foregoing, the findings of fact, opinions, and recommendations of the investigating officer are approved.

GEORGE Z. WATSON

Copy to:
OJAG (Code 11, Admiralty)
Naval Station San Diego

Each authority to whom you route a JAGMAN Investigation forwards it by endorsement. If an authority decides the investigation has major errors, that endorser can turn the report back down the chain for further inquiry or for corrections. However, unless the errors are especially severe, each endorser will normally correct the mistakes in the report (and those in any prior endorsements), approve or disapprove of the conclusions and recommendations, and *send the package on*. Otherwise, the delay could be extensive.

This process doesn't mean you're completely off the hook for any errors you may have made in the investigation. After forwarding the report, the endorser will send a copy of the endorsement *back down the chain* to your commanding officer's reporting senior(s), first. On a staff, an endorsement will usually go on the read board, so that many eyes will see seniors' criticisms of the report you've written. The endorsement will eventually get back to your own commanding officer and finally to you. You can be sure that your boss will notice (and certainly not appreciate) any mistakes you've made. For all these reasons, do your best to make the report as good as it can be, and consider having some lawyer review it, informally, before you submit it.

As the 0-6 JAG at a major type command commented, too often an investigating officer will call up the staff JAG when first seeing the endorsement and ask, "Why didn't you call me? Why did you have to put the gig in print? My skipper is going to hit the overhead when he sees this!" You have to remember that once it's in print, it's official, and that the staff JAG works for the 0-6 or flag, not for you. (The process is slightly different in the Marine Corps. Marine legal officers commented that they make a policy of doing the same review for the battalion officer as they do for the general, thus solving perceived problems before an investigation reaches the general's desk.)

What will the endorser look at? Anything and everything suggested above, and perhaps other details too. Before submitting your report, check it over one last time to make sure you've met all the requirements. If you can say yes to all the questions in the checklist below, you can be pretty sure you have a decent report.

Checklist on JAGMAN Investigations

- Does your report "answer the mail"? Have you carried out what the appointing order directed you to do?
- Do all the parts mesh? Does the preliminary statement properly introduce the rest of the report? Do the findings describe the basic facts? Do the opinions and recommendations logically follow through?
- Does every fact have an enclosure and every opinion a reference?
- Are the opinions and recommendations reasonable?
- Has the investigation been as thorough as you could reasonably expect?
- Is the report technically complete and correct in all its details? Have you classified it correctly? Have you identified all the witnesses? Are all the enclosures in place, properly marked, and highlighted? Are all the copies (including reproduced copies of enclosures) readable? Have you made enough copies of the report?
- Have you shown this report to someone else (a knowledgeable reader and good critic)? Can that person follow it all? Does it make sense to him or her?
- Does the report needlessly present a poor image of your command or any individuals involved in the investigation?
- If you were the officer charged with seeing to it that the government's interest had been looked after, would you think all required duties and responsibilities had been carried out?
- On the other hand, if you were the person whose acts were under investigation, would you think you had gotten a complete hearing and a fair shake?

I keep six honest serving men
(They taught me all I knew);
Their names are What and Why and When
And How and Where and Who.

—Rudyard Kipling

10

Writing for the News Media

Who besides official journalists or public affairs officers needs to know about news writing? Quite a number of people, as it turns out: COs who want to tell the good story of their commands and get their people recognition; COs, XOs, and CDOs who may have to approve and release news stories; Marine Corps Unit Information Officers (UIOs) putting out information on their units; and many Navy officers who, on their ships, air squadrons, or other stations, are assigned as collateral duty public affairs officers (PAOs).

Some of the latter part-time PAOs have a great deal to say about the importance of writing good news releases, along with other aspects of their jobs. For example, the educational services officer on an amphibious assault ship commented on how his PAO work affected those aboard. He began putting an article in the base newspaper every month—the CO loved it. Coming back from Beirut, 300 award recipients spelled out the ship's hull number on the flight deck for a photo, which appeared in the Norfolk and Little Creek base newspapers—the awardees loved it. He went into the engine rooms during an inspection and got another article with photos into the base paper—and the snipes (who *never* had recognition) loved it too.

Besides enhancing crew morale and pleasing the CO, news or feature writing can do real service in informing the public, not only the public of families and friends served by base newspapers but also the wider naval audience reached by such papers and magazines as *Navy Times, All Hands, Naval Aviation News, Naval Reservist News, Leatherneck*, and *Marines*. Of course there are also many civilian outlets for naval news, from the local paper and other local media on up. Articles that reach the publics that these forums serve do inestimable benefit for us all.

News writing is distinctly different from most of the other writing spoken of in this book. It requires a "wholly different style," according to the CO of a training command. Part of the difference lies in the nature of the subject matter. While there are different kinds of news writing, and some elements are more important to one kind than another, any genuine news item should contain all or most of these basic ingredients:

- Something must HAPPEN!
- It must be timely.
- It must be significant.
- It must have local interest.

The item will be even more valuable as news if it contains

- Humor
- Conflict
- Human interest
- Well-known personalities
- Suspense

Recognizing news is one thing; finding it is another. Some stories will come to a writer as gifts. But you will obtain most of your significant news only by lots of leg work, a little ingenuity, some imagination, and an organized routine. Don't wait for news to find you. Go seek it out.

Military writers make use of two standard kinds of journalistic writing: (1) news releases and (2) features. These writings differ primarily in *the way they deal with reader interest.*

The news release follows the order of *decreasing* interest, the so-called "inverted pyramid," in which you assume a reader might stop anywhere in the story. A writer begins the story with a basic summary of an event—the most crucial facts—and then expands on those facts.

In contrast, the feature story generally tries to intrigue readers by dangling incidental facts or using special techniques, and then leads them to and through the more important information. The feature story assumes level or *increasing* interest. A simple diagram will illustrate the difference:

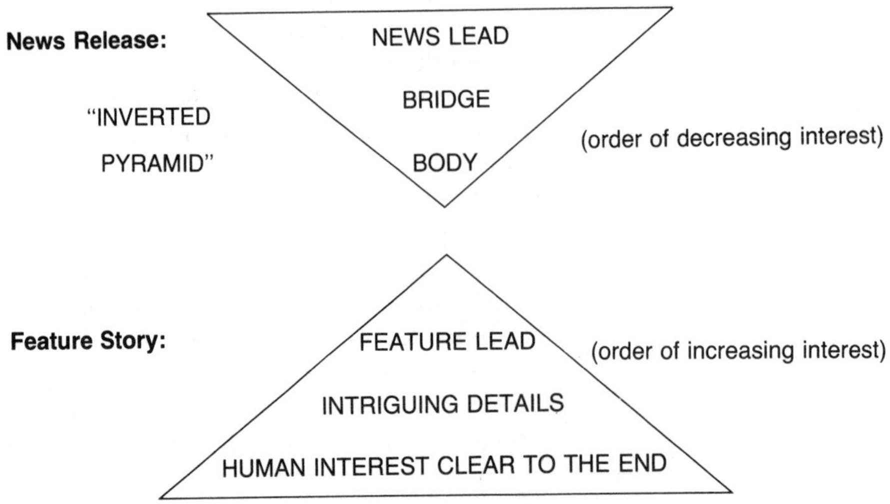

The news release and feature require sharply different techniques, each of them having been perfected over decades of journalistic practice. Both are very useful for naval writers to learn, not only for use in news writing but also for the spin-offs they have in day-to-day staff and organizational writing. Let's look at each of them in some detail.

The News Release

News releases have three parts—the lead, the bridge, and the body. Most important of these is the lead.

Write an Accurate Summary Lead

Although reader interest is always a consideration, you don't design a lead primarily to get a reader to read a story. Headlines have more of that function, and subject matter itself is probably the most important factor in determining which news stories any particular person reads. Rather than being an enticement, a lead is better defined as an effective summary that spills all the basic facts at once, allowing the reader to scan the paper and decide which stories to read through for more details.

A good lead, then, offers the basic information of the story in quick summary form. To write a lead well requires strong craftsmanship. It is usually a single sentence of some 25–30 words and can be of several types, each of which has special usefulness. You categorize a lead by which of the 5Ws and 1H it emphasizes (although more than one of these should appear in it, just one receives special emphasis). Is it a *who, what, where, when, why,* or *how* lead?

Before writing a lead, list the *who, what, where, when, why,* and *how* of a story. Then consider the story from your audience's viewpoint. Which emphasis will likely have most impact on your reader? Which might be most interesting, or hardest hitting? Theoretically, by emphasizing any one of these aspects, you could compose six different summary leads. However, "when" and "where," important as they are to a news story, don't usually provide the best leads. On the other hand, there are two different kinds of "who" leads. Altogether, you have five strong possible leads for a story:

A WHAT Lead—usually the most important element in hard news stories:

> A revised version of the Former Spouses' Protection Act was enacted with the 1985 Defense Authorization bill.

A WHO Lead—especially useful if the *who* is well known:

> Secretary of Defense Caspar Weinberger yesterday urged military people to help the Red Cross raise money to aid famine victims in Africa.

An IMPERSONAL WHO Lead—used if the "who" is not well known; the person is identified in the bridge or the body of the story:

Navy wrestlers won four of the 17 medals taken by U.S. wrestlers at the Conseil International du Sport Militaire in December.

A WHY Lead—"why" is sometimes the most interesting element:

Because of a shortage of instructors in the Naval Dental School, the student-instructor ratio will be increased to 16–1 next month.

A HOW Lead—sometimes the "how" is the strongest possible lead:

By dropping a bomb down the chimney, an escaped arsonist blew up the town judge's home yesterday.

Remember—don't get bogged down in secondary details or get tangled in the chronology of events in a lead; let those elements follow in the body.

Compose a "Bridge" as an Effective Link

The bridge is a sentence or two that links the summary information in the lead to the detailed information of the body. Although not always required, it helps a writer avoid cluttering the lead with secondary facts. The bridge serves the lead, for the kind of lead usually determines the type of bridge that follows.

For example, a bridge following an "impersonal who" lead provides complete identification of the individuals mentioned in the lead:

Lead: An off-duty Marine gate guard stationed here saved a 10-year old boy from drowning just off the seawall near the base gym.

Bridge: By jumping off the seawall and swimming 50 yards, Corporal Sam Jones saved the life of the unidentified youngster, who had fallen off a sailboat.

Another common purpose is to tell the source of information given in the lead and to supply additional information:

Lead: Vandals in the students' barracks destroyed nearly $12,000 worth of fire protection equipment in the last six months, leaving their fellow students to the risk of injury or death.

Bridge: According to Base Fire Chief Charles W. Smith, vandals have torn down smoke detectors, bells, and pull stations that contractors installed in the barracks about six months ago. In addition, 211 fire extinguishers had to be replaced, the chief said.

A bridge following a lead that omits some of the 5Ws simply adds other information.

Lead: The harbor tug *Wobegon* (YTB 472) rescued two men from a disabled motorboat that was drifting to sea on the ebb tide early Saturday morning.

Bridge: The motorboat had been without power for three hours when the *Wobegon* appeared about 4:30 AM, a half-mile southeast of

> Fort Sumter, Charleston, S.C. The two men in the boat, who were not identified, got the tug's attention by a flashlight SOS.

Other bridges tie a lead back to earlier stories on the same subject or simply add additional facts.

In the Body, Add Details in Descending Order of Importance

In the body, elaborate on the elements given in the lead and bridge by adding details, in-depth discussion, chronology of events, or quotes on what occurred. In essence, the body *retells in detail and descending order of importance* the summary facts given in the lead.

Remember these important principles when writing the body of a news release. First, an editor with limited space who wants to use your story will cut from the bottom. Make sure no essential material is left to the end, and place the most important information in paragraphs immediately succeeding the lead and bridge. Again, write in descending order of importance, with minor details left for the end.

Second, remember that newspaper columns are very narrow. Dense blocks of type inhibit reading wherever encountered, but narrow columns of news type can make reading even more difficult than usual. Limit your paragraphs to two or three sentences in length.

Don't Forget the Heading

Once you've composed a news release complete with lead, bridge, and body, don't overlook one other part—a news release *heading.* A good heading can mean the difference between good material being used, lost, or thrown out. Include in this heading five basic items:

1. The *name of the command.* Identifies the releasing authority.
2. The *contact individual* within the command. Your name and phone number are very important—they tell the editor how to reach you to clarify information, to confirm some aspect of the release, etc.
3. The *telephone number* of the command or contact individual.
4. A *"slug"* or *title* to give the editor an idea of the story content.
5. The *release date and time.* Note the following common terms:
   - FOR IMMEDIATE RELEASE—for hot items
   - FOR GENERAL RELEASE—for feature and other items with no time element
   - HOLD FOR RELEASE UNTIL—for items mailed in advance of the time/date when the public can be informed
   - DO NOT USE AFTER—for items not accurate or pertinent after a certain date (such as publicizing an open house, etc.)

Don't include a cover letter for your release—that's too much official clout, and editors don't have time to read a cover letter anyway. The paper will recognize you're submitting a news release by reading the heading and the title "News Release."

Figure 10.1 is a good short news release, heading and all.

Figure 10.1 A News Release from a Navy Ship. This release, complete on one page, tells its story quickly and well.

USS THEODORE ROOSEVELT (CVN-71)

PUBLIC AFFAIRS OFFICE
FPO NEW YORK 09599-2871
(A) 546-7402
(C) 804-444-7402

For Immediate Release 10 January 1988

TWO MEN RESCUED FROM ATLANTIC

ABOARD USS THEODORE ROOSEVELT (CVN-71)...The nuclear aircraft carrier USS THEODORE ROOSEVELT rescued two 24-year-old men from the Atlantic Ocean 10 January after they had drifted with the wreckage of their trimaran for four-and-a-half days.

Joseph Donald Buffkin, Jr., and John Wirth Frederico were rescued 20 nautical miles from San Salvador Island at 7:06 pm after being spotted from the 98,000-ton THEODORE ROOSEVELT by the ship's starboard lookout, Seaman Rodney Jackson.

"I saw a light off the starboard side and reported it to the bridge," said Jackson, an Alabama native who has been in the Navy for a year-and-a-half. "The officer of the deck identified the signal as an SOS so we turned the ship around."

The trimaran sailboat overturned and broke apart in heavy weather according to Buffkin. "We had sold our cars and bought the boat to island hop. We set out from Jacksonville and have been sailing around down here since October."

Buffkin and Frederico spent 96 hours holding on to the crippled hull. By diving down and entering the compartment they located food and water. On the last of their excursions they found the flashlight that helped save their lives.

After being brought aboard the Navy's newest aircraft carrier they were examined by the ship's medical staff, fed and allowed to rest. Suffering only minor cuts and bruises in their ordeal, they were flown to Guantanamo Bay, Cuba.

The Feature Story

Many naval stories—especially those written in weekly base papers—are feature stories. Commercial newspapers usually cover hard news, while base newspapers, having limited staff resources, simply can't be as up-to-date as other news sources.

Timeliness is still important in some instances. A story about a ship returning from deployment should come out in the base paper within a week of the event; the same for changes of command, etc. But in most cases the interest in such stories is no longer on the event itself but on some special aspect of it. So instead of a "hard news" release, you would write a "feature story" and send it either to a base newspaper, or, if it is good enough, to a journal like *All Hands*, *Surface Warfare*, or *Marines*. These magazines aren't interested in "hard news" but rather in human interest, humor, technical information, and military or institutional facts of life. As one writer put it, "Feature stories are the readers' gravy in the meat and potato world of news. They add a human dimension to what is sometimes perceived as an impersonal approach to reporting the news of the day" (JOC Jon Cabot, *Direction*, Spring 1983).

Feature stories on Navy and Marine Corps subjects can help humanize the services for nonnaval audiences. This type of reporting helps citizens relate to and understand men and women in the service. On the other hand, feature stories that specifically target service members and their families—most of the features in base newspapers—help us relate to and understand one another. They deal with our tasks, jobs, environments, desires, loves, challenges, and predicaments. Moreover, by giving fitting recognition to the dedication and deeds of service members and their families, news features help boost individual and unit morale.

The task of the feature writer, then, is first to find that special story worth telling, and then to tell it in a way that will prick interest. As a result, the whole approach of a feature story differs from that of the news release.

Writing Feature Leads

The feature lead serves a different purpose than the news lead. Unlike the news lead, it does not deliver all the basic facts at once—instead, it attempts above all to get readers interested, to grip them and make them want to learn more. Many different leads can introduce feature stories—there is no standard formula based upon the 5Ws. Nor is there a necessary "lead-bridge-body" structure, but instead, (1) a lead to intrigue followed by (2) secondary interest, often leading to (3) a story and reader climax. Maybe such a formula is impractical in all cases, but at the least material of sustained interest should follow the lead, and a well-crafted ending should wrap up the story. (The emphasis on the ending is distinctive of the feature; in contrast, the hard news release just ends. You shouldn't spend any special time on its ending, for an editor is likely to cut off the last few paragraphs to save space anyway.)

The following paragraphs illustrate several popular kinds of feature leads—leads connected with several different kinds of stories. These examples are just a few of many possibilities.

The SUMMARY lead leads off with fascinating facts. It resembles a news lead, but is more interesting. This example is from a story on what the Navy is doing to control the cost of spare parts.

> A 4-cent diode cost the Navy $110. A 67-cent bolt was priced at $17.59. A $15 claw hammer was marked up to $435.
>
> Such overcharging seems impossible, but the Navy and other military services did pay the inflated prices for these and many other items.

The NARRATIVE OR DESCRIPTIVE lead sets the mood, stirs emotions, and gets a reader into the story. This lead introduces a feature about the Grenada operation.

> Not until about 40 hours before H-hour were commanding officers of the ships told what the mission in Grenada would be—to evacuate U.S. citizens, neutralize any resistance, stabilize the situation, and maintain the peace. That didn't leave much time to get the ships ready. On board USS Guam (LPH 9), . . .

The TEASER lead captures a reader's interest by promising something interesting, without telling the reader what the story is about. The reader learns more of the subject as the story continues. The story below was about the Navy's first aircraft, the A-1, but it doesn't name the aircraft until later.

> It was a light, delicate aircraft, but in its short life it survived several crashes. And like most pioneers, it had its share of failures and accomplishments.

The QUOTATION lead is suitable for historical stories or recent events. Use it rarely, and only with dynamic and short quotes.

> "You really don't know what freedom is until you have had to escape from Communist captivity," said Navy Lt. Deiter A. Dengler, an escapee from a Viet Cong prison camp.

The DIRECT ADDRESS lead states or implies the word "you" somewhere in the first paragraph.

> If you write a rubber check at a stateside commissary, you'll have to pay a $10 service charge and stand the chance of facing a judge, either civil or military.

On Writing the Rest of the Feature

As with the news release lead, authorities often advise that you write the feature lead first, before writing a story. The lead will often set the stage for the rest of the article, suggesting a logical structure.

How you go about writing the rest of the story varies. "The bottom line in feature writing," said JOC Jon Cabot in the Spring 1983 *Direction*, "is adding personality or character to any given subject. The easiest way to take a topic and featurize it is to think in terms of putting the topic on a stage, much like an actor. You then move the topic across the stage through the effective use of quotes and anecdotes until you come to the end of the stage or your summary."

Colorful writing and freedom of composition are not only permissible but encouraged in feature writing. This subjectivity differs from writing news releases, in which journalists do their best to be (and to appear to be) objective. "Straight news" writers see to it that no opinions remain unattributed, and they scrutinize their adjectives to ensure no bias has crept in. They do their best to disappear from the story.

In contrast, writers of feature stories are allowed, even encouraged, to state opinions (they usually receive by-lines, not only to give them credit for their stories but also to identify the source of whatever opinions appear). They are also encouraged to write colorfully to keep the interest up. Writers can use several techniques—looking at events from differing points of view, making intriguing comparisons and contrasts, using striking quotations—the possibilities are endless. The best way to learn to write features is probably to read features and to study the techniques in stories that especially interest you.

The end of a good feature shows as much craft as the beginning. One good way to end is with a choice quotation from an interview; another favorite method is to summarize the key points of the story and comment on their impact. A good feature story keeps the interest of the reader to the very end and if possible surprises or delights the reader even in the conclusion itself.

Here's an example of a feature story written by a collateral-duty PAO aboard a destroyer. Published in *Soundings*, the base newspaper in Norfolk, it is a good example of a standard feature that a part-time PAO would write. After the heading, the story begins with a quotation lead, and then proceeds to tell its story, keeping up interest with details about the Cape Verde Islands and an adept use of several quotations, including a good one to end the story. (Remember that this release would be *double-spaced* on an actual news release form.)

NEWS RELEASE

USS COMTE DE GRASSE (DD 974)
Lt. Joe DiRenzo III, Public Affairs Officer
Phone: 804-444-7552
"Comte de Grasse Makes Port Visit to the Cape Verde Islands"
FOR GENERAL RELEASE

"It is a distinguished pleasure and privilege to host the USS Comte de Grasse (DD 974) here in the islands," commented U.S. Ambassador Vernon D. Penner, Jr., during a luncheon on board the ship as it rested at anchor in the Cape Verde Islands. "We have had other ships, but nothing like this magnificent vessel," continued Penner.

The USS Comte de Grasse, having just left the Mediterranean Sea and duties with the U.S. Sixth Fleet, had traveled more than 1,500 miles to this tiny group of islands 385 miles west of Senegal.

Under the command of Cmdr. Russell J. Lindstedt II, the officers and crew were treated to a port visit vastly different from any they had seen during their five and one-half months in the Mediterranean.

With several small fishing boats on either side, the Comte de Grasse anchored off the port city of Mindelo. "Mindelo's ties with the U.S. are rich ones," commented the ambassador.

"Mindelo is the sister city of Bedford, Massachusetts, and has many exchanges with Bedford," continued Ambassador Penner. "Overall, our ties to this country extend over 200 years and have been strengthened by visits like this." Many Cape Verdeans were part of the U.S. armed forces in World War I and World War II, he added.

The ambassador's visit was one of the several official calls Cmdr. Lindstedt made and received. "These people have awaited your arrival for a while," added Penner. "The embassy received a lot of calls to host the captain. I only wish your stay could be longer."

Cape Verde became an independent nation on July 5, 1978. Until granted independence, the country was a Portuguese colony. The new government of Cape Verde is working hard to improve the standard of living for all Cape Verdeans. "They are developing, getting more trade and more currency," continued Penner. "Just last year several new hotels opened."

In addition to the ambassador's luncheon, the ship hosted Cmdr. Amancio Lopez, commander of the Cape Verde Navy, and his flag deputy Subtente Amante Da Rosa, and gave them a tour of the ship.

The commander remarked through an interpreter, "I have always wanted to see a U.S. warship and meet the crew. It was a pleasurable experience and one I will remember for a long time." Added Lopez, "This one ship is longer than our whole Navy."

Figure 10.2 is the first page of another feature release. Put out by a Marine Corps officer stationed at the Naval Academy, it discusses the special significance for the Marine Corps of an upcoming graduation at that institution.

News Style vs. Official Style

Whether you compose hard news releases or features, and whether you write for civilian or military sources, remember to write in "news" style, not official. Here are a few pointers on news style.

Avoid Acronyms

Far too many people send out press releases full of unidentified acronyms. Proper news style is to use as few acronyms as possible, whether identified or unidentified. Even if a story is intended for a Navy or Marine Corps audience, spell out all acronyms the first time—but then *use them as little as possible.* To save space (and help the reader), look for a generic term: "the wing" instead of COMASWWINGPAC, or "the training group" in place of FASOTRAGRUPAC.

Figure 10.2 A Marine Corps Release, Ashore. This is the first page of a graduation release of several pages.

DEPARTMENT OF THE NAVY
U.S. NAVAL ACADEMY
MARINE CORPS REPRESENTATIVE
ANNAPOLIS, MD 21402-5044

NEWS RELEASE
7 Apr 1987
By Capt. Keith Oliver, USMC
(301) 267-3377

NAVAL ACADEMY TIED TO CORPS

ANNAPOLIS, Md. -- Commissioning week is just around the corner at the U.S. Naval Academy, and amid the pageantry of military parades, the springtime charm of Annapolis, and the roar of the Blue Angels, 173 Marine second lieutenants will assume their duties of office.

The new Leathernecks, representing nearly 17 per cent of the graduating Class of '87, signify that, for the fifth year in a row, the Marine Corps has "made quota" at this institution nestled on the banks of the Severn River.

Included in that number are the Brigade Commander (student body president), several former enlisted Marines, and a plethora of scholar-athletes who have distinguished themselves in every area from electrical engineering to lacrosse.

Serving as role models for these aspiring combat leaders are 45 field- and company-grade officers and one gunnery sergeant whose duties entail teaching, coaching, staff work, and, routinely, the acquisition, care, and feeding of future Marine officers.

[more]

Remember, many readers may have just joined the service, and others are civilian employees or dependents with little service knowledge. Even among long-time service members, will a submariner understand aviation acronyms? Will an infantry Marine follow Pentagon budget terms?

Stay Away from Jargon

Of course, avoid Navy and Marine Corps jargon, and technical terms like "displacement," but realize that Navy ratings can be jargon too. What would the public think of a "mess management specialist"? It's best to call that person MS2 Jones, and briefly explain the job she does. Better yet, quote MS2 Jones explaining her own rating.

Use Media Abbreviations for Military Ranks and Other Titles

Another characteristic of news style is that it uses special abbreviations for military ranks—Rear Adm. instead of RADM, for example, and Lt. Cmdr. instead of LCDR. Navy personnel should refer to *JO 3&2* for a complete listing of military ranks; virtually the same list appears in the *Associated Press Stylebook and Libel Manual* under "Military Titles." However, Marine PAOs use slightly different abbreviations for Marine ranks on external news releases than those listed in either of the above publications. See the "Marine Corps—Unique Style Guide," Appendix H, Vol. II of the Marine Corps Public Affairs Manual for these abbreviations.

Capitalize Much Less

Realize that you capitalize much less in news writing than in official documents. When writing for a newspaper or magazine, lowercase such occupational titles as "commanding officer," and capitalize the rank or job of "captain" only when immediately preceding a name. News style doesn't use all caps or italics for the names of vessels, either.

Be Particularly Careful with Quotation and Attribution

Besides adopting slightly different styles, news writers have to pay particular attention to the use of quotations. Clearly, there are good times to use quotations (when there are unique, surprising, or striking statements; important quotes by important officials; etc.) and other times when it's best not to (when you're dealing with simple, factual material, for instance, or when the quote does nothing to enliven the story). The important point to cover here is the issue of attribution, or how to state the source of information.

Of course you need not cite a source for everything that is common knowledge, but for information that is subject to argument or involves policy, you must keep yourself out of trouble by citing specific sources. Use "he said" or the equivalent at least once per paragraph when citing such data. For variety, insert such attribution between sentences or phrases.

Incidentally, do not be reluctant to use that specific word "said" (as in "he said" or "she said" or "they said") as many times as you wish. Perhaps you can occasionally substitute an equally neutral word like "remarked," "stated," "added," or "commented," but be on your guard. Some substitute terms ("charged," "asserted," or "argued," for instance) can imply a particular emotional stance on the part of the person quoted that you do not intend. Similarly, if you report that a commanding officer "claimed" or "maintained" something, the reader may infer you don't quite believe him. Be very sensitive to the nuances of the words you use.

Direct quotes always need attribution, and of course any direct quotes should be *absolutely accurate.* Make sure you know *exactly* what was said, especially when quoting directly. You'll be surprised how much trouble a slight misquoting can cause, and how much it can upset the person misquoted.

Be aware of one slight exception to this rule of accuracy: if a speaker uses improper English (sentence fragments; bad grammar; lots of "ands," "ifs," or "buts"; agreement errors, etc.)—the accepted practice is to clean up the syntax for the speaker. Indeed, some COs even let you make up comments for them—as long as they can review the story before release.

Here are some examples of various way to attribute quotes. Besides noting the method of attribution, also pay careful attention to the punctuation and capitalization in the passages below:

The Basic Information:

Captain Charles B. Stevens made the following statement: "For 20 years we have provided the Navy with the best possible communications officers and radiomen."

• With Direct Attribution in a Complete Sentence:

"For 20 years we have provided the Navy with the best possible communications officers and radiomen," the captain said.

or

Captain Charles B. Stevens, commanding officer of the communications school, said, "For 20 years we have provided the Navy with the best possible communications officers and radiomen."

or

"For 20 years," the captain said, "we have provided the Navy with the best possible communications officers and radiomen."

• With Direct Attribution, but Using Just Part of the Quote:

The captain said the school has "provided the Navy with the best possible communications officers and radiomen."

or

The school has provided the Navy with "the best possible communications officers and radiomen," the captain said.

- **Using Indirect Quotation (Minor Rewriting but Same Meaning):**

The communications school has aimed at providing top communication officers and radiomen for the Navy, the captain said.

or

The captain said the school has always aimed at providing the Navy with the best communications officers and radiomen.

For Further Style Guidance

For further guidance, see the *The Associated Press Stylebook and Libel Manual*, the guide that most Navy and Marine Corps journalists and public affairs officers use for news style. This book is perhaps the best quick reference dictionary on the style of news writing available; it also has excellent advice on punctuation, word usage, capitalization in news writing, and many other news writing matters.

Distributing the Story

Obviously, writing a story does no good if it doesn't get to the right outlets or doesn't get there in time. Your story will likely get only as far as a well-thought-out distribution list. Determine the public you are targeting, and release information to the media that service that public.

Besides the local daily and weekly press (including base newspapers), don't overlook radio and TV outlets. Also consider sending releases to the house organs of various industrial and service organizations. Often Navy and Marine Corps subjects will be of great interest to these publications.

Many press releases compete at the editorial offices of service-wide publications. When considering whether to send an article to such official magazines as *All Hands* or *Wifeline* or *Leatherneck* or the commercial newspaper *Navy Times*, you need to ask yourself, "If I were in the Indian Ocean on deployment and saw this story appear in a publication, would it whet my interest?" If so, send it in.

Two other possible outlets for items having especially *wide* interest are the "Navy News Service" and "Headquarters Marine Corps News" (MCNEWS). These weekly "wire services" of the Navy and Marine Corps include much service-wide news as well as some public affairs guidance. You've seen products of one or both of these wire services posted on bulletin boards or in the message files, and base newspapers often run stories from these services. Both encourage submission of releases that have Navy-wide or Corps-wide interest.

When deployed, if you wonder whether an article or particular subject would be acceptable in a wire service, a call or routine message sent to the Fleet Public Affairs Officer (say, at SIXTHFLT or SEVENTHFLT) can answer your question. As that same officer is always on the lookout for articles or photos, be sure to send that officer a copy of your final release as well.

Find out where to send copy and what the deadlines are; realize that commercial papers are extremely time sensitive. Often a town paper will publish a fairly mediocre article that arrives well before the deadline before a top-notch one that arrives just barely on time. You might consider tailoring releases to specific markets (highlighting special local interest, for example). Although probably not worthwhile for all your releases, taking special care to craft a release for a particular publication, group of publications, or geographic area can sometimes get articles placed that would otherwise reach only the circular file.

Finally, don't forget the Naval Information Offices (NAVINFOs). These six Navy offices in different parts of the country coordinate media relations throughout a whole region. The offices accept releases from fleet units and fleet centers and market them. If the sailors you're writing about have forgotten their hometown newspapers' names, or even if you know the papers' names, you can send the story to the NAVINFO in, say, Dallas for a paper in Texas, or to the office in Atlanta for somewhere in the Southeast. Knowing which local papers will use the story, that office will send it where it is most likely to get published, doing your marketing work for you. For more on NAVINFOs, how they work, and what they can do for you, look into SECNAVINST 5720.44.

After preparing a release and getting releasing approval from your CO, prepare your distribution list from the following lists of media:

Local Newspapers
Wire Services
Local Radio and TV Outlets
Base Newspapers
Service Magazines and Newspapers
Type Commander Publications
Local House Organs
Local Service Organization Publications
Local Reserve Unit Publications
Fleet Hometown News Center
Fleet Public Affairs Officer, especially when deployed

A Note on Photos

Send black-and-white photographs with a story whenever possible. Photos (especially good quality pictures) will often convince an editor to publish a story.

Remember that in public affairs photography, the *individual* is the important subject. Strive for *an identity* first; then the job, equipment, or background of the individual can usually appear in a photo without overshadowing the subject.

On the other hand, editors always look for pictures full of action and interest. Stress to your photographer that you want *action* shots. Instead of the ship's sailor of the year receiving a certificate from the commanding officer, have your photographer shoot the sailor on the job.

Before you release a photo, ask yourself if anything in it detracts from the main subject. Does equipment or heavy shadow obstruct the faces? Could the photo be taken from a better angle? Is it in poor taste? Is it unflattering to the subject? If the answer to any of these questions is yes, throw it out and have it reshot. Not having a photo at all is better than using one of poor quality.

Be especially careful that the service members depicted present a positive image of the military, including its grooming and uniform standards. Any success you feel from having a story published will quickly disappear when the CO notices one of his sailors has appeared before the world with an inch of hair over his collar.

Also avoid:

- flag poles, trees, and other objects growing out of a subject's head.
- human limbs cut off at unnatural spots.
- idle hands: don't let them hang motionless at the subject's sides.
- people staring at the camera.
- dark backgrounds, especially when the subjects have dark hair.
- still and formal poses, or "line-up" shots.
- "hand-shakers," also known as "grip 'n' grins": look instead for action and the unusual in your photos.

Finally, be sure the prints are no smaller than 5×7 inches. Use pieces of cardboard for backing, and place the prints in a sturdy envelope. When possible include four or five different views and both horizontal and vertical formats to give layout editors some leeway when designing the page for your story. Make sure to include a *double-spaced caption* just under the photo (or taped to the back). The caption should include the full names (and ranks/rates or titles if appropriate) of depicted individuals, and explain what is going on in the photo. Give the photographer a photo credit here too. Follow this example:

CAPTION

SN Mike W. Adams catches up on some damage control maintenance while USS Biddle (CG 34) is in port. A leading seaman in the ship's first division, Adams often performs duties required of a petty officer third or second class. (Photo by JO2 Mark Osburn)

Other Pointers

Short items in magazines or newspapers often have surprising impact—a top-notch paragraph by itself may catch the eye, or a striking photo with a deep caption (long cutline). Remember that the release itself should be easily readable—stay away from OCR or other unreadable typeface on your releases.

When you are deployed, base papers back home will be glad to get your copy. Friends and families will be delighted to see what you're doing. Indeed, for them, getting information published when you're deployed is probably more important than when you're at your home station.

Identify all the people in your stories (full rank or title, first name, middle initial, and last name), and be sure the names are accurate. Always make sure that the CO's name is in the story you write, along with the full name of the command. On the other hand, remember that people, not ranks, make news. A lieutenant has no more news value than a seaman. Don't feel you have to mention the division officer and chief of every seaman you talk to. If you use quotes to enliven your story (not a bad idea), don't feel you must restrict your quotes to the CO or others in authority. The sailor can have something of interest to say too.

Finally, make sure the appropriate officials have reviewed and okay'd your story before it goes anywhere. At a minimum, ask the PAO who should see your story; if there is no PAO, consult your XO for releasing guidance.

Resources for News Writing

Get familiar with the pertinent sources below (and others mentioned in chapter 7) if you aren't already.

- *Journalist 3&2* and *Journalist 1&C.* These rate training manuals for Navy journalists are comprehensive guides for writing news releases and feature stories, for distributing those stories, and for much, much more. Begin with these books; they are excellent general guides and can be of great help to anyone working part time or full time in the area of news writing.
- *The Associated Press Stylebook and Libel Manual.* This book is *the* standard guide to news style for most American magazines and newspapers. It is also the universally accepted PAO style guide.
- Rene J. Cappon, *The Word: An Associated Press Guide to Good News Writing.* Rather than a dictionary, this writing text is especially good on news writing.
- Martin L. Gibson, *Editing in the Electronic Era,* 2nd ed. (Ames, Iowa: The Iowa State University Press, 1984). This book covers such subjects as getting a good start, trimming the fat, using the king's English, and writing headlines; newspaper layout, photographs and cutlines, editing symbols, the copy editor, and the electronic newsroom.
- Floyd K. Baskette, Jack Z. Sissors, and Brian S. Brooks, *The Art of Editing,* 4th edition (New York: Macmillan, 1986). The authors cover copy-editing skills, headline-writing skills, and editing for other media.
- SECNAVINST 5720.44. The basic Public Affairs Officer regulation for both the Navy and Marine Corps.
- MCO P5720.61, Marine Corps Public Affairs Manual, Vol. II. This publication, which references SECNAVINST 5720.44, is the specific Marine Corps PAO manual for internal and external media.
- Fleet Instructions. Almost every fleet or type commander issues written guidance on news writing (and has full-time PAOs who will be glad to give you advice and written guidance).
- *Military Media Review.* The DOD magazine for journalists and public affairs officers. It gives out excellent advice on how to write stories, on writing style, on who takes what kinds of stories, etc.
- "Roster Stories." Fleet Hometown News Center, Norfolk, produces "fill in the blank" releases tailored for various occasions. For example, the "USMCR Toys for Tots" program includes sample fill-in-the-blank releases for nationwide use by on-the-scene coordinators.
- Weapons and equipment fact sheets and Topical Issues, printed by HQMC (PAM) and updated regularly.
- The Navy Editor Service. This monthly package of feature stories, line art, photographs, and other information is for use by ship and station

editors and is most useful for those putting out a newsletter or other publication. (The Navy Editor Service is different from the Captain's Call Kit, which is put out automatically for commanding officers and is for internal use only.) Those desiring the service should write a letter of request on command letterhead, have it signed by someone with "by direction" authority, include the proper mailing address and SNDL, and send the letter to Navy Editor Service, 601 N. Fairfax, Suite 230, Alexandria, VA 22314.

• "PANCOs." Most Marines are within shouting distance of a public affairs office or at least a recruiting station. For example, cities from Macon, Georgia, to Richmond, Virginia, rate a Public Affairs NCO ("PANCO") who can help the uninitiated through the wickets. Another source of help is the U.S. Marine Corps Combat Correspondents Association. Members located nationwide (mostly former or retired Marine public affairs people) are available to assist. Write the Executive Director, USMCCCA, Inc., 1035 Hazen Drive, San Marcos, CA 92069.

Finally, here is a list of the major service-wide magazines.

Navy:

- *All Hands*
- *Wifeline*
- *Naval Aviation News*
- *Surface Warfare*
- *Fathom* (Naval Surface Safety Review)
- *Approach* (Naval Aviation Safety Review)
- *Mech* (Naval Aviation Maintenance Safety Review)
- *Wings of Gold*
- *Shipmate*
- *Tailhook*
- *Naval Reservist News*
- *Naval Reserve Association News*
- *Chaplain Corps Newsletter*

Marine Corps:

- *Leatherneck*
- *Marines*
- *Marine Corps Gazette*

> A Marine willing to terminate his career in a firefight should be no less willing to terminate it through the candid expression of his professional convictions, constructively offered. . . . The real issue is not the risk to the critic, but the risk to the Corps if there are no critics.
>
> —Col Gordon D. Batcheller, *Marine Corps Gazette,* May 1987

11

The Professional Article

So you're thinking of writing an article for a professional journal. Perhaps your spouse has remarked, as one commander's did, "Why grouse so much to me? Why not write for *Proceedings* if you're so bothered by this?" Or maybe a shipmate has commented on one of your notions, "You know, that's an excellent idea, and I've never seen it spelled out anywhere. You ought to write it up." With such encouragement, should you take some extra hours over the next several weeks to dig into this subject and write an article for a professional military journal? The time and effort are a big sacrifice—and what real good will it do?

Of course, you'd like to see your name in print—always a motive for authors—and you wouldn't mind picking up a few extra bucks. Then there's the remote possibility that writing this article would do your career some good. Someone up the line might see it and think, "There's someone who might make a good administrative assistant, speechwriter, or aide." There's simply a professional advantage in being identified as a service member who expresses ideas well. A pattern of authorship sometimes has even larger consequences. Reportedly, Lieutenant Colonel Rommel "wrote his way to the command of a Panzer division and an eventual field marshal's baton with his *Infantry Attacks*" (LtCol J. W. Hammond, Jr., "The Responsibility to Write," *Marine Corps Gazette,* January 1970, p. 28).

However, when researching this book, I found very few Navy or Marine Corps authors who thought their publishing would significantly help their careers. On the contrary, the number of times officers commented about the *dangers* of publishing (with warnings like "Be careful when publishing. . . . It's hard for officials to look at what you write with objectivity," or "You can say almost anything—but get it clear in your own mind the *price* you may have to pay") suggests that you should get straight the main reason for writing for publication. These officers didn't write articles for personal prestige, career advancement, or monetary reward, primarily. Instead, they wrote for the good of the profession.

Why We Need Professional Journals

Because of the nature of naval service, we may need professional argument and open forums more than other professions. Why not just live by official doctrine and official reports? By their very nature, official reports tend to limit expression of views. As then LtCol G. D. Batcheller pointed out in an essay published in the *Marine Corps Gazette* ("For the Sake of the Corps, Write!" February 1984), all official reports "go through the chain of command. This [review process] has an inhibiting effect on all participants. . . . Critical candor becomes the first casualty. A satisfactory answer to 'Whose ox does this gore?' is a hurdle that any critical comment must clear if it is to survive the editorial ax. The more senior the ox, the less goring allowed" (p. 56).

"Writing is the way to reach those people when they are not at hand and you have no way of getting to them. Talking is like a 24-pdr muzzle loader: terrifically effective at very short range. Writing is like an airplane or a missile: It permits you to be effective over the horizons of space and of time."—Frank Uhlig, Publisher of *Naval War College Review*, unpublished speech

Batcheller went on to argue that since reports are usually staff efforts, signed by committees, and because the signers become liable for the product, putting critical views forward is difficult. "Something you may feel with great conviction may not be shared by the officer who has to sign the document. You may be reluctant to ask him to buy into your misery; he may be unwilling to do so" (p. 56).

As a result, the official information received at the top of the chain of command may be limited in value. As Admiral Rickover once commented, "Always rely on the chain of command to transmit and implement your instructions; but if you rely on the chain of command for your information about what's going on, you're dead" (Admiral Rickover was quoted by R. James Woolsey, former Under Secretary of the Navy; the quote was published in the April 1984 *Marine Corps Gazette*). Clearly, many senior officials are insulated from criticism by their positions, and therefore badly need to hear some *un*official views, on occasion. One place to hear forthright expressions of personal opinion is professional journals.

Not only commanders but all naval professionals need to have as informed a perspective as possible. True, we all read official publications that help us stay informed of late developments and broaden our perspective on naval service. But unofficial sources help greatly here too. Most naval personnel at sea would know very little about larger developments in the services without such forums as Naval Institute *Proceedings*, *Marine Corps Gazette*, *Navy Times*, and *Naval War College Review*.

"Never underestimate the power of a crank letter."—Navy Captain

Informational articles in such forums keep readers abreast of new developments in hardware, strategy, tactics, logistics, and many personnel-related topics. The magazines mentioned above publish persuasive articles to plant ideas, open discussion, and help readers to think of their jobs in new ways. Some pieces are "seminal" articles; they initiate whole programs and courses of action. Others do good work by "nudging" policy or thought. As Frank Uhlig, publisher of the *Naval War College Review*,

> **Opportunities for New Authors to Write**
>
> **Should you hesitate to write because of lack of seniority? Absolutely not. Most military journals—and particularly *Proceedings* and the *Gazette*—actively encourage junior authors and go out of their way to help those with promising ideas to improve their articles. They open their pages to enlisted service members, civil servants, and young officers. They even hold contests to stimulate new authors to try their hands at writing essays.**
>
> **If anything, because of editors' encouragement of junior authors, someone who is *not* senior will have a marked advantage in getting an article published, especially the very first one. After that, you're an old hand, and will have to sweat and struggle like the rest of us.**

pointed out, even if you don't convince your readers immediately, you get readers to begin thinking about what you're thinking about—a process that can be effective too.

So do your service a favor, and consider putting your good ideas or experience in print. How should you proceed? The following pages present brief guidance gleaned from conversations with many military authors and editors and from published articles on this subject.

Besides reading these pages, if you think either now or later in your career you might have something to say of value to the profession, then the very best way you can prepare is to start *reading*. Read books on naval topics; read naval and other military journals; and read beyond strictly military subjects too. The most thoughtful authors know the wide contexts of their subjects. They speak across boundaries of disciplines, and they draw analogies from widely varying fields and eras. They read literature of many differing kinds and have wide civic interests. In short, the best naval *writers* are good general *readers* first.

Writing a Professional Article

Like most writing, professional writing involves a series of discrete processes.

Decide on Your Focus

The basic question is one of focus. First decide whether you know something that your reader doesn't and that is significant or interesting enough to attract attention. Writing well depends above all on *having something to say*.

One good piece of advice to authors is to concentrate on a specific area—limit your subject. Don't try to refight the Battle of the Falklands in 2,000 words or attempt to explain the Navy and Marine Corps budget process even in 5,000. Not only are such subjects impossible to cover in such short space, but narrowing the subject to something you *really are an expert in* will help you to speak authoritatively. Stay in your area of expertise, and write on a subject with which you're familiar.

That doesn't mean you have to have twenty years of experience before you write. As a senior military journal editor pointed out, midshipmen sometimes have held their own with officers ten years their seniors by writing about what it's like to be led by good or bad leaders, or by revealing their thoughts upon first stepping into leadership roles. The midshipmen could speak with credibility and sharpness when they stayed close to their own certain knowledge. Of course, as you gain experience, you can range much farther afield. But new authors should start with what is close to home.

Look at What Kinds of Articles Journals Publish

Having selected a subject, consider the kind of forum you're trying to write for. Locate at least three or four possibilities—journals will often send you back copies as well as a writing guide or information sheet for authors. If you can, analyze several back issues, taking a careful look at what each journal publishes, especially the kind of articles it has put out recently. What's the style, length, and content of the articles? For whom do they seem to be written? Not only will such analysis help you decide whether your article can fit into that journal, but it may give you several ideas on good methods of support, ways to begin and end, the best use of anecdotes and quotations, etc.

Remember that a journal normally has several different sections. *Proceedings*, for instance, has "Professional Notes," "Nobody Asked Me But," and "Leadership Forum" as well as feature articles. The *Marine Corps Gazette* is similar—each issue has several sections, and besides full-length articles of about 2,500–5,000 words, it publishes shorter ones of 500–1,500. Some of the latter involve opinion or argument ("Commentary on the Corps"), while others are professional notes ("Strategy and Tactics," "Weapons and Equipment," etc.), or short historical vignettes. Typically the editorial review process differs for different sections of a journal; getting a piece into the shorter sections is sometimes a bit less difficult.

Do Any Necessary Research

Of course, you must have excellent support for whatever kind of article you write. Your reader rightly expects you to have rich and detailed knowledge or experience—assets that make you worth listening to. "Skimming the top" simply won't do.

Regardless how much you think you already know about your subject, become familiar with its wider context by reading published sources, including past articles related to your topic. Besides giving you more information and assuring you of the quality of your ideas, these sources will help you orient your article in the current professional discussion.

You may find that you need to do additional research, in which case follow the counsel on research given in chapter 1. Or you may conclude you already have sufficient arguments and data at hand. Whether you need to do further research is a judgment call on your part. The test of whether you have enough to present your topic fully is often the very first draft.

Draft the Article—Get the Content Down

Content is, of course, the key to any article. Journal editors have great patience with authors who have dynamic ideas, even if those authors can't write very well. As the *Gazette*'s "Writing Guide" comments, "We'll gladly accept a good idea written with a pencil stub on wrapping paper." Not everyone would go quite *that* far ("It's much easier to edit if it's typed, double-spaced, with one-inch margins," responded one harassed *Proceedings* editor), but if the content is good enough, almost all editors will go out of their way by offering pointers, reviewing revised drafts, and editing the final product heavily.

On the other hand, if you have problems in the content, whatever catchy introductions and other stylistic dressing-up you add won't help. One prominent military journal editor complained about bad content even in articles submitted from war colleges. Though an article by definition is conceptual and not "completed staff work," still, he argued, it must at least nod toward real-world issues like cost, manpower, priorities, and so on. The author must think deeply, do some basic research, and then have subject-matter experts review the essay. Too often, the editor continued, such critical spadework has not been done.

Therefore, when writing a professional article, concentrate on the *basic idea* and *its proof* (if yours is an argumentative essay) or on a *sharp presentation of content and data* (if it is an informative piece). Here are some of the questions that *Proceedings* editors often ask of an article that crosses their desks:

— Is the subject relevant?
— Is its focus sharp and the topic limited?
— Is the topic timely?
— Does the author know what he or she is talking about?
— Is the logic sound?
— Has the research been thorough?
— Is the thought sequence easy to follow?
— Do the main points emerge clearly from the details?
— Are the explanations clear and convincing?
— Are the details interesting?
— Has the writer had experts criticize this paper?

Editors can fix the grammar, and they can help an author with an introduction, a closing, and the whole style of a piece. But a miner mines raw materials only to recover some precious metal within. Make sure your essay has good *substance* to begin with. Focus on capturing that substance in your first draft or drafts.

Revise Your Article for Content

After getting a good draft down, work it over again (wait a couple of days first—you'll be surprised how different it all looks). Flesh out your ideas and generally rework the piece. You may find your thesis has to be modified or that your organization needs rethinking. Much of your effort will be adding details, examples, and illustrations, and looking at your logic. All of this work can be tedious, but if your first draft was successful, you can often revise a section at a time till you've substantially revised the whole article.

Of course, *double-check all your facts.* Remember, yours is the final responsibility for what you say. Magazines usually rely on your subject-matter expertise and do not check the basic accuracy of all that they publish.

Here are some other tests for the content of your article, once you're in the revision stage:

• Is your idea sound? Is it so clearly presented that it seems self-evident to the reader?

• In an argumentative article, have you taken a strong stand, adopted a definite point of view?

• Do you have sufficient support? Do you present justification for all superlatives and evidence for all generalizations? Evidence can be facts, descriptions, graphs, tables, anecdotes, and many other things. When deciding how much to say, follow this general rule: *don't say everything you know* about the subject, but *do say everything the reader needs to know* in order to understand and to buy your main point. On the other hand, too much is probably better than too little. Editors can cut much more easily than they can add information.

• Have you included quotations (if available)? Quotes can add both interest and credibility to your article. Look for expressions that perfectly capture the issue at hand, or supporting statements that carry weight because of the authority of the person who uttered them. Don't clutter your manuscript with long quotes that only restate what you are trying to prove, but look for the *telling* comment, the *penetrating* phrase. (Work on pithy writing in your own prose too.)

• Have you documented all special sources and data? Editors are wary of any unsupported assertions.

• Are your examples clear? Have you taken into account the specific audience you are writing for and its level of understanding? Unless you are writing for technical journals, most of your readers will probably not be very knowledgeable in your topic. Make sure you explain difficult concepts and technical terms.

• Have you clarified your argument's *relevance*? That is, have you also made clear your argument's consequences and put those consequences in terms your readers can identify with?

• Have you refuted any opponents' likely arguments (usually after adducing positive support)?

• Finally, if you have criticized a policy or program, have you also offered constructive recommendations? Avoid criticizing a policy or procedure without suggesting an alternative—unless you are simply saying, *Stop it! Right now!*

Taking the Emotion Out

You may find yourself very much emotionally engaged in your argument. Such involvement in itself can be either good or bad, depending on how you address your readers. Colonel John Greenwood of the *Marine Corps Gazette* suggests you make the assumption that those you are writing to are intelligent and as patriotic and conscientious as you are. That attitude will take any viciousness or pent-up frustration out of your argument. Put the audience on the same side as you are; assume that readers are reasonable and open to argument, and you'll avoid being too strident or on edge in your tone.

Admittedly, sometimes even this attitude isn't enough. The emotion that affects you can be very powerful, not only clouding your view but inhibiting you altogether from writing with a reasonable tone. An officer was so greatly worked up over the "Women in the Military" issue as to be literally unable to write on the topic *at all* without sounding vindictive, or defensive, or both. Apparently the bare mention of any word involving gender triggered a deep emotional reaction. It was only by altering the very terms being dealt with—so that instead of saying "men" and "women" the officer spoke in terms of "the incoming group" and "the current group"—that this writer was able to get the emotion out and successfully complete the article.

***Don't* refrain from writing an article just because you're charged up about it. Emotion has a great deal of psychic power, energy that you can channel into highly effective (and vitally needed) communication. *Do* recognize that you may be overwrought and, because of your emotional engagement, may be seeing only one side of the issue. Besides doing what you can to see the matter objectively, get several outside reviews from professionals who are not steamed up like you are. Going through a review process not only can make your article better, but it can also provide a learning experience as to how to communicate with others.**

Revise Your Article for Style

Once satisfied with the basic content, work on your style. Although journals edit articles before publishing them, an editor is more likely to publish a polished article than a dull, awkward, and mistake-riddled one. Here are some points to remember:

• Is the writing vivid, or does it sound like a training manual or an official instruction? If the latter, try *writing the way you speak*. That approach will freshen up your language. Virtually no one *talks* bureaucratese—so if you talk out your article, the writing will usually be clearer, simpler, and more natural.

• Make sure you use the *active voice*. Virtually all military journals mention this point. None of them wants all that impersonal and long-winded discourse so common to navalese—"it is recommended that," "the suggestion is made to," "the argument is offered that," etc. Instead of wading through such bilge, most readers will simply turn the page or put the magazine down entirely.

• Don't repeat yourself unnecessarily. Yes, an old stand-by in public speaking (and military instruction) is to "say what you're going to say, say it, and then say that you've said it." Such repetition can help when you're giving briefings, which depend on the ear and on memory. But military authors tend to repeat themselves overmuch in their writing, and also to add too much background and context. As a result, military journals often cut two or three pages *from both ends* of an article.

• Watch for long sentences and cut them back (an average of about 17 words per sentence is ideal, according to some experts). Keep the paragraphs short, too. Cut out all words, sentences, or paragraphs that are dull, repetitive, or unnecessary. Shortening will help sharpen your point.

• Work on rhythm and phrasing, reading aloud to listen to your prose. Strive for exactly the right word choice. Work for the truly vivid example and for clearness in your explanation.

• Try using subheads in your article, perhaps every five to seven paragraphs or so, depending on the content. Subdivision will help keep the reader oriented and might attract readers who are just browsing through.

• Finally, avoid jargon, buzz words, and navalisms. Define all important terms. Avoid unnecessary abbreviations and acronyms. Define what acronyms you absolutely must use the first time you use them, as in tactical action officer (TAO), remotely piloted vehicle (RPV), or airborne early warning (AEW). Then you can use these acronyms in succeeding sentences, as long as they aren't several paragraphs apart. Vary subsequent references by interspersing other, simpler nouns ("the officer," "the vehicle," "the concept", etc.) to keep from overusing the acronym.

"The trick is to make your essay jump out of the stack of 90 or so that the staff readers (including me) must screen—with a grabby title, snappy motto, riveting lead paragraph, and challenging arguments. You want to grab the reader by the stacking swivel, move him deftly from Point A to Point B, and convince him that the trip was worth his time and effort."—Col John Miller, USMC (Retired), Managing Editor, U.S. Naval Institute *Proceedings*

Consider Including Graphics

See if you can add any graphics support. Good graphics can make your argument much more readable and interesting and can incline the editorial board in your favor. Photos, charts, tables, maps, and diagrams are all good possibilities—and sometimes a staff artist can fix your rough sketches. Of course, think in terms of lively illustrations meant for magazines, not dull charts from a training manual. Don't overlook the possibility that you might have the perfect material on hand or be able to get it quickly. Although not all articles include illustrative material, it may help sell your article. If you have an idea for artwork but can't get it yourself, let the editors know. A magazine (like *Proceedings* or *Marine Corps Gazette*, particularly) can often illustrate your article with photographs from its own files.

Get Good Critiques, and Then Revise Again

Once you have a good draft, get some good criticism. How much, and from whom? One frequent contributor to *Proceedings* argues that you should find ten people who know a lot about your subject and have them tear your article apart. He always does. As a result, he finds that his material sails through editorial staffs—and he looks a lot smarter, too.

Maybe you can't get ten—but get some experts to review your work. To make sure you are not speaking over your readers' heads, have some nonexperts read your article as well.

Then revise your essay once more.

Get the Required Security and Policy Review

Normally, service members and Department of Defense civilians must clear articles for security through their local public affairs offices prior to submission and must include a signed statement of clearance with the article. Although some journals will assume responsibility for a security review, the author must usually get the article cleared. Don't regard a security review as antagonistic; do your homework ahead of time.

Not only security but policy may be an issue. For one thing, be careful about using the privileged information your job gives access to, even if it is unclassified. Such information may not be intended for public distribution. Wise authors make a practice of getting the material they use from some standard naval source and then citing that source in their articles.

For another thing, recognize that readers may have difficulty separating your own view from that of the office that you occupy. Even with a useful disclaimer on your part—"Opinions, conclusions, and recommendations expressed or implied within are solely those of the author and do not necessarily represent the views of . . ."—people will often assume that the stance you take is official because of your official position. Talk to experienced authors around your duty station or community if you envision any problems in this area.

Another difficult subject is how to handle legitimate dissent within such a hierarchical and honor-bound institution as the military. On this subject, a senior officer once gave this even-handed advice:

> Your oath of office doesn't cease when sitting at the typewriter. You have a professional obligation (1) not to reveal any classified information, (2) to be responsible and objective, and not harmful to the service, (3) to learn the current rules for getting articles cleared for policy as well as security, and (4) never to sandbag your boss (send a courtesy copy to your boss when your article has been prepared for publication).
>
> On the other hand, remember that it is not possible to say "good morning" without some fellow in Washington objecting to it. Yes, follow the rules, but there are times to put your blind eye to the telescope.

A magazine editor suggested, "Try to stay within the regs, but don't be slavish to them. If you run into review problems, contact the editor. Maybe he can help."

Final Review

As a final review, check all figures, dates, names, titles, footnotes, quotations (especially quotations—and against the original source) and other material to make sure you have not made inadvertent errors. Also check grammar, mechanics, spelling, and punctuation.

Format the Article, Type it, and Send It In

• Double-check the exact format required by the journal you're sending the article to. (As stated above, most journals will send out a sheet describing what they look for, including format and number of copies. Also, usually a journal will list its specific format requirements in each issue, somewhere near the title page.) Some journals require footnotes; others ask you to work documentation into your text as done in this chapter. Technical journals will often ask you to submit an abstract. There are many other idiosyncratic requirements—again, check the particular journal you're writing for.

• Unless informed otherwise, submit your article typewritten and double-spaced on while 8½″ × 11″ bond paper (one side of the page only). Don't use script or all caps. Make your margins at least one inch at top, bottom, and right, and an inch and a half at the left (some journals require a three-inch top margin on the first page). List your name, rank, office, and phone at the beginning or end of your article, and number your pages. Always mail manuscripts of more than five pages flat, with a paper clip. Include a cover letter of no more than a page in length. Remember to include a self-addressed, stamped return envelope.

• Send tables or graphs to illustrate your article, and make sure they are in black ink, not photocopy. If you send photos for magazines other than *Proceedings* (which prefers color slides), make your photos black and white, glossy finish, and 8″ × 10″ if possible. Identify pictured individuals on a separate sheet (writing on the back of a photo can damage it). For all illustrations, include a suggested caption. The caption should explain the illustration, relate it to the text as appropriate, but not repeat the exact words of the text.

• Remember that most journals ask authors not to submit material to more than one journal at a time, regarding multiple submissions as unprofessional.

• Be sure to proof the final copy very carefully before sending it in.

Consider These Naval and Other Military Journals

Below are the four major professional magazines or journals that provide forums for expression of opinion on the naval profession:

- U.S. Naval Institute *Proceedings*
- *Marine Corps Gazette*
- *Naval War College Review*
- *Naval History*

Here are some other naval magazines that might also be worth looking to, if you have suitable material (they are written mostly by staff):

- *Leatherneck*
- *Naval Aviation News*
- *Submarine Review*
- *Seapower*
- *Surface Warfare*
- *Navy Civil Engineer*

Of course, several professional magazines are oriented to nonnaval military topics. If you plan to do a good deal of writing and know others locally who are also interested, your ship or unit can order the helpful booklet *Markets for the Military Writer*. Put out every three years or so by the U.S. Army's public affairs headquarters, this publication lists and describes dozens of official and commercial journals that publish military-oriented topics. Contact the Print Media Branch, Command Information Division, Office of the Chief of Public Affairs (HQ, Department of the Army, SAPA-CI-PM, Washington, DC 20310) to order the pamphlet.

Converting a Paper into an Article

Many professional military articles originate in a classroom, but what makes a good student paper is not what makes a good article. The paper typically has a particular instructor as the intended audience (an expert who is already interested in the topic), and part of the paper's purpose is to show off the student's research. So the paper burgeons with buzzwords and stumbles with weighty footnotes. To interest journal readers who have never so much as thought about the subject before, the author must spread a much wider net by cutting back mere documentation and enlivening crucial support.

Typically, those who've written a good paper at Newport, Quantico, Monterey, or some other naval school have little conception of how much it takes to write successfully to a general professional audience. Normally they must describe their subjects much more simply (and visually) than they did in the original essay. They must also change the terms they use; the terminology and acronyms that work for experts are often gibberish for others.

In fact, so specialized has military terminology become that when writing for a broad military audience, an author does best to assume that the readers aren't in the service *at all.* As Frank Uhlig of the *Naval War College Review* once put it, "Assume that the people reading your article are intelligent and interested *laymen*. A destroyer officer and a fighter pilot both belong to the same navy, but neither is likely to know very much about the other's business. The same is true if you are aiming at people in other services, or civilians, only more so."

Adding intriguing introductions, simpler and fuller explanations, descriptive language, simplified terms, and striking conclusions may help to transform a paper into a journal article. Readers can always put the magazine down when what you have written does not engage them—so you must work for relevance, interest, even charm throughout the article.

What follow are examples of openings or "leads," exemplifications or illustrations, and conclusions or "sign-offs." These examples are somewhat artificial; they have been taken out of context and are necessarily brief. Nevertheless, they show the principles in action.

Openings or "Leads"

A good beginning not only attracts the reader's attention but also draws the reader immediately into important material. A "lead" can be a sentence, a phrase, or a paragraph. On a professional note, the lead will often be very short, for when describing new programs or recent developments you can sometimes count on ready reader interest. In contrast, the lead for a feature article will occasionally extend over several paragraphs. Even there you shouldn't lose motion. Craft the lead to draw the reader quickly into the meat of the article. See the examples below.

Open with **an anecdote** that pertinently introduces your topic:

Attention-getting anecdote

A scientist and an engineer were put in a room across from a bag of gold. They were told they could have the bag when they moved across the room. They could go as fast as they wanted provided they went no more than half the remaining distance with each move. The scientist, recognizing the impossibility of the situation, left the room. The engineer, on the other hand, moved across the room until he was within arm's reach of the bag. At this point, he declared that he had gone far enough for an engineering approximation, grabbed the bag, and left.

introduces the topic.

In developing its weapons, the Navy's goal frequently is to build a state-of-the-art system on the cutting edge of technology, rather than a simpler system that is good enough to get the job done. The result is that developmental work is always halfway finished, and its goals are never reached.

—LCDR Eric Johns, USN. "Perfect is the Enemy of Good Enough," U.S. Naval Institute *Proceedings* (October 1988): 37.

Open with **a striking statement:**

Arresting statement *leads to* *article's central query*

"Free a man to fight!" The battle cry of World War II justified the inclusion of women in the Marine Corps, the other armed forces, and war-related industries. Today's Marine Corps integrates women into the force structure more completely than ever before. They serve in virtually all echelons of command in all noncombat-related military occupational specialties (MOSs). But do women truly have a place in a Corps whose doctrine designs it to be a highly mobile amphibious fighting force?

—Staff Sergeant Martha B. Hall, USMC. "Is There a Place for the Woman Marine?" U.S. Naval Institute *Proceedings* (November 1988): 112.

. . . or open with **an arresting question:**

Arresting question leads to subjects of discussion.

Because one missile may sink a ship, naval officers often ask:

I know I can use force in self-defense if my ship is actually attacked. *But do I have to take the first hit?*

This paper discusses how international law, Navy Regulations and naval rules of engagement (ROE) answer this question for the on-scene commander. It also deals with the more general question sometimes asked by the President and other national command authorities: Are there circumstances when the United States may use force first?

—George Bunn. "International Law and the Use of Force in Peacetime: Do U.S. Ships Have to Take the First Hit?" *Naval War College Review* (May–June 1986): 69.

Open professional articles **by getting right to the point.** Here **a brief comparison** sets the stage:

Comparable civilian circumstances suggest Navy changes.

The civil aviation community has been debating the three-man cockpit issue for years. Now, labor relations notwithstanding, it appears that in the future most commercial cockpits will have two-man crews. Maybe it's time the Navy reviews its cockpit manning policies for the P-3 Orion airplane.

—CDR John V. DeThomas, USN. "Are Two Heads Better Than Three in a P-3?" U.S. Naval Institute *Proceedings* (January 1983): 108.

. . . and here the author locates the context **in recent articles:**

One problem's solution has other benefits.

The problem of continuity in units assigned to the northern NATO commitment has been discussed in recent GAZETTE articles. The Marine Corps Reserve could take a major step in solving the problem of continuity by establishing a Marine amphibious brigade (MAB) dedicated to a cold weather environment. Establishing such a cold weather unit would increase preparedness to fight a Soviet invasion and at the same time greatly enhance the individual reservist's sense of mission. . . . If properly trained and organized, the Reserves could greatly enhance the Marine Corps' ability to deploy and fight on short notice in the arctic environment.

—Capt Eric J. Green, USMC. "Continuity in Arctic Units." *Marine Corps Gazette* (February 1986): 36.

Open with an **offer of something new:**

Personal interest leads to

Implied question: "How does she handle?"

A new class of ship always excites a shiphandler. When the new ship is a gas turbine–powered, high performance cruiser built on the superb lines of a *Spruance* (DD-963)-class destroyer, the chance to drive is especially welcome. The *Ticonderoga* (CG-47) class is now entering the fleet in significant numbers: five are active and four are set to commission this year. It is time to enter the forum with a few thoughts about handling the new Aegis cruisers.

—LCDR James Stavridis, USN. "Handling a *Ticonderoga*." U.S. Naval Institute *Proceedings* (January 1987): 107.

. . . or open by citing **a pertinent historical precedent:**

Startling opening

connected to recent events

introduces the topic

Deliberately killing oneself while crashing a bomb-laden vehicle into an enemy target is a mode of warfare alien to U.S. doctrine and morality. In 1983, however, when a suicidal driver slammed his truck, carrying the equivalent of 12,000 pounds of TNT, into the Marine compound in Beirut, Americans learned that kamikazi-type tactics are still quite acceptable to others. More recently, the Iranians have made threats, broadcast over Tehran radio, that "martyrdom-seeking" volunteers have been practicing suicide missions on dummy enemy ships . . . and that their naval forces are fully prepared to take action against the United States. Such threats have to be taken quite seriously.

—Steven M. Shaker. "Suicidal Boat and Robot Craft Attacks." U.S. Naval Institute *Proceedings* (August 1988): 96.

Illustrations and Examples

Making bare facts or general statements meaningful can require special methods, such as visualization, comparison, exemplification, and so on. The possibilities are numberless, but the techniques below are common.

Use statistics creatively to make your point. Strategic use of statistics may prove conclusive. Do your best to make your figures comprehensible to your reader, with comparisons, multiplications, or other such manipulation (as long as you do it honestly). Also make sure to list your source, as in the example below.

A selection board scenario

There is great pressure to reduce defense expenses. People in powerful positions are more and more often heard commenting that "something has got to give" —the tremendous cost of maintaining our modern defense establishment must somehow be reduced. Consequently, they look askance at the fact that each of the Navy captains who must be retired from active duty at 26–30 years of service is entitled to a pension (on the average) of about $40,000 per year for perhaps as long as 27.1 more years. By the Bureau of Naval Personnel (BuPers) official estimate, this totals *seen in its financial ramifications*

$1,087,468 over the remainder of his life. Multiplying this number by the 250 senior captains who retired in 1986 (again, a BuPers estimate), it appears that their flag selection board added about $280,000,000 to our national debt.

—CAPT Edward L. Beach, USN (Retired). "Up Or Out: A Financial Disaster." U.S. Naval Institute *Proceedings* (June 1987): 54.

Use examples to support your assertions. Examples that support your points will both illustrate what you mean and tend to convince by accumulation. In the example below, the authors drive their points home by narrating telling incidents with the same general import from three different armed services.

Author's point, proved by . . .

Navy example,

Army example,

Royal Navy example.

In addition, a disturbing set of events occurred which seemed to reflect doubt on the advisability of using polyester materials for naval uniforms. A chief petty officer wearing double-knit khakis was severely burned when exposed to flash fire in a ship's fireroom. Safety Center experiments showed that corfam shoes burned and melted when subjected to flame. A U.S. Army aviator wearing a Nomex flight suit received fatal burns following a crash traceable to the melted nylon undershorts and undershirt he was wearing. (His Nomex flight suit was intact and his copilot, wearing Nomex with cotton undergarments, was only slightly injured.) In more recent experience, Royal Navy crewmen wearing polyester coveralls suffered severely aggravated polyester slag burns during the Falklands Conflict.

—LT David M. Kennedy, USN, and LT William R. C. Stewart III, Medical Corps, USNR. "That Dangerous Polyester Look." U.S. Naval Institute *Proceedings* (January 1984): 97.

Here a more eminent author uses **the same technique:**

Author's point, shown by . . .

Aegis example,

Perry-*class example,*

Israeli example,

Gulf of Sidra example.

Even more important, we are getting perhaps the best quality product in recent memory on the waterfront. The Aegis antiair warfare cruiser is revolutionizing air defense of the battle force. The *Perry*-class frigates working with SH-60B helicopters are providing us with the most potent and cost-effective above-surface antisubmarine warfare platforms in history. The 91 to 0 kill ratio the Israeli Air Force achieved with our equipment over Syrian MIGs in 1982 attests to the effectiveness of our air-to-air missile inventory. Our recent flawless operations in the Gulf of Sidra and against Libyan terrorist targets on shore demonstrate our capabilities against very sophisticated air defenses.

—John Lehman. "Successful Naval Strategy in the Pacific: How We Are Achieving It. How We Can Afford It." *Naval War College Review* (Winter 1987): 26.

Use **bullet format** in articles as well as point papers:

Author's thesis

For years the Pacific has been looked at as a subsidiary theater, secondary to our Nation's interest in Europe. There are, of course, historical reasons for this. While those reasons may have been valid in their day, they are no longer. We are now on the verge of the "Age of the Pacific."

supported by four specific instances.

• The economies of Japan, Korea, Taiwan, and Singapore have had unprecedented growth for the past 10 years.
• Since 1980, trade with the Pacific East Asia region has outstripped trade with the European community; $185 billion in two-way trade last year.
• Roughly 62 percent of the people in the world will live in the Pacific region which accounts for 60 percent of the world's gross national product.
• Return on investment in the region is on the average higher than anywhere else in the world, and the Pacific has vast potential markets and large resources.

—ADM James A. Lyons, Jr., USN. "A Peacetime Strategy for the Pacific." *Naval War College Review* (Winter 1987): 45.

Use **multiple illustrations** to make clear what you mean:

Culminating, dramatic point

Finally, a commander must have the capability of being completely *ruthless*. He need not be cruel-natured, but he must be capable of relieving his best friend who, although hard working and loyal, has proved incompetent. He must be capable of driving his men until they drop, then insisting that they completely dig-in a position before allowing them any rest. He must be capable of forcing them to wear restrictive, uncomfortable NBC protective clothing for days on end, even though there is no apparent chemical threat. He must be able to close his ears and his heart to the screams of anguish from innocent women and children, the victims of war, and deny them food and medicines when he must conserve his meager supply for his own troops. The battlefield of the future will be no place for the faint-hearted. Only the hardest of heart will survive.

illustrated by increasingly dramatic instances.

Restatement

—Maj Kenneth A. Nette, CD, PPCLI, USMC. "A Philosophy of Command." *Marine Corps Gazette* (December 1983): 50.

Closings or "Sign-Offs"

A good closing or "sign-off" to an article will usually lead back in some way either to the heart of the article or to some special high point in it. It may summarize, call to action, or challenge the reader. Whatever the approach, the best closing provides a "sense of an ending," releasing the reader's attention gracefully but with a final flick of the wrist. At the *very* end (the last sentence or words), you might hark back to the introduction, cite a historical quotation, or make some kind of appeal.

Close with a **summary:**

Generalization

Keeping in mind the sources of available navigational information and ensuring that your entire plotting team is aware of them are the true marks of the professional navigator. Using vertical angles, horizontal angles, and relative bearings to establish the ship's position may seem archaic compared to Loran or satellite receivers. But when

Summary, which admits apparent incongruity

Article's central contention, & famous phrase	the electricity-dependent equipment fails, a reliable, dusty sextant and a skilled navigator may be the best combination to steer the ship clear of harm's way.

—QMC H. Bradley McCracken, USN. ". . . A Tall Ship and a *Hill* to Steer Her By." U.S. Naval Institute *Proceedings* (September 1988): 104.

Close with a **conclusion:**

General conclusions	The overall goal of this ten-year strategic plan for training is to win in combat. Many people will disagree with individual programs; few can find fault with the goal. Moreover, without some agenda, without some vision, without some cohesive goal, Navy training will continue in its fragmented
Return to "baseball" scenario used in introduction	fashion. The Chief of Naval Operations is right; training is important. It is too important to employ the home run philosophy in developing training programs. The U.S. Navy must be so well trained that any opponent will be deterred from ever trying us.
Strong wrap-up	This is not baseball. We need vision.

—CDR Miles A. Libbey III, USN. "A Strategic Plan for Training." U.S. Naval Institute *Proceedings* (October 1983): 93.

Close by **citing an authority:**

Summary	The story of our POW experience in Vietnam, accepting a modicum of failure, is one of undaunted, unremitting courage. Even a fleeting profile of POW opinion demonstrates that the Code of Conduct
Citing of authority	proved to be sound doctrine. Capt Jim Mulligan put the Code in final perspective:
Conclusive last sentence	It can't answer everything, but it sets the rules. If you don't have any moral guts or personal integrity, the Code is not going to give them to you. But most military people have them someplace inside, and the Code of Conduct brings them out.

—Maj Terrence P. Murray, USMC. "Code of Conduct—A Sound Doctrine." *Marine Corps Gazette* (December 1983): 62.

. . . or by **citing historical precedent:**

Return to article's beginning,	In the early days of World War II, we failed to anticipate the actions of our enemies. Thousands of Americans died as a result. Among these legions were many merchant mariners and civilians who lost their lives in an obscure operational backwater—ironically,
pointing out historical mistakes.	a backwater that lies on the very shores of our continental United States. It would be painful to relearn these lessons from a new generation of enemy
Present actions to take	sailors by repeating the mistakes of our history. Through creative planning and use of our Reserve forces, we can prepare for a future enemy campaign in the Gulf of Mexico. This strategic imperative is crucial for our Nation's ability to maintain the

to prevent future mistakes.	industrial tempo that wartime will demand: a major loss of the vast resources of the Gulf coast could spell tragedy in any future, major conflict.

—LT William J. Cox, USNR. "The Gulf of Mexico: A Forgotten Frontier in the 1980s." *Naval War College Review* (Summer 1987): 75.

Close by illustrating **how success is close at hand:**

Summary	History clearly shows us the utility of smaller vessels in support of major fleet elements; we can have this small boat capacity at a cost which does not force us to weaken other vital defense projects, and we can have it quickly.
Intriguing cost as conclusion	For less than $175 million, the Navy could have 24 new patrol combatants by early 1985.

—LCDR R. D. Jacobs, USNR. "In Search of . . . Patrol Combatants." U.S. Naval Institute *Proceedings* (September 1983): 127.

Close by **calling to action:**

Reminder of article title	When blood is spilled again on the decks, as it inevitably will be during future conflict, let us hope that Navy surgeons will be in a position to respond, both effectively and skillfully.
Call for action	The time for taking action is now.

—CAPT Arthur M. Smith, Medical Corps, USNR. "Blood on the Decks." U.S. Naval Institute *Proceedings* (July 1988): 65.

Or close with **some combination of the above:**

Summary of proposals	The three security measures outlined above—random searches, random interviews, and a security awareness program—provide the core for an active security program that is both effective and practical. Until the Navy or DOD directs the implementation of these or similar measurers, the security of our classified information is being left basically to individual commands and organizations.
A warning against ominous historical precedent	As the Walker case amply demonstrated, the impact of espionage operations is not solely contained in the command where the spying originated. Indeed, in the Walker case, the effect was and continues to be felt worldwide.
Call to action	If we are to get serious about protecting classified information and preventing future Walkers or Pollards from operating, we need to change our attitudes towards security and not only recognize the threat, but do something about it. Implementing the measures outlined above would be a beginning.

—CAPT E. D. Smith, Jr., USN. "The Security Dilemma." *Naval War College Review* (Autumn 1988): 64.

Handbook

The guidelines suggested here reflect current military and professional writing practices, having been developed by reference to both official and unofficial sources. The Department of the Navy Correspondence Manual, Marine Corps documents of various sorts, and the Air Force pamphlet *Tongue and Quill* have been chief sources for this section.

Because practices differ from place to place within the services, naval writers should also follow whatever guides have been developed locally and are standardized throughout a command, service, or service community.

This short section, of course, can't cover everything. Besides this handbook, every professional should have close at hand a college-level (hardbound) dictionary and a complete handbook. Other useful books might include a thesaurus, a word-division guide, and a short reference manual. Most of these resources are available at the local servmart. You should also have ready access to the Correspondence Manual, any desk-top guide your command may have put out, and handy desk planners such as the Navy Leader Planning Guide (NAVPERS 15255 series). See "The Well-Stocked Desk" on page 348.

Numbers

In general, **spell out whole numbers below 10** (one, three, eight), **but write numbers 10 and above as figures** (10, 17, 347). Otherwise:

Spell Out

Numbers that begin a sentence:
Twelve stevedores loaded the vessel.
Twenty-five games remain.

Numbers used in connection with serious or dignified subjects, especially in formal writing:
The Thirteen Colonies
The Ten Commandments
The Eighty-second Congress
Fourscore and seven years . . .

Numbers of 100 or less preceding a compound modifier containing a figure (spell out to avoid confusion):
Two ¼-inch pipes
three 30-year-old destroyers
seventeen 8-inch guns
but
155 20-year-old aircraft

Indefinite expressions of round numbers:
a thousand and one reasons
thirteenth-century architecture
the early eighties
but
the 1980s (*or* the 80s)

Numbers of a million and up (for easy grasp of large numbers):
$15 million
$1.9 million
300 billion
but
$15,000
316,965

Fractions that stand alone:
one-third the cost
but
¾-inch boards

The plurals of numbers used with other plurals:
two fours
sixty fifteens

Write in Figures any Numbers Expressing

Age:
a 5-year-old child
She is 18 years old.
but
He's in his eighties (*not* his '80s or 80s)

Time:
before 10:00 AM
0900 (*not* 0900 hours)
4 o'clock in the afternoon (*not* 4 o'clock PM)

after 9:30 PM
15 years 4 months 13 days

Dates:

15 October 1988 *or* 15 Oct 88 *[if you abbreviate the year, also abbreviate the month]*
June 1989 or June 22, 1989 (*not* June, 1989 *or* June 22d, 1989)
10 January to 24 May 1987
Class of 1943 or Class of '43
23d of February
1st, 2d, 3d, and 4th of the month
but
Fourth of July—the holiday

Money:

Give the cabbie $20.
They sent a bill for $55,787.00.
a $50 bill
It costs $8.65.
65 yen; 2.5 francs, etc.

Measurements:

8 meters wide
about 15 yards long
8 by 12 inches
9 gallons
15.5 bushels
3,500 acres
7 feet by 7 feet 8 inches
¼- to ½-inch margin

Numbers used as numbers:

You have to multiply by 4.
Pick a number between 1 and 10.

Miscellaneous numbers:

speed: The ship can do 35 knots.
The aircraft can fly at 525 miles per hour.
sizes: He has a size 34 waist.
temperature: It reached 102 degrees today.
degrees: The ship had a 5-degree list, and it rolled 25 degrees to port.
percentages: The number of voters increased by 200 percent.
ratio: a ratio of 3 to 2 *or* a 3-to-2 ratio
vote: a vote of 15 to 13
scores: They won by a score of 7 to 4.
or She bowled a score of 225.
or Navy beat Air Force by 12 points.
or It was Navy 75, Army 0.

Various numerical abbreviations:

No. 152
£22 4s. 6d.
No. 77
212 B.C.
Genesis 24:8
lines 6 and 7
pages 137–138

paragraph 13
A.D. 13–15
Chapter 15

In Any Case

Treat related numbers in the same set alike:

The $800,000 increase in income taxes followed a $2,000,000 boost in property taxes. *[Since the thousands are written out, so are the millions.]*

Two out of twenty-five Marines were wounded. *[The second number is spelled out since the first one is.]*

He wrote checks of $10.50, $121.00, and $.50.

Express numbers in a series in figures if any number is 10 or more; spell them out if all are under 10.

The command sent 70 instructions, 5 notices, and 1500 messages.
She bought three gloves, three balls, and one bat.

Designate plurals by adding s, and form numerical form of first, second, fourth, etc., by adding *st, d, th,* etc.

built in the 1970s
temperature in the 20s
1st, 2d, 3d, 4th, and 5th
their 25th year of marriage
the 100th aircraft

Numbers Used in Titles of Military Units

Navy Units

Spell out all numbers in the address element of naval messages:

— 1 to 19 as one word (SEVEN or TWELVE or NINETEEN):

COMCARDIV FIVE
CRUDESGRU TWELVE

— 20 and up as:

COMDESRON FIVE ZERO
TASK UNIT ONE FIVE THREE PT FOUR PT TWO

Spell out naval fleets:

Sixth Fleet

Spell out naval districts:

Twelfth Naval District

Spell out unit numbers in a letterhead, especially if the numbers are small:

Naval Reserve Readiness Command Region Ten
Mobile Technical Unit Nine
Helicopter Anti-Submarine Squadron Eighty Five

But note that increasingly in correspondence numbers of units are written as figures:

Naval Security Group 1
Submarine Development Group 1 Detachment Alameda

Write as figures hull numbers of ships*:

USS GEORGE C. MARSHALL (SSBN 654)
USS SHREVEPORT (LPD 12)
USS KITTY HAWK (CV 63)

Write as figures task unit designations*:

Task Force 62
Commander, Task Group 62.3 (CTG 62.3)
*(*But see the rule for the address elements of naval messages.*)

Marine Corps Units

U.S. Marine Corps units are designated by using letters for companies and batteries; Arabic numerals for divisions, regiments, battalions, platoons, and squads; and Roman numerals for forces:

Company B
1st Marine Division (1st MarDiv)
Marine Fighter Squadron 212 (VMF-212)
III Marine Expeditionary Force (III MEF)
2d Squad

See HQO 5216.6 for more examples.

Normally, use figures for all Marine Corps units rather than spelling out the numbers:

2d Marine Expeditionary Brigade
III Marine Expeditionary Force (3d MarDiv)
Marine Aircraft Group 42 (MAG-42)
Marine Heavy Helicopter Squadron 772 Detachment A (HMH 772 Det A)
4th Marine Aircraft Wing

Exception: Spell out a numbered unit if the number begins a sentence:

First Platoon will be inspected on Thursday.
Third Marine Expeditionary Force (III MEF) will embark for Africa.

Army Units

Use figures for all army units but corps and numbered armies. Use Roman numerals for corps, and spell out numbered armies:

82d Infantry Regiment
7th AAA Brigade
2d Infantry Division
III Corps
2d Army Group
First Army

Air Force Units

Use figures for units up to and including air divisions. Use figures for numbered air forces only if using the abbreviation *AF.*

31st Combat Support Group; 31 CSG
22d Tactical Fighter Wing; 22 TFW
934th Air Division; 934 AD
Ninth Air Force; 9 AF
Fifth Air Force; 5 AF

Capitalization

The First Word

Capitalize the first word of every sentence and other expression used as a sentence:

The umpire called the batter out.
Stop! First get the gun. The M-16, in the locker.
The case is solved. Without a question.

Capitalize the first word in quoted sentences and in direct quotations or questions within sentences:

That was his argument. "No two ships could be on exactly the same bearing at the same distance at the same time."
The chief said, "Bring the two seamen up here."
Both recruits had one worry: What could they tell the drill sergeant?

Don't capitalize fragmentary or incomplete quotations:

— She argued with the stipulation that military personnel "must be covered even while exercising."
— Lincoln asked "whether that nation, or any nation so conceived and so dedicated, can long endure."

Capitalize the first word of each item in a series of sentences that is introduced by a complete sentence:

Two results follow on the decision to send combatants to such a distant location: First, food will have to be obtained locally. Second, all the other pipelines—ammunition, repair parts, crew reliefs for personnel, mail, etc.—will be greatly extended.

Do not capitalize if the series completes the sentence that introduces it:

— The decision means that
  a. some foodstuffs will have to be obtained locally, and
  b. all the other pipelines will be greatly extended.
— Officers present raised several issues: per diem, BOQ space, and transportation back to base.

Capitalize the first word of a parenthetical sentence that stands on its own (and place the period within the final parenthesis):

The three surface line officers discussed the DD's capabilities. (It was old but carried lots of guns.)

Do not capitalize the first word of such a sentence if the sentence does not stand on its own:

— The three midshipmen (they had failed English 101) reported for extra instruction Wednesday afternoon.

Also do not capitalize the first word in a parenthetical expression that is not a sentence (unless you have some other reason to capitalize it):

— The admiral started up the hallway (out to E Ring) but stopped suddenly.

— The course instructor (Professor Gilliland) took the roll.

Capitalize the first word of an independent clause following a colon if the expression following is clearly the more dominant element, or if it is introduced by a word such as *Note, Warning, Caution*, etc. Otherwise, use lowercase.

The rule is: Check every third automobile.

Warning: This drum contains highly corrosive material.

but

Whatever the case, the enemy will not retreat: this line is critical to their supplies and communications.

Proper vs. Common Nouns

Capitalize proper nouns, that is, the names of specific persons, offices, places, and things:

Athens
New York
Martin Luther King
The Bowery
Messenger of the Watch
Officer Candidate School
Egypt
Judith Smith-McKee
Master at Arms

Capitalize a common noun or adjective that forms an essential part of a proper noun. Normally use lower case for the common noun alone when used as a substitute for the name of a place:

Naval War College; the college
Jefferson Memorial; the memorial
University of Kansas; the university
Suez Canal; the canal
Golden Gate Bridge; the bridge

Military and Naval Terms

Capitalize the following widely used terms in the Navy and Marine Corps; lowercase common nouns as indicated:

Department of the Navy; Navy Department; DON

United States Navy; the Navy (*always* capitalized if used in reference to the U.S. Navy); a Navy regulation; a Navy officer *but* foreign navies; a sailor, an officer, a chief, etc.

Marine Corps; the Marines; the Corps; a Marine Corps officer; a Marine; *but* a sergeant, a corporal, etc.

Armed Forces; *but* armed services

Naval Academy; the Academy; *but* service academies
Brigade of Midshipmen; the Brigade; *but* the midshipman
Naval Reserve; Marine Corps Reserve; the Reserves; *but* a reserve officer
Pensacola Naval Air Station; Naval Military Personnel Command; *but* naval air stations; naval personnel; naval aviation; naval terms
The term "naval" has reference to both the Navy and the Marine Corps. See General Simmons's explanation on page 51.

Names of Naval Ships

Use all capitals for naval vessels, except in journalism and professional articles.
USS CALIFORNIA (CGN 36)
USS GEORGE WASHINGTON CARVER (SSBN 656)

Military and Naval Ranks and Titles

Capitalize military ranks when used with a proper noun. Do not capitalize when they stand alone:
Admiral Nimitz was remembered; *but* the admiral was spoken of
Sergeant Gonzalez was cited; *but* the sergeant was commended
Senior Chief Oko gave the orders; *but* the senior chief took charge
Airman Adams worked hard; *but* the airman handled the details
Note 1: Capitalize the word "captain" when referring to the captain of a ship, whatever the officer's rank:
— The Captain ordered us to . . .
— According to the Captain, the beach is . . .
Note 2: When referring to a particular military member in official documents, first identify by full grade and full name (usually first name, middle initial, and last name), and subsequently just by short title and last name, both capitalized:
— Lieutenant Jennifer J. Johnson brought up school quotas. Concerned with timely application, LT Johnson argued . . .
— Sergeant Major George R. Wood . . . SgtMaj Wood
— Chief Boatswain's Mate George Sand . . . BMC Sand or Chief Sand

Capitalize billet or organizational titles when used with a proper name, when used in place of a proper name, or when such usage is customary. But don't capitalize generic job descriptions.
The Administrative Officer will escort you to your quarters.
Few of them had negative things to say about the Leading Petty Officer, SK1 Lemoine.
She earned the designation "Naval Flight Officer."
We need good courses if we're going to train good communications officers.

Capitalize the names of departments within an organization, such as specific departments or divisions aboard ship or departments in a Marine combat unit. Do not capitalize the common nouns that refer to them.

I think he works in the Weapons Department of the frigate that's in port.
Requisition all supplies through the Supply Department in the Headquarters and Service Battalion.
We'll want to get the department heads and division officers in on this.

National Government Offices and Titles

Always capitalize the reference to a head of state or assistant head of state:

President Reagan; the President; *but* presidents have often
Vice-President Quayle; the Vice-President
Prime Minister Margaret Thatcher; the Prime Minister

Capitalize the titles of U.S. Government officials, and the names of U.S. Government bodies, buildings, and documents:

U.S. Government; the Federal Government; the Government
U.S. Congress; Congress; Congressman Smith; *but* a congressman from Wyoming; congressional matters
U.S. Senate; the Senate; Senator Arthur; *but* a senator on the committee
U.S. House of Representatives; the House; Representative Macuso; the Speaker; *but* a representative from Minnesota
Supreme Court; Justice Powell; *but* a justice
U.S. Constitution; the Constitution; *but* constitutional
the Capitol; the White House; the Jefferson Memorial; the memorial
the Department of Defense; Defense Department; DOD

Local Government Terms and Titles

Capitalize the full names of state or local organizations, but not the short names for them.

the New Orleans City Council; *but* the city council's task
the Ohio State Legislature convened; *but* the legislature adjourned
The capital of Maryland is in Annapolis.

Capitalize the titles of state or local officials when the titles are used with the name, but when used alone, lowercase them.

Mayor Stephanie Alison addressed the meeting; *but* the mayor spoke
Lieutenant Governor Jefferson presided; *but* the lieutenant governor's job
they contacted Sheriff Delahoussaye; *but* the sheriff arrived

Capitalize the terms "state," "city," "county," "ward," etc., only if part of the corporate name, with this exception: also capitalize a traditional name for a state or city:

New York State; the state of New York
New York City; the city of New York
Kansas City; the city
Oswego County; the county
Third Ward; the ward

traditional names:
the Empire State
the Sunflower State
the Windy City
also:
the Fifty States
it was good to get back to the States

Educational Terms

Capitalize the proper names of schools, colleges, and academic departments. Do *not* capitalize common nouns that refer to them:
University of New Orleans; *but* the university
Department of Mathematics; *but* the math department
Officer Indoctrination School; OIS; *but* the school

Capitalize the name of a class, but not the member of the class; capitalize specific course titles, but not the common noun referring to them, and not areas of study:
the Third Class; *but* third classman
the Junior Class; *but* a junior
English 410, Classics of Greece and Rome; but the classics course
Mary is studying physics at UCLA.

Capitalize academic degrees (including abbreviations) that follow a person's name, or whenever using the complete title of the degree:
he has a Ph.D. in Engineering; *but* he holds a doctoral degree
Amy Johnson, M.A.; *but* Amy holds a master's degree
A Naval Academy graduate is awarded a Bachelor of Science (B.S.) even if he or she majors in history.
George Gray, M.D; *not* Mr. George Gray, M.D. *or* Dr. George Gray, M.D.

History

Capitalize names of important historical events, periods, or documents:
the Korean War
the Tet Offensive
the Battle of the Bulge
the Renaissance
the Sixteenth Century; *but* the sixteen hundreds
Magna Charta

Laws, Acts, Documents, Bills, and Treaties

Capitalize the official names of laws but not the common nouns that refer to them:
Public Law 165; *but* the law
Sherman Antitrust Act; *but* the act
Marine Corps Manual; *but* the manual

the Unequal Treaties; *but* the treaties
Article 31 of Naval Regulations; *but* the article

Days, Months, Holidays, and Seasons

Capitalize all but seasons:
Wednesday, Thursday
February, March
Memorial Day; Easter; New Year's Day; Fourth of July (the Fourth)
but
fall, winter, spring, summer, autumn

Compass Directions

Capitalize compass directions used to indicate geographical regions, or when part of names:
the Midwest
the West Coast
Northwestern Mutual
The Democrats want to carry the South.
The battalion deployed to the Middle East.
He enrolled at East Texas State University.
Do not capitalize compass directions used just to indicate direction or position:
— The fleet was northwest of Hawaii.
— Proceed south to Point Alfa; then go southeast.
— The enemy patrols in the northern sector are thin.

Races, Peoples, Languages, Nations, and Religions

Capitalize all:
Caucasian; Japanese; European
French; Indo-European; Russian
the Soviet Union; Venezuela; Angola; the Virgin Islands
Roman Catholic; Methodist; Buddhist

Organizations, Corporations, and Commercial Products

Capitalize the name of an organization, but not the common noun that refers to it:
Rand Corporation; the corporation; the company
the Veterans Administration; the VA; the administration; veterans' benefits
the Republican party; the party; Republicans
A concept such as "democracy" is not capitalized, except when part of a proper noun such as "the Democratic party." Someone who

believes in democracy is a democrat (not in caps) and may also be a member of the party by that name, i.e., a Democrat (capitalized). However, that person might also be a Republican. The word "party" is always lowercased, e.g., the Socialist party.

Capitalize the name of departments within an organization, but not the common noun that refers to them:

Cassius Jones of the Accounting Department; *but* Mr. Jones of accounting will speak to you.

I'm applying for a position in maintenance.

Capitalize trade names, variety names, and names of market grades and brands, but don't capitalize the common nouns that follow these names:

Nabisco crackers
a Pendleton shirt
Seth Thomas clock
Zenith television set

Don't capitalize one-time trade names or proper or place names that through usage have become generic. But check a dictionary if in doubt.

venetian blinds
pasteurize
neoprene

Punctuation

Use the Apostrophe

In contractions where letters have been omitted:

can't
isn't
won't
it's
she'll
should've

To form possessives of nouns:

Add 's to all singular nouns:

the officer's stateroom
CDR Jones's schedule
yesterday's menu
the boss's office

Add 's to plural nouns not ending in s:

men's gymnasium
alumni's gathering

Add only the apostrophe to plural nouns ending in s:

engineers' estimates
officers' formation
boys' and girls' rooms

To form plurals of letters and figures:

ten a's

four m's
two 4's

It is becoming increasingly common to omit the apostrophe following figures and acronyms (multiple letters). In this case:

Omit the apostrophe to indicate plurals of figures or acronyms:

the 1980s
three Boeing 747s
two MEUs
many PAOs

Use an apostrophe with such letters and figures—singular or plural—to show possession:

The 727's front wheels blew out. [One 727 had its wheels blow out.]

The F-18s' wings iced up. [Several F-18s had their wings ice up.]

The FFG's bow was buckled. [One FFG had a buckled bow.]

The BTs' schooling had proved inadequate. [Several BTs had poor schooling.]

Whichever style you use, make sure you are consistent within any one document.

As single quotation marks to indicate a quote within a quote:

The survivor said, "I thought the gig had gone until I heard someone say, 'Let's look one more time around the anchor chain.' "

Do *not* use the apostrophe with the possessive forms of personal pronouns, but *do* use the apostrophe with the possessive forms of indefinite pronouns:

ours
hers
yours
its
theirs
ours
anybody's
everyone's
someone's

Watch possible confusion between it's *(it is) and the pronoun* its:

Wrong: *Its* clear that the patrol boat has turned off *it's* searchlights.

Right: *It's* the only way we can get the telescope to *its* destination.

Use the Asterisk

To refer readers to footnotes at the bottom of a page:*

*Like this. Asterisks follow all punctuation marks (including quotation marks).

To mark the omission of one or more paragraphs:

A line of asterisks (seven per line) or periods can be used to indicate the omission:

* * * * * * *

Use Brackets

To insert brief editorial comments or explanations in direct quotations:

"The French Admiral [Darlan] disagreed."

"Order those troops [the Marines] to return to the front."

With *sic* to mark an error of spelling, usage, or fact within a quotation:

"Practically speaking, the Navy and Marine Corps have lived, worked, and fought together since their enception [*sic*]."

The sic tells the reader that what may seem an error on your part is a faithful copy of the original material. A sic can comprise a strong criticism, saying in effect, "See the errors this guy makes?" In some circumstances you may want to correct a minor error in a quotation and leave out the sic.

To signify parentheses within parentheses:

The board president then ended the meeting (although only after the officers [LCDR Arthur and LTJG Gregg] had departed).

If your typewriter or word processor doesn't have brackets, either leave spaces and draw brackets freehand, or use parentheses instead, as in the examples of JAG Manual Investigations in this text.

Use the Colon

After a main clause to introduce a list or some other summation, if "as follows" or "the following" is expressed or implicit in the clause before the colon:

The order of entry will be the following: Colonel McDaniel, Major Mazzeno, and Professor White. ("The following" is explicit.)

The inspection party found two discrepancies: loose wiring in the overhead and a leaking faucet. ("As follows" is implicit.)

Do not use a colon between a verb and its object or complement, or between a preposition and its object.

Right: They visited three new ports: Marseilles, Barcelona, and Cadiz.

Wrong: They traveled through: Denver, Colorado Springs, and Pueblo.

Wrong: Public hearings have been scheduled on: August 26, September 3, and October 8.

To join two independent clauses when the second illustrates or explains the first:

After plebe year, you begin to feel like a prisoner on good conduct: all those privileges they had once taken away they now begin to give back one by one.

It was cold that night; the mercury dropped to thirty below.

Note the difference between the colon and the semicolon: the colon introduces items to follow; a semicolon separates coordinate sentence elements, that is, two complete sentences whose ideas are very closely tied together.

To express the preposition *to* in a ratio:

2:1

5:3

To punctuate the salutation in a business letter:

Dear Mrs. Parsons:

Dear Corporal Smith:

To separate hours from minutes in 12-hour clock time:

3:01

12:15

10:45

To separate the place of publication from the name of the publisher in a bibliography entry:

New Orleans: Pelican Press, 1989.

Use the Comma

To separate an introductory subordinate clause or a long prepositional phrase from the clause it modifies:

If the Major approves, we will send out the briefing package this afternoon.

When you come to Poydras Street, turn right.

During the extended firefights near My Tho, the boats were not reinforced.

To set off words that introduce quotations, as long as the word "say" (or a substitute) is included:

The steward said, "Dinner is served."

He replied, "Give her the orders."

The admiral asked, "Does anyone have a question?"

Note 1: Use a colon instead of a comma if the word "say" or a substitute is omitted, or if that word takes an object prior to the quotation:

— The captain turned: "Who gave that order?"

— The captain said these words distinctly: "Who gave that order?"

Note 2: No comma is necessary if the quotation functions as an integral part of the sentence:

The argument "might makes right" is immoral.

To set off introductory words such as "Yes," "No," or "Oh":

No, we didn't fly that low.

Oh, you must mean the ship's boat.

To separate a series of modifiers:

The recruits were young, scared, and homesick.

To separate three or more words in a series, including the word before the final "and," "or," or "nor":

She issues food, equipment, and clothing.

Move the people in any way you can—on cars, planes, trains, or buses.

To separate parallel phrases or clauses:

She has excellent writing skills, works hard, and is a very quick study.

To separate parallel adjectives:

a hard, cold winter

a shiny, brittle material

If the order of the adjectives can be reversed, or if and *can stand between them, then the adjectives are parallel and a comma should separate them.* Do not *use a comma if the second adjective and the noun form a single concept:*

— a light blue dress

— a new video recorder

To separate two or more independent clauses in a compound sentence if they are joined by a simple conjunction such as *or, nor, and,* or *but.* (You can omit the comma when the statements are short and closely related.)

There are several districts, and each district has its own commandant.

"Either I'll go by plane, or I won't go at all."

The shooting started and all the ships reversed course.

Do not use a comma before a coordinating conjunction that joins compound subjects, compound verbs, or phrases.

Wrong: The Congressman, and his staff, walked up the gangplank.

Wrong: The inspection team tested the procedures, and found no discrepancies.

Right: The aviators and their maintenance staffs looked on smugly.

To follow transitional words and phrases such as *however, that is, namely, therefore, for example, moreover,* and *i.e.* Use a comma after these terms when they interrupt the flow of the sentence. The type of punctuation used *before* them is determined by the strength of the interruption.

She bought all the groceries; however, she forgot to go to the bank.

He had been decorated in battle—nevertheless, he still opposed the war.

Moreover, the sea state was very high.

When such words are used to be emphatic, do not set them off with commas.

— There are therefore no missiles at all left in the magazine.

Before *for*, when *for* is used as a conjunction:

He did not issue the order, for the troops had not yet rested.

To set off a noun or phrase in direct address:

Mr. Chairman, the committee has voted.

Congresswoman Phillips, we ask your assistance.

I enjoyed my tour of the ship, Ensign Alfred, and I appreciate your hospitality.

To set off words or phrases that are appositives (explanatory equivalents):

Captain Robichaux, the skipper of the ship, has been in the Navy for ten years.

Peter Elshire, the courteous professor, explained the phrase.

To set off words or phrases in contrast when introduced by *not* or *but*:

The women, not the men, have offered leadership here.

Classes are not held in the portables, but in the main building.

The sergeant is known for his successes, not his failures.

To set off parenthetic words, phrases, or clauses (commas in pairs have the force of weak parentheses):

There is, my friend, no alternative.

Plan B, on the other hand, may have some merit.

The recommendations, developed months ago, have not yet been implemented.

Use the comma with "nonrestrictive clauses"—clauses that are parenthetical are called nonrestrictive. Clauses that limit or modify the meaning of a sentence in a way that is not parenthetical—which are essential to the sentence's meaning—are called "restrictive" and are not set off by commas.

Nonrestrictive—use commas:

The lieutenant, who was wounded, was left behind. *There was only one lieutenant in the area. The phrase is not essential to the sentence, but just adds information.*

Restrictive—no commas:

The lieutenant who was wounded was left behind. *Tells which lieutenant of several was left behind. The phrase is necessary to identify which lieutenant is being referred to.*

To set off interrupting words, phrases, or clauses when they break the flow of a sentence:

The price they paid, in fact, was twice as much as advertised elsewhere.
The senior chief, you know, has the ear of the CO.
She knew that the butcher, too, was likely to quit his job.

To indicate the omission of an understood word or words:

Before those encounters, we used the tactic again and again; afterward, never. *The second comma takes the place of* we used it.

To set off afterthoughts:

It will get out of the channel by 1700, won't it?
The general has been given the VIP suite, I hope.

To separate words or figures that might otherwise be misread or misunderstood:

To Charles, Jeffrey was friendly.
Out of 50, 22 actually graduated.
What the target is, is now clear.
Just before, the boat docked successfully.

To separate repeated words:

It was a deep, deep depression.
Now, now. Settle down.

To separate thousands, millions, etc., in numbers of four or more digits:

17,854
4,880,000
2,900

After the date of the month when the date is expressed in conventional civilian terms (military style uses no commas in dates):

Civilian Style: November 17, 1988
Military Style: 17 November 1988
In a sentence: He lived in Boulder from December 13, 1967 to March 22, 1969.

To separate parts of an address (but no comma precedes the ZIP Code):

The telegram was delivered to 1177 Louisiana Street, Lawrence, Kansas 66044.

To separate parts of the titles of bases, stations, or other military installations:

He was to report to Naval Air Station, Memphis, on October 1st.
The ship left Naval Station, Charleston, at 2000.

Omit the comma with the shortened name of a military facility or installation:

— MCAS Beaufort
— NAS Key West
— MCB Camp Lejeune

To set off names of states and foreign countries when used with other place names (use the comma before and after):

She moved from Dalhart, Texas, to Kansas City.
The squadron arrived in Atsugi, Japan, on 15 December.

To separate some titles and following personal names: Jr. and Sr. are set off by commas, and so are academic degrees. But 2d, 3d and II, III are not.

Henry Ford II
Rolando Smith, Jr.
George Thomas Kennedy, Esq.
Jennifer Dunn, M.A.
John Houston, Ph.D.

Between a title and the name of an organization, and between different levels within an organization:

Sandra Estoff, Corporal, USMC
Henry Dean, Lieutenant Commander, JAGC, USN
Director, Strategic Sealift
Chairman, House Armed Services Committee
Commanding Officer, Company A, 1st Battalion, 2d Marines

Use the Dash

To indicate a sudden break or abrupt change in thought:

Order two copies of the document—no, on second thought, order a whole case.

The change to the Awards Manual should be—no, will be—published by year's end.

To set off emphatically (stronger than commas) words or phrases of explanation that you want to emphasize:

The boat crew—every petty officer—acted competently in the crisis.

Make sure if you set off a word or phrase in the middle of a sentence that you put dashes on both sides *of it.*

To set off nonessential explanatory clauses when those clauses contain internal commas:

All of these subjects—English, history, and philosophy—are in the humanities.

To set off single words:

He's after just one thing—guns.

Before a clause that summarizes a series of words or phrases:

The Navy and the Marine Corps—together, these services comprise the Department of the Navy.

Before the source of a quotation or credit line:

I have not yet begun to fight.
—John Paul Jones

Occasionally, to indicate emphasis:

The F-16s must be moved—but to somewhere else in Europe.

If your typewriter or word processor has no dash, make the dash with two hyphens and no space before or after--like this.

Use the Exclamation Point

To mark surprise, incredulity, admiration, appeal, irony, or other *strong* emotion:

What a beautiful sight!

Great! I don't have to go.

Get going! The ship leaves the pier in five minutes!

Use a comma after mild *interjections; end mildly exclamatory sentences with a period:*

— Oh, it seems the ship got underway early.

— I wish you success.

To mark a statement made with particular emphasis or force, including an order or command:

"Cease fire! Cease fire!"

"All stop! All back full! Sound the collision alarm!"

Place an exclamation point within a closing quotation mark only if it belongs to the quoted material:

He shouted, "All aboard!"

"I never, never heard the captain say, 'Return to port'!"

Remember that exclamation marks and dashes quickly lose effectiveness if overused.

Use the Hyphen

To join two or more words serving as a single adjective before a noun:

two-story house

well-bred person

up-to-date report

Such words are not hyphenated when they follow the noun:

— Charles is well bred.

— This report is up to date.

Do not *use a hyphen to connect an adverb ending in* ly *and an adjective, or the adverb* very *and an adjective.*

— an easily mastered task

— a very attractive person

When describing family relationships involving great- and -in-law:

brother-in-law

great-grandfather

To join compound numbers, and when writing out a fraction:

sixty-six

one-fifth of the crew

twenty-eight

six and one-third kilometers

With the prefixes ex- (meaning former), self-, all-, quasi-, and the suffixes -elect and -designate:

ex-governor

all-American

quasi-complete
self-made
president-elect
ambassador-designate

To avoid mispronunciation, or to make clear what word you mean:

His re-creation of the old village was complete.
The draftsman re-marked the plans.
The two engineers co-operated the plant.

To connect geographically descriptive terms:

Latin-American
Anglo-Irish

To link two numbers that represent a continuous sequence when they are not introduced by the words "from" or "between":

the 1980-88 time frame *but* between the years 1980 and 1988
pages 1-55 *but* from page 1 to page 55.

To join single capital letters to nouns or participles:

A-bomb
X-ray
U-shaped

To indicate continuation of a word divided at the end of a line:

The ships fall into three categories: combat, repair, and supply ships.

Always consult a dictionary if you are not sure where the syllable breaks are, and attempt to place at least three letters on each line.

To connect numerals with their units of measure (watch possible confusion here):

Right: The sailors maintained an extraordinary 80-hour work week.

Right: They required 10-inch-thick metal plates. (The number comprises part of a unit of measure, is a part of a compound adjective.)

Right: They required 10 inch-thick metal plates. (The number modifies plates. Inch-thick is the compound adjective.)

Wrong: They required 10 inch thick metal plates. (The meaning is unclear.)

When carrying a modifier over to a later word (this is called a "suspended hyphen"):

two-, four-, and six-gun vessels
low-, moderate-, and high-income families

In military usage, link the numerical designation of aviation squadrons and groups to the abbreviated title of the unit by a hyphen:

VF-33
HM-15
MAG-32

Do *not* use a hyphen when the full name for the unit is written out, nor with ground units, nor with the hull designators for Navy ships, nor to separate the names of an exercise from the year in which it occurs:

Fighter Squadron Thirty Three
USS WISCONSIN (BB 64)

Speaking Authoritatively

UNITED STATES GOVERNMENT

MEMORANDUM

TO: Editor, All Hands Magazine DATE: 28 July 1966

FROM: LT B. A. SILVER, USN, USS BULLOCH COUNTY (LST509)

1. BUPERS states in my orders that my ship is LST-509. My yeoman from YN "B" School says it's LST509. NavPers 10241-D YN1&C says it's LST 509, and so do I.

Thank you

B. A. SILVER

4th MEB
Marine Attack Squadron 223
USS FULTON (AS 11)
Bold Eagle 86

Use Parentheses

To set off explanatory material (a single word, phrase, or entire sentence) that is not essential to the main point of the sentence. If constructed properly, the material between parentheses can always be deleted without harming the logical or grammatical structure of the sentence.

A ship's gig (from the CARL VINSON, it turned out) had just cast off from the landing.

The result (see fig. 15) is impressive.

To enclose a parenthetical clause where the interruption is too great to be indicated by commas:

His boat (the fastest in the country, no doubt) won three prizes last year.

Parentheses signal a stronger interruption than commas. On the other hand, dashes give much more emphasis than either commas or parentheses to interrupting material:

— Let's make sure that *all* the military services—don't forget the Marine Corps—get invited to the conference.

To enclose numbers or letters designating items in a series:

You will observe that the sword is (1) old fashioned, (2) still sharp, and (3) unusually light for its size.

Normally the stations on the phone line will be (a) port lookout, (b) starboard lookout, (c) after lookout, (d) QMOW, and (e) combat.

Place a period outside parentheses at the end of a sentence, unless the words within the parentheses comprise a complete sentence:

Individual incomes in the northeast (chart 7), which have not been discussed, are greater than those in the southeast (chart 8).

Inspecting officers listened to all the petty officers' complaints. (In fact, they even talked to some nonrated men.)

Place periods, commas, and other punctuation within the parentheses if they belong to the parenthetical clause or phrase; place them outside the parentheses if they belong to the words of the rest of the sentence:

Certain types of vessels (destroyers, cruisers, carriers, frigates, etc.) are known as "combatants."

You've met the senior admiral (Admiral Heyward), I believe?

Use the Period

To end declarative and mildly imperative sentences. Use exclamation points where greater emphasis is desired.

The Marines stood at attention.

Stand at attention.

Get the rifle up here. Hurry!

To end an indirect question:

She asked if the tax reduction was an illusion.

To follow abbreviations, unless by usage the period is customarily omitted (as with organizations, agencies, and terms known by their initials):

etc.
O.A.S.
Rev.
gal.
Mr.
but
DOD
ICC
UFO
CONUS
EAOS

Normally abbreviate United States as U.S., *without a space between the periods.*

To form an ellipsis—three spaced periods (with a space between each) that indicate omission of one or more words within a quoted passage:

Fourscore and seven years ago our fathers brought forth upon this continent a new nation . . . dedicated to the proposition that all men are created equal.

If the omission ends with a period, use four spaced periods (three to show the omission, and one to mark the end of the sentence).

—We have come to dedicate a portion of that field as a final resting-place. . . .

If only a fragment of a sentence is quoted within another sentence, you need not use ellipses to signify the omission of words:

— The speaker cited the principle of "government of the people, by the people and for the people" at the conclusion of her talk.

As a decimal point:

.05
$9.40
10.7%

Use the Question Mark

After a sentence that asks a direct question:

Who gave that order?
When did the broadcast go down?

Punctuate indirect *questions as you would direct statements, that is,* without *question marks:*

Right: Would you have time for me to stop by the exchange? (direct question)
Wrong: He asked her if she would have time to stop by the exchange? (indirect question)
Right: The petty officer asked Lieutenant Humphrey if he could go on liberty at 1300. (indirect question)

When a question is involved in a quotation, follow this rule: If the quotation alone comprises the question, leave the question mark within *the quotation marks. But if the whole sentence that encloses the quotation is a question, place the question mark* outside *the quotation marks.*

— The lieutenant asked, "Who gave the order?"
— Did the lieutenant say, "The screen commander"?

To indicate doubt or uncertainty as to the correctness of the preceding word, figure, or date:

The ship is 125 (?) feet long.
John Johnston, 1556 (?)–1633

Use Quotation Marks

To enclose a direct quotation, the exact words of a speaker or writer:

He said, "Hold your fire."
"I say again," shouted the captain into the mike, "come aboard."
General Lejeune argued, "The relation between officers and enlisted men should in no sense be that of superior and inferior . . . but rather that of teacher and scholar."

If the passage is five or more lines, set it off from the rest of the text and indent it as a block quotation without quotation marks. Also *see p. 328* *for the use of periods as ellipses to indicate omission of short passages.* *See p. 319* *on using asterisks for longer omissions.*

To enclose slang expressions, nicknames, words used ironically, slogans, humor, or poor grammar:

They resented being regarded as the "fall guys."

We have heard lots about "Flower Power" since the Sixties.

To indicate the titles of short works (such as poems, songs, essays, articles) and parts of longer works (chapters, lessons, topics, sections):

He remembered reading Kipling's "If."

Sybil Stockdale's part of *In Love and War* begins with Chapter 2, "The Navy Wife."

Dvozak made the spiritual "Goin' Home" the theme of *The New World Symphony.*

His essay, "The Classics, the Military, and the Missing Modern Element," has just been published by the journal *Observer.*

As seen above, longer works (such as books, names of newspapers, magazines, symphonies, and operas) are underlined or italicized.

To enclose titles of completed but unpublished works like reports, dissertations, and manuscripts:

Evidently, none of the.members of the committee had read "The State of the Shipyards after the Building of the 600-ship Navy."

Although her dissertation, "John Milton and the Concept of Right Reason," was excellent, she had difficulty getting it published.

With any matter following expressions such as "the word," "the term," "marked," "endorsed," "entitled," "designated," "classified," and "signed," when the exact message is quoted:

The directive, entitled "Revised Damage Control Policy," has been revised.

The envelope was marked "Top Secret"; he feared to open it.

His letter was signed "With Best Wishes, Tom."

Classified just "For Official Use Only," the document seemed unimportant.

The petty officer was designated "Jack of the Dust."

Use single quotation marks to enclose a quotation within a quotation:

"The airman was heard to say, 'Let's forget the inspection and take off early.' "

Always place commas and periods inside the quotation marks:

"The colonel may say 'We can't afford it,' and he ought to know."

Always place colons and semicolons outside:

Mrs. Joseph argued, "The professor isn't in yet"; she obviously didn't want the student to go into the office.

Place question marks and exclamation points inside or outside, depending on whether they apply just to the quotation or to the whole sentence:

"Is this the correct form?" he asked.

What is the meaning of the "balance of payments"?

She exclaimed, "You can't pay them that much!"

Use the Semicolon

To separate independent clauses in a compound sentence when you don't want to use a coordinating conjunction (and, or, nor, for, but, or yet):

The repair is finished; the ship sails today.

To connect two independent clauses that are closely related and joined by a conjunctive adverb such as *however, consequently, therefore, nevertheless, thus, moreover,* etc.:

They argued as hard as they could; however, the contractor remained unconvinced.

The admiral had attended the briefing; therefore, he had his aides gather the charts.

Normally, a comma follows the linking adverb, as above.

To separate elements in a complex series if the elements themselves include commas:

Included in the battle group were NEW JERSEY, a battleship; TOPEKA, a cruiser; and several destroyers and other escorts.

To precede words or abbreviations that introduce a summary or explanation of what has gone before in the sentence:

The regatta included a wide variety of vessels; for example, sailboats, launches, and yachts mingled in the holiday atmosphere of a race.

Use the Underscore

For the names of trains, aircraft, and spacecraft:

The Orient Express

Challenger

Enola Gay

Civilian practice is to use the underscore for ships too, or sometimes (depending on which handbook you use) to use italics for ships' names:

U.S.S. Saratoga or U.S.S. *Saratoga*; S.S. Titanic or S.S. *Titanic*

However, consistent Navy and Marine Corps practice is to use all caps, and no periods in USS or USNS:

USS ENTERPRISE (CVN 65)

USNS H.H. ARNOLD

USS DAVID R. RAY (DD 971)

To underscore the titles of whole published works: books, pamphlets, magazines, newspapers, plays, movies, symphonies, operas, long poems, essays, lectures, sermons, and reports:

U.S. Naval Institute Proceedings

Richard McKenna's The Sand Pebbles

The Washington Post

For sections or parts of published works (chapters, parts, etc.), for short stories and short plays, and for titles of unpublished works (like manuscripts and dissertations), use quotation marks:

— I liked the article in Money, "Affording College."

— One of Frank O'Connor's finest stories is "My Oedipus Complex."

To refer to words, numbers, symbols, and words used as such:

The word omitted has only one m.

The verbs attribute and contribute are often confused.

Quotation marks are also used for the same purpose, but be consistent in your usage.

The verbs "attribute" and "contribute" are often confused.

For emphasizing (sparingly) certain words, phrases, or sentences:
What do we need to focus all our efforts on? Damage control.
Italics are used for most of the same purposes as the underscore—but not in the same document. Again: be consistent.

Abbreviations and Acronyms

Several sources for guidance on abbreviations exist. Chapter 9 of the *GPO Style Manual* contains some general guidelines, but common military practices differ significantly from GPO rules. For the Marine Corps, Chapter 6 of the Individual Records and Administration Manual (IRAM) is the principal reference for abbreviations. For the Navy, the most comprehensive guide is the *Dictionary of Naval Abbreviations*, ed. Bill Wedertz, 3rd edition (Annapolis: Naval Institute Press, 1984). See below for abbreviations of Navy and Marine Corps forces, exercises, and ranks; abbreviations of days, months, and states; and abbreviations commonly used in naval messages.

General Rules on Use of Abbreviations and Acronyms

"In the last BOQ I went into, there were almost no bachelors, very few officers, and it's questionable it could be defined as quarters. But still it's called a BOQ. . . ."—Lieutenant Commander

- Do not introduce an abbreviation or acronym *at all* unless you will use it more than once. *Put clarity before economy.*
- If you do plan to use an acronym several times, spell out the complete term on first use and follow it by the acronym in parentheses, like this: Marine Corps Development and Education Command (MCDEC). Use the acronym consistently from then on in place of the full term.
- Don't use an acronym or other abbreviation once on page one, and then not again until pages later. The reader may have forgotten its meaning.
- Except in task organization designations (e.g., Task Unit 15.3.2 or Task Element 5.3.2.1), do not use periods with military abbreviations and acronyms. Instead, run the letters together without separation, as in SECNAV or HQMC. However, do separate the unit title from the numerical designation, as in COMCARDIV THREE or COMCRUDESGRU EIGHT.
- Designate the plural of an acronym by a lower case *s* following the acronym, as in "several FFs" (several fast frigates) or "twenty RMs" (twenty radiomen). In the case of possessives, use apostrophes according to standard rules, e.g., "CNO's desires are . . ." or "FLETRAGRU's position was . . ." or "the DDs' line of bearing was . . ." (CNO and FLETRAGRU are singular, but there are several destroyers, all on a line of bearing).

Typical Abbreviations of Navy Forces

Below are common abbreviations of U.S. Navy forces. Note the consistent use of ALL CAPS in Navy abbreviations.

SECNAV, ASSTSECNAV, UNSECNAV
OPNAV
CNO and VCNO and DCNO
COMNAVMILPERSCOM
COMNAVSURFLANT
COMCRUDESGRU FOUR
USS ROOSEVELT

Typical Abbreviations of Marine Corps Forces

Here are common abbreviations of U.S. Marine Corps forces. Note the practice of using both lowercase and uppercase letters except where the abbreviation is made up entirely of the initial letters of major words. Note also the use of numbers. See HQO 5216.6 for further instruction.

HQMC
USMC
FMFLant
MedEvac
CG III MAF
BLT 2/3
7th Mar
CG 1st MarDiv
24th MAU
2d MAW
CG FMFPac

Abbreviation of Exercises

Both the Navy and Marine Corps abbreviate the names of exercises, but typically the Navy uses all caps, while the Marine Corps capitalizes only the first word in each noun:

Navy: RIMPAC 88
PACSUBICEX 1–86
Marine Corps: Exercise Bold Eagle
Team Spirit 86

Abbreviations of Navy and Coast Guard Enlisted Ranks

Pay Grade E-1 through E-3 Titles	*Abbreviation*
Airman Recruit, Airman Apprentice, Airman	AR, AA, AN
Constructionman Recruit, Constructionman Apprentice, Constructionman	CR, CA, CN

(*continued*)

Dentalman Recruit, etc.	DR, DA, DN
Fireman Recruit, etc.	FR, FA, FN
Hospitalman Recruit, etc.	HR, HA, HN
Seaman Recruit, etc.	SR, SA, SN

Higher Pay Grades	*Title*	*Abbreviation*
E-4	Petty Officer Third Class	PO3
E-5	Petty Officer Second Class	PO2
E-6	Petty Officer First Class	PO1
E-7	Chief Petty Officer	CPO
E-8	Senior Chief Petty Officer	SCPO
E-9	Master Chief Petty Officer	MCPO
E-9	Master Chief Petty Officer of the Navy/Coast Guard	MCPON or MCPO-CG

Abbreviations of Marine Corps Enlisted Ranks

E-1	Private	Pvt
E-2	Private First Class	PFC
E-3	Lance Corporal	LCpl
E-4	Corporal	Cpl
E-5	Sergeant	Sgt
E-6	Staff Sergeant	SSgt
E-7	Gunnery Sergeant	GySgt
E-8	Master Sergeant	MSgt
E-8	First Sergeant	1stSgt
E-9	Master Gunnery Sergeant	MGySgt
E-9	Sergeant Major	SgtMaj
E-9	Sergeant Major of the Marine Corps	SgtMaj

Abbreviations of Navy and Coast Guard Officer Ranks

W-1	Warrant Officer	WO
W-2	Chief Warrant Officer	CWO W2
W-3	Chief Warrant Officer	CWO W3
W-4	Chief Warrant Officer	CWO W4
O-1	Ensign	ENS
O-2	Lieutenant Junior Grade	LTJG
O-3	Lieutenant	LT
O-4	Lieutenant Commander	LCDR
O-5	Commander	CDR
O-6	Captain	CAPT
O-7	Rear Admiral (Lower Half)	RADM
O-8	Rear Admiral (Upper Half)	RADM
O-9	Vice Admiral	VADM
O-10	Admiral	ADM

Abbreviations of Marine Corps Officer Ranks

W-1	Warrant Officer	WO-1
W-2	Chief Warrant Officer	CWO-2
W-3	Chief Warrant Officer	CWO-3
W-4	Chief Warrant Officer	CWO-4
O-1	Second Lieutenant	2dLt
O-2	First Lieutenant	1stLt
O-3	Captain	Capt
O-4	Major	Maj
O-5	Lieutenant Colonel	LtCol
O-6	Colonel	Col
O-7	Brigadier General	BGen
O-8	Major General	MajGen
O-9	Lieutenant General	LtGen
O-10	General	Gen

Abbreviations of Days and Months

Days	*Months*	
Mon	Jan	Jul
Tues	Feb	Aug
Wed	Mar	Sep
Thurs	Apr	Oct
Fri	May	Nov
Sat	Jun	Dec
Sun		

State Abbreviations

Alabama	AL	Alaska	AK
Arizona	AZ	Arkansas	AR
California	CA	Colorado	CO
Connecticut	CT	Delaware	DE
Florida	FL	Georgia	GA
Hawaii	HI	Idaho	ID
Illinois	IL	Indiana	IN
Iowa	IA	Kansas	KS
Kentucky	KY	Louisiana	LA
Maine	ME	Maryland	MD
Massachusetts	MA	Michigan	MI
Minnesota	MN	Mississippi	MS
Missouri	MO	Montana	MT
Nebraska	NE	Nevada	NV
New Hampshire	NH	New Jersey	NJ
New Mexico	NM	New York	NY
North Carolina	NC	North Dakota	ND
Ohio	OH	Oklahoma	OK

Oregon	OR	Pennsylvania	PA
Rhode Island	RI	South Carolina	SC
South Dakota	SD	Tennessee	TN
Texas	TX	Utah	UT
Vermont	VT	Virginia	VA
Washington	WA	West Virginia	WV
Wisconsin	WI	Wyoming	WY
Territories and Districts			
District of Columbia	DC	Guam	GU
Puerto Rico	PR	Virgin Islands	VI

Standard Message Abbreviations

Below is an unofficial list of standard, well-recognized abbreviations widely used in naval messages. Again, for Marine Corps abbreviations, see Chapter 6 of the IRAM.

AAW	Antiair Warfare
ABBREV/ABBRV	Abbreviation
ABD	Aboard
ABT	About
A/C	Aircraft
ACDU	Active Duty
ACFT	Aircraft
ACKN	Acknowledge
ADDEE	Addressee
ADDL	Additional
ADMIN	Administrative
ADP	Automated Data Processing
ADTAKE	Advise Action Taken
AEW	Airborne Early Warning
AF	Air Force
AFFIRM	Affirmative
AIG	Address Indicator Group
AKA	Also Known As
ALCON	All Concerned
ALT	Alternate
	Altitude
AMEND	Amendment
AMMO	Ammunition
AMPN	Amplification
AMT	Amount
ANS	Answer
AOR	Area Of Responsibility
APL	Allowance Parts List
APPL/APPS	Application/Applications
APPROX	Approximately

APPT	Appoint
ARR	Arrive, Arrival
ART	Article
ARTY	Artillery
ASAP	As Soon As Possible
ASN	Assistant Secretary of the Navy
ASST	Assist, Assistant
ASUW	Antisurface Warfare
ASW	Antisubmarine Warfare
ATA	Actual Time of Arrival
ATD	Actual Time of Departure
ATK	Attack
ATP	Allied Tactical Publication
ATTN	Attention
AUTH	Authorized
AUTO	Automatic
AVAIL	Availability
	Available
AVG	Average
AVN	Autovon
	Aviation
AWD	Award
BCST	Broadcast
BD	Board
BI	Background Investigation
BLDG	Building
BN	Battalion
BOQ	Bachelor Officers' Quarters
BT	Break, Bathythermograph
BTWN	Between
BZ	Well Done
CAD	Collective Address Designator
CAL	Calibrate, Calibration
CANC/CANX	Cancel/Canceled
CAPT	Captain
CASCOR	Casualty Correction
CASREP	Casualty Report
CDO	Command Duty Officer
CDR	Commander
CHAP	Chaplain
	Chapter
CHENG	Chief Engineer
CHG/CHGS	Change/Changes
CHOP	Change of Operational Control
CINC	Commander-In-Chief
CIV	Civilian

CLNC	Clearance
CMC	Commandant of the Marine Corps
CMD	Command
CMS	Communications Security Material System
CNBZN	Cannibalization
CNO	Chief of Naval Operations
CNR	Chief of Naval Reserve
CNX	Cancel, Canceled
CO	Commanding Officer
CODEL	Congressional Delegation
COG	Cognizance
COMDR	Commodore
COMM/COMMS	Communications
COMMO	Commodore Communications Officer
COMSEC	Communications Security
CONF	Conference Confidential
CONGRATS	Congratulations
CONGRINT	Congressional Interest, Letter of Congressional Interest, Congressional Inquiry
CONUS	Continental United States
COORD	Coordinate, Coordination
CORR	Correct, Correction
CORRESP	Correspondence
COSAL	Consolidated Shipboard Allowance List
CPA	Closest Point of Approach
CRYPTO	Cryptographic
CSO	Chief Staff Officer Combat Systems Officer
CTE	Commander, Task Element
CTF	Commander, Task Force
CTG	Commander, Task Group
CTR	Center
CTU	Commander, Task Unit
CV	Carrier
CVBG	Carrier Battle Group
CWO	Chief Warrant Officer
CY	Cycle Year
DC	Damage Control
DECL/DECLAS	Declassify, Declassified
DEF	Defense
DEFCON	Defense Condition
DEG	Degree, Degrees
DEP	Depart, Departure
DEPT	Department

DESIG	Designated, Designator
DET	Detach, Detachment
DG	Downgrade, Downgraded
DIRLAUTH	Direct Liaison Authorized
DISB	Disbursing
DISCH	Discharge
DIV	Division
DOA	Dead On Arrival
DOB	Date Of Birth
DOD	Department Of Defense
DON	Department Of the Navy
DOR	Date Of Rank
DTD	Dated
DTG	Date-Time-Group
DWNGRD	Downgrading Classification
EA	Executive Assistant
EAOS	Expiration of Active Obligated Service
ECM	Electronic Countermeasures
EDD	Estimated Delivery Date Estimated Departure Date
EFF	Effective
EFTO	Encrypted For Transmission Only
EIC	Equipment Identification Code
EMCON	Emission Control
EMERG	Emergency
EMI	Electromagnetic Interference
EMPSKD	Employment Schedule
ENCL	Enclosure
END	Endorse, Endorsement
ENG	Engineering
ENGR	Engineer
ENL	Enlisted, Enlistment
ENR	En Route
EOD	Explosive Ordnance Disposal
EQUIP/EQPT	Equipment
EST	Estimate, Estimated
ETA	Estimated Time of Arrival
ETC	Estimated Time of Completion
ETD	Estimated Time of Departure
ETR	Estimated Time of Repair
EVAL	Evaluation
EW	Electronic Warfare
EX	Exercise
EXPL	Explanation Explosive

FAX	Facsimile
FBM	Fleet Ballistic Missile
FCST	Forecast
FLT	Fleet
	Flight
FM	From
FMF	Fleet Marine Force
FOL	Follow, Following
FOLBY	Followed By
FORAC	For Action
FOUO	For Official Use Only
FPO	Fleet Post Office
FR	From
FREQ	Frequency
FRP	For Record Purposes
FT	Foot
	Fort
FWD	Forward
FY	Fiscal Year
FYI	For Your Information
GFP	Government Furnished Property
GMT	Greenwich Mean Time
	General Military Training
GOVT	Government
GQ	General Quarters
GRP	Group
GRUCOM	Group Command
GTR	Government Transportation Request
HE	High Explosive
HELO	Helicopter
HF	High Frequency
HOSP	Hospital
HQ	Headquarters
HR	Hour
HSTL	Hostile
HVY	Heavy
IAW	In Accordance With
ICO	In the Case Of
	In Concern Of
ICW	In Conjunction With
ID	Identification
ID'D	Identified
IG	Inspector General
IMA	Intermediate Maintenance Activity
IMMED	Immediate
IMPT	Important

INDEF	Indefinite
INDIV	Individual
INFO	Information
INOP	Inoperative
INSP	Inspect, Inspection
INST	Instruction
INTEL	Intelligence
IOT	In Order To
IR	Infrared
IRT	In Reference/Reply/Response To
ISIC	Immediate Superior In Chain of Command
ITE	In The Event of
ITO	In Terms Of
IVO	In View Of
JAG	Judge Advocate General
JAGMAN	JAG Manual
JCS	Joint Chiefs of Staff
JOOD	Junior Officer Of the Deck
JOTS	Joint Operational Tactical System
JR	Junior
KIA	Killed In Action
KT	Knot, Knots
KUDO	Compliments, Praise
LANG	Language
LANT	Atlantic
LAT	Latitude
LDO	Limited Duty Officer
LDR	Leader
LF	Low Frequency
LIMDIS	Limited Distribution
LMT	Local Mean Time
LOA	Letter Of Appreciation
LOC	Letter Of Commendation
LOG	Logistics, Logistical
LOGREQ	Logistics Request
LOI	Letter of Instruction
LONG	Longitude
LPO	Leading Petty Officer
LTR	Letter
LV	Leave
M&R	Maintenance And Repair
MAD	Magnetic Anomaly Detection Message Address Directory
MAG	Marine Aircraft Group Military Assistance Group
MAINT	Maintenance

MATL	Material
MAW	Marine Air Wing
MAX	Maximum
MBR	Member
MCM	Mine Countermeasures
MEB	Marine Expeditionary Brigade
MED	Mediterannean
MEDEVAC	Medical Evacuation
MEF	Marine Expeditionary Force Middle East Force
MEMO	Memorandum
MEU	Marine Expeditionary Unit
MF	Medium Frequency
MFR	Memo For Record
MGMT	Management
MGR	Manager
MIA	Missing In Action
MID/MIDN	Midshipman
MIL	Military
MILDET	Military Detachment
MIN/MNM	Minimum
MISC	Miscellaneous
MOA	Memorandum Of Agreement
MOB	Mobilization
MOD	Modification
MON/MO	Month
MOS	Military Occupational Specialty
MOTU	Mobile Training Unit
MOU	Memorandum Of Understanding
MOVREP	Movement Report
MPN	Military Personnel—Navy
MSC	Military Sealift Command
MSG	Message
MSL	Missile
MSM	Meritorious Service Medal
MSN	Mission
NA	Not Applicable
NAC	National Agency Check
NAF	Naval Air Facility
NAM	Navy Achievement Medal
NAS	Naval Air Station
NATL	National
NAV	Navy, Naval
NAVGRAM	Navy Telegram
NAVRES	Naval Reserve
NAVSTA	Naval Station
NBC	Nuclear, Biological, & Chemical

NBR/NMBR	Number
NCM	Navy Commendation Medal
NEC	Naval Enlisted Classification Code
NEG/NEGAT	Negative
NET	Not Earlier Than
NFO	Naval Flight Officer
NGFS	Naval Gunfire Support
NIS	Naval Investigative Service Not In Service Not In Stock
NLT	Not Later Than
NMPC	Naval Military Personnel Command
NOBC	Naval Officer Billet Code
NOFORN	No Foreign Eyes Authorized
NOTAL	Not To All nor needed by all
NR	Number
NS	Naval Station
NSA	National Security Agency National Shipping Authority Naval Support Activity
NSC	Naval Supply Center
NTC	Naval Training Center
NTDS	Naval Tactical Data System
NWP	Naval Warfare Publication
OADR	Originating Agency's Determination Required
OBE	Overcome, Overtaken By Events
OBS	Observe, Observation
OCA	Operational Control Authority
OFCR/OFF	Officer
OFLD	Offload
OIC/OINC	Officer In Charge
OJT	On the Job Training
OMIGOD	Oh, No!
ONBD	On Board
ONLD	Onload
OOC	Out Of Commission
OOD	Officer Of the Deck
OP	Operation
OPCON	Operational Control
OPLAN	Operation Plan
OPNAV	Office of the Chief of Naval Operations
OPNL	Operational
OPORD	Operation Order
OPS	Operations
OPSEC	Operational Security
OPSKED	Operations Schedule

ORD	Order
ORG	Organization
ORI	Operational Readiness Inspection
ORIG	Originator
OSD	Office of the Secretary of Defense
OTC	Officer in Tactical Command
OTSR	Optimum Track Ship Routing
OVHL	Overhaul
PAC	Pacific
PAO	Public Affairs Officer
PARA	Paragraph
PAREN/UNPAREN	Begin Parenthesis/End Parenthesis
PASEP	Pass/Passed Separately
PAX	Passenger, Passengers
PCO	Prospective Commanding Officer
PCS	Permanent Change of Station
PCT	Percentage
PD	Period
PEBD	Pay Entry Base Date
PERGRA	Permission Granted
PERS	Personnel
PFT	Physical Fitness Testing or Training
PGM	Program
PHIB	Amphibious
PHONCON	Telephone Conversation
PHOTO	Photograph
PHYS	Physical, Physical Examination
PIM	Point and Intended Movement
PLA	Plain Language Address
PLAD	Plain Language Address Directory
PLS	Please
PMS	Planned Maintenance System
POAM/POA&M	Plan of Action and Milestones
POC	Point Of Contact
POD	Plan Of the Day
POM	Planned Overseas Movement Program Objective Memorandum
POSIT	Position
POSS	Possible, Possibility
PREP	Prepare, Preparation
PRI	Primary Priority
PROB	Probable, Probably
PROV	Provide
PRT	Physical Readiness Testing or Training
PSA	Personnel Support Activity
PSD	Personnel Support Detachment

PT	Physical Therapy Physical Training Point, Period
PUB	Publication
PVST	Port Visit
PXO	Prospective Executive Officer
QA	Quality Assurance
QUAL	Quality, Qualify, Qualification
QUES	Question
QUOTE/UNQUOTE	Quotation/End of Quotation
QTR	Quarter
QTRS	Quarters
QTY	Quantity
R&D	Research And Development
RCMD	Recommend
RCV/RCVD	Receive/Received
RDD	Required Delivery Date
RDO	Radio
RDVU	Rendezvous
REF	Refer, Reference
REG	Regular Regulation
REGS	Regulations
REQ	Request
REQN	Requisition
REP	Representative
RES	Reserve
RESP	Responsible
REV/REVD	Revise/Revised
RFS	Ready For Sea
RMKS	Remarks
ROE	Rules Of Engagement
ROH	Regular Overhaul
RPR	Repair
RPT	Report Repeat
RQD/RQRD	Required
RQMT	Requirement
RQN	Requisition
RQR	Require
RQST	Request
RQSTD	Requested
RTB	Return To Base
RVW/RVWD	Review/Reviewed
SAM	Surface-to-Air Missile
SAR	Search And Rescue

SAT	Satisfactory Security Alert Team
SATCOM	Satellite Communications
SATNAV	Satellite Navigation
SATO	Scheduled Airline Traffic Office
SCTY	Security
SEC	Secondary
SECDEF	Secretary of Defense
SECNAV	Secretary of the Navy
SECRET	Secret
SECT	Section
SELRES	Selected Reserve
SEPCOR	Separate Correspondence
SEPMSG	Separate Message
SER	Serial Service
SIMA	Shore Intermediate Maintenance Activity
SINS	Shipboard Inertial Navigation System
SITREP	Situation Report
SKED	Schedule
SNDL	Standard Navy Distribution List
SNM	Subject Named Member
SNO	Subject Named Officer
SNR	Senior
SOA	Speed Of Advance
SOE	Schedule Of Events
SOM	Standard Operating Manual
SOP	Standard Operating Procedure
SOPA	Senior Officer Present Afloat
SPCL	Special
SPCM	Special Courts-Martial
SPD	Speed
SPDLTR	Speedletter
SPECAT	Special Category
SQD	Squad
SQDN/SQDRN	Squadron
SR	Senior
SRB	Selective Reenlistment Bonus
SSIC	Standard Subject Identification Code
SSN	Nuclear Fleet Attack Submarine Social Security Number
ST	State
STA	Station
STK	Strike
STND	Standard
SUB	Submarine
SUBJ	Subject

SUM	Summary
SUP	Supply
SUPP	Supplement
SURF	Surface
SUSP	Suspend, Suspended
SVC/SVCS	Service/Services
SWO	Surface Warfare Officer
TA/TECH ASSIST	Technical Assist
TACAIR	Tactical Air
TAD	Temporary Assigned Duty
TAO	Tactical Action Officer
TDY	Temporary Duty
TECH	Technical
TECHMAN	Technical Manual
TELCON	Telephone Conversation
TEMP	Temporary
TGT	Target
THRU	Through
TOVR	Turnover
TRANS	Transportation
TRE	Training Readiness Evaluation
TRNG	Training
TS	Top Secret
TTY	Teletype
TVL	Travel
TYCOM	Type Commander
UA	Unauthorized Absence
UCMJ	Uniform Code of Military Justice
UIC	Unit Identification Code
UNCLAS	Unclassified
UNK/UNKN	Unknown
UNODIR	Unless Otherwise Directed
UNPAREN	End of Parenthesis
UNQUOTE	End of Quotation
UNREP	Underway Replenishment
UNSAT	Unsatisfactory
UPK	Upkeep
U/W	Underway
VCTY	Vicinity
VDS	Variable-Depth Sonar
VEH	Vehicle
VERTREP	Vertical Replenishment
VHA	Variable Housing Allowance
W/	With
WIA	Wounded In Action

WO	Warrant Officer
W/O	Without
WPNS	Weapons
WRT	With Regard To
WX	Weather
XDECK	Crossdeck
XFER	Transfer
XMIT	Transmit
XMPT/XMT	Exempt
XMSN	Transmission
XO	Executive Officer
XSIT	Transit
YR	Year

The Well-Stocked Desk

Just as no carpenter would be without saw, hammer, and nails, so every naval writer should have at his or her fingertips tools essential to writing, tools in addition to the text you're reading from. Many of them are in the supply system—some, in fact, may be picked up at the local Servmart. But we often forget to do so.

Experienced writers learn they can dispense with one or two of them after years at the trade, but they'll still want them somewhere about the office. What follows is a good general list—add to your short bookshelf with gouges or useful tips as you find them. See specialized sections of this text for reference to good books or articles on news writing, professional writing, speaking and briefing, JAGMAN Investigations, etc.

For Every Desk

Correspondence Manual

- Department of the Navy Correspondence Manual, SECNAVINST 5216.5C. Have a copy on hand, or ready access to one.

Dictionary. Use a standard collegiate (hardbound) dictionary, not a pocket dictionary. The following are excellent:

- *Webster's Ninth New Collegiate Dictionary* (or latest edition)
- *Random House Dictionary*, current edition
- *The American Heritage Dictionary*, current edition

Handbook of Grammar and Mechanics. The short handbook in this text doesn't cover everything. Besides grammar and usage (punctuation, capitalization, use of numbers, etc.), handbooks usually cover style, general writing guidance, résumé writing, and other things having to do with writing. See such handbooks, too, for guidance on documentation, including footnotes or endnotes, the number-reference method, and bibliographies. Here are some good ones:

- *Harbrace College Handbook*, current edition, eds. John C. Hodges and Mary Whitten
- *New English Handbook*, current edition, ed. Hans Guth
- *Scott, Foresman Handbook for Writers*, current edition, eds. Hairston and Ruszkiewicz
- *GPO Style Manual*. Although this book is primarily a typesetter's and printer's manual, some naval writers still swear by its sections on proofreader's marks, capitalization, spelling, compound words, hyphenation, punctuation, abbreviations, and signs and symbols. Note that naval practice in some areas differs from GPO guidance.
- *Chicago Manual of Style*. Chicago: Univ. of Chicago Press, current edition. Another classic reference text for the same kinds of things as listed above under *GPO Style Manual*.

For Some Desks

Word Division Guide

- *Word Division Supplement* to the *GPO Style Manual*. 8th ed., Washington, D.C., 1984. Tells you how to divide words at the end of a line.

Short Reference Manual

- *Gregg Reference Manual*, current edition, ed. W. A. Sabin. Some authors swear by this one.

Guide on Performance Evaluations

- *Phrases for Performance Evaluations*. A standard best-seller.
- Several other texts are available.

Desk Planner

- Navy Leader Planning Guide, NAVPERS 15255 series, published annually. Contains a yearly calendar with pertinent administrative dates, an index to instructions on personnel, and some phone numbers. Automatically distributed to most Navy commands annually.

Thesaurus (Dictionary of synonyms and antonyms)

- *Random House Thesaurus*.
- *Roget's: The New Thesaurus, No. II*, Houghton-Mifflin, 1980.
- *Webster's Collegiate Thesaurus*, G. & C. Merriam Co., 1975.

Permissions

Grateful acknowledgment is made to all those who provided letters, memos, evaluations, etc., from which real-life examples have been drawn. In addition, the following are acknowledged for providing permission to reprint previously published material:

Baker, Brent, CAPT, USN. "The Public Affairs Front." U.S. Naval Institute *Proceedings* (September 1988): 116–17.

Batcheller, Gordon D., LtCol, USMC. "For the Sake of the Corps, Write!" *Marine Corps Gazette* (February 1984): 56.

Beach, Edward L., CAPT, USN (Ret.). "Up Or Out: A Financial Disaster." U.S. Naval Institute *Proceedings* (June 1987): 54.

Blair, Carvel, CAPT, USN. "Effective Writing, Navy or Civilian." U.S. Naval Institute *Proceedings* (July 1968): 131.

Broome, Jack. *Make Another Signal*. London: William Kimber, 1973.

Bunn, George. "International Law and the Use of Force in Peacetime: Do U.S. Ships Have to Take the First Hit?" *Naval War College Review* (May–June 1986): 69.

Coonts, Stephen P. *Flight of the Intruder*. Annapolis: Naval Institute Press, 1986. Copyright © 1986 by Stephen P. Coonts.

Cox, William J., LT, USNR. "The Gulf of Mexico: A Forgotten Frontier in the 1980s." *Naval War College Review* (Summer 1987): 75.

DeThomas, John V., CDR, USN. "Are Two Heads Better Than Three in a P-3?" U.S. Naval Institute *Proceedings* (January 1983): 108.

Green, Eric J., Capt, USMC. "Continuity in Arctic Units." *Marine Corps Gazette* (February 1986): 36.

Hall, Martha B., SSgt, USMC. "Is There a Place for the Woman Marine?" U.S. Naval Institute *Proceedings* (November 1988): 112.

Hammond, J. W., Jr., LtCol, USMC. "The Responsibility to Write." *Marine Corps Gazette* (January 1970): 28.

Hayward, Thomas B., ADM, USN. "CNO Speaks Out: Why the *Nimitz* Aircraft Carrier." *Surface Warfare* (May 1982): 11.

Jacobs, R. D., LCDR, USNR. "In Search of . . . Patrol Combatants." U.S. Naval Institute *Proceedings* (September 1983): 127.

Johns, Eric, LCDR, USN. "Perfect is the Enemy of Good Enough." U.S. Naval Institute *Proceedings* (October 1988): 37.

Kelso, Frank B., II, ADM, USN. Remarks to the Texas Daily Newspaper Association, 25 July 1986. "Navy Excellence: A Story to Tell." CINCLANTFLT (2 December 1986).

Kennedy, David M., LT, USN, and LT William R. C. Stewart III, Medical Corps, USNR. "That Dangerous Polyester Look." U.S. Naval Institute *Proceedings* (January 1984): 97.

Lehman, John. "Successful Naval Strategy in the Pacific: How We Are Achieving It. How We Can Afford It." *Naval War College Review* (Winter 1987): 26.

Libbey, Miles A., III, CDR, USN. "A Strategic Plan for Training." U.S. Naval Institute *Proceedings* (October 1983): 93.

Lyons, James A., Jr., ADM, USN. "A Peacetime Strategy for the Pacific." *Naval War College Review* (Winter 1987): 45.

McCracken H., Bradley, QMC, USN. ". . . A Tall Ship and a *Hill* to Steer Her By." U.S. Naval Institute *Proceedings* (September 1988): 104.

Morison, Samuel Eliot. "Notes on Writing Naval (*not* Navy) English." *The American Neptune* (January 1949): 10.

Murray, Terrence P., Maj, USMC. "Code of Conduct—A Sound Doctrine." *Marine Corps Gazette* (December 1983): 62.

Nette, Kenneth A., Maj, CD, PPCLI, USMC. "A Philosophy of Command." *Marine Corps Gazette* (December 1983): 50.

Shaker, Steven M. "Suicidal Boat and Robot Craft Attacks." U.S. Naval Institute *Proceedings* (August 1988): 96.

Smith, Arthur M., CAPT, Medical Corps, USNR. "Blood on the Decks." U.S. Naval Institute *Proceedings* (July 1988): 65.

Smith, E. D., Jr., CAPT, USN. "The Security Dilemma." *Naval War College Review* (Autumn 1988): 64.

Stavridis, James, LCDR, USN "Handling a *Ticonderoga*." U.S. Naval Institute *Proceedings* (January 1987): 107.

Webb, James H., Jr. "Role of American Seapower." *Defense Issues* Vol. 2 No. 58: 2.

Weinberger, Caspar W. NL 102 course booklet. U.S. Naval Academy, 1986.

Wouk, Herman. *The Caine Mutiny*. New York: Pocket Books, 1951.

Index

About the Author

A captain in the Naval Reserve, Robert Shenk began his naval career in 1965 as communications officer in the *Harry E. Hubbard* (DD 748). He then served with River Patrol Division 535 in the Republic of Vietnam. Earning his Ph.D. from the University of Kansas in 1976, he continued to serve in various naval reserve units and returned to active duty with the Navy in 1979 to teach writing and literature at the Air Force and Naval Academies. He is currently a professor of English at the University of New Orleans. Shenk is the editor of *The Left-Handed Monkey Wrench: Stories and Essays by Richard McKenna* (Naval Institute Press) and McKenna's *The Sand Pebbles* (CNL, Naval Institute Press) and author of *The Sinners Progress: A Study of Madness in English Renaissance Drama* (Universität Salzburg) and numerous articles about Renaissance literature, education in the military, and writing.

The Naval Institute Press is the book-publishing arm of the U.S. Naval Institute, a private, nonprofit professional society for members of the sea services and civilians who share an interest in naval and maritime affairs. Established in 1873 at the U.S. Naval Academy in Annapolis, Maryland, where its offices remain today, the Naval Institute has more than 100,000 members worldwide.

Members of the Naval Insitute receive the influential monthly magazine *Proceedings* and discounts on fine nautical prints, ship and aircraft photos, and subscriptions to the quarterly *Naval History* magazine. They also have access to the transcripts of the Institute's Oral History Program and get discounted admission to any of the Institute-sponsored seminars regularly offered around the country.

The Naval Institute's book-publishing program, begun in 1898 with basic guides to naval practices, has broadened its scope in recent years to include books of more general interest. Now the Naval Institute Press publishes more than forty new titles each year, ranging from how-to books on boating and navigation to battle histories, biographies, ship and aircraft guides, and novels. Institute members receive discounts on the Press's more than 375 books.

Full-time students are eligible for special half-price membership rates. Life memberships are also available.

For a free catalog describing the Naval Institute Press books currently available, and for further information about U.S. Naval Institute membership, please write to:

THE NAVAL INSTITUTE PRESS

GUIDE TO NAVAL WRITING

Designed by Alan Carter

Set in Trump and Helvetica
by Byrd Data Imaging, Inc., Richmond, Virginia

Printed on 50-lb. Decision Opaque
and bound in Kivar
by The Maple-Vail Book Manufacturing Group,
Binghamton, New York